The Gallup Poll

Public Opinion 1999

Other Gallup Poll Publications Available from Scholarly Resources

The Gallup Poll: Public Opinion Annual Series

1998 (ISBN 0-8420-2698-3)
1997 (ISBN-0-8420-2597-9)
1996 (ISBN-0-8420-2596-0)
1995 (ISBN-0-8420-2595-2)
1994 (ISBN-0-8420-2560-X)
1993 (ISBN-0-8420-2483-2)
1992 (ISBN-0-8420-2463-8)
1991 (ISBN-0-8420-2397-6)
1990 (ISBN-0-8420-2368-2)
1989 (ISBN-0-8420-2344-5)
1988 (ISBN-0-8420-2330-5)

1987 (ISBN-0-8420-2292-9)
1986 (ISBN-0-8420-2274-0)
1985 (ISBN-0-8420-2249-X)
1984 (ISBN-0-8420-2234-1)
1983 (ISBN-0-8420-2220-1)
1982 (ISBN-0-8420-2214-7)
1981 (ISBN-0-8420-2200-7)
1980 (ISBN-0-8420-2181-7)
1979 (ISBN-0-8420-2170-1)
1978 (ISBN-0-8420-2159-0)
1972–77 (ISBN-0-8420-2129-9, 2 vols.)
1935–71 (ISBN-0-394-47270-5, 3 vols.)

International Polls

The International Gallup Polls: Public Opinion, 1979
ISBN-0-8420-2180-9 (1981)

The International Gallup Polls: Public Opinion, 1978
ISBN-0-8420-2162-0 (1980)

The Gallup International Public Opinion Polls:
France, 1939, 1944–1975
2 volumes ISBN-0-394-40998-1 (1976)

The Gallup International Public Opinion Polls:
Great Britain, 1937–1975
2 volumes ISBN 0-394-40992-2 (1976)

The Gallup Poll

Public Opinion 1999

George Gallup, Jr.

SR Scholarly Resources Inc.
Wilmington, Delaware

ACKNOWLEDGMENTS

The preparation of this volume has involved the dedication, skills, and efforts of many devoted individuals to whom I am indebted. At The Gallup Organization, gratitude is owed to James Clifton, president and CEO; Alec Gallup, co-chairman; and The Gallup Poll staff, including Frank Newport, editor-in-chief; David Moore and Lydia Saad, managing editors; Judy Nelson, operations manager; and Leslie McAneny, editor of *The Gallup Poll Monthly*. At Scholarly Resources, I would like to thank Ann M. Aydelotte, who edited, proofread, and indexed this volume; James L. Preston, production manager; and Carolyn J. Travers, managing editor. At Type Shoppe II Productions Ltd., my appreciation goes to Lydia A. Wagner, Penelope Hollingsworth, Michelle Gladu, and Shirl' Eklund for their typesetting and design expertise. Finally, I wish to thank Professor Fred L. Israel of the City College of New York for his invaluable work as the principal coordinator of this publication.

G. G., Jr.

♾ The paper used in this publication meets the minimum requirements of the American National Standard for permanence of paper for printed library materials, Z39.48, 1984.

Scholarly Resources Inc.
104 Greenhill Avenue
Wilmington, DE 19805-1897
www.scholarly.com

Library of Congress Catalog Card Number: 79-56557
International Standard Serial Number: 0195-962X
International Standard Book Number: 0-8420-2699-1

CONTENTS

THE SAMPLE

Although most Gallup Poll findings are based on telephone interviews, a significant proportion is based on interviews conducted in person in the home. The majority of the findings reported in Gallup Poll surveys is based on samples consisting of a minimum of 1,000 interviews. The total number, however, may exceed 1,000, or even 1,500, interviews, where the survey specifications call for reporting the responses of low-incidence population groups such as young public-school parents or Hispanics.

Design of the Sample for Telephone Surveys

The findings from the telephone surveys are based on Gallup's standard national telephone samples, consisting of unclustered directory-assisted, random-digit telephone samples utilizing a proportionate, stratified sampling design. The random-digit aspect of the sample is used to avoid "listing" bias. Numerous studies have shown that households with unlisted telephone numbers are different from listed households. "Unlistedness" is due to household mobility or to customer requests to prevent publication of the telephone number. To avoid this source of bias, a random-digit procedure designed to provide representation of both listed and unlisted (including not-yet-listed) numbers is used.

Telephone numbers for the continental United States are stratified into four regions of the country and, within each region, further arranged into three size-of-community strata. The sample of telephone numbers produced by the described method is representative of all telephone households within the continental United States.

Only working banks of telephone numbers are selected. Eliminating nonworking banks from the sample increases the likelihood that any sampled telephone number will be associated with a residence.

Within each contacted household, an interview is sought with the youngest man 18 years of age or older who is at home. If no man is home, an interview is sought with the oldest woman at home. This method of respondent selection within households produces an age distribution by sex that closely approximates the age distribution by sex of the total population.

Up to three calls are made to each selected telephone number to complete an interview. The time of day and the day of the week for callbacks are varied to maximize the chances of finding a respondent at home. All interviews are conducted on weekends or weekday evenings in order to contact potential respondents among the working population.

The final sample is weighted so that the distribution of the sample matches current estimates derived from the U.S. Census Bureau's Current Population Survey (CPS) for the adult population living in telephone households in the continental United States.

Design of the Sample for Personal Surveys

The design of the sample for personal (face-to-face) surveys is that of a replicated area probability sample down to the block level in the case of urban areas and to segments of townships in the case of rural areas.

After stratifying the nation geographically and by size of community according to information derived from the most recent census, over 350 different sampling locations are selected on a mathematically random basis from within cities, towns, and counties that, in turn, have been selected on a mathematically random basis.

The interviewers are given no leeway in selecting the areas in which they are to conduct their interviews. Each interviewer is given a map on which a specific starting point is marked and is instructed to contact households according to a predetermined travel pattern. At each occupied dwelling unit, the interviewer selects respondents by following a systematic procedure that is repeated until the assigned number of interviews has been completed.

Weighting Procedures

After the survey data have been collected and processed, each respondent is assigned a weight so that the demographic characteristics of the total weighted sample of respondents match the latest estimates of the demographic characteristics of the adult population available from the U.S. Census Bureau. Telephone surveys are weighted to match the characteristics of the adult population living in households with access to a telephone. The weighting of personal interview data includes a factor to improve the representation of the kind of people who are less likely to be found at home.

The procedures described above are designed to produce samples approximating the adult civilian population (18 and older) living in private households (that is, excluding those in prisons, hospitals, hotels, religious and educational institutions, and those living on reservations or military bases)—and in the case of telephone surveys, households with access to a telephone. Survey percentages may be applied to census estimates of the size of these populations to project percentages into numbers of people. The manner in which the sample is drawn also produces a sample that approximates the distribution of private households in the United States. Therefore, survey results also can be projected to numbers of households.

Sampling Tolerances

In interpreting survey results, it should be borne in mind that all sample surveys are subject to sampling error—that is, the extent to which the results may differ from what would be obtained if the whole population surveyed had been interviewed. The size of such sampling errors depends largely on the number of interviews.

The following tables may be used in estimating the sampling error of any percentage. The computed allowances have taken into account the effect of the sample design upon sampling error. They may be interpreted as indicating the range (plus or minus the figure shown) within which the results of repeated samplings in the same time period could be expected to vary, 95 percent of the time, assuming the same sampling procedure, the same interviewers, and the same questionnaire.

Table A shows how much allowance should be made for the sampling error of a percentage. Let us say a reported percentage is 33 for a group that includes 1,000 respondents. First, we go to the row headed "Percentages near 30" and then go across to the column headed "1,000." The number here is 4, which means that the 33 percent obtained in the sample is subject to a sampling error of plus or minus 4 points. Another way of saying it is that very probably (95 chances out of 100) the average of repeated samplings would be somewhere between 29 and 37, with the most likely figure being the 33 obtained.

In comparing survey results in two samples, such as for men and women, the question arises as to how large must a difference between them be before one can be reasonably sure that it reflects a real difference. In Tables B and C, the number of points that must be allowed for in such comparisons is indicated. Table B is for percentages near 20 or 80, and Table C is for percentages near 50. For percentages in between, the error to be allowed for is between those shown in the two tables.

TABLE A
Recommended Allowance for Sampling Error of a Percentage

	In Percentage Points (at 95 in 100 confidence level)* Sample Size					
	1,000	750	600	400	200	100
Percentages near 10	2	3	3	4	5	7
Percentages near 20	3	4	4	5	7	9
Percentages near 30	4	4	4	6	8	10
Percentages near 40	4	4	5	6	8	11
Percentages near 50	4	4	5	6	8	11
Percentages near 60	4	4	5	6	8	11
Percentages near 70	4	4	4	6	8	10
Percentages near 80	3	4	4	5	7	9
Percentages near 90	2	3	3	4	5	7

*The chances are 95 in 100 that the sampling error is not larger than the figures shown.

TABLE B
Recommended Allowance for Sampling Error of the Difference

Size of sample	In Percentage Points (at 95 in 100 confidence level)* Percentages near 20 or percentages near 80			
	750	600	400	200
750	5			
600	5	6		
400	6	6	7	
200	8	8	8	10

*The chances are 95 in 100 that the sampling error is not larger than the figures shown.

TABLE C
Recommended Allowance for Sampling Error of the Difference

Size of sample	In Percentage Points (at 95 in 100 confidence level)* Percentages near 50			
	750	600	400	200
750	6			
600	7	7		
400	7	8	8	
200	10	10	10	12

*The chances are 95 in 100 that the sampling error is not larger than the figures shown.

Here is an example of how the tables would be used: Let us say that 50 percent of men respond a certain way and 40 percent of women also respond that way, for a difference of 10 percentage points between them. Can we say with any assurance that the 10-point difference reflects a real difference between men and women on the question? The sample contains approximately 600 men and 600 women.

Since the percentages are near 50, we consult Table C, and since the two samples are about 600 persons each, we look for the number in the column headed "600" that is also in the row designated "600." We find the number 7 here. This means that the allowance for error should be 7 points, and that in concluding that the percentage among men is somewhere between 3 and 17 points higher than the percentage among women, we should be wrong only about 5 percent of the time. In other words, we can conclude with considerable confidence that a difference exists in the direction observed and that it amounts to at least 3 percentage points.

If, in another case, men's responses amount to 22 percent and women's 24 percent, we consult Table B because these percentages are near 20. We look for the number in the column headed "600" that is also in the row designated "600" and see that the number is 6. Obviously, then, the 2-point difference is inconclusive.

GALLUP POLL ACCURACY RECORD

Presidential Elections

	Candidates	Final Gallup Survey*	Election Result*	Gallup Deviation
1996	Clinton	52.0	50.1	+1.9
	Dole	41.0	41.4	−0.4
	Perot	7.0	8.5	−1.5
1992	Clinton	49.0	43.3	+5.7
	Bush	37.0	37.7	−0.7
	Perot	14.0	19.0	−5.0
1988	Bush	56.0	53.9	+2.1
	Dukakis	44.0	46.1	−2.1
1984	Reagan	59.0	59.2	−0.2
	Mondale	41.0	40.8	+0.2
1980	Reagan	47.0	50.8	−3.8
	Carter	44.0	41.0	+3.0
	Anderson	8.0	6.6	+1.4
	Other	1.0	1.6	−0.6
1976	Carter	48.0	50.1	−2.1
	Ford	49.0	48.1	+0.9
	McCarthy	2.0	0.9	+1.1
	Other	1.0	0.9	+0.1
1972	Nixon	62.0	61.8	+0.2
	McGovern	38.0	38.2	−0.2
1968	Nixon	43.0	43.5	−0.5
	Humphrey	42.0	42.9	−0.9
	Wallace	15.0	13.6	+1.4
1964	Johnson	64.0	61.3	+2.7
	Goldwater	36.0	38.7	−2.7
1960	Kennedy	51.0	50.1	+0.9
	Nixon	49.0	49.9	−0.9

1956	Eisenhower	59.5	57.8	+1.7
	Stevenson	40.5	42.2	−1.7
1952	Eisenhower	51.0	55.4	−4.4
	Stevenson	49.0	44.6	+4.4
1948	Truman	44.5	49.5	−5.0
	Dewey	49.5	45.1	+4.4
	Wallace	4.0	2.4	+1.6
	Other	2.0	3.0	−1.0
1944	Roosevelt	51.5	53.8	−2.3
	Dewey	48.5	46.2	+2.3
1940	Roosevelt	52.0	55.0	−3.0
	Willkie	48.0	45.0	+3.0
1936	Roosevelt	55.7	62.5	−6.8
	Landon	44.3	37.5	+6.8

*To allow direct comparisons with Gallup's reported estimates, the official election results are shown as the division of the major party (or three-party) vote in thirteen of the sixteen elections, and the vote for all parties including "other" in the 1948, 1976, and 1980 contests.

Trend in Deviation
(For Each Candidate)

Elections	Average Error
1936–1948	3.6%
1952–1964	2.4%
1968–1996	1.5%
1936–1996 (Overall)	2.2%

GALLUP POLL ACCURACY RECORD

Congressional Elections
(Midterm)

	Parties	*Final Gallup Survey*	*Election Result*	*Gallup Deviation*
1994	Republican	53.5	53.5	±0.0
	Democratic	46.5	46.5	±0.0
1990	Democratic	54.0	54.1	−0.1
	Republican	46.0	45.9	+0.1
1986*				
1982	Democratic	55.0	56.1	−1.1
	Republican	45.0	43.9	+1.1
1978	Democratic	55.0	54.6	+0.4
	Republican	45.0	45.4	−0.4
1974	Democratic	60.0	58.9	+1.1
	Republican	40.0	41.1	−1.1
1970	Democratic	53.0	54.3	−1.3
	Republican	47.0	45.7	+1.3
1966	Democratic	52.5	51.9	+0.6
	Republican	47.5	48.1	−0.6
1962	Democratic	55.5	52.7	+2.8
	Republican	44.5	47.3	−2.8
1958	Democratic	57.0	56.5	+0.5
	Republican	43.0	43.5	−0.5
1954	Democratic	51.5	52.7	−1.2
	Republican	48.5	47.3	+1.2
1950	Democratic	51.0	50.3	+0.7
	Republican	49.0	49.7	−0.7
1946	Republican	58.0	54.3	+3.7
	Democratic	42.0	45.7	−3.7

1942	Democratic	52.0	48.0	+4.0
	Republican	48.0	52.0	−4.0
1938	Democratic	54.0	50.8	+3.2
	Republican	46.0	49.2	−3.2

*No final congressional survey.

Trend in Deviation
(For Each Party)

Elections	Average Error
1938–1946	3.6%
1950–1970	1.2%
1974–1994	0.5%
1938–1994 (Overall)	1.5%

CHRONOLOGY

This chronology is provided to enable the reader to relate poll results to specific events, or series of events, that may have influenced public opinion.

1998

On December 19 the Republican-led House of Representatives voted largely along party lines to impeach President Bill Clinton in the Monica Lewinsky sex-and-perjury scandal. Following an eight-month inquiry by Independent Counsel Kenneth Starr, the House approved two articles of impeachment accusing Clinton of lying under oath and of obstructing justice by attempting to cover up a sexual affair with Lewinsky, a former White House intern. Clinton thus became the second president impeached in the history of the United States. Despite the scandal, Clinton continued to maintain high public support for his job performance. Gallup Polls throughout the year showed that Americans expressed "scandal fatigue" as they criticized Starr and Congress for pressing on with their inquiries.

In other news, U.S. financial markets soared for a fourth straight year despite a currency crisis in Southeast Asia and despite major economic declines in Russia, Brazil, and Argentina. The Dow Jones Industrial Average recorded a fourth consecutive rise in excess of 20%.

1999

January 7   Chief Justice William Rehnquist opens President Clinton's impeachment trial in the Senate.

January 13   Michael Jordan, considered to be among the all-time greatest basketball players, retires from professional basketball.

January 19   President Clinton delivers his annual State of the Union address as his impeachment trial proceeds.

January 25	The National Association of Realtors reports that sales of existing homes in 1998 jumped 13.5% from the previous year.
January 26	John Paul II arrives in St. Louis to begin the papal visit to the United States.
January 27	The Senate votes to continue President Clinton's trial and agrees, along party lines, to hear three witnesses.
January 29	The Commerce Department reports that the gross domestic product (GDP) grew, after inflation adjustments, at an annual rate of 3.9% in 1998.
February 1	President Clinton presents to Congress a $1.77-trillion budget for fiscal year 2000, an increase of 2.2% over the 1999 budget.
February 4	The Senate rejects hearing live witnesses in the president's impeachment trial but votes instead to allow the House's prosecution team to present videotaped excerpts from depositions.
February 5	The Labor Department reports that the January unemployment figures remained at 4.3%, the lowest rate since 1970.
February 7	King Hussein of Jordan dies in his forty-sixth year as that nation's monarch.
February 12	After a five-week trial, the Senate votes to acquit President Clinton of impeachment charges in the Lewinsky scandal.
February 23	The Serbs and ethnic Albanians agree in principle to an accord that would end their year-old conflict in Yugoslavia.
March 2	Texas Governor George W. Bush announces that he will seek the Republican presidential nomination in 2000.
March 6	The *New York Times* reports a major Chinese theft of nuclear technology from American weapons laboratories in the 1980s.
March 10	Elizabeth Dole, former head of the American Red Cross, announces that she is considering a run for the Republican presidential nomination in 2000.
March 16	Steve Forbes declares his candidacy for the Republican presidential nomination in 2000.
March 18	Ethnic Albanian representatives sign a peace accord aimed at ending the conflict between Yugoslavia and the ethnic Albanian

Kosovo Liberation Army. Serbia rejects the agreement because it includes plans for a NATO force to maintain peace in Kosovo.

March 24   NATO launches air strikes against Serb targets in Yugoslavia at the start of a sustained bombing campaign, but the Serbs continue their assault on Kosovo's ethnic Albanians.

March 29   The Dow Jones Industrial Average closes above the 10,000 mark for the first time.

March 31   NATO's air strikes against Yugoslavia enter their second week. The Serbs force a massive flight of refugees from Kosovo.

April 2   The unemployment rate in March dropped to 4.2%, a twenty-nine-year low.

April 8   The nations bordering on Yugoslavia struggle with an influx of thousands of ethnic Albanian refugees who have been driven from their homes in Kosovo. NATO planes bomb Belgrade.

April 14   The NATO bombing campaign in Yugoslavia concludes its third week. Daily air strikes take place along with increasing international efforts at finding a political resolution to the situation in Kosovo.

April 20   In Littleton, Colorado, two teenagers storm Columbine High School and, in a five-hour rampage, kill a teacher and twelve students and wound more than thirty others before killing themselves.

April 23   NATO celebrates its fiftieth anniversary as air strikes in Yugoslavia enter the second month.

April 27   A search for a resolution of the Yugoslavian situation intensifies. Russia now plays a greater role in attempting to reach a settlement.

May 1   Yugoslavia releases three captured American soldiers while NATO vows to continue the bombing.

May 3   Tornadoes cause severe damage in South Dakota, Nebraska, Kansas, Oklahoma, and Texas.

May 7   NATO's accidental bombing of the Chinese embassy in Belgrade sparks mass protests in China.

May 22   Serbian forces accelerate their expulsion of ethnic Albanians from Kosovo.

May 24	The International Criminal Tribunal at The Hague indicts Yugoslavian President Slobodan Milosevic for war crimes.
June 3	Yugoslavia accepts a Kosovo peace plan.
June 4	The unemployment rate dropped to 4.2% in May from 4.3% in April.
June 9	NATO ends its seventy-eight-day bombing campaign, which began in March after Yugoslavia rejected a peace settlement.
June 12	Russian troops, in a surprise move, enter Kosovo in advance of the NATO peacekeeping force.
June 16	Vice President Al Gore declares his candidacy for the Democratic presidential nomination in 2000.
June 29	President Clinton announces a plan to restructure the Medicare program.
June 30	Texas Governor Bush reveals that he has raised an unprecedented $36 million in the first half of 1999 for his presidential bid.
July 5	NATO and Russia reach an agreement about peacekeeping troops in Kosovo.
July 16	John F. Kennedy, Jr., along with his wife and sister-in-law, are killed when their plane crashes in the ocean off Martha's Vineyard, Massachusetts.
July 23	King Hassan II of Morocco, the longest-ruling monarch in the Arab world, dies.
August 9	Russian President Boris Yeltsin names Vladimir Putin as premier and his political heir.
August 11	President Clinton offers to commute the sentences of sixteen Puerto Rican nationalists who were involved in a bombing campaign in the United States from 1974 through 1983.
August 17	A major earthquake kills more than 20,000 people in Turkey.
August 24	The Federal Reserve Board raises interest rates in an attempt to curb inflation.
August 25	The FBI admits to using pyrotechnic tear gas in its 1993 assault on the Branch Davidian cult's compound in Waco, Texas.
September 7	Viacom intends to purchase CBS in the largest-ever media merger.

September 8	Former Senator Bill Bradley of New Jersey announces his candidacy for the 2000 Democratic presidential nomination.
September 23	President Clinton vetoes a Republican tax-cut bill.
September 27	Arizona Senator John McCain declares his candidacy for the 2000 Republican presidential nomination.
October 1	Fifty years of Communist rule are commemorated in China.
October 13	The Senate rejects the Nuclear Test Ban Treaty.
October 20	Elizabeth Dole withdraws her name from the Republican party's nominating process.
October 25	Patrick Buchanan leaves the Republican party to seek the presidential nomination of the Reform party.
October 31	An EgyptAir jet bound for Cairo crashes about thirty minutes after taking off from New York City, killing all 217 people on board.
November 5	In the government's antitrust suit, a federal judge finds the Microsoft Corporation to be a "monopoly power."
November 7	The unemployment rate fell to 4.1% in October, the lowest since January 1970.
November 15	China and the United States sign a wideranging trade agreement.
November 16	The Federal Reserve Board again raises interest rates in an effort to curb inflation.
November 23	First Lady Hillary Rodham Clinton announces that she will seek the Democratic Senate seat from New York in 2000.
November 30	The World Trade Organization meets in Seattle amid fierce protests from the public.
December 14	Control of the Panama Canal is formally handed over by the United States to the nation of Panama.
December 16	The Commerce Department reports that the U.S. trade deficit reached a record high in October.
December 31	Boris Yeltsin resigns as Russia's president.
	The world celebrates the new millennium.

GALLUP REGIONS

EAST

New England
Maine
New Hampshire
Vermont
Massachusetts
Rhode Island
Connecticut

Mid-Atlantic
New York
New Jersey
Pennsylvania
Maryland
Delaware
West Virginia
District of Columbia

MIDWEST

East Central
Ohio
Michigan
Indiana
Illinois

West Central
Wisconsin
Minnesota
Iowa
Missouri
North Dakota
South Dakota
Nebraska
Kansas

SOUTH

Southeast
Virginia
North Carolina
South Carolina
Georgia
Florida
Kentucky
Tennessee
Alabama
Mississippi

Southwest
Arkansas
Louisiana
Oklahoma
Texas

WEST

Mountain
Montana
Arizona
Colorado
Idaho
Wyoming
Utah
Nevada
New Mexico

Pacific
California
Oregon
Washington
Hawaii
Alaska

President Clinton's Impeachment Trial

JANUARY 16

Interviewing Dates: 1/8–10/99
CNN/*USA Today*/Gallup Poll
Survey #GO 125722

As you may know, removing a president from office involves two major steps in Congress. First, the House of Representatives must vote on whether there is enough evidence to bring a president to trial before the Senate; this step is called impeachment. Next, the Senate must vote on whether to remove the president from office, or not. The House has now impeached Bill Clinton and the case has been sent to the Senate for trial. What do you want your senators to do—vote in favor of convicting Clinton and removing him from office, or vote against convicting Clinton so he will remain in office?

In favor of convicting 32%
Against convicting 63
No opinion 5

	In favor of convicting	Against convicting	No opinion
By Sex			
Male	36%	60%	4%
Female	29	66	5
By Ethnic Background			
White	35	60	5
Nonwhite	15	84	1
Black	8	91	1
By Education			
Postgraduate	43	53	4
College Graduate	45	51	4
College Incomplete	29	66	5
No College	28	68	4
By Region			
East	26	69	5
Midwest	33	65	2
South	39	55	6
West	28	67	5
By Age			
18–29 Years	27	70	3
30–49 Years	36	59	5
50–64 Years	34	62	4
65 Years and Over	28	66	6

By Household Income

	In favor of convicting	Against convicting	No opinion
$75,000 and Over	41	55	4
$50,000 and Over	41	54	5
$30,000–$49,999	30	67	3
$20,000–$29,999	32	64	4
Under $20,000	17	80	3

By Politics

Republicans	63	30	7
Democrats	7	90	3
Independents	34	62	4

By Political Ideology

Conservative	49	46	5
Moderate	25	71	4
Liberal	13	83	4

Selected National Trend

	In favor of convicting	Against convicting	No opinion
1999*			
January 8–10	32%	63%	5%
January 6**	33	63	4
1998			
December 19–20	29	68	3
December 15–16†	34	63	3
December 12–13†	35	61	4
December 4–6†	33	65	2
November 20–22†	33	64	3
November 13–15†	30	68	2
October 23–25†	30	63	7
October 9–12†	31	63	6

*The same question was asked between January 15–17, 1999: vote in favor of convicting, 36%; vote against convicting, 61%; no opinion, 3%.
**Question wording: *If the Senate holds a trial, what would you want your senators to do . . . ?*
†Question wording: *If the House does vote to impeach Clinton and send the case to the Senate for trial, what would you want your senators to do . . . ?*

Now I'm going to read the two charges against Bill Clinton for which he was impeached by the House of Representatives and is now on trial for in the Senate. As I read each one, please say, regardless of your view about removing him from office, whether you think that charge against Clinton is true or not true:

The charge that Bill Clinton committed perjury by providing false and misleading testimony about his relationship with Monica Lewinsky to Ken Starr's grand jury?

True	79%
Not true	17
No opinion	4

	True	Not true	No opinion
By Sex			
Male	80%	17%	3%
Female	77	18	5
By Ethnic Background			
White	82	14	4
Nonwhite	60	32	8
Black	56	37	7
By Education			
Postgraduate	82	15	3
College Graduate	90	8	2
College Incomplete	81	17	2
No College	73	20	7
By Region			
East	83	15	2
Midwest	76	19	5
South	77	18	5
West	78	16	6
By Age			
18–29 Years	81	18	1
30–49 Years	84	14	2
50–64 Years	79	16	5
65 Years and Over	62	25	13
By Household Income			
$75,000 and Over	88	9	3
$50,000 and Over	88	10	2
$30,000–$49,999	83	14	3
$20,000–$29,999	76	20	4
Under $20,000	60	29	11

By Politics

Republicans	95	5	*
Democrats	63	29	8
Independents	81	16	3

By Political Ideology

Conservative	84	12	4
Moderate	76	20	4
Liberal	75	22	3

*Less than 1%

The charge that Bill Clinton obstructed justice by trying to influence the testimony of Monica Lewinsky, his secretary, and others in the Paula Jones lawsuit?

True	53%
Not true	40
No opinion	7

	True	Not true	No opinion
By Sex			
Male	55%	40%	5%
Female	51	41	8
By Ethnic Background			
White	56	38	6
Nonwhite	33	57	10
Black	30	61	9
By Education			
Postgraduate	57	38	5
College Graduate	62	33	5
College Incomplete	59	38	3
No College	44	45	11
By Region			
East	49	43	8
Midwest	55	39	6
South	58	36	6
West	47	47	6
By Age			
18–29 Years	51	45	4
30–49 Years	57	39	4
50–64 Years	55	37	8
65 Years and Over	43	42	15

By Household Income

$75,000 and Over	62	36	2
$50,000 and Over	61	36	3
$30,000–$49,999	50	43	7
$20,000–$29,999	52	43	5
Under $20,000	43	46	11

By Politics

Republicans	80	15	5
Democrats	28	64	8
Independents	55	38	7

By Political Ideology

Conservative	66	27	7
Moderate	45	48	7
Liberal	41	54	5

Now, for each of those charges, I would like you to tell me whether you think that, if true, the offense is or is not serious enough to justify Bill Clinton's removal from office by the Senate:

The charge that Bill Clinton committed perjury by providing false and misleading testimony about his relationship with Monica Lewinsky to Ken Starr's grand jury?

Serious enough	40%
Not serious enough	58
No opinion	2

	Serious enough	Not serious enough	No opinion
By Sex			
Male	43%	56%	1%
Female	38	59	3
By Ethnic Background			
White	44	54	2
Nonwhite	21	77	2
Black	12	85	3
By Education			
Postgraduate	46	53	1
College Graduate	52	48	*
College Incomplete	39	59	2
No College	36	61	3

By Region

East	36	63	1
Midwest	39	60	1
South	48	49	3
West	35	62	3

By Age

18–29 Years	39	61	*
30–49 Years	44	55	1
50–64 Years	41	56	3
65 Years and Over	32	61	7

By Household Income

$75,000 and Over	44	55	1
$50,000 and Over	47	52	1
$30,000–$49,999	41	59	*
$20,000–$29,999	38	59	3
Under $20,000	25	68	7

By Politics

Republicans	70	28	2
Democrats	14	84	2
Independents	43	55	2

By Political Ideology

Conservative	55	43	2
Moderate	35	62	3
Liberal	18	81	1

*Less than 1%

The charge that Bill Clinton obstructed justice by trying to influence the testimony of Monica Lewinsky, his secretary, and others in the Paula Jones lawsuit?

Serious enough	41%
Not serious enough	56
No opinion	3

	Serious enough	Not serious enough	No opinion
By Sex			
Male	46%	52%	2%
Female	37	59	4
By Ethnic Background			
White	44	53	3
Nonwhite	26	71	3
Black	21	75	4

By Education

Postgraduate	47	50	3
College Graduate	53	46	1
College Incomplete	43	56	1
No College	35	59	6

By Region

East	39	58	3
Midwest	40	58	2
South	45	51	4
West	38	59	3

By Age

18–29 Years	44	56	*
30–49 Years	43	56	1
50–64 Years	42	55	3
65 Years and Over	32	53	15

By Household Income

$75,000 and Over	48	49	3
$50,000 and Over	47	50	3
$30,000–$49,999	41	58	1
$20,000–$29,999	40	58	2
Under $20,000	29	64	7

By Politics

Republicans	67	29	4
Democrats	15	80	5
Independents	46	52	2

By Political Ideology

Conservative	54	43	3
Moderate	36	61	3
Liberal	22	74	4

*Less than 1%

Note: As the historic impeachment trial of Bill Clinton gets under way in the U.S. Senate, a new Gallup Poll finds that the American public agrees with the House contention that the president committed perjury and that he obstructed justice. On the other hand, respondents do not agree that these offenses, even if true, are severe enough to cause the Senate to convict Clinton and remove him from office.

The fact that they believe that President Clinton lied and broke laws is not a new finding. The public came to the conclusion early last year that he was not telling the truth about his relationship with Monica Lewinsky. Within a few weeks of Clinton's late January statement that he had not had "sexual relations with that woman," a majority of the public (67%) said that in fact they believed that he probably or definitely had. Additionally, by April of last year, about six in ten said that Clinton had "probably" or "definitely" lied under oath.

In Gallup's most recent poll, conducted January 8–10, respondents were asked directly about the central charges contained in the two articles of impeachment passed by the House of Representatives. On both counts, the public agrees that the charges are true. Specifically, 79% believe that the charge that Clinton committed perjury by lying under oath to a grand jury is true, and 53% agree that he obstructed justice in trying to influence the testimony of Lewinsky, his secretary, and others in the Paula Jones lawsuit.

In this sense, it is clear that the public is in sync with the basic premise of the case being brought to the Senate by the House managers. At the same time, Americans diverge from the conclusions of the House in terms of the implications of these presidential misdeeds. They do not believe that these offenses rise to the level of being impeachable: only about four in ten say that even if the charges embodied in the articles of impeachment are true, they should warrant Clinton's being convicted and removed from office. And, when asked specifically, only one-third want their senators to vote to convict Clinton and remove him from office, a number that has held essentially steady for the past three months.

The poll asked the survey respondents who oppose removing Clinton from office (63% of the public) why they feel this way. Out of a list of nine read, the three most important reasons were: 1) Clinton is doing a good job running the country (perceived to be either the most important reason or a major reason by 87%); 2) the charges deal with sexual matters (76%); and 3) the public supports Clinton's government policies (73%).

Consistent with their views about the truth of the charges, only 33% of those opposed to Clinton's removal say that the "fact that Clinton did not break any laws" constitutes an important reason why they oppose his removal, while 70%

say that the fact that "the laws Clinton broke are not serious enough to remove him from office" is important.

In short, the lack of public enthusiasm for impeaching Clinton is not centered on the belief that he did anything illegal. Rather, the majority appear to oppose his removal because they do not believe that the laws he broke are significant enough to warrant his being the first president in U.S. history to be removed from office through the impeachment process—particularly a president who is perceived to be doing an excellent job. In fact, the "good job running the country" theme is strongly echoed in other data from the most recent poll. Clinton's approval rating (at 67%) remains remarkably stable and high. And the public's rating of the economy (at 41% "very good," 48% "somewhat good") is also very high and even more positive now than it was as recently as last summer.

JANUARY 30

Interviewing Date: 1/27/99*
CNN/*USA Today*/Gallup Poll
Survey #GO 126430

As you may know, the Senate today [January 27] voted on whether to end the Clinton impeachment trial immediately, or whether to continue the trial. The Senate voted to continue the trial. Do you approve or disapprove of that decision?

Approve... 41%
Disapprove.. 57
No opinion... 2

	Approve	Dis-approve	No opinion
By Sex			
Male.............................	44%	55%	1%
Female	39	59	2

*For results based on a sample of this size, one can say with 95% confidence that the error attributable to sampling and other random effects could be ±4 percentage points.

By Age

	Approve	Disapprove	No opinion
18–29 Years	46	53	1
30–49 Years	41	57	2
50 Years and Over	38	60	2

By Politics

	Approve	Disapprove	No opinion
Republicans	75	25	*
Democrats	14	85	1
Independents	39	57	4

By Clinton Approval

	Approve	Disapprove	No opinion
Approve	22	77	1
Disapprove	83	15	2

*Less than 1%

In addition, the Senate today voted in favor of having three witnesses in the Clinton impeachment trial give testimony to the Senate in private. These witnesses would be Monica Lewinsky, Vernon Jordan, and Sidney Blumenthal. Do you approve or disapprove of that decision?

Approve 44%
Disapprove 54
No opinion 2

	Approve	Dis- approve	No opinion
By Sex			
Male	41%	57%	2%
Female	46	51	3
By Age			
18–29 Years	45	54	1
30–49 Years	44	53	3
50 Years and Over	42	56	2
By Politics			
Republicans	72	26	2
Democrats	26	73	1
Independents	38	58	4
By Clinton Approval			
Approve	27	71	2
Disapprove	79	19	2
By Senate Decision Not to End Trial			
Approve	80	18	2
Disapprove	19	80	1

Do you approve or disapprove of the way each of the following is handling the impeachment proceedings against Bill Clinton:

The Republicans in the Senate?

Approve 33%
Disapprove 57
No opinion 10

	Approve	Dis- approve	No opinion
By Sex			
Male	38%	56%	6%
Female	29	57	14
By Age			
18–29 Years	34	57	9
30–49 Years	31	59	10
50 Years and Over	34	55	11
By Politics			
Republicans	65	28	7
Democrats	13	81	6
Independents	26	58	16
By Clinton Approval			
Approve	19	72	9
Disapprove	62	26	12
By Senate Decision Not to End Trial			
Approve	64	24	12
Disapprove	11	82	7

Selected National Trend

	Approve	Dis- approve	No opinion
1999			
January 8–10	36%	54%	10%
1998			
December 15–16	38	56	6
December 4–6	32	61	7
November 20–22	34	58	8
November 13–15	31	62	7
October 9–12	38	55	7
October 6–7	34	58	8
September 23–24*	32	59	9

September 11–12*	43	48	9
August 10–12*	33	52	15
February 13–15*	44	44	12

*Question wording: *Do you approve or disapprove of the way each of the following has handled the controversy over Bill Clinton and Monica Lewinsky?*

The Democrats in the Senate?

Approve	45%
Disapprove	45
No opinion	10

	Approve	Dis-approve	No opinion
By Sex			
Male	45%	48%	7%
Female	45	42	13
By Age			
18–29 Years	38	50	12
30–49 Years	45	44	11
50 Years and Over	49	43	8
By Politics			
Republicans	16	78	6
Democrats	73	20	7
Independents	43	42	15
By Clinton Approval			
Approve	61	30	9
Disapprove	13	77	10
By Senate Decision Not to End Trial			
Approve	22	68	10
Disapprove	63	28	9

Selected National Trend

	Approve	Dis-approve	No opinion
1999			
January 8–10	53%	36%	11%
1998			
December 15–16	52	40	8
December 4–6	47	44	9
November 20–22	44	46	10

November 13–15	44	46	10
October 9–12	44	46	10
October 6–7	44	45	11
September 23–24*	45	41	14
September 11–12*	43	44	13
August 10–12*	44	39	17

*Question wording: *Do you approve or disapprove of the way each of the following has handled the controversy over Bill Clinton and Monica Lewinsky?*

Note: A new Gallup survey finds that four in ten Americans (41%) approve of the Senate vote to continue, rather than immediately dismiss, the Clinton impeachment trial. A similar number (44%) approves of the decision to introduce witnesses into the process. However, more respondents—just over half—disapprove of each action.

Supported by only one Democrat, Senate Republicans voted on Wednesday [January 27] to kill a motion to dismiss the impeachment trial and subsequently adopted one allowing House managers to privately depose three witnesses—former intern Monica Lewinsky, Clinton friend Vernon Jordan, and White House aide Sidney Blumenthal. Public support in the new poll for extension and expansion of the impeachment trial is somewhat higher than support for removing Bill Clinton from office has been throughout the impeachment process. Last week, Gallup found only 33% saying that they want their senators to vote to convict and remove Clinton, while 66% opposed conviction and removal.

The relatively broad support for the Senate's actions seen in this week's poll could reflect some Americans' feelings that there should be a fuller deliberation of the charges, even if they personally want the outcome to be favorable to Clinton. This notion is supported by two other findings in the poll. First, reaction to Clinton's refusal to answer ten questions posed to him last week by a group of Senate Republicans was somewhat negative, with 52% disapproving of his decision and 43% approving. And second, when presented with summaries of two opposing views heard during this week's debate over dismissal of the trial, respondents are almost evenly divided. Just over one-half (52%) agree with the Democratic argument that "the Senate should end the trial now because it is certain Bill Clinton will not be convicted and removed from office, regardless of what happens in the trial." Just under one-half (46%) agree with the Republican argument that "the Senate should continue the trial, because the Senate can only fulfill its Constitutional duties by continuing, regardless of whether the outcome already seems clear."

The partisanship of this week's Senate debate may have taken a toll on the image of Senate Democrats, who were previously seen in a positive light by a majority of Americans. Presently, 45% approve of the way that Senate Democrats are handling the impeachment proceedings, and 45% disapprove. While these percentages are similar to ratings that the House Democrats received throughout the fall, today's ratings represent an 8-point drop in approval for the Senate Democrats from those of earlier this month, when 53% approved and only 36% disapproved of their approach. However, the Democrats' image remains superior to that of the Senate Republicans, for whom only 33% approve and 57% disapprove of the job that they are doing. Meanwhile, Clinton's presidential job rating remains unaffected, at 67%.

FEBRUARY 9

Interviewing Dates: 1/22–24/99
CNN/*USA Today*/Gallup Poll
Survey #GO 126280

When the Senate begins to debate the impeachment issues, do you think it should open the debate to the public and to coverage by the news media, or conduct the debate in private?

Open the debate 49%
Conduct it in private 49
No opinion 2

	Open the debate	Conduct it in private	No opinion
By Politics			
Republicans	48%	51%	1%
Democrats	47	51	2
Independents	51	47	2

Note: As the U.S. Senate deliberates the fate of Bill Clinton's presidency, Americans are split on whether those deliberations should be held in open session or behind closed doors. Unlike regular Senate business, the rules for President Clinton's trial require debate among senators to be conducted in private, much like a jury in a regular trial. However, an impeachment trial is the rare case in American law where the jury is allowed to set the rules for the trial, and senators have the option of voting to open deliberations to public scrutiny. They rejected that option on February 9 by a vote of 59 in favor of public deliberations to 41 opposed. Supporters of public deliberations needed 67 votes, or two-thirds of the Senate, to change the rules for the trial.

In the latest Gallup Poll, Americans are split evenly on whether the deliberations should be public or private, with 49% supporting public deliberations and 49% supporting the current practice of private ones. Unlike many other issues relating to impeachment, there are virtually no partisan differences on this one: Republicans are as evenly split as Democrats.

FEBRUARY 11

Interviewing Date: 2/9/99*
CNN/*USA Today*/Gallup Poll
Survey #GO 126687

If the Senate votes not to convict and remove Bill Clinton from office, how would you want the senators from your state to vote on a possible resolution to formally censure Bill Clinton for his actions in this matter—would you want them to vote in favor of a resolution to formally censure Clinton, or vote against a resolution to formally censure Clinton?

In favor 57%
Against.. 34
No opinion 9

	In favor	Against	No opinion
By Politics			
Republicans	72%	21%	7%
Democrats	47	43	10
Independents	53	36	11

*Based on one-night poll: margin of error ±4 percentage points with additional possible error due to limitations of polls conducted in only one night

By Clinton Approval

Approve	52	39	9
Disapprove	68	24	8

Regardless of your view on whether Clinton should be removed from office, do you approve or disapprove of the way the U.S. Senate is handling the impeachment trial of Bill Clinton?

Approve	33%
Disapprove	61
No opinion	6

	Approve	Dis- approve	No opinion
By Politics			
Republicans	44%	51%	5%
Democrats	20	76	4
Independents	36	56	8
By Clinton Approval			
Approve	29	67	4
Disapprove	46	46	8

So far, do you think Bill Clinton has or has not gotten a fair trial in the Senate?

Yes, fair	62%
Not fair	32
No opinion	6

	Yes, fair	Not fair	No opinion
By Politics			
Republicans	87%	9%	4%
Democrats	39	55	6
Independents	63	29	8
By Clinton Approval			
Approve	52	42	6
Disapprove	90	7	3

Now I'm going to read the two charges against Bill Clinton for which he was impeached by the House of Representatives and is now on trial in the Senate. As I read each one, please say, regardless of your view about removing him from office, whether you think that charge against Clinton is true or not true:

The charge that Bill Clinton committed perjury by providing false and misleading testimony about his relationship with Monica Lewinsky to Ken Starr's grand jury?

True	73%
Not true	24
No opinion	3

	True	Not true	No opinion
By Politics			
Republicans	91%	8%	1%
Democrats	51	46	3
Independents	79	17	4
By Clinton Approval			
Approve	63	33	4
Disapprove	99	1	*

*Less than 1%

The charge that Bill Clinton obstructed justice by trying to influence the testimony of Monica Lewinsky, his secretary, and others in the Paula Jones lawsuit?

True	49%
Not true	45
No opinion	6

	True	Not true	No opinion
By Politics			
Republicans	76%	19%	5%
Democrats	25	68	7
Independents	49	43	8
By Clinton Approval			
Approve	32	61	7
Disapprove	92	4	4

In terms of the wording of a censure resolution that might be passed by the Senate, would each of the following types of censure be acceptable to you, or not:

A censure which states that Clinton committed crimes in the Lewinsky matter?

Acceptable 51%
Not acceptable 47
No opinion 2

	Acceptable	Not acceptable	No opinion
By Politics			
Republicans	73%	24%	3%
Democrats....................	26	72	2
Independents...............	56	42	2
By Clinton Approval			
Approve	40	58	2
Disapprove..................	79	18	3

A censure which condemns Clinton's behavior in the Lewinsky matter but does not state that he committed any crimes?

Acceptable 44%
Not acceptable 54
No opinion 2

	Acceptable	Not acceptable	No opinion
By Politics			
Republicans	18%	82%	*
Democrats....................	65	33	2
Independents...............	45	53	2
By Clinton Approval			
Approve	58	41	1
Disapprove..................	12	88	*

*Less than 1%

If the Senate votes not to remove Bill Clinton from office, would you feel that Clinton will have received sufficient punishment for his behavior in the Lewinsky matter, or that Clinton will have gotten off without any real punishment?

Sufficient punishment..................................... 49%
Gotten off 45

Neither; other (volunteered) 2
No opinion.. 4

	Sufficient punishment	Gotten off	Neither; other; no opinion
By Politics			
Republicans	23%	75%	2%
Democrats....................	72	23	5
Independents...............	48	42	10
By Clinton Approval			
Approve	64	29	7
Disapprove..................	12	87	1

Note: Gallup Poll trends throughout the entire impeachment debate have shown one consistent belief: the American people do not want Bill Clinton removed from office for his behavior relating to the Lewinsky scandal. The support for impeachment and removal consistently reflects the view of about one-third of the public, while a solid two-thirds are opposed to removing the president from office.

These numbers remain consistent despite an overwhelming belief that Clinton did commit some level of wrongdoing. In the latest Gallup Poll, 73% believe that he did commit perjury during his grand jury testimony about his relationship with Monica Lewinsky. However, the public is split on whether the president committed obstruction of justice by trying to influence the testimony of Lewinsky and his key aides in the Paula Jones lawsuit. Forty-nine percent believe that the charge is true, while 45% believe that he is innocent.

Given that Americans believe that President Clinton did do something wrong but do not want him removed from office, what kind of consequences can the public support? Fifty-seven percent say that their senators should vote in favor of a resolution censuring Clinton for his actions, while 34% oppose censure.

Survey respondents were also asked about two possible censure alternatives. A slim majority support exists for a resolution that would state that Clinton committed crimes in the Lewinsky matter. Fifty-one percent support the concept, with 47% opposed, and Republicans firmly support this alternative. The situation changes if the resolution merely condemns Clinton's actions but says that no crimes were committed. Republican support for that proposal drops, with the result that only 44% of respondents would find that resolution acceptable, while 54% would find it unacceptable.

Has the trial been punishment enough, considering Clinton's known desire to ensure a positive place in the history books? Again, Americans are split, with 49% saying that the president has already been punished enough and 45% believing that he will have escaped without any real punishment if he is not removed from office.

And did Clinton receive a fair trial? Sixty-two percent say yes, while 32% say no. However, Americans do not like the way that the Senate conducted that trial. In mid-January, 45% of those polled agreed with the senators' handling of the trial and 45% disapproved. However, after the decision to call witnesses, including Lewinsky, the public's opinion of the Senate shifted. Today, 61% of those polled disapprove of the Senate's handling of the trial, while 31% approve.

FEBRUARY 12
THE GENDER GAP—AN ANALYSIS*

Bill Clinton went into the historic Senate impeachment vote today with a stronger position among women in the American population than among men—despite the fact that the impeachment controversy centered on allegations of sexual harassment and an admitted affair with a White House intern half the president's age. In Gallup's most recent poll before the impeachment proceedings, conducted on February 9:

	Should be convicted and removed	Should not be convicted and removed
Men	38%	59%
Women	25	72

This type of gender gap was a significant factor historically in Clinton's two presidential victories, with women voters forming the core of his sup-

*This analysis was written by Frank Newport, Editor in Chief, The Gallup Poll.

port. The nature of the situations that gave birth to the impeachment process—involving allegations of illicit propositions and affairs with women—could have been hypothesized to have caused a diminution of the female skew in his support. That, as can be seen above, did not occur.

Clinton also continues to enjoy stronger support among Democrats than he does opposition among Republicans. This situation among rank-and-file Democrats and Republicans nationwide thus mirrors the final vote in the Senate on Friday [February 12], in which Democrats were unanimous in voting against conviction on both charges, while ten and five Republicans broke ranks and voted with Democrats on the perjury and obstruction of justice charges, respectively. Mathematically, coupling these Democratic and Republican patterns with the fact that independents are strongly against conviction and removal creates the situation in which two-thirds of the overall population supported Clinton's staying in office in the February 9 poll.

	Should be convicted and removed	Should not be convicted and removed
Republicans	67%	32%
Democrats	7	91
Independents	25	70

FEBRUARY 12
THE TRIAL—AN ANALYSIS*

The Senate trial is over and President William Jefferson Clinton has been acquitted. Gallup Poll trends during the impeachment process consistently showed about one-third of Americans supporting Clinton's impeachment and removal, with two-thirds opposed. That basic proportionate split in the American population stayed constant up through Gallup's final pre-vote poll conducted on Tuesday night [February 9], thus suggesting that the final Senate vote on Friday [February 12] was in accord with the will of the American people.

*This analysis was written by Mark Gillespie, Senior Broadcast Producer, The Gallup Poll.

The trial itself still did not necessarily sit well with the American people. As the Senate trial progressed, the public's opinion of the trial process became more negative as early bipartisanship turned into disputes over witness testimony and a potential censure resolution. In mid-January, the Senate's trial approval rating stood at 45%, with a disapproval rate of 45%. However, in the CNN/ *USA Today*/Gallup Poll conducted on February 9, the disapproval rate rose to 61%, with only 33% approving of the Senate's handling of the trial.

Despite that, Americans still believe President Clinton received a fair trial: 62% of Americans believe his trial was conducted fairly. That number includes the majority of Republicans, who may also believe the trial was too fair to the president since the House managers were blocked from calling many potential witnesses to testify against the president. Thirty-two percent of Americans believe the trial was not conducted fairly.

Since the Senate failed to convict and will apparently not agree on a formal censure motion, the question remains, was the House impeachment and Senate trial enough of a punishment for Clinton? His desire for a place in history is well known, but the stigma of impeachment will now be a key part of that legacy. Forty-nine percent of Americans believe that the process today is sufficient punishment for the president, but 45% believe he "got away" with the crimes of perjury and obstruction of justice.

FEBRUARY 15

Interviewing Dates: 2/12–13/99
CNN/*USA Today*/Gallup Poll
Survey #GO 126688

Do you approve or disapprove of the way Bill Clinton is handling his job as president?

Approve	68%
Disapprove	30
No opinion	2

	Approve	Dis-approve	No opinion
By Politics			
Republicans	35%	62%	3%
Democrats	91	8	1
Independents	69	28	3
By Senate Acquittal			
Approve	92	6	2
Disapprove	22	75	3

Selected National Trend

	Approve	Dis-approve	No opinion
1999			
February 9	70%	27%	3%
February 4–8	65	33	2
January 27	67	31	2
January 22–24	69	29	2
January 15–17	69	29	2
January 8–10	67	30	3
January 6	63	34	3

Thinking about Bill Clinton as a person, do you have a positive or negative opinion of him?

Positive	35%
Negative	57
No opinion	8

	Positive	Negative	No opinion
By Politics			
Republicans	13%	83%	4%
Democrats	57	34	9
Independents	30	61	9
By Senate Acquittal			
Approve	53	37	10
Disapprove	3	94	3

Selected National Trend

	Positive	Negative	No opinion
1999			
January 22–24	40%	53%	7%
January 15–17	41	54	5

December 15–16.........	46	50	4
October 9–12*............	53	45	2
September 23–24........	38	55	7
September 11–12........	36	58	6

*Based on half sample

As you may know, the Senate today [February 12] voted to acquit Bill Clinton of both articles of impeachment, which means he will remain in office. Do you approve or disapprove of that decision?

Approve..	64%
Disapprove..	34
No opinion..	2

By Politics

	Approve	Dis-approve	No opinion
Republicans................	30%	68%	2%
Democrats...................	89	10	1
Independents...............	66	32	2

Do you think the Senate's decision today vindicates or does not vindicate Bill Clinton in the matters for which he was impeached?

Yes, vindicates..	39%
Does not vindicate..	53
No opinion..	8

	Yes, vindicates	Does not vindicate	No opinion
By Politics			
Republicans................	21%	73%	6%
Democrats...................	57	33	10
Independents...............	36	57	7
By Senate Acquittal			
Approve......................	53	38	9
Disapprove.................	15	79	6

Which of the following best describes your own reaction to the Senate's decision to not convict and remove Bill Clinton from office— delighted, pleased, displeased, or angry?

Delighted..	18%
Pleased..	41
Displeased..	25
Angry..	14
Don't care one way or the other (volunteered).....................................	1
None; other (volunteered)..............................	1
No opinion..	*

*Less than 1%

	Delighted	Pleased	Dis-pleased	Angry*
By Politics				
Republicans.....	5%	17%	47%	29%
Democrats.......	30	56	9	3
Independents...	17	43	24	12
By Senate Acquittal				
Approve..........	28	62	6	**
Disapprove......	**	2	58	39

*"Don't care," "none," "other," and "no opinion" —at 4% or less—are omitted.
**Less than 1%

Which would you rather see the Senate now do—debate a resolution to formally censure Bill Clinton for his actions, or drop the matter entirely?

Censure Clinton..	26%
Drop the matter..	73
No opinion..	1

	Censure Clinton	Drop the matter	No opinion
By Politics			
Republicans................	41%	57%	2%
Democrats...................	15	85	*
Independents...............	25	74	1
By Senate Acquittal			
Approve......................	13	87	*
Disapprove.................	50	48	2

*Less than 1%

After the Senate vote, Bill Clinton made a public statement in which he said he was "profoundly sorry" for his actions which led to the events of the past year. Do you think Clinton was sincere or not sincere when he said that?

Yes, sincere			57%
Not sincere			41
No opinion			2

	Yes, sincere	Not sincere	No opinion
By Politics			
Republicans	28%	71%	1%
Democrats	80	19	1
Independents	56	40	4
By Senate Acquittal			
Approve	79	19	2
Disapprove	16	83	1

If Bill Clinton knew for certain that he could commit adultery again and get away with lying about it if necessary, do you think he would or would not do it again?

Yes, would do it again			54%
Would not			42
No opinion			4

	Yes, would do it again	Would not	No opinion
By Politics			
Republicans	81%	17%	2%
Democrats	32	62	6
Independents	57	38	5
By Senate Acquittal			
Approve	35	59	6
Disapprove	91	9	*

*Less than 1%

Note: The initial reaction of Americans to the historic Senate vote on Friday [February 12] to acquit President Bill Clinton is positive. Polls for many months have indicated that the public did not want Clinton to be impeached or convicted and removed from office. The last Gallup Poll conducted before the vote—on Tuesday, February 9—showed that 66% wanted their senators to vote to acquit. In a poll conducted on Friday and Saturday, February 12–13, immediately after the verdict, the public says essentially the same thing: 64% approve of the vote.

Two previous congressional decisions—the vote by the House Judiciary Committee to recommend impeachment to the House and the House impeachment vote itself—went counter to the majority of the public's wishes. This weekend, the Senate came back in line with the majority opinion, and 63% of those polled this weekend say that the public's wishes have prevailed in Washington.

At the same time, despite the support for the Senate vote, there is a strong feeling that the entire process itself has harmed the country. Given a four-part choice, 74% of those polled this weekend say that the process has been harmful (32% very harmful, 42% somewhat harmful). And when respondents were asked to rate each of a list of individuals and concepts as either winners or losers as a result of the scandal, the American public comes out on the negative side, with 52% saying that the public lost in the deal, compared to only 42% who reply that it was a winner.

The vote on Friday means that Clinton, unless there are unanticipated revelations or events between now and January 2001, will survive this historic challenge to his presidency. Where does this leave him as he surveys the remaining twenty-three months of his term? On the plus side, the president's job approval ratings remain high (at 68% this weekend), continuing the trend of high ratings that began last year after the crisis first came to the public's attention. Additionally, Clinton is seen as a winner in the process by 58%, while only 38% see him as a loser (only the Democrats in Congress get a higher "winning" percentage).

The majority also is not interested in seeing Clinton charged in criminal court by Kenneth Starr, either while Clinton stays in office or after he leaves. And, as far as the public is concerned, censure should be a dead issue: only 26% want the Senate to pursue censure when it returns to session, while 73% say that the matter of censure should be dropped completely. Moreover, a majority (57%) also believes that the president was sincere on Friday when he said in his brief Rose Garden statement that he was "profoundly sorry" for his actions.

Nevertheless, the data from the most recent poll clearly show that Clinton has emerged from the past year's events with many problems. As polling has shown consistently for the year, significantly less than a majority of the public says that Clinton is honest and trustworthy—less honest, in fact, than either party in Congress. The public also holds the president in low personal regard: only 35% have a positive opinion of Clinton as a person. And despite the dislike of the partisanship and the low approval numbers given Independent Counsel Ken Starr this past year, the public also clearly thinks that Clinton is ultimately at fault for what has transpired. Given a choice, 73% say that he brought it on himself, while only 24% see him as the victim of an unfair investigation.

The public also clearly feels that Clinton has diminished the Office of the Presidency. By June 1994, 35% said that Clinton had lowered the stature of the presidency compared to previous chief executives. Now, this past weekend when the same question was asked again, that "lowered" number is up to 59%. And perhaps as an indicator of the cynicism with which the public views this president, when asked if Clinton would commit adultery again if he knew for certain that he could "get away with lying about it if necessary," 54% say that he would.

The bottom line: the public agrees with the Senate vote, does not want further indictments against Clinton, and does not even want (now that the vote has been taken) the Senate's time to be taken up with censure. Clinton himself now sits in a diminished position in the minds of the American public—viewed as not honest, held in low personal regard, seen as having brought the troubles on himself, perceived as having lowered the stature of the presidency, and viewed as a person who, despite it all, might well commit adultery again if given the opportunity.

FEBRUARY 19

Interviewing Dates: 2/4–8/99
CNN/*USA Today*/Gallup Poll
Survey #GO 126611

Still thinking about the Clinton investigation and impeachment process, overall, do you feel the news media have acted responsibly or irresponsibly in this matter?

Responsibly 48%
Irresponsibly 50
No opinion 2

	Re-sponsibly	Irre-sponsibly	No opinion
By Politics			
Republicans	44%	53%	3%
Democrats...................	47	50	3
Independents...............	51	47	2

Overall, would you say the media in this country have been biased in favor of Bill Clinton, or biased against Bill Clinton?

Biased in favor.. 40%
Biased against him... 37
Not biased (volunteered) 16
No opinion 7

	Biased in favor	Biased against him	Not biased	No opinion
By Politics				
Republicans.....	63%	21%	10%	6%
Democrats.......	25	48	19	8
Independents ...	37	38	18	7

Note: The news media covering the Clinton impeachment process receive somewhat higher marks from the American public now than they did when the crisis first broke a year ago. About one-half of those interviewed in a Gallup Poll conducted on February 4–8 say that the media have acted responsibly in the matter. While these numbers may not seem like a spectacular vote of confidence, they mark a significant uptick from the responses to the same question asked on January 28, 1998, when only 37% said that the news media were acting responsibly in what then were the initial, developing stages of the Lewinsky revelations.

At the same time, confirming previous Gallup studies of perception of bias in the media, Republicans and Democrats each tend to think that the news media are biased against their positions. Republicans say that the media have been biased in favor of Bill Clinton, while Democrats say that the news media have been biased against him. Republicans feel stronger about their views, however, with 63% of those identifying with the GOP saying that the media have displayed a pro-Clinton bias, while only 48% of Democrats reply that the media have displayed an anti-Clinton bias. When independents' views are averaged in, the net total for the whole country is a rough break-even on this issue of media bias: 40% say that the media are biased in favor of Clinton, while 37% say that they are biased against him.

DECEMBER 21

Interviewing Dates: 12/9–12/99
CNN/*USA Today*/Gallup Poll
Survey #GO 129321

As you may know, removing a president from office involves two major steps in Congress. First, the House of Representatives must vote on whether there is enough evidence to bring a president to trial before the Senate; this step is called impeachment. Next, the Senate must vote on whether to remove the president from office, or not. As you may know, the House of Representatives impeached Bill Clinton last December, after which the matter was sent to the U.S. Senate, where they acquitted Clinton on both articles. Thinking back on the first action, do you approve or disapprove of the House decision to vote in favor of impeaching Clinton and sending the case to the Senate for trial?

Approve 50%
Disapprove.. 49
No opinion 1

	Approve	Dis-approve	No opinion
By Politics			
Republicans	79%	21%	*
Democrats....................	23	77	*
Independents...............	50	47	3

*Less than 1%

Now we'd like you to think about the second action, where the Senate voted to acquit Bill Clinton of both articles of impeachment,

meaning he remained in office. Do you approve or disapprove of that decision?

Approve 57%
Disapprove.. 42
No opinion 1

	Approve	Dis-approve	No opinion
By Politics			
Republicans	32%	67%	1%
Democrats....................	84	16	*
Independents...............	53	44	3

*Less than 1%

Selected National Trend

	Approve	Dis-approve	No opinion
1999			
March 12–14................	61%	37%	2%
February 12–13...........	64	34	2

From what you have read or heard, do you think that Congress did or did not conduct its review of the charges against Bill Clinton in a fair and impartial manner?

Yes, fair 44%
Not fair 52
No opinion 4

	Yes, fair	Not fair	No opinion
By Politics			
Republicans	59%	39%	2%
Democrats....................	33	64	3
Independents...............	41	53	6

Do you think Bill Clinton should or should not be charged in a court of law with a crime for these matters, after he leaves office?

Should.. 35%
Should not 62
No opinion 3

	Should	Should not	No opinion
By Politics			
Republicans	56%	41%	3%
Democrats....................	13	85	2
Independents...............	36	59	5

How harmful, if at all, do you feel the impeachment process of Bill Clinton was to the country—very harmful, somewhat harmful, not too harmful, or not harmful at all?

	Dec. 9–12, 1999	Feb. 12–13, 1999
Very harmful	27%	32%
Somewhat harmful	37	42
Not too harmful	18	16
Not harmful at all	17	10
No opinion	1	*

*Less than 1%

Note: One year has gone by since the House of Representatives passed its resolution of impeachment of President Bill Clinton on December 19, 1998, and in the space of that year, Americans have become significantly less negative toward the historic House decision. In a poll conducted immediately after the House's vote to impeach Clinton, on December 19 and 20 of last year, only 35% approved of the vote. Now, in a poll conducted on December 9–12 of this year, 50% approve, moving the balance of the nation's sentiment to a break-even position rather than the roughly 2-to-1 opposition that prevailed last year. The change has occurred across the political spectrum, although the percentage of independents and of Democrats who approve of impeachment has increased slightly more than the percentage of Republicans.

There has been much less change in the public's view of the Senate's ultimate decision to acquit Clinton. In February and March of this year, after the Senate vote, Gallup Polls showed that 61% to 64% of the public approved of the decision to acquit. Now, in the most recent survey, 57% approve, while 42% disapprove, making only a slight change over the past nine months. Perhaps part of the reason why respondents are more approving of the House vote to impeach and send the trial to the Senate is that, in looking back, they are less certain now than earlier this year that the process was harmful to the country. In February, just after the Senate vote that ended the process, 32% said that it had been very harmful to the country, and 42% said that it had been somewhat harmful. Now, those numbers have both dropped: 27% find it very harmful, and 37% somewhat harmful. In broader terms, those who say that impeachment has been at least somewhat harmful to the nation has dropped by 10 percentage points.

Two other questions about impeachment similarly show little change. Only about one-third (35%) now say that Clinton should be charged in a court of law for a crime in the impeachment-related matters after he leaves office, actually slightly lower than the 39% who thought that way last February. Moreover, respondents remain more negative than positive in response to questions asking if Congress conducted its review of the charges against Clinton in a fair and impartial manner. By a 52%-to-44% margin, they say that Congress did not, and these numbers are very little changed from a poll conducted in the middle of the House deliberations in October 1998.

Kosovo Crisis

FEBRUARY 22

Interviewing Dates: 2/19–21/99
CNN/*USA Today*/Gallup Poll
Survey #GO 126799

If a peace agreement is reached, NATO has proposed sending 30,000 peacekeeping troops to Kosovo, including about 4,000 U.S. troops. Would you favor or oppose the United States committing its troops as part of that peacekeeping force in Kosovo?

Favor	54%
Oppose	40
No opinion	6

	Favor	Oppose	No opinion
By Politics			
Republicans	53%	44%	3%
Democrats	58	36	6
Independents	52	40	8

Note: With negotiators for Serbs and ethnic Albanians still trying to reach a peace agreement for Yugoslavia's troubled Kosovo region, Americans appear willing to support the use of U.S. troops as part of a NATO peacekeeping force. In a new Gallup Poll, 54% favor participation by U.S. troops in a peacekeeping role, with 40% opposing such a mission. Support for the mission is strong across party lines, with Republicans, Democrats, and independents all in favor. However, 78% believe that President Bill Clinton should seek approval from Congress before deploying U.S. forces in the region. Support for the other option—the threat of NATO air strikes against Serb targets if the talks do not produce an agreement—wavers significantly. Only 43% support U.S. participation in NATO air strikes, while 45% oppose it.

Comparing the support for a peacekeeping mission in Kosovo to the U.S. peacekeeping role in Bosnia, Gallup Poll data from November 1995 show opposition to that mission before it started. Forty-nine percent of Americans opposed the use of U.S. troops in Bosnia, with 47% favoring the mission.

Despite its recent prominence in the news, more than one-half of those polled do not know where Kosovo is located. The weekend Gallup Poll asked respondents to choose which of four geographic areas best described Kosovo. While 42% were able to accurately place Kosovo in the Balkans region of Central Europe, 26% believed that it was a part of the former Soviet Union, 8% placed Kosovo in either Africa or Southeast Asia, and 24% answered "don't know." Support for a possible U.S. role in Kosovo is higher among those who know where to find Kosovo: 61% of this aware group support the use of U.S. troops in a peacekeeping role, while 36% disapprove. Of the rest, 49% approve of the peacekeeping mission, while 42% are critical of the U.S. role.

MARCH 24

Interviewing Dates: 3/19–21/99
CNN/*USA Today*/Gallup Poll
Survey #GO 127182

Do you think the United States needs to be involved in Kosovo in order to protect its own interests, or don't you think so?

Yes, needs to be 42%
Don't think so 50
No opinion 8

	Yes needs to be	Don't think so	No opinion
By Politics			
Republicans	34%	59%	7%
Democrats..................	53	39	8
Independents..............	36	55	9

Selected National Trend

	Yes, needs to be	Don't think so	No opinion
1999			
February 19–21...........	37%	55%	8%
1995			
November 27*	36	52	12
June 5–6*...................	30	63	7
1994			
February 7*.................	32	59	9

*Question wording: *Do you think the United States needs to be involved in Bosnia in order to protect its own interests, or don't you think so?*

Do you think the United States has a moral obligation to help keep the peace in Kosovo, or not?

Yes, has 58%
Has not.. 37
No opinion.. 5

	Yes, has	Has not	No opinion
By Politics			
Republicans	48%	44%	8%
Democrats..................	70	25	5
Independents..............	53	44	3

Selected National Trend

	Yes, has	Has not	No opinion
1999			
February 19–21...........	52%	43%	5%
1995			
November 27*	53	40	7

*Question wording: *Do you think the United States has a moral obligation to help keep the peace in Bosnia, or not?*

Note: A Gallup Poll taken in anticipation of NATO military action over Kosovo finds tepid public support for U.S. military involvement in that region. Less than one-half of the public (46%) currently favors U.S. participation in NATO air and missile attacks. Nearly as many Americans (43%) are opposed to this possible U.S. intervention.

U.S. public support for air and missile strikes today is roughly the same as four weeks ago. In a February Gallup Poll, 43% favored and 45% opposed U.S. participation in NATO attacks provoked by the continued failure of the Yugoslavian Serbs and Kosovo's ethnic Albanian majority to reach a peace agreement.

Over the same time period, however, public support for two possible justifications for U.S. intervention has slightly increased. Today, 42% of Americans, compared to 37% last month, believe that the United States needs to be involved in Kosovo to protect its own interests. Similarly, 58% today, compared to 52% in February, believe that the United States has a moral obligation to help keep the peace in Kosovo.

The current balance of opinion toward a NATO air and missile attack is similar to public support for U.S. involvement with international military operations in the Balkans at other times this decade. In one of Gallup's earliest questions on this subject in August 1992, just 49% of Americans thought that the United States should participate in UN air strikes against Serbian forces in Bosnia in order to stop their blocking of relief efforts to Sarajevo; 39% were opposed. More recently, in December 1997, 49% approved and 43% disapproved of the presence of U.S. troops in Bosnia as part of a United Nations peacekeeping force.

Relative to other issues in the news over the past few years, respondents today are paying scant attention to the Kosovo situation. About one-third (36%) are following the situation closely, while the rest are paying little to no attention, thus putting interest in the issue on a par with the current Microsoft Corporation trial. By comparison, the Monica Lewinsky scandal, the 1997 United Parcel Service strike, and the beginning of the 1991 Gulf War were all followed closely by eight in ten Americans. Among the minority who are paying close attention to Kosovo, support for U.S. participation in NATO air strikes is relatively high, at 58%. Those not paying close attention oppose U.S. involvement by a 46%-to-39% margin.

Although the question has not been updated since 1995, the Gallup Poll in that year found American support for U.S. involvement in peacekeeping activities in the Balkans largely evaporating when respondents were presented with the possibility that American soldiers might be killed. If that sentiment continues to hold, U.S. participation in air or ground attacks (as opposed to cruise missile attacks) could be politically risky.

It should be noted, moreover, that public reluctance to involve the United States in military conflict is not unusual. A look into Gallup's archives reveals majority opposition to U.S. military involvement at the early stages of the Persian Gulf crisis in 1990, Indo-China in 1954, and World War II in 1941. Of course, Americans became much more supportive of U.S. involvement in each case once military action actually began.

APRIL 2

Interviewing Dates: 3/30–31/99
CNN/*USA Today*/Gallup Poll
Survey #GO 127287

Do you believe the United States, through its participation in the current NATO air attacks, will or will not accomplish its objectives in Kosovo?

	March 30–31, 1999	March 25, 1999
Yes, will	41%	44%
Will not	47	40
Has no objectives (volunteered)	1	2
No opinion	11	14

March 30–31, 1999

	Yes, will	Will not	Has no objectives; no opinion
By Sex			
Male	41%	51%	8%
Female	42	43	15
By Ethnic Background			
White	40	49	11
Nonwhite	46	36	18
Black	51	30	19
By Education			
Postgraduate	33	56	11
College Graduate	35	55	10
College Incomplete	46	45	9
No College	41	43	16
By Region			
East	40	47	13
Midwest	43	46	11
South	45	43	12
West	35	54	11
By Age			
18–29 Years	48	43	9
30–49 Years	45	46	9
50–64 Years	31	52	17
65 Years and Over	34	48	18
By Household Income			
$75,000 and Over	38	54	8
$50,000 and Over	41	51	8
$30,000–$49,999	45	45	10
$20,000–$29,999	40	46	14
Under $20,000	39	45	16

By Politics

Republicans	36	57	7
Democrats	50	36	14
Independents	36	50	14

By Political Ideology

Conservative	37	52	11
Moderate	43	45	12
Liberal	45	41	14

Regarding the situation in Kosovo, are you very confident, somewhat confident, not too confident, or not at all confident that:

The United States will be able to accomplish its goals with very few or no American casualties?

Very confident	14%
Somewhat confident	38
Not too confident	28
Not at all confident	16
No opinion	4

	Very confident	Somewhat confident	Not too confident	Not at all confident*
By Sex				
Male	17%	33%	28%	20%
Female	13	42	28	12
By Ethnic Background				
White	14	38	29	16
Nonwhite	18	33	26	15
Black	18	36	23	14
By Education				
Postgraduate	10	35	33	18
College Graduate	8	34	32	24
College Incomplete	16	42	24	16
No College	17	36	29	13
By Region				
East	11	38	31	15
Midwest	17	43	26	12
South	16	34	28	17
West	13	36	28	20

By Age

18–29 Years	22	43	26	8
30–49 Years	13	38	28	17
50–64 Years	12	32	28	23
65 Years and Over	13	36	31	15

By Household Income

$75,000 and Over	10	35	28	24
$50,000 and Over	14	34	31	20
$30,000–$49,999	12	42	28	14
$20,000–$29,999	12	41	29	12
Under $20,000	22	36	26	13

By Politics

Republicans	13	32	34	19
Democrats	20	43	26	8
Independents	10	37	26	22

By Political Ideology

Conservative	14	32	32	21
Moderate	14	41	26	14
Liberal	17	39	29	8

*"No opinion"—at 9% or less—is omitted.

Selected National Trend

	Very confident	Somewhat confident	Not too confident	Not at all confident*
Feb. 1999	18%	36%	25%	14%
Dec. 1995**	12	28	29	28
Oct. 1994†	23	44	19	13
Sept. 1994†	21	40	22	14
Dec. 1992‡	27	37	22	10

*"No opinion"—at 7% or less—is omitted.
**Question wording: *Regarding the situation in Bosnia . . .*
†Question wording: *Regarding the situation in Haiti . . .*
‡Question wording: *Regarding the situation in Somalia . . .*

The United States will be able to accomplish its goals without sending in U.S. ground troops?

Very confident.. 9%
Somewhat confident 34
Not too confident... 31
Not at all confident 22
No opinion.. 4

	Very con- fident	Some- what con- fident	Not too con- fident	Not at all con- fident*
By Sex				
Male	11%	31%	30%	26%
Female.............	8	37	31	19
By Ethnic Background				
White..............	9	35	31	22
Nonwhite.........	13	32	28	21
Black	15	31	28	19
By Education				
Postgraduate....	6	28	38	27
College				
Graduate......	5	27	38	28
College				
Incomplete...	10	36	28	21
No College	11	36	28	20
By Region				
East.................	6	34	38	19
Midwest	11	36	34	15
South	12	34	25	24
West	6	34	25	31
By Age				
18–29 Years	11	41	29	17
30–49 Years	9	31	33	24
50–64 Years	10	30	32	25
65 Years				
and Over......	8	37	25	22
By Household Income				
$75,000				
and Over......	3	29	35	32
$50,000				
and Over......	5	31	34	28
$30,000–				
$49,999	16	32	28	22
$20,000–				
$29,999	9	35	32	18
Under				
$20,000	9	39	30	17

By Politics				
Republicans.....	5	30	36	27
Democrats	16	39	24	17
Independents ...	5	33	33	24
By Political Ideology				
Conservative ...	11	32	32	23
Moderate	7	38	30	21
Liberal.............	10	32	28	23

*"No opinion"—at 8% or less—is omitted.

From what you've heard or read, do you think the current NATO military action in Yugoslavia has made the situation in that region better or worse?

Better 22%
Worse... 64
No difference (volunteered) 6
No opinion... 8

	Better	Worse	No difference	No opinion
By Politics				
Republicans.....	18%	70%	6%	6%
Democrats	29	57	4	10
Independents ...	18	66	7	9

Looking ahead to when the current NATO military action in Yugoslavia has ended, do you think it will have made the situation in that region better or worse?

Better 53%
Worse... 36
No difference (volunteered) 5
No opinion... 6

	Better	Worse	No difference	No opinion
By Politics				
Republicans.....	45%	47%	4%	4%
Democrats	63	28	3	6
Independents ...	48	37	7	8

In your view, whose actions are more responsible for the large number of ethnic Albanian refugees now leaving Kosovo—the Serbian government's actions, or the NATO alliance's actions?

Serbian government.. 67%
NATO alliance 19
Both equally (volunteered)............................ 4
Neither; other (volunteered) 1
No opinion.. 9

	Serbian government	NATO alliance	Both; neither; other	No opinion
By Politics				
Republicans.....	68%	17%	7%	8%
Democrats	69	19	3	9
Independents ...	62	19	7	12

Next, I'm going to read some possible reasons for U.S. military involvement in Yugoslavia. Please say whether you think each one is serious enough to justify the current U.S. military air strikes in the region:

Serbian attacks on civilians in Kosovo?

Yes, justifies air strikes 65%
Does not.. 30
No opinion.. 5

	Yes, justifies air strikes	Does not	No opinion
By Politics			
Republicans	60%	35%	5%
Democrats...................	72	24	4
Independents...............	63	31	6

The threat to U.S. strategic interests in Europe?

Yes, justifies air strikes 47%
Does not.. 45
No opinion.. 8

	Yes, justifies air strikes	Does not	No opinion
By Politics			
Republicans	37%	56%	7%
Democrats...................	60	34	6
Independents...............	41	49	10

Note: A new Gallup Poll finds little change in public support for the U.S. role in the NATO military offensive in Yugoslavia, compared to when the air and missile strikes began one week ago. Fifty-three percent of those polled on the nights of March 30 and 31 favor U.S. involvement in the mission aimed at ending alleged Serb oppression of ethnic Albanians in the Yugoslavian province of Kosovo, up just slightly from 50% in a survey taken on the night of March 25.

There are a few new indications that Americans are growing cynical about the effectiveness of an air war in Yugoslavia. In particular, there has been a drop in public confidence that the United States can accomplish its objectives through NATO air attacks, from 44% last week to 41% today. At the same time, there has been an 8-point rise in the percentage who would favor sending in U.S. ground troops if the air and missile strikes alone prove ineffective, from 31% last week to 39% today. Just as the public seems split over the effectiveness of the current air attacks, it is divided in its evaluation of the Clinton administration's foreign policy leadership on this issue. Forty-six percent believe that the administration's objectives in the Kosovo situation are clear, while 47% disagree.

In the aftermath of the loss of an F-117 stealth fighter plane, reportedly shot down by Serbian antiaircraft fire, the public's belief that the NATO mission will result in few or no American casualties has not changed. Fifty-two percent of those polled this week believe that the mission will be accomplished with few or no American casualties, while 44% are not confident that casualties can be avoided. In the March 25 poll, 54% were confident that casualties could be kept to a minimum. Whether that confidence is sustained now that American soldiers have been taken as prisoners of war remains to be seen.

As thousands of ethnic Albanian refugees stream across the border into Macedonia and other neighboring countries, 64% say that the NATO air strikes have made the situation in Yugoslavia worse. However, 67% blame the Serbian government's actions for causing the problem; and 58% believe that the Serbs have been using all possible means, including "ethnic cleansing" and mass killings, to remove the ethnic Albanians from Kosovo. Two in three Americans polled believe that the killings alone justify the NATO air strikes, along with the possibility that the Serb aggression could spread to neighboring countries. Finally, 53% believe that the NATO mission will eventually improve the situation in Yugoslavia.

However, the mission has cost President Bill Clinton some of his credibility. While his overall approval ratings continue to hold strong at 64%, his foreign policy approval rating has dropped to 54%, down from 60% in a poll taken in the weekend before the air strikes began.

APRIL 29

Interviewing Dates: 4/26–27/99
CNN/*USA Today*/Gallup Poll
Survey #GO 127538

From what you have heard or read, do you think the Clinton administration has a clear and well-thought-out policy on the Kosovo situation, or don't you think so?

Yes, has clear policy.. 38%
Don't think so 54
No opinion 8

	Yes, has clear policy	Don't think so	No opinion
By Sex			
Male.............................	37%	58%	5%
Female	38	51	11
By Ethnic Background			
White	36	56	8
Nonwhite	45	44	11
Black............................	50	39	11
By Education			
Postgraduate	31	63	6
College Graduate.........	37	56	7
College Incomplete.....	33	58	9
No College..................	42	49	9
By Region			
East..............................	43	49	8
Midwest......................	34	60	6
South...........................	39	50	11
West............................	33	60	7
By Age			
18–29 Years................	40	51	9
30–49 Years................	34	58	8
50–64 Years................	39	55	6
65 Years and Over......	40	49	11

	Yes, has clear policy	Don't think so	No opinion
By Household Income			
$75,000 and Over	35	60	5
$50,000 and Over	33	62	5
$30,000–$49,999........	36	58	6
$20,000–$29,999........	42	52	6
Under $20,000............	41	43	16
By Politics			
Republicans	26	70	4
Democrats...................	53	39	8
Independents...............	31	57	12
By Political Ideology			
Conservative...............	29	64	7
Moderate.....................	40	52	8
Liberal	47	44	9

Selected National Trend

	Yes, has clear policy	Don't think so	No opinion
1999			
April 13–14.................	41%	51%	8%
April 6–7.....................	39	50	11
March 30–31...............	46	47	7

If the current NATO air and missile strikes are not effective in achieving the United States' objectives in Kosovo, would you favor or oppose President Clinton sending U.S. ground troops into the region along with troops from other NATO countries?*

Favor.. 40%
Oppose.. 56
No opinion.. 4

*Based on half sample

	Favor	Oppose	No opinion
By Politics			
Republicans	38%	59%	3%
Democrats...................	48	46	6
Independents...............	36	61	3

Selected National Trend

	Favor	Oppose	No opinion
1999			
April 13–14.................	52%	45%	3%
April 6–7.....................	47	47	6

March 30–31............... 39	57	4	
March 25*................... 31	65	4	

1994

April 16–18**............. 41	53	6

*Question wording: . . . *sending U.S. ground troops into the region to stop the Serbian attacks on Kosovo?*
**Question wording: . . . *sending U.S. ground troops into Bosnia to join ground troops from other West European countries?*

From what you've heard and read, do you think the current NATO military action in Yugoslavia has been a success or a failure?

Success	35%
Failure..	47
Too soon to tell (volunteered)	9
No opinion...	9

	Success	Failure	Too soon to tell	No opinion
By Politics				
Republicans.....	28%	59%	6%	7%
Democrats	45	35	12	8
Independents ...	29	52	9	10

Selected National Trend

	Success	Failure	Too soon to tell	No opinion
1999				
April 13–14.....	37%	46%	9%	8%
April 6–7	37	41	15	7

Looking ahead to when the NATO military action in Yugoslavia has ended, do you think it will be a success or a failure?

Success	49%
Failure..	37
Too soon to tell (volunteered)	6
No opinion...	8

	Success	Failure	Too soon to tell	No opinion
By Politics				
Republicans.....	41%	48%	5%	6%
Democrats	65	22	6	7

Independents ... 40	45	6	9

Selected National Trend

	Success	Failure	Too soon to tell	No opinion
1999				
April 13–14.....	51%	35%	8%	6%
April 6–7	50	35	8	7

Do you favor or oppose a call-up of U.S. military reservists to assist in the NATO air war on Yugoslavia?

Favor...	46%
Oppose..	50
No opinion...	4

	Favor	Oppose	No opinion
By Politics			
Republicans	42%	55%	3%
Democrats...................	54	41	5
Independents...............	41	55	4

Note: There has been a significant downturn in the American people's support for the possible introduction of ground troops into the Kosovo situation. Additionally, support for the current air strikes and for the way in which President Bill Clinton is handling the situation is also slipping, and less than one-half of the public favors the announced call-up of military reservists.

While support for both air strikes and ground troops had been rising steadily from mid-March through a mid-April poll, the current survey finds that support levels for both actions are down. In this poll, 56% support the current U.S. and NATO air and missile attacks, down from 61% on April 13–14.

Perhaps more important for U.S. and NATO policy decision-makers, support for the introduction of ground troops—if the air strikes are not successful—is down significantly. In mid-April, 52% of the public said that they would favor the introduction of ground troops if the strikes did not achieve U.S. objectives. In the most recent poll, that percentage has fallen to only 40% approval, with 56% saying that they are opposed.

One reason for this downturn in public support may be continuing low levels of optimism about the impact of current or future military actions in the region. In the current poll, only 35% say that the NATO actions have been a success to date, and, further, only 49% say that the NATO actions will ultimately achieve their objectives. Despite the heavy publicity and numerous justifications presented over the past month by both the U.S. administration and NATO leaders, these numbers have essentially not changed.

MAY 4

Interviewing Dates: 4/30–5/2/99
CNN/*USA Today*/Gallup Poll
Survey #GO 127557

Do you favor or oppose sending U.S ground troops along with troops from other NATO countries to serve in a combat situation in the region?

Favor	40%
Oppose	55
No opinion	5

	Favor	Oppose	No opinion
By Politics			
Republicans	38%	59%	3%
Democrats	45	50	5
Independents	37	58	5

Selected National Trend

	Favor	Oppose	No opinion
1999			
April 26–27	36%	60%	4%
April 13–14	43	53	4
April 6–7	41	54	5

If a peace agreement is worked out between the Yugoslavian Serbs and Kosovo's ethnic Albanian majority, would you favor or oppose sending U.S. ground troops along with troops from other countries to serve as peacekeepers in the region?

Favor	67%
Oppose	31
No opinion	2

	Favor	Oppose	No opinion
By Politics			
Republicans	62%	37%	1%
Democrats	74	22	4
Independents	63	35	2

Do you approve or disapprove of the way Congress is handling the situation in Kosovo?

Approve	41%
Disapprove	45
No opinion	14

	Approve	Dis-approve	No opinion
By Politics			
Republicans	41%	46%	13%
Democrats	47	41	12
Independents	35	49	16

How confident are you in Bill Clinton as a military leader—very confident, somewhat confident, not too confident, or not confident at all?

Very confident	16%
Somewhat confident	40
Not too confident	18
Not confident at all	26
No opinion	*

*Less than 1%

	Very con-fident	Some-what con-fident	Not too con-fident	Not con-fident at all*
By Politics				
Republicans	5%	22%	22%	51%
Democrats	30	49	15	5
Independents	11	45	18	25

*"No opinion"—at 1% or less—is omitted.

Overall, whom do you have more confidence in to set the United States' military policy toward Yugoslavia—President Clinton, or the Republican leaders in Congress?

Clinton 43%
Republican leaders 42
Other (volunteered) 11
No opinion 4

	Clinton	Republican leaders	Other	No opinion
By Politics				
Republicans.....	15%	74%	8%	3%
Democrats	70	20	5	5
Independents ...	37	41	18	4

Note: After five weeks of the NATO air strike campaign against Serbian forces in Yugoslavia, a majority of Americans continues to support U.S. involvement in that action, with a new Gallup Poll showing 58% in favor and 36% opposed—little changed from last week, and about the same as a month ago. The current poll also shows that while Americans continue to oppose the deployment of U.S. ground combat troops in the conflict by a 55%-to-40% margin, they would nevertheless favor sending U.S. ground troops to Kosovo as part of an international peacekeeping effort. Should a peace agreement be reached between the Serbs and Kosovars, they would support a U.S. peacekeeping role by better than a 2-to-1 margin, with 67% in favor and only 31% opposed.

These attitudes about U.S. involvement in Kosovo are not highly partisan, with at least one-half of Democrats, Republicans, and independents all aligned on the same side of the various issues—approving the air strikes, opposing ground combat troops, and supporting the proposal for U.S. peacekeeping troops if peace is first achieved. There are some partisan differences, with Democrats most supportive and Republicans least supportive of the Clinton administration's policies, but only when President Bill Clinton's name is specifically mentioned do majorities of Republicans and Democrats disagree.

Thus, for example, 50% of Republicans support U.S. involvement in the NATO air campaign, compared with 57% of independents and 66% of Democrats. While these results reveal a 16 percentage-point difference between Republicans and Democrats, the differences are much larger when respondents are asked about Clinton directly. Only 36% of Republicans approve of Clinton's handling of the situation in Kosovo, compared with 51% of independents and 74% of Democrats—a Republican-Democratic gap of 38 percentage points. The partisan gap increases to 52 points when respondents are asked how much confidence they have in Clinton as a military leader: 27% of Republicans are very or somewhat confident, compared with 56% of independents and 79% of Democrats.

Oddly enough, when respondents are asked to evaluate Congress's handling of the situation in Kosovo, the responses are virtually nonpartisan. Overall, 41% express approval, with 47% approval among Democrats, 35% among independents, and 41% among Republicans. In that question, however, the fact that Republicans control Congress is not mentioned. Later, when asked whether they have more confidence in Clinton or the Republican leaders in Congress to set U.S. military policy toward Yugoslavia, the respondents are evenly divided—43% in favor of Clinton, 42% in favor of the Republican congressional leaders. But the partisan differences here are large: only 15% of Republicans choose Clinton, compared with 70% of Democrats, a 55-point gap. Similarly, just 20% of Democrats choose the Republican leaders in Congress, compared with 74% of Republicans, a 54-point gap. Independents are about evenly divided between Clinton and the Republicans in Congress, with 41% favoring the GOP leaders and 37% opting for Clinton.

MAY 11

Interviewing Dates: 5/7–9/99
CNN/*USA Today*/Gallup Poll
Survey #GO 127650

So far, do you think the military action against Yugoslavia by the United States and NATO has been too aggressive, about right, or not aggressive enough?

Too aggressive.. 24%
About right 44
Not aggressive enough 27
No opinion... 5

	Too aggressive	About right	Not aggressive enough	No opinion
By Politics				
Republicans.....	24%	41%	29%	6%
Democrats	19	53	25	3
Independents ...	29	40	27	4

Which of the following approaches to reaching a peace agreement in Yugoslavia would you prefer to see the United States take—continue the current military action against Yugoslavia until Slobodan Milosevic complies with peace terms that are acceptable to NATO, or stop the military action and focus on a diplomatic effort to reach a peace agreement?

Continue military action.................................. 48%
Stop and focus on peace 48
Neither; other (volunteered) 3
No opinion... 1

	Continue military action	Stop and focus on peace	Neither; other	No opinion
By Politics				
Republicans.....	48%	48%	2%	2%
Democrats	51	47	1	1
Independents ...	45	49	5	1

Note: As the United States and NATO issue apologies for the errant bomb that struck China's embassy in Belgrade on May 8, a new Gallup Poll shows that a slim majority of Americans continues to support the NATO air strikes on Yugoslavia. The poll was conducted on May 7–9, and most of the interviews came after the attack that left three Chinese journalists dead. Support for the NATO mission is at 55%, while the percentage of Americans opposed to the mission is at 38%. These support and opposition percentages have been running at roughly this level for a number of weeks, suggesting that it will take major changes or events to produce a significant shift in public opinion at this point in the military operations.

Americans also are split over whether the attacks have been too strong or not strong enough. One in four (24%) believes that the air strikes have been too aggressive, and about the same percentage (27%) believe that the rules of engagement have not been aggressive enough. Another 44% view the level of air strikes as "about right."

Public support for Bill Clinton's handling of the Kosovo crisis also remains consistent, with 55% approving of the president's actions—a result that has remained steady since late April. From a broader perspective, the new poll also shows that Clinton's overall job approval rating is constant at 60%, unchanged since early April.

In a question asked for the first time by Gallup interviewers this weekend, Americans were given the chance to speak out on their favored approach for the future of the mission—whether to continue the air strikes and simultaneously pursue peace terms acceptable to NATO, or to declare a cease-fire and focus on diplomatic efforts to reach a peace agreement. NATO and U.S. officials have stated unequivocally that they stand behind the first approach, but poll respondents are split on the issue, with 48% favoring continued attacks and 48% supporting a cease-fire and diplomatic efforts.

MAY 12

Interviewing Dates: 5/7–9/99
CNN/*USA Today*/Gallup Poll
Survey #GO 127652

I'd like to get your overall opinion of some people in the news. As I read each name, please say if you have a favorable or unfavorable opinion of this person, or if you have never heard of him:

Jesse Jackson?

Favorable... 70%
Unfavorable... 22
No opinion... 8

	Favorable	Un-favorable	No opinion
By Politics			
Republicans	56%	36%	8%
Democrats	84	11	5
Independents	70	20	10

Selected National Trend

	Favorable	Un-favorable	No opinion
Feb. 19–21, 1999	59%	31%	10%
July 20–23, 1995	47	40	13
April 17–19, 1995	38	55	7
May 7–10, 1992	46	42	12

Serbian leader Slobodan Milosevic?

Favorable	3%
Unfavorable	76
No opinion	10
Never heard of	11

	Favorable	Un-favorable	No opinion	Never heard of
By Politics				
Republicans	4%	79%	8%	9%
Democrats	2	76	8	14
Independents	2	74	13	11

Do you believe that one of the objectives of U.S. and NATO military action in Yugoslavia should or should not be the removal of Slobodan Milosevic from power?

Should	79%
Should not	15
No opinion	6

	Should	Should not	No opinion
By Politics			
Republicans	77%	17%	6%
Democrats	84	12	4
Independents	77	14	9

As you may know, several hundred ethnic Albanian refugees from Kosovo have been brought to the United States. Do you support or oppose the decision to bring them here to the United States?

Support	66%
Oppose	30
No opinion	4

	Support	Oppose	No opinion
By Politics			
Republicans	65%	32%	3%
Democrats	68	29	3
Independents	65	30	5

As you may know, the refugees are being temporarily housed at military bases, but some will be placed with American families. If given the chance, would you open your home to a Kosovo refugee family, or not?

Yes, would	39%
Would not	57
No opinion	4

	Yes, would	Would not	No opinion
By Politics			
Republicans	35%	60%	5%
Democrats	39	56	5
Independents	41	55	4

Note: By better than a 2-to-1 majority (66% to 30%), Americans support the decision of the Clinton administration to bring several hundred ethnic Albanian refugees from Kosovo to the United States. Also, about four in ten (39%) say that if given the chance, they would open their homes to a Kosovar refugee family.

This positive reaction to admitting Kosovar refugees into the United States is partly related to whether Americans support U.S. involvement in the NATO air strikes against Yugoslavia. Overall, 55% support such involvement; and, among these people, three-quarters support the decision to bring Kosovar refugees to the United States. Among the 38% who oppose U.S. involvement in the air strikes, support is lower, although still more than one-half agree with the decision. When it comes to opening their homes to the refugees, however, policy differences are not an important consideration: 42% who support U.S. policy in

Kosovo would make their homes available, compared with 35% of those who oppose U.S. policy.

The current poll also shows that reaction to the acceptance of refugees in the United States is not highly politicized. While Democrats are much more likely than either independents or Republicans to support U.S. involvement in the NATO air strikes, about two-thirds of each of these partisan groups support the decision to bring the refugees to this country. Furthermore, about the same number of each group—from 37% to 42%—would be willing to open their homes to refugee families.

MAY 26

Interviewing Dates: 5/23–24/99
CNN/*USA Today*/Gallup Poll
Survey #GO 127701

As you may know, the military alliance of Western countries called NATO has launched air and missile attacks against Serbian military targets in Yugoslavia. Do you favor or oppose the United States being a part of that military action?

Favor.. 49%
Oppose.. 47
No opinion.. 4

	Favor	Oppose	No opinion
By Sex			
Male............................	49%	47%	4%
Female	50	46	4
By Ethnic Background			
White	51	46	3
Nonwhite	43	49	8
Black...........................	42	50	8
By Education			
Postgraduate	62	34	4
College Graduate........	50	46	4
College Incomplete.....	51	46	3
No College..................	45	50	5
By Region			
East.............................	54	45	1
Midwest.......................	50	46	4
South...........................	47	46	7
West............................	47	49	4
By Age			
18–29 Years................	47	48	5
30–49 Years................	52	45	3
50–64 Years................	58	39	3
65 Years and Over......	37	57	6
By Household Income			
$75,000 and Over	48	49	3
$50,000 and Over	53	45	2
$30,000–$49,999........	57	40	3
$20,000–$29,999........	42	52	6
Under $20,000............	39	55	6
By Politics			
Republicans	46	52	2
Democrats...................	54	40	6
Independents...............	48	47	5
By Political Ideology			
Conservative...............	44	53	3
Moderate......................	53	42	5
Liberal	56	42	2

Selected National Trend

	Favor	Oppose	No opinion
1999			
May 7–9......................	55%	38%	7%
April 30–May 2*	58	36	6
April 26–27.................	56	40	4
April 21......................	51	39	10
April 13–14................	61	35	4
April 6–7....................	58	36	6
March 30–31..............	53	41	6
March 25....................	50	39	11

*Based on half sample

How confident are you in President Clinton's ability to handle the situation in Kosovo— very confident, somewhat confident, not too confident, or not at all confident?

Very confident... 17%
Somewhat confident....................................... 40
Not too confident.. 17
Not at all confident... 25
No opinion... 1

	Very con-fident	Some-what con-fident	Not too con-fident	Not at all con-fident*
By Politics				
Republicans.....	8%	26%	24%	42%
Democrats.......	32	53	9	6
Independents...	14	39	17	28

*"No opinion"—at 2% or less—is omitted.

Selected National Trend

	Very con-fident	Some-what con-fident	Not too con-fident	Not at all con-fident*
1999				
March 30–31...	27%	39%	20%	13%
1995				
Nov. 27**........	21	42	19	15
June 5–6**......	13	38	28	18

*"No opinion"—at 3% or less—is omitted.
**Question wording: . . . *handle the situation in Bosnia*

As you may know, the NATO countries participating in the attack on Yugoslavia have a number of options right now. For each of the following possible options, please say whether you would approve or disapprove if the United States and NATO decided to take that course of action today:

If the United States and NATO were to send in ground troops to serve in a combat situation?

Approve 39%
Disapprove.. 58
No opinion 3

	Approve	Dis-approve	No opinion
By Politics			
Republicans	36%	63%	1%
Democrats....................	46	50	4
Independents...............	36	61	3

If the United States and NATO were to temporarily suspend the air strikes and attempt to resolve the matter through negotiations and other means?

Approve 82%
Disapprove.. 15
No opinion 3

	Approve	Dis-approve	No opinion
By Politics			
Republicans	85%	13%	2%
Democrats....................	85	13	2
Independents..............	78	18	4

If the United States and NATO were to permanently end all military action and make no further effort to help the refugees return to Kosovo?

Approve 25%
Disapprove.. 71
No opinion 4

	Approve	Dis-approve	No opinion
By Politics			
Republicans	20%	76%	4%
Democrats....................	24	73	3
Independents..............	28	67	5

Thinking about the U.S. and NATO military action against Yugoslavia, would you say that the United States and NATO are doing everything possible to conduct the air strikes in a way that minimizes the number of civilian casualties, or that the United States and NATO could do more to minimize the number of civilian casualties being caused by the air strikes?

Doing everything possible.............................. 48%
Could do more 46
No opinion 6

	Doing everything possible	Could do more	No opinion
By Politics			
Republicans	49%	44%	7%
Democrats....................	52	42	6
Independents..............	45	49	6

Note: American support for U.S. involvement in the Kosovo situation has dropped to its lowest point since the NATO air attacks began two months ago, and the vast majority of Americans now favor a cease-fire in order to resolve the situation through negotiations. Perhaps partially as a result of the souring mood on Kosovo, President Bill Clinton's job approval rating has fallen to its lowest level since August 1996.

A new Gallup Poll shows that approval for U.S. participation in the air strikes against Serbia is essentially at a break-even point—49% of Americans approve, and 47% disapprove. This figure is down from the 55% who approved two weeks ago, on May 7–9, and marks the lowest level of support since March 25, the day after the strikes began, when support levels were at 50%. Even at that point, however, opposition was at only 39%, with 11% having no opinion. In the current poll, the percentage of those with no opinion is only 4%.

Confidence in President Clinton's ability to handle the situation in Kosovo has also dropped from late March. At that point, 66% of respondents were very or somewhat confident in his ability to handle the situation. Now, that number has dropped to 57%, with 42% saying that they are not confident. This lack of confidence is no doubt reflected in Clinton's overall job approval, which, at 53%, is at its lowest level since August 1996. The president's job approval was consistently in the 60% range during 1998 and, twice in late 1998 and in early February of this year, rose to 70% or higher. In recent weeks, however, his approval rating has been at just 60%, and thus the current 53% reading represents a drop of 7 points in only two weeks. The poll was conducted on Sunday and Monday nights of this week and may reflect the fallout not only from the Kosovo situation but also the continuing revelations concerning the allegations that the Chinese may have stolen American nuclear secrets.

JUNE 7

Interviewing Dates: 6/4–5/99
CNN/*USA Today*/Gallup Poll
Survey #GO 127853

In view of the developments since we entered the fighting in Yugoslavia, do you think the United States made a mistake sending military forces to fight in Yugoslavia?

Yes... 43%
No 53
No opinion... 4

	Yes	No	No opinion
By Politics			
Republicans	58%	41%	1%
Democrats...................	30	65	5
Independents..............	43	52	5

Overall, which side do you think has won more of what they wanted in the peace agreement— the United States and NATO, or the Serbs in Yugoslavia?

United States and NATO................................ 50%
Serbs in Yugoslavia....................................... 26
Neither (volunteered) 8
Both; mixed (volunteered)............................. 1
No opinion... 15

	United States and NATO	Serbs in Yugoslavia	Neither; both; mixed	No opinion
By Politics				
Republicans.....	44%	33%	7%	16%
Democrats	63	14	9	14
Independents ...	43	32	10	15

Do you feel the United States and its NATO allies should continue military action in Yugoslavia until Slobodan Milosevic is removed from power, or not?

Yes, continue until he is removed 63%
Do not continue 33
No opinion... 4

	Yes, continue	Do not continue	No opinion
By Politics			
Republicans	56%	39%	5%
Democrats...................	69	26	5
Independents..............	62	35	3

Looking ahead, do you think it is more likely that Slobodan Milosevic will comply with the terms of the agreement, or that he will violate the terms of the agreement?

Will comply with terms 19%
Will violate terms 73
No opinion 8

	Will comply with terms	Will violate terms	No opinion
By Politics			
Republicans	14%	80%	6%
Democrats...................	24	67	9
Independents..............	19	73	8

Would you favor or oppose the United States using federal funds to help rebuild:

The area that the refugees will return to in Kosovo?

Favor.. 58%
Oppose... 39
No opinion 3

	Favor	Oppose	No opinion
By Politics			
Republicans	50%	47%	3%
Democrats...................	67	29	4
Independents..............	56	40	4

The Serbian areas bombed by the United States in Yugoslavia?

Favor.. 37%
Oppose... 60
No opinion 3

	Favor	Oppose	No opinion
By Politics			
Republicans	31%	67%	2%
Democrats...................	43	52	5
Independents..............	35	62	3

Note: The initial reaction of the American public to the proposed peace settlement in the Kosovo crisis is positive, but wary. In the latest Gallup Poll, 61% of the public approve of the plan, while only 13% oppose it. About one-fourth do not know enough about it to be able to evaluate it. The talks about the specific implementation of the agreement broke down on Sunday [June 6], but even before these details became known, almost three-quarters of Americans said that Yugoslavian leader Slobodan Milosevic could not be trusted to comply with the agreement's terms.

Reinforcing this evident distrust of the Yugoslavian leader, 63% of those interviewed think that NATO and the United States should continue the military action until Milosevic is totally removed from power. One reason that Americans may feel it is important to remove leaders of countries that the United States opposes in military action could be lessons learned from the Persian Gulf War: 76% of Americans in 1991, after the end of the conflict, thought that Saddam Hussein should have been removed from power.

JUNE 11

Interviewing Date: 6/10/99, between 8:15 P.M. and 9:00 P.M. EST
CNN/*USA Today*/Gallup Poll
Survey #GO 127914

Do you consider President Clinton's recent actions concerning Kosovo to be a significant U.S. foreign policy achievement, or don't you think so?

	Total	Speech watchers
Yes, significant	46%	48%
Don't think so	48	51
No opinion	6	1

	Yes, significant	Don't think so	No opinion
By Politics			
Republicans	35%	62%	3%
Democrats...................	62	29	9
Independents..............	40	53	7

All in all, do you think the situation in Kosovo was worth going to war over, or not?

	Total	Speech watchers
Yes, worth going	47%	48%
Not worth going	47	47
No opinion	6	5

	Yes, worth going	Not worth going	No opinion
By Politics			
Republicans	40%	57%	3%
Democrats	53	36	11
Independents	49	48	3

Do you favor or oppose sending 7,000 U.S. ground troops along with troops from other countries to serve as peacekeepers in Kosovo?

Favor	53%
Oppose	43
No opinion	4

	Favor	Oppose	No opinion
By Politics			
Republicans	47%	51%	2%
Democrats	66	29	5
Independents	47	49	4

Thinking again about the peace agreement that has just been signed, do you think that peace agreement probably will work or probably will break down?

	Total	Speech watchers
Probably work	38%	43%
Probably break down	55	54
No opinion	7	3

	Probably work	Probably break down	No opinion
By Politics			
Republicans	31%	64%	5%
Democrats	47	46	7
Independents	35	57	8

Note: Key findings from a Gallup Poll conducted immediately after President Bill Clinton's televised address to the nation on Thursday night [June 10] about the peace agreement in Kosovo may be broken down into four points. First, Americans do not have a strong sense that the apparently successful conclusion of the military action in Kosovo, accompanied by the agreement that Yugoslavian troops will leave Kosovo and that the Kosovar Albanian refugees can return, has constituted a highly significant or even necessary achievement. In fact, the public is split down the middle on the issue of whether or not the situation in Kosovo was worth going to war over: 47% say that it was, but 47% say that it was not. These results can be contrasted to the 80% who said that the Persian Gulf situation was worth going to war over after its successful completion in early 1991. Moreover, only 46% now say that President Clinton's recent actions concerning Kosovo are a "significant U.S. foreign policy achievement," while 48% say that they are not.

Second, the American public does not have a great deal of confidence that the peace agreement will hold. Over one-half (55%) believe that the peace agreement will probably break down, while only 38% say that it will probably work.

Third, although the basic peace agreement itself is overwhelmingly favored, by a 60%-to-12% margin (28% have no opinion), only 53% favor the introduction of ground troops into Kosovo to serve as peacekeepers. Furthermore, there is considerable pessimism about what will transpire once U.S. and NATO ground troops are on location. Seventy-two percent of those interviewed on Thursday night say that it is somewhat or very likely that the situation will turn out to be a long-term commitment of U.S. troops, and 52% find it likely that the U.S. ground troops will suffer a significant number of casualties.

And fourth, perceptions of President Clinton's handling of the situation in Kosovo have not enjoyed the "bounce" from the peace accord that might be expected. Approval of the way that he is handling the situation is essentially the same now as it was when the military action began over two months ago: 55% approve, while 35% disapprove. Although this poll was conducted after the conclusion of Clinton's speech to the nation on

Thursday night, only 18% of those interviewed watched some or all of it, while another 20% watched only a little, and a full 62% had seen none of it.

JUNE 15

Interviewing Dates: 6/11–13/99
CNN/*USA Today*/Gallup Poll
Survey #GO 127916

Do you approve or disapprove of the way President Clinton is handling the situation in Kosovo?

Approve	57%
Disapprove	38
No opinion	5

	Approve	Dis-approve	No opinion
By Sex			
Male	57%	40%	3%
Female	57	36	7
By Ethnic Background			
White	55	40	5
Nonwhite	66	26	8
Black	70	23	7
By Education			
Postgraduate	56	41	3
College Graduate	53	43	4
College Incomplete	58	37	5
No College	58	35	7
By Region			
East	61	32	7
Midwest	57	40	3
South	54	41	5
West	57	37	6
By Age			
18–29 Years	52	40	8
30–49 Years	57	39	4
50–64 Years	61	37	2
65 Years and Over	59	34	7

	Approve	Dis-approve	No opinion
By Household Income			
$75,000 and Over	56	40	4
$50,000 and Over	53	44	3
$30,000–$49,999	62	33	5
$20,000–$29,999	53	37	10
Under $20,000	64	30	6
By Politics			
Republicans	39	56	5
Democrats	77	18	5
Independents	53	41	6
By Political Ideology			
Conservative	46	47	7
Moderate	65	32	3
Liberal	65	28	7

Selected National Trend

	Approve	Dis-approve	No opinion
1999			
June 10	55%	35%	10%
June 4–5	56	39	5
May 7–9	55	35	10
April 30–			
May 2	54	41	5
April 26–27	54	41	5
April 13–14	61	34	5
April 6–7	58	35	7
March 25	58	32	10

How much credit do you think President Clinton deserves for the peace agreement that was reached in Kosovo—a great deal, a moderate amount, not much, or none at all?

Great deal	20%
Moderate amount	47
Not much	21
None at all	10
No opinion	2

	Great deal	Moderate amount	Not much	None at all*
By Politics				
Republicans	13%	40%	31%	15%
Democrats	28	58	10	3
Independents	20	43	23	12

*"No opinion"—at 2% or less—is omitted.

As you may know, the Serbian leader Slobodan Milosevic has agreed to the terms of a peace plan which has led to the end of NATO bombing in Yugoslavia. From what you know or have heard, do you favor or oppose the terms of this peace agreement?

Favor.. 65%
Oppose... 14
Not familiar with it (volunteered) 17
No opinion.. 4

	Favor	Oppose	Not familiar with it	No opinion
By Sex				
Male	68%	17%	12%	3%
Female.............	64	10	21	5
By Ethnic Background				
White...............	65	13	18	4
Nonwhite.........	69	15	13	3
Black	68	16	14	2
By Education				
Postgraduate....	74	16	8	2
College Graduate......	62	17	16	5
College Incomplete...	61	12	23	4
No College	67	14	15	4
By Region				
East.................	67	16	13	4
Midwest	69	12	15	4
South	63	13	20	4
West	63	12	20	5
By Age				
18–29 Years	64	9	23	4
30–49 Years	65	14	17	4
50–64 Years	70	19	9	2
65 Years and Over......	67	12	16	5
By Household Income				
$75,000 and Over......	69	14	15	2
$50,000 and Over......	67	15	15	3
$30,000– $49,999	67	12	18	3
$20,000– $29,999	73	10	14	3
Under $20,000	62	15	18	5
By Politics				
Republicans.....	57	15	22	6
Democrats	73	12	14	1
Independents ...	65	14	16	5
By Political Ideology				
Conservative ...	58	16	21	5
Moderate	71	12	15	2
Liberal.............	74	11	12	3

Selected National Trend

	Favor	Oppose	Not familiar with it	No opinion
1999				
June 11–13	65%	14%	17%	4%
June 10	60	12	23	5
June 4–5	61	13	23	3

Do you favor or oppose the presence of U.S. ground troops, along with troops from other countries, in an international peacekeeping force in Kosovo?

Favor.. 66%
Oppose... 31
No opinion.. 3

	Favor	Oppose	No opinion
By Politics			
Republicans	54%	43%	3%
Democrats...................	77	18	5
Independents...............	66	31	3

Do you think the outcome of the air strikes in Kosovo represents a victory for the United States, or not?

Yes, victory 40%
No 53
Too soon to tell (volunteered) 4
No opinion.. 3

	Yes, victory	No	Too soon to tell	No opinion
By Politics				
Republicans.....	34%	58%	4%	4%
Democrats.......	54	39	5	2
Independents...	33	60	3	4

Do you think the recent military action in Yugoslavia will or will not prevent other governments around the world from committing human rights atrocities such as mass killings or ethnic cleansing?

Yes, will prevent..	33%
Will not prevent..	63
No opinion..	4

	Yes, will prevent	Will not prevent	No opinion
By Politics			
Republicans................	31%	67%	2%
Democrats...................	39	56	5
Independents..............	30	66	4

Thinking about the chances for a secure peace in Yugoslavia while Slobodan Milosevic is still president, do you think it is possible for peace to be maintained while he remains president, or do you think it is possible for peace to be maintained only if he is removed as president?

While he remains...	22%
If he is removed...	71
No opinion..	7

	While he remains	If he is removed	No opinion
By Politics			
Republicans................	19%	75%	6%
Democrats...................	21	72	7
Independents..............	24	68	8

Note: Americans are giving Bill Clinton minimal credit for achieving the peaceful solution to the conflict in Kosovo and are doubtful that the military action will serve to deter aggression in similar situations in the future. The public is also strongly skeptical about the possibility of peace in the region as long as Slobodan Milosevic remains in power.

President Clinton on Thursday night [June 10] declared the result of the military action to be a victory for the United States, but only 40% of respondents in the Gallup Poll conducted this weekend agree with him. These results vary by partisanship, but not as much as might be expected. Fifty-four percent of Democrats say that the situation represents a victory, while only 34% of Republicans and 33% of independents agree. These results occur despite the fact that 65% of those polled favor the peace agreement itself, and almost exactly the same number favor the presence of U.S. ground troops along with troops from other countries in the international peacekeeping force in Kosovo.

One reason why the action is not very likely to be seen as a victory may rest with the fact that the public tends to believe, by almost a 2-to-1 margin, that the war in Kosovo will not help deter similar atrocities from being committed in the future. Sixty-three percent say that the action will not prevent such atrocities, while only 33% say that it will.

All of the events that have occurred since the March 24 beginning of the air and missile attacks have done little to change how respondents rate President Clinton, either in terms of the overall job that he is doing or, more specifically, in terms of his handling of the situation in Kosovo. Clinton now has a 60% job approval rating, which is actually down slightly from the ratings that he received either before or just after the military action began. Similarly, his 57% approval rating for his handling of the situation in Kosovo is virtually the same as those he received just after the action began. Only 20% of the public gives Clinton a great deal of credit for the peace agreement reached in Kosovo (47% say that he deserves a moderate amount of credit), and only 43% say that the Clinton administration has a clear and well-thought-out policy on the Kosovo situation.

As for Yugoslavian leader Slobodan Milosevic, the American public is deeply skeptical that lasting peace will be possible while he is still in power: 71% say that peace will be possible in the region only if Milosevic leaves office. There is strong agreement with one policy set out by President Clinton relating to the Yugoslavian leader: 70% say that U.S. economic aid to help rebuild the Serbian areas of Yugoslavia bombed by NATO forces should be provided only when Milosevic is removed from power—the same sentiment expressed by Clinton in his speech last Thursday night.

JUNE 24

Interviewing Dates: 6/11–13/99
CNN/*USA Today*/Gallup Poll
Survey #GO 127916

Do you think it will be best for the future of the country if we take an active part in world affairs, or if we stay out of world affairs?

Take active part	61%
Stay out	34
No opinion	5

	Take active part	Stay out	No opinion
By Sex			
Male	63%	33%	4%
Female	59	36	5
By Ethnic Background			
White	61	34	5
Nonwhite	57	36	7
Black	52	40	8
By Education			
Postgraduate	75	20	5
College Graduate	65	29	6
College Incomplete	67	31	2
No College	51	42	7
By Region			
East	66	28	6
Midwest	58	39	3
South	54	41	5
West	69	26	5

	Take active part	Stay out	No opinion
By Age			
18–29 Years	55	43	2
30–49 Years	64	32	4
50–64 Years	68	28	4
65 Years and Over	53	36	11
By Household Income			
$75,000 and Over	72	25	3
$50,000 and Over	67	30	3
$30,000–$49,999	66	31	3
$20,000–$29,999	52	41	7
Under $20,000	54	40	6
By Politics			
Republicans	61	34	5
Democrats	66	29	5
Independents	56	39	5
By Political Ideology			
Conservative	54	39	7
Moderate	67	30	3
Liberal	64	31	5

Selected National Trend

	Take active part	Stay out	No opinion
April 30–			
May 2, 1999	69%	28%	3%
October 1998	61	28	11
1994	65	29	6
1990	62	28	10
1986	64	27	9
1982	54	35	11
1978	59	29	12
1974	66	24	10
1973	66	31	3
1956	71	25	4
1955	72	21	7
1954	69	25	6
1953	71	21	8
1952	68	23	9
1950	66	25	9
1949	68	25	7
1948	70	24	6
1947	68	25	7

Do you generally approve or disapprove of American troops participating in peacekeeping forces under the United Nations command?*

	Approve		
Approve			75%
Disapprove			24
No opinion			1

*Based on half sample

By Politics	Approve	Dis-approve	No opinion
Republicans	67%	32%	1%
Democrats	87	13	*
Independents	72	27	1

*Less than 1%

Do you generally approve or disapprove of American troops participating in peacekeeping forces under NATO command?

Approve			69%
Disapprove			29
No opinion			2

*Based on half sample

By Politics	Approve	Dis-approve	No opinion
Republicans	63%	33%	4%
Democrats	76	22	2
Independents	68	31	1

Which of the following statements do you agree with more—the United States only uses military air strikes for vital strategic and moral purposes, or the United States sometimes goes too far in using military air strikes for purposes that are less than vital?

For vital purposes			46%
For purposes less than vital			51
No opinion			3

By Politics	For vital purposes	For purposes less than vital	No opinion
Republicans	40%	57%	3%
Democrats	53	45	2
Independents	45	52	3

Now we'd like you to think about the use of the U.S. military in the past few years to stop human rights atrocities such as mass killings or ethnic cleansing. Do you think the United States should use the U.S. military more often, about the same, or less often than it has been to stop these kinds of atrocities?

More often			24%
About the same			43
Less often			29
No opinion			4

By Politics	More often	About the same	Less often	No opinion
Republicans	21%	41%	32%	6%
Democrats	27	47	22	4
Independents	25	42	31	2

Note: A new Gallup Poll on foreign policy attitudes finds Americans to be decidedly internationalist in the wake of NATO air strikes in Yugoslavia. Most of the public (61%) continues to say that the United States should maintain an active role in world affairs rather than stay out. An even higher share favors U.S. participation in multinational peacekeeping forces, including 69% who approve of U.S. troops serving under NATO command. Two-thirds also believe that the United States should continue to respond to international human rights atrocities with military force.

These internationalist sentiments seem generally consistent with recent public reaction to the Kosovo intervention. The latest Gallup survey finds that despite some doubts about the short-term success of the conflict, the public is generally optimistic about the long-term impact that the NATO air strikes will have in Yugoslavia. Short term, only 40% consider the air strikes a victory for the United States, while 53% do not, and only 22% believe that it is possible for peace to be maintained in Yugoslavia as long as its president, Slobodan Milosevic, is still in power. Nevertheless, 64% are very or somewhat confident that the U.S. effort to establish peace in Kosovo will succeed, and a similar number believes that it can be done with few or no American casualties.

Perhaps as a result of this optimism that peace will ultimately prevail, two-thirds of Americans indicate that they would favor the use of the military abroad in the future to deal with situations similar to Kosovo. This figure includes 43% who believe that the United States should continue to use military force at the same level as in the past few years to stop human rights atrocities such as mass killings or ethnic cleansing. An additional 24% believe that the United States should use the military in these cases more often than it has in the past, while only 29% think that the United States should use the military less often for these purposes.

Poll Trends

PRESIDENT CLINTON: JOB APPROVAL

Do you approve or disapprove of the way Bill Clinton is handling his job as president?

	Approve	Dis-approve	No opinion
December 20–21	57%	36%	7%
December 9–12	56	41	3
November 18–21	59	36	5
November 4–7	58	38	4
October 21–24	59	36	5
October 8–10	56	39	5
September 23–26	59	38	3
September 10–14	60	38	2
August 24–26	60	35	5
August 16–18	59	36	5
August 3–4	60	35	5
July 22–25	64	31	5
July 16–18	58	38	4
July 13–14	59	37	4
June 25–27*	57	41	2
June 11–13	60	37	3
June 4–5	60	35	5
May 23–24	53	42	5
May 7–9	60	35	5
April 30–May 2	60	36	4
April 26–27	60	35	5
April 13–14	60	36	4
April 6–7	59	35	6
March 30–31	64	32	4
March 19–21	64	33	3
March 12–14	62	35	3
March 5–7	68	28	4
February 26–28	66	31	3
February 19–21	66	30	4
February 12–13	68	30	2
February 9	70	27	3
February 4–8	65	33	2
January 27	67	31	2
January 22–24	69	29	2
January 15–17	69	29	2
January 8–10	67	30	3
January 6	63	34	3

PRESIDENT CLINTON: ISSUES APPROVAL

Now, thinking about some issues, do you approve or disapprove of the way Bill Clinton is handling:

Foreign affairs?

	Approve	Dis-approve	No opinion
June 4–5	55%	40%	5%
April 26–27	50	43	7

		Dis-approve	No opinion
April 6–7	55	38	7
March 30–31	54	40	6
March 19–21	60	30	10
January 15–17	64	32	4

The economy?

	Approve	Dis-approve	No opinion
June 4–5	74%	20%	6%
April 26–27	72	22	6
April 6–7	73	18	9
March 30–31	78	16	6
March 19–21	80	12	8
January 15–17	81	15	4

Crime?

	Approve	Dis-approve	No opinion
January 15–17	66%	28%	6%

Education?

	Approve	Dis-approve	No opinion
January 15–17	69%	28%	3%

The environment?

	Approve	Dis-approve	No opinion
January 15–17	69%	22%	9%

Health-care policy?

	Approve	Dis-approve	No opinion
January 15–17	52%	42%	6%

Medicare?

	Approve	Dis-approve	No opinion
January 15–17	53%	37%	10%

Poverty and homelessness?

	Approve	Dis-approve	No opinion
January 15–17	47%	43%	10%

Race relations?

	Approve	Dis-approve	No opinion
January 15–17	76%	15%	9%

The situation in Iraq?

	Approve	Dis-approve	No opinion
January 15–17	56%	39%	5%

Social Security?

	Approve	Dis-approve	No opinion
January 15–17	56%	37%	7%

Taxes?

	Approve	Dis-approve	No opinion
January 15–17	58%	37%	5%

Federal budget deficit?

	Approve	Dis-approve	No opinion
January 15–17	68%	23%	9%

HILLARY RODHAM CLINTON: JOB APPROVAL

Do you approve or disapprove of the way Hillary Rodham Clinton is handling her job as First Lady?

	Approve	Dis-approve	No opinion
November 18–21	66%	30%	4%
May 23–24	71	23	6
February 19–21	80	17	3

PEOPLE IN THE NEWS: FAVORABILITY RATINGS

I'd like to get your overall opinion of some people in the news. As I read each name, please say if you have a favorable or unfavorable opinion of this person, or if you have never heard of him or her:

Bill Clinton?

	Favorable	Un-favorable	No opinion
December 9–12	45%	53%	2%
September 23–26	54	45	1
August 3–4	52	46	2

July 22–25 57	41	2
June 25–27................. 48	50	2
April 30–		
May 2...................... 53	45	2
April 13–14................ 51	47	2
March 5–7................... 54	43	3
February 19–21........... 55	43	2
February 4–8............... 55	44	1
January 8–10.............. 58	40	2

Al Gore?

	Favorable	Un-favorable	No opinion
December 9–12...........	54%	42%	4%
October 21–24	58	36	6
October 8–10	54	42	4
September 23–26........	55	40	5
August 16–18	58	37	5
August 3–4	52	40	8
July 22–25	53	35	12
June 25–27.................	56	39	5
April 30–			
May 2......................	55	37	8
April 13–14................	54	39	7
February 19–21...........	59	33	8
February 4–8..............	61	31	8

Hillary Rodham Clinton?

	Favorable	Un-favorable	No opinion
December 9–12...........	48%	48%	4%
September 23–26........	56	40	4
August 3–4	56	41	3
July 22–25	62	35	3
June 25–27.................	56	42	2
March 5–7...................	65	31	4
February 19–21...........	65	30	5
February 4–8..............	66	31	3

Texas Governor George W. Bush?

	Favorable	Un-favorable	No opinion	Never heard of
Dec. 9–12........	68%	25%	6%	1%
Oct. 21–24.......	71	21	7	1
Oct. 8–10.........	70	25	4	1
Sept. 23–26	71	22	6	1
Aug. 16–18......	68	21	10	1
June 25–27	69	16	11	4
April 13–14.....	73	15	9	3
Feb. 19–21	69	12	14	5

Israeli Prime Minister Benjamin Netanyahu?

	Favorable	Un-favorable	No opinion	Never heard of
May 7–9	34%	20%	27%	19%

Palestinian leader Yassar Arafat?

	Favorable	Un-favorable	No opinion	Never heard of
May 7–9	26%	44%	24%	6%

Arizona Senator John McCain?

	Favorable	Un-favorable	No opinion	Never heard of
Dec. 9–12........	57%	11%	18%	14%
Oct. 21–24.......	37	12	21	30
April 13–14.....	35	12	25	28
Feb. 19–21	27	8	21	44

Former Red Cross President Elizabeth Dole?

	Favorable	Un-favorable	No opinion	Never heard of
Aug.16–18.......	69%	16%	11%	4%
April 13–14.....	74	13	9	4
Feb. 19–21	75	10	9	6

The Republican party?

	Favorable	Un-favorable	No opinion
November 18–21	50%	44%	6%
April 30–			
May 2......................	47	44	9
February 19–21...........	45	46	9
February 12–13...........	40	54	6
February 4–8...............	45	47	8
January 8–10..............	40	52	8

The Democratic party?

	Favorable	Un-favorable	No opinion
November 18–21	51%	41%	8%
April 30–May 2	53	37	10
February 19–21...........	55	37	8
February 12–13...........	56	38	6
February 4–8...............	57	37	6
January 8–10..............	57	35	8

Secretary of State Madeleine Albright?

	Favorable	Un-favorable	No opinion	Never heard of
April 13–14.....	61%	22%	12%	5%

Monica Lewinsky?

	Favorable	Un-favorable	No opinion
March 5–7	15%	79%	6%
February 19–21	16	73	11

Independent Counsel Kenneth Starr?

	Favorable	Un-favorable	No opinion	Never heard of
March 5–7	24%	66%	6%	4%
Feb. 19–21	31	62	4	3
Feb. 4–8	30	61	6	3

Political commentator Pat Buchanan?

	Favorable	Un-favorable	No opinion	Never heard of
Oct. 21–24	27%	51%	16%	6%
Oct. 8–9	29	52	13	6
Sept. 23–26	32	45	15	8
March 5–7	31	40	20	9

Former Tennessee Governor Lamar Alexander?

	Favorable	Un-favorable	No opinion	Never heard of
March 5–7	17%	15%	32%	36%

Former New Jersey Senator Bill Bradley?

	Favorable	Un-favorable	No opinion	Never heard of
Dec. 9–12	68%	25%	6%	1%
Oct. 21–24	52	16	20	12
Oct. 8–10	53	20	18	9
Sept. 23–26	44	14	21	21
Aug. 16–18	48	11	23	18
April 13–14	46	10	24	20
Feb. 19–21	38	9	20	33

Speaker of the House Dennis Hastert?

	Favorable	Un-favorable	No opinion	Never heard of
Sept. 10–14	23%	7%	48%	22%
Feb. 19–21	31	10	27	32

Senate Republican Leader Trent Lott?

	Favorable	Un-favorable	No opinion	Never heard of
Feb. 19–21	30%	26%	17%	27%
Jan. 8–10	30	26	21	23

Linda Tripp?

	Favorable	Un-favorable	No opinion	Never heard of
Feb. 19–21	11%	76%	7%	6%

House Judiciary Committee Chairman Henry Hyde?

	Favorable	Un-favorable	No opinion	Never heard of
Feb. 19–21	34%	30%	16%	20%

Ohio Congressman John Kasich?

	Favorable	Un-favorable	No opinion	Never heard of
Feb. 19–21	16%	8%	23%	53%

Former Vice President Dan Quayle?

	Favorable	Un-favorable	No opinion	Never heard of
Feb. 19–21	46%	44%	10%	*

*Less than 1%

Businessman Steve Forbes?

	Favorable	Un-favorable	No opinion	Never heard of
Oct. 21–24	42%	26%	18%	14%
Aug. 16–18	46	23	20	11
Feb. 19–21	49	13	22	16

New Hampshire Senator Bob Smith?

	Favorable	Un-favorable	No opinion	Never heard of
Feb. 19–21	13%	8%	20%	59%

Chairman of the Family Research Council Gary Bauer?

	Favorable	Un-favorable	No opinion	Never heard of
Feb. 19–21	14%	8%	17%	61%

Massachusetts Senator John Kerry?

	Favorable	Un-favorable	No opinion	Never heard of
Feb. 19–21	30%	9%	22%	39%

Microsoft chairman Bill Gates?

	Favorable	Un-favorable	No opinion	Never heard of
July 23–25	64%	15%	15%	6%
March 30–31	59	18	22	1

| Feb. 26–28 ...... 62 | 16 | 18 | 4 |
| Feb. 8–9 .... 66 | 18 | 13 | 3 |

Federal Reserve chairman Alan Greenspan?

	Favorable	Un-favorable	No opinion	Never heard of
Aug. 16–18......	50%	13%	16%	21%

Ross Perot?

	Favorable	Un-favorable	No opinion	Never heard of
Sept. 23–26	35%	54%	9%	2%

Supreme Court Chief Justice William Rehnquist?

	Favorable	Un-favorable	No opinion	Never heard of
Jan. 8–10	51%	8%	23%	18%

Businessman Donald Trump?

	Favorable	Un-favorable	No opinion	Never heard of
Oct. 8–10.........	33%	58%	7%	2%
Sept. 23–26	41	47	9	3

Minnesota Governor Jesse Ventura?

	Favorable	Un-favorable	No opinion	Never heard of
Oct. 8–10.........	37%	45%	11%	7%
Sept. 23–26	51	25	12	12

Former Connecticut Senator Lowell Weicker?

	Favorable	Un-favorable	No opinion	Never heard of
Sept. 23–26	13%	12%	18%	57%

House Republican Whip Tom DeLay?

	Favorable	Un-favorable	No opinion	Never heard of
Sept. 10–14	17%	11%	54%	18%

House Republican Leader Dick Armey?

	Favorable	Un-favorable	No opinion	Never heard of
Sept. 10–14	20%	14%	49%	17%

PRESIDENT CLINTON: PERSONAL CHARACTERISTICS

I'm going to read some personal characteristics and qualities. As I read each one, please say whether you think it applies or does not apply to Bill Clinton:

Can get things done?

	Applies	Does not apply	No opinion
January 15–17.............	82%	17%	1%

Honest and trustworthy?

	Applies	Does not apply	No opinion
January 15–17.............	24%	74%	2%

Shares your values?

	Applies	Does not apply	No opinion
January 15–17.............	35%	62%	3%

CONGRESS: JOB APPROVAL

Do you approve or disapprove of the way Congress is handling its job?

	Approve	Dis-approve	No opinion
Sept. 23–26.................	37%	56%	7%
June 11–13..................	41	53	6
April 13–14.................	45	47	8
February 12–13...........	41	54	5
January 15–17.............	50	46	4

SATISFACTION INDEX

In general, are you satisfied or dissatisfied with the way things are going in the United States at this time?

	Satisfied	Dis-satisfied	No opinion
September 23–26........	52%	45%	3%

August 24–26	62	35	3
June 11–13	55	42	3
May 23–24	51	46	3
April 26–27	51	45	4
April 13–14	58	39	3
February 12–13	71	26	3
January 15–17	70	26	4

ECONOMIC CONDITIONS

How would you rate economic conditions in this country today—excellent, good, only fair, or poor?

	Excellent	Good	Fair	Poor*
Oct. 21–24	16%	49%	27%	8%
Sept. 10–14	20	47	24	8
Aug. 24–26	14	50	28	7
June 4–5	18	56	21	5
Jan. 15–17	14	55	27	4

*"No opinion"—at 1% or less—is omitted.

Right now, do you think that economic conditions in the country as a whole are getting better or getting worse?

	Better	Worse	Same (volunteered)	No opinion
Oct. 21–24	52%	34%	11%	3%
Sept. 10–14	59	29	9	3
Aug. 24–26	54	31	12	3
June 4–5	60	27	9	4
Jan. 15–17	63	28	6	3

PERSONAL FINANCES

We are interested in how people's financial situation may have changed. Would you say that you are financially better off now than you were a year ago, or are you financially worse off now?

	Better off	Worse off	Same (volunteered)	No opinion
Oct. 21–24	56%	24%	19%	1%
Aug. 24–26	53	25	22	*
June 4–5	57	22	20	1
Jan. 15–17	58	21	21	*

*Less than 1%

Now, looking ahead, do you expect that at this time next year you will be financially better off than now, or worse off than now?

	Better off	Worse off	Same (volunteered)	No opinion
Oct. 21–24	68%	12%	13%	7%
Aug. 24–26	67	13	16	4
June 4–5	67	17	12	4
Jan. 15–17	68	14	14	4

Politics and Government

JANUARY 8
TRUST IN FEDERAL GOVERNMENT

Interviewing Dates: 12/28–29/98
CNN/*USA Today*/Gallup Poll
Survey #GO 125579

How much trust and confidence do you have in our federal government in Washington when it comes to handling each of the following—a great deal, a fair amount, not very much, or none at all:

International problems?

Great deal	22%
Fair amount	54
Not very much	18
None at all	5
No opinion	1

	Great deal	Fair amount	Not very much	None at all*
By Politics				
Republicans	19%	54%	20%	7%
Democrats	30	55	11	3
Independents	16	52	24	6

*"No opinion"—at 2% or less—is omitted.

Selected National Trend

	Great deal	Fair amount	Not very much	None at all*
May 1997	10%	53%	23%	7%
June 1976	8	48	33	7
April 1974	24	49	18	4
May 1972	20	55	20	2

*"No opinion"—at 7% or less—is omitted.

Domestic problems?

Great deal	9%
Fair amount	52
Not very much	30
None at all	7
No opinion	2

	Great deal	Fair amount	Not very much	None at all*
By Politics				
Republicans	7%	53%	33%	7%
Democrats	13	55	23	6
Independents	7	53	33	7

*"No opinion"—at 3% or less—is omitted.

Selected National Trend

	Great deal	Fair amount	Not very much	None at all*
May 1997	6%	45%	36%	11%

June 1976 5	44	42	7
April 1974 9	42	36	8
May 1972 11	59	26	3

*"No opinion"—at 5% or less—is omitted.

As you know, our federal government is made up of three branches: an Executive branch, headed by the President; a Judicial branch, headed by the U.S. Supreme Court; and a Legislative branch, made up of the U.S. Senate and House of Representatives. How much trust and confidence do you have at this time in each of the following—a great deal, a fair amount, not very much, or none at all:

The Executive branch, headed by the President?

Great deal	24%
Fair amount..	39
Not very much	23
None at all	12
No opinion..	2

By Politics

	Great deal	Fair amount	Not very much	None at all*
Republicans.....	8%	31%	33%	27%
Democrats	40	45	11	3
Independents ...	21	38	28	11

*"No opinion"—at 2% or less—is omitted.

Selected National Trend

	Great deal	Fair amount	Not very much	None at all*
May 1997	13%	49%	27%	9%
June 1976	12	28	36	20
April 1974	13	28	36	20
May 1972	24	49	20	4

*"No opinion"—at 4% or less—is omitted.

The Judicial branch, headed by the U.S. Supreme Court?

Great deal	27%
Fair amount..	51
Not very much	16

None at all	4
No opinion..	2

	Great deal	Fair amount	Not very much	None at all*
By Politics				
Republicans.....	31%	53%	11%	5%
Democrats	27	47	20	3
Independents ...	23	55	16	4

*"No opinion"—at 3% or less—is omitted.

Selected National Trend

	Great deal	Fair amount	Not very much	None at all*
May 1997	19%	52%	22%	5%
June 1976	16	47	26	6
April 1974	17	54	20	5
May 1972	17	49	24	7

*"No opinion"—at 5% or less—is omitted.

The Legislative branch, consisting of the U.S. Senate and House of Representatives?

Great deal	13%
Fair amount..	48
Not very much	30
None at all	7
No opinion..	2

	Great deal	Fair amount	Not very much	None at all*
By Politics				
Republicans.....	24%	55%	17%	3%
Democrats	9	45	36	8
Independents ...	9	45	34	9

*"No opinion"—at 3% or less—is omitted.

Selected National Trend

	Great deal	Fair amount	Not very much	None at all*
May 1997	6%	48%	36%	8%
June 1976	9	52	31	6
April 1974	13	55	24	4
May 1972	13	58	22	3

*"No opinion"—at 4% or less—is omitted.

How much trust and confidence do you have in the government of the state where you live when it comes to handling state problems—a great deal, a fair amount, not very much, or none at all?

Great deal	29%
Fair amount	51
Not very much	15
None at all	4
No opinion	1

	Great deal	Fair amount	Not very much	None at all*
By Politics				
Republicans	36%	51%	11%	2%
Democrats	25	54	15	5
Independents	27	48	19	3

*"No opinion"—at 3% or less—is omitted.

Selected National Trend

	Great deal	Fair amount	Not very much	None at all*
May 1997	18%	50%	25%	6%
June 1976	13	59	19	7
April 1974	16	59	17	3
May 1972	15	48	27	6

*"No opinion"—at 5% or less—is omitted.

And how much trust and confidence do you have in the local government in the area where you live when it comes to handling local problems—a great deal, a fair amount, not very much, or none at all?

Great deal	23%
Fair amount	54
Not very much	16
None at all	5
No opinion	2

	Great deal	Fair amount	Not very much	None at all*
By Politics				
Republicans	24%	56%	14%	4%
Democrats	23	54	19	3
Independents	21	55	16	6

*"No opinion"—at 2% or less—is omitted.

Selected National Trend

	Great deal	Fair amount	Not very much	None at all*
May 1997	21%	48%	21%	7%
June 1976	13	52	23	9
April 1974	16	55	16	8
May 1972	12	51	26	7

*"No opinion"—at 5% or less—is omitted.

In general, how much trust and confidence do you have in the mass media, such as newspapers, television, and radio, when it comes to reporting the news fully, accurately, and fairly—a great deal, a fair amount, not very much, or none at all?

Great deal	11%
Fair amount	44
Not very much	35
None at all	9
No opinion	1

	Great deal	Fair amount	Not very much	None at all*
By Politics				
Republicans	11%	41%	36%	12%
Democrats	15	44	33	8
Independents	7	46	37	8

*"No opinion"—at 2% or less—is omitted.

Selected National Trend

	Great deal	Fair amount	Not very much	None at all*
May 1997	10%	43%	31%	15%
June 1976	18	54	22	4
April 1974	21	48	21	8
May 1972	18	50	24	6

*"No opinion"—at 2% or less—is omitted.

Finally, how much trust and confidence do you have in general in men and women in political life in this country who either hold or are running for public office—a great deal, a fair amount, not very much, or none at all?

Great deal	7%
Fair amount	56

Not very much 31
None at all 4
No opinion 2

	Great deal	Fair amount	Not very much	None at all*
By Politics				
Republicans.....	8%	61%	27%	3%
Democrats	10	58	28	3
Independents ...	4	50	37	5

*"No opinion"—at 4% or less—is omitted.

Selected National Trend

	Great deal	Fair amount	Not very much	None at all*
May 1997	5%	52%	37%	5%
June 1976	6	58	28	4
April 1974	7	61	24	4
May 1972	7	58	27	5

*"No opinion"—at 4% or less—is omitted.

Note: Despite the continuing controversy over whether and how Congress should deal with impeachment charges against Bill Clinton and how the president should be punished for his admittedly inappropriate relationship with Monica Lewinsky, Americans continue to express high levels of confidence in all three branches of the federal government as well as in state and local governments, in the news media, and in the men and women who hold public office. This reaction is much different from the Watergate era, when President Richard Nixon was forced to resign. At that time, public confidence in the federal government, especially the Executive branch, dropped significantly.

According to a Gallup Poll conducted after Christmas and before the New Year, 76% of the public hold either a great deal or fair amount of confidence in the federal government in Washington to handle international problems, up from 63% a year ago. And 61% have a similarly high level of confidence in the government to handle domestic problems, up from 51% in mid-1997 but still 9 percentage points lower than in 1972. Confidence in the Executive branch is also high, at 63%, but essentially unchanged from a year and

one-half ago, while confidence in the Legislative branch has climbed by 7 points to 61%. Respondents express their greatest confidence in the Judicial branch, with 78% giving a high rating, also up 7 points from mid-1997.

These high ratings may surprise some observers, who have argued that the impeachment of the president and the year-long focus on charges against him have exacerbated a cycle of distrust toward the American political system. But the poll suggests that the past year's events have not led to an erosion of public confidence and that the overall level of confidence and trust in the government is robust. If any change has occurred in the past year and one-half, it has been in a positive direction.

It is true, however, that current trust in the government is somewhat lower than in the years preceding the Watergate controversy, which led to the resignation of President Nixon. In 1972, when these readings were first taken, 73% held a high level of trust in the Executive branch. Two years later, in the aftermath of the Watergate hearings and shortly before Nixon resigned, just 41% held a high level of trust in that branch. But trust did not rebound quickly, reaching only 40% in 1976, toward the end of Gerald Ford's brief tenure as president. Even today it is about 10 points lower than the pre-Watergate levels.

The most dramatic change over the past quarter of a century is found in the public's currently high level of trust in state and local governments. In 1972, 63% held a high level of trust in both their state and their local governments. During the Watergate crisis, this trust increased by several percentage points. And in the latest poll, about eight in ten express high trust in their state governments (80%) and their local governments (77%).

During the three readings of public confidence in the news media in the 1970s, about seven in ten expressed a high level of confidence that the news was reported accurately and fairly. But by the next reading in mid-1997, some two decades later, barely one-half (53%) held that level of confidence in the news media. Current poll results are about the same, at 55%. It was apparently not Watergate but events since then that have led to the somewhat lower ratings for the media.

The three polls in the 1970s as well as the two polls in the 1990s all suggest that the public holds a surprisingly high and consistent level of trust and confidence in those who commit themselves to public office. In the 1970s between 64% and 68% held a great deal or a fair amount of confidence in men and women who either hold or are running for office. In mid-1997 the number had dropped somewhat to 57%, but in the current poll, trust has climbed back to 63%.

MARCH 29
PREJUDICE IN POLITICS

Interviewing Dates: 2/19–21/99
CNN/*USA Today*/Gallup Poll
Survey #GO 126799

Between now and the year 2000 political conventions, there will be discussion about the qualifications of presidential candidates— their education, age, religion, race, and so on. If your party nominated a generally well-qualified person for president who happened to be one of the following, would you vote for that person:

Jewish?

Yes.. 92%
No 6
No opinion.. 2

Selected National Trend

	Yes	No	No opinion
July 10–13, 1987	89%	6%	5%
April 29–			
May 2, 1983.............	88	7	5
July 21–24, 1978	82	12	6
March 12–17, 1969.....	86	8	6
April 19–24, 1967.......	82	13	5
July 16–21, 1965	80	15	5
August 15–20, 1963 ...	77	17	6
August 24–29, 1961 ...	68	23	9
Dec. 10–15, 1959........	72	22	6
Sept. 10–15, 1958.......	63	29	8
July 30–			
Aug. 4, 1958	62	28	10
Feb. 10–15, 1937	46	47	7

An atheist?

Yes.. 49%
No 48
No opinion.. 3

Selected National Trend

	Yes	No	No opinion
Aug. 10–13, 1987	44%	48%	8%
April 29–			
May 2, 1983.............	42	51	7
July 21–24, 1978	40	53	7
Dec. 10–15, 1959........	22	74	4
Sept. 10–15, 1958.......	18	77	5
July 30–			
Aug. 4, 1958	18	75	7

Black?

Yes.. 95%
No 4
No opinion.. 1

Selected National Trend

	Yes	No	No opinion
Jan. 4–			
Feb. 28, 1997	93%	4%	3%
July 10–13, 1987	79	13	8
July 27–30, 1984	77	16	7
April 29–			
May 2, 1983.............	77	16	7
July 21–24, 1978	77	18	5
Oct. 8–11, 1971	69	23	8
March 12–17, 1969.....	66	24	10
April 19–24, 1967.......	53	41	6
July 16–21, 1965	59	34	7
Aug. 15–20, 1963	48	45	7
Aug. 24–29, 1961	50	41	9
Dec. 10–15, 1959........	49	46	5
Sept. 10–15, 1958.......	38	54	8
July 30–			
Aug. 4, 1958.............	37	53	10

A Catholic?

Yes.. 94%
No 4
No opinion.. 2

Selected National Trend

	Yes	No	No opinion
April 29–			
May 2, 1983	92%	5%	3%
July 21–24, 1978	91	4	5
March 12–17, 1969	87	7	6
April 19–24, 1967	90	8	2
July 16–21, 1965	87	10	3
Aug. 15–20, 1963	84	13	3
Aug. 24–29, 1961	82	13	5
May 26–31, 1960	71	21	8
Dec. 10–15, 1959	70	25	5
April 2–7, 1959	70	21	9
Sept. 10–15, 1958	67	27	6
July 30–			
Aug. 4, 1958	69	24	7
July 10–15, 1958	72	24	4
May 7–12, 1958	72	21	7
April 16–21, 1958	70	22	8
May 31–			
June 5, 1956	72	22	6
Jan. 20–25, 1955	69	23	8
March 27–			
April 2, 1940	61	33	6
Feb. 3–8, 1937	60	30	10

A homosexual?

Yes	59%
No	37
No opinion	4

Selected National Trend

	Yes	No	No opinion
April 29–			
May 2, 1983	29%	64%	7%
July 21–24, 1978	26	66	8

A woman?

Yes	92%
No	7
No opinion	1

Selected National Trend

	Yes	No	No opinion
July 10–13, 1987	82%	12%	6%

July 27–30, 1984	78	17	5
April 29–			
May 2, 1983	80	16	4
July 21–24, 1978	76	19	5
Aug. 15–18, 1975	73	23	4
July 15–18, 1971	66	29	5
March 12–17, 1969	53	40	7
April 19–24, 1967	57	39	4
Aug. 15–20, 1963	55	41	4
Dec. 10–15, 1959	57	39	4
Sept. 10–15, 1958	54	41	5
Feb. 10–15, 1955	52	44	4
Sept. 25–30, 1949	48	48	4
Nov. 23–28, 1945	33	55	12
Jan. 27–			
Feb. 1, 1937	33	64	3

A Baptist?

Yes	94%
No	4
No opinion	2

Selected National Trend

	Yes	No	No opinion
April 19–24, 1967	95%	3%	2%
Dec. 10–15, 1959	94	3	3
Sept. 10–15, 1958	93	4	3
July 30–			
Aug. 4, 1958	92	2	6

A Mormon?

	Feb. 19–21, 1999	April 19–24, 1967
Yes	79%	75%
No	17	17
No opinion	4	8

Note: It has become less and less acceptable in recent years—both legally and normatively—for Americans to overtly take into account such characteristics as race, gender, religious preference, or sexual orientation in making decisions on hiring or firing employees. Perhaps not surprisingly, then, a new Gallup Poll demonstrates that the public is less willing now than in the past to express an unwillingness to vote for candidates for president on the basis of these same types of characteristics. Still, the poll shows that members of certain groups, including atheists, homosexuals, and Mormons, may find that these characteristics, even today, could be taken as negative factors by a sizeable portion of the U.S. population.

Gallup began asking Americans about their willingness to vote for individuals with various demographic and religious characteristics over sixty years ago. At that time, in 1937, there was considerable reluctance on the part of the American population to vote for either a Jew, a woman, or a Catholic: 46% said that they would vote for a Jew for president, 60% for a Catholic for president, and 33% for a woman for president. Of these groups, only one has had a member actually become president in the intervening years: John F. Kennedy, a Catholic, who was elected in 1960. There have been no female or Jewish presidents.

Still, the theoretical acceptance of members of all three categories has risen steadily over time. The acceptance of a Catholic for president took its biggest leap forward with the election of Kennedy, jumping from 71% in 1960 to 82% in 1961. By 1967, the acceptance of a Catholic had risen to 90%, and it is now at 94% in Gallup's most recent poll, taken in February. The acceptance of a Jewish candidate for president also rose into the 80% range in 1965 and is now at 92%, leaving 6% who say that they would not vote for a Jew for president. Of particular relevance this year, with the potential candidacy of Elizabeth Dole, is the acceptance of a woman for president, which rose from 33% in 1937 to 82% in 1987 and to 92% this year. (Seven percent of the population would not vote for a woman for president.)

Gallup has tested five other groups in this presidential vote scenario over the years. Being an atheist is still not widely acceptable to the American public. The latest poll shows that only 49% would vote for an atheist for president, making this group the most discriminated-against of the eight tested. Moreover, the idea of voting for a homosexual for president remains unacceptable to 37% of the population, placing it second to atheist on the unacceptable list. Fifty-nine percent would vote for a homosexual, which is up significantly from 26% in 1978, when the question was first asked. Furthermore, the willingness to vote for a black for president was at 37% in 1958, when Gallup first in-cluded the category in its survey tests. That number rose through the 1960s and into the 1970s, although as recently as 1987 only 79% said that they would vote for a black person for president. By 1997 that number had risen to 93% and is now at 95%.

Two other religious groups have been tested by Gallup. Americans are very accepting of a Baptist in the White House (of which there have been two—Jimmy Carter and Bill Clinton), but significantly less accepting of a Mormon. "Baptist" was first included in the lists in 1958, with 92% acceptance, which has risen slightly, to 94% who say that they would accept a Baptist today. The idea of a Mormon as president, however, draws reactions from Americans that are more negative. Seventy-nine percent would vote for a Mormon for president, while 17% would not. Interestingly, this number has not changed significantly over time; 75% of those polled said that they would vote for a Mormon thirty-two years ago, in 1967, only 4 percentage points lower than the current figure.

APRIL 9
THE INDEPENDENT VOTER—
AN ANALYSIS*

Despite the continued strength of the two-party system in U.S. elections, more people of voting age today consider themselves politically independent than identify with either the Republican or Democratic party. This finding is not new, but has been apparent in Gallup's national telephone surveys for most of the 1990s.

Today, 38% of Americans age 18 and older consider themselves politically "independent" of either major party. Among this group, only 1–2% indicates belonging to a specific third party while the rest are unaffiliated. A slightly smaller percentage of Americans, 34%, consider themselves Democrats today while the smallest share, 28%, identify as Republicans. These figures are based on over 10,000 telephone interviews conducted by the Gallup Poll in the first quarter of 1999 and have a margin of error of less than 1 percentage point.

*This analysis was written by Lydia Saad, Managing Editor, The Gallup Poll.

Partisanship Steady in Recent Years

A pattern by which political independents outnumber Democrats by 3 to 4 points, and Republicans trail Democrats by 5 to 6 points, has been in place for most of President Clinton's term in office. The major exception came in 1994 and 1995—the glory years for the Republican majority in Congress—when the percentage of Americans identifying with the Republican party reached almost as high as the Democratic figure. Even during this time period, however, independents outnumbered Democrats by a few percentage points. In 1996, by contrast, the percentage of self-declared independents fell at the same time Democratic percentages increased, perhaps due to the highly partisan nature of a presidential election year combined with Bill Clinton's popularity:

	Repub- lican	Demo- cratic	Inde- pendent	Demo- cratic lead
1999*	28%	34%	38%	6
1998	29	34	37	5
1997	29	34	37	5
1996	30	35	35	5
1995	30	31	39	1
1994	30	32	38	2
1993	29	34	37	5
1992	29	34	37	5
1991	33	31	36	–2
1990	33	35	32	2
1989	33	35	32	2
1988	30	35	35	5

*First quarter only

Independents See Good in Both Parties

Eschewing party membership should not necessarily be viewed as a sign that independents reject what the Republican or Democratic party stands for. Indeed, when asked this January to express their feelings toward each party on a 10-point scale, a majority of political independents viewed both parties favorably. Even though the poll was taken in the midst of the highly partisan impeachment proceedings against Bill Clinton, 58% of independents at the time said that they had a favorable view of the Republican party and 70% felt favorably toward the Democratic party.

Most members of the Republican and Democratic parties, on the other hand, view the opposing party in negative terms:

View of Republican Party

	Repub- lican	Demo- cratic	Inde- pendent
Favorable	91%	29%	58%
Unfavorable	8	68	34

View of Democratic Party

Favorable	43%	94%	70%
Unfavorable	56	5	23

Furthermore, when asked if they lean toward one of the major two parties, approximately three out of four independents interviewed thus far in 1999 are willing to say they identify with either the Republicans or Democrats while only one-quarter—representing about 9% of all Americans—insist they are truly independent, and lean to neither party.

Women Favor Democratic Party

Much is often made of the "gender gap" in American politics, with women perceived to be more favorable than men toward the Democratic party. While not overwhelming, a significant gender difference in partisanship is seen in Gallup's polls taken from January through March of this year. Women identify themselves as Democrats by a 10-point margin, 37% vs. 27%. By comparison, men identify as Democrats by just 2 points, 32% vs. 30%:

	Men	Women
Republican	30%	27%
Democratic	32	37
Independent	38	36

Political Independence Highest among Young Adults

The current pattern of party identification across various age groups in U.S. society is similar to what Gallup has seen in earlier years. Young adults, age 18–29, are the most inclined to consider themselves independents, while senior citizens, those age 65 and older, are most likely to be Democrats.

Americans who are approximately the same age as the Baby Boom generation, 30–49, are the most evenly divided of all age groups in affiliation between the Republican and Democratic parties:

	18–29	30–49	50–64	65+
Republican	24%	30%	28%	28%
Democratic	35	33	34	38
Independent	41	37	38	34

Independent Percentages Took Off after Vietnam and Watergate

In longer historical terms, Gallup records indicate that the percentage of Americans calling themselves independent jumped at two key intervals. One was between 1964 and 1968, spanning the period when the Vietnam War became a major political controversy. Over this period the percentage calling themselves independent increased from 22% to 27%. A second shift toward political independence was seen in the post-Watergate period between 1972 and 1975, when the number of unaffiliated respondents in Gallup surveys increased from 29% to 33%.

The balance of power between the two major parties has also shifted in the past several decades. From 1968 until Ronald Reagan's second term in office, only one-quarter of Americans identified themselves as Republicans, while the percentage calling themselves Democrats ranged from 43% to 47%. Then, in 1984, the Republicans saw a 6-percentage-point shift in their favor, bumping their percentages up from one-quarter to roughly one-third of Americans. While this level of support for Republicans was sustained throughout the Republican administration of George Bush, it appears that the Grand Old Party has lost some of this ground under the Clinton presidency.

It should be noted that Gallup measures of political party identification prior to 1988 rely on in-person rather than telephone surveys, and that the two methods of interviewing have been shown to produce slightly different results. Therefore, special care needs to be taken in making pre-1988 and post-1988 comparisons of party affiliation.

MAY 27
AL GORE

Interviewing Dates: 5/23–24/99
CNN/*USA Today*/Gallup Poll
Survey #GO 127701

Looking ahead to the presidential election in November of next year, if Al Gore is the Democratic nominee for president in 2000, how likely is it that you would vote for him—extremely likely, very likely, fairly likely, not too likely, or not at all likely?

Extremely likely	14%
Very likely	12
Fairly likely	16
Not too likely	15
Not at all likely	40
No opinion	3

	Extremely likely	Very likely	Fairly likely	Not too, not at all likely*
By Politics				
Republicans	1%	3%	6%	90%
Democrats	35	24	21	19
Independents	9	9	19	58

*"No opinion"—at 5% or less—is omitted.

Next, please say whether you think Al Gore would do a good job or not a good job of handling each of the following issues if he were to become president:

The economy?

Good job	50%
Not a good job	43
No opinion	7

	Good job	Not a good job	No opinion
By Politics			
Republicans	25%	68%	7%
Democrats	81	14	5
Independents	44	46	10

Foreign affairs?

Good job	37%
Not a good job	53
No opinion	10

	Good job	Not a good job	No opinion
By Politics			
Republicans	16%	77%	7%

| Democrats | 61 | 28 | 11 |
| Independents | 33 | 54 | 13 |

Education?

Good job		63%
Not a good job		29
No opinion		8

	Good job	Not a good job	No opinion
By Politics			
Republicans	44%	47%	9%
Democrats	87	11	2
Independents	60	30	10

Taxes?

Good job		38%
Not a good job		52
No opinion		10

	Good job	Not a good job	No opinion
By Politics			
Republicans	16%	77%	7%
Democrats	64	28	8
Independents	34	53	13

The environment?

Good job		69%
Not a good job		25
No opinion		6

	Good job	Not a good job	No opinion
By Politics			
Republicans	57%	39%	4%
Democrats	86	10	4
Independents	66	27	7

For each of the following statements about Al Gore, please say whether you think it is true or not true:

His positions on environmental issues are too extreme?

True	35%
Not true	57
No opinion	8

He is a tax-and-spend liberal?

True	50%
Not true	37
No opinion	13

His stands on the issues would be too close to Clinton's?

True	57%
Not true	37
No opinion	6

He went too far in defending Clinton during the Monica Lewinsky controversy?

True	44%
Not true	51
No opinion	5

He engaged in unethical fund-raising activities during the last presidential campaign?

True	48%
Not true	38
No opinion	14

He doesn't inspire you?

True	64%
Not true	33
No opinion	3

He lacks vision for how to solve the big problems facing the country?

True	54%
Not true	37
No opinion	9

Summary of "True" Replies about Al Gore
(By Political Affiliation)

	Republicans	Democrats	Independents
Environmental positions	62%	16%	30%
As tax-and-spend liberal	72	26	51
As too close to Clinton	74	39	59
Lewinsky controversy	62	21	47
Unethical fund-raising	68	29	48

Doesn't inspire you 85   36   68
Lacks vision................ 77   33   55

Asked for each "true" reply in the previous question: Does each of the following make you less likely to vote for Al Gore for president in 2000, or not:

His positions on environmental issues are too extreme?

Yes, less likely.. 27%
Not less likely.. 8
Not true.. 57
No opinion.. 8

He is a tax-and-spend liberal?

Yes, less likely.. 38%
Not less likely.. 12
Not true.. 37
No opinion.. 13

His stands on the issues would be too close to Clinton's?

Yes, less likely.. 38%
Not less likely.. 19
Not true.. 37
No opinion.. 6

He went too far in defending Clinton during the Monica Lewinsky controversy?

Yes, less likely.. 31%
Not less likely.. 13
Not true.. 51
No opinion.. 5

He engaged in unethical fund-raising activities during the last presidential campaign?

Yes, less likely.. 34%
Not less likely.. 14
Not true.. 38
No opinion.. 14

He doesn't inspire you?

Yes, less likely.. 48%
Not less likely.. 16
Not true.. 33
No opinion.. 3

He lacks vision for how to solve the big problems facing the country?

Yes, less likely.. 43%
Not less likely.. 11
Not true.. 37
No opinion.. 9

Summary of "Yes, Less Likely" Replies about Al Gore
(By Political Affiliation)

	Repub-licans	Demo-crats	Inde-pendents
Environmental positions	53%	8%	23%
As tax-and-spend liberal.....................	64	14	38
As too close to Clinton....................	64	11	40
Lewinsky controversy	52	8	33
Unethical fund-raising	59	14	32
Doesn't inspire you	73	20	51
Lacks vision................	70	18	44

Here are some different statements about Al Gore. For each one, please say whether you think it is true or not true:

He is honest and trustworthy?

True 56%
Not true.. 36
No opinion.. 8

He is a good husband and father?

True 79%
Not true.. 2
No opinion.. 19

He cares about the needs of people like you?

True 54%
Not true.. 40
No opinion.. 6

He has the necessary experience to be president?

True 59%

Not true.. 37

No opinion.. 4

As president he would continue the policies of the Clinton administration?

True 72%

Not true.. 22

No opinion.. 6

Summary of "True" Replies about Al Gore
(By Political Affiliation)

	Repub-licans	Demo-crats	Inde-pendents
Honest and trustworthy	41%	80%	50%
Good husband and father	76	88	75
Cares about people	37	83	46
Has experience	44	83	54
Continue Clinton's policies	81	72	67

Asked for each "true" reply in the previous question: Does each of the following make you more likely to vote for Al Gore for president in 2000, or not:

He is honest and trustworthy?

Yes, more likely 44%

Not more likely.. 12

Not true.. 36

No opinion.. 8

He is a good husband and father?

Yes, more likely 44%

Not more likely.. 35

Not true.. 2

No opinion.. 19

He cares about the needs of people like you?

Yes, more likely 42%

Not more likely.. 12

Not true.. 40

No opinion.. 6

He has the necessary experience to be president?

Yes, more likely 42%

Not more likely.. 17

Not true.. 37

No opinion.. 4

As president he would continue the policies of the Clinton administration?

Yes, more likely 30%

Not more likely.. 42

Not true.. 22

No opinion.. 6

Summary of "More Likely" Replies about Al Gore
(By Political Affiliation)

	Repub-licans	Demo-crats	Inde-pendents
Honest and trustworthy	29%	71%	36%
Good husband and father	32	63	39
Cares about people	20	74	34
Has experience	19	76	34
Continue Clinton's policies	13	55	24

Note: According to the latest Gallup Poll, Vice President Al Gore continues to trail Texas Governor George W. Bush by double digits in a hypothetical contest for president, with 54% of Americans saying that they would vote for Bush, and 40% for Gore. Among the group of respondents whom Gallup classifies as "regular voters"—people who are currently registered to vote and who voted in the 1996 presidential election—Bush's lead is marginally better at 56% to 40%.

However badly Gore is currently doing in the general election race, it does not appear as though the Democrats are ready to abandon him as their nominee. The poll shows that if all Democrats could vote in a national primary, they would support Gore over former New Jersey Senator Bill Bradley, the only other announced Democratic candidate, by about a 2-to-1 margin (59% to 30%). In the last two polls, taken after all other major potential Democratic candidates made clear their intentions not to run, Gore's lead over Bradley ranged from a 20-point lead in mid-April (54% to 34%) to better than a 40-point lead at the end of April (66% to 23%).

Some Gore supporters have suggested that the vice president's poor showing in the polls is not of great concern right now, pointing out that Vice President George Bush also lagged in the polls in 1987–88 before going on to win the presidency. The elder Bush trailed Gary Hart by about 8 to 10 percentage points in the spring of 1987 and then later trailed the eventual Democratic nominee, Michael Dukakis, by 17 points as late as May in the election year.

Whether or not it is a "curse" to be a vice president, as some analysts have suggested, there are at the very least special problems facing a sitting vice president who runs for president. On the one hand, Americans expect the vice president to be loyal to the policies of the chief executive, who, after all, originally chose the vice president to be part of his team. On the other hand, they also expect any candidate for the presidency to show his or her own original and independent side. This tension between loyalty and independence has beleaguered every sitting vice president who has run for president in the past half century—Richard Nixon in 1960, Hubert Humphrey in 1968, George Bush in 1988, and Al Gore today. While Bush was successful in his bid, neither Nixon nor Humphrey was able to establish a compelling image as a presidential candidate in his own right, and both lost to their opponents by very close margins. (Nixon eventually went on to win, but not as a sitting vice president.)

Gore's problems today are not unlike those faced, and eventually overcome, by Bush in 1987–88, but there is some evidence that Gore is in worse shape than was Bush at this time in the election cycle, when Bush was a sitting vice president and trying to launch his candidacy. In May 1987, Americans were asked (with no opponent mentioned) how likely they were to vote for Bush in the general election. Overall, 50% said that they would be extremely or very likely to do so. In the latest poll, a similar question was asked about Gore, again without mentioning an opponent, and just 26% say that they are extremely or very likely to vote for Gore. Only 19% in 1987 said that they would not be likely to vote for Bush in the presidential election, while today more than one-half (55%) are not likely to vote for Gore. These results suggest that Gore's image problem is considerably larger than was Bush's twelve years ago.

Most Americans (about two thirds or more) think that Gore would do a good job in handling the issues of education and the environment, but clear majorities think that he would not do a good job in handling foreign affairs or taxes. Respondents are more ambivalent on how he would handle the economy, with 50% saying that he would do a good job and 43% saying that he would not.

Perhaps the most serious negative assessment that Gore receives from the American public deals with his inability to inspire people. In the poll, respondents were asked to assess Gore in seven areas: whether his positions on environmental issues are too extreme, whether he is a tax-and-spend liberal, how close his positions on the issues are to Bill Clinton's, whether he went too far in defending Clinton in the Monica Lewinsky controversy, whether he engaged in unethical fundraising in the last presidential campaign, whether he has a vision for solving the big problems facing the country, and how substantial is his ability to inspire people. This last item has emerged as Gore's biggest liability.

Overall, 64% say that Gore does not inspire them, and three-quarters of these people say that as a consequence of that failing, they are less likely to vote for him for president. Thus, about one-half of the American people are negatively affected in their vote by their perception that Gore is not an inspirational leader. Close behind is the general perception that Gore does not have a vision for dealing with the larger issues: over one-half say that he has no such vision, and about eight in ten of these say that this lack of vision makes them less likely to vote for Gore.

Most political observers believe that Gore is almost certain to be the Democratic party's nominee in 2000, due primarily to his close association with President Clinton, but this association also has its drawbacks. Among the general public, 38% would be less likely to vote for Gore as president because they think his policies would be too close to

Clinton's, while 30% would be more likely to vote for Gore because he would continue the policies of the Clinton administration. On balance, at this point in the campaign, Gore's association with Clinton would appear to be a net disadvantage among the general public, despite the obvious advantage that it gives the vice president in obtaining the Democratic nomination.

JUNE 5
HILLARY RODHAM CLINTON

Interviewing Dates: 5/23–24/99
CNN/*USA Today*/Gallup Poll
Survey #GO 127701

There has been some discussion of Hillary Rodham Clinton possibly running for the Senate in New York next year. Would you personally like to see Hillary Clinton run for the Senate in New York, or not?

Yes.. 44%
No 47
No opinion.. 9

	Yes	No	No opinion
By Politics			
Republicans	25%	69%	6%
Democrats	65	26	9
Independents	41	47	12

If Hillary Clinton decides to run for the Senate and it turns out that her campaign interferes with her duties as First Lady, how concerned would you be that the duties of First Lady are not being properly met—very concerned, somewhat concerned, not too concerned, or not concerned at all?

Very concerned... 15%
Somewhat concerned...................................... 20
Not too concerned 30
Not concerned at all.. 34
No opinion.. 1

	Very concerned	Somewhat concerned	Not too concerned	Not concerned at all*
By Politics				
Republicans	19%	17%	29%	34%
Democrats	11	21	37	31
Independents	16	20	25	37

*"No opinion"—at 2% or less—is omitted.

Note: Hillary Rodham Clinton's announcement on Friday [June 4] that she will set up an exploratory committee for a possible 2000 Senate bid in New York comes at a time when she enjoys exceptionally high image ratings from the American public. Gallup surveys taken this spring show that two in three respondents hold a favorable view of her personally, and an even higher percentage approves of the job that she is doing as First Lady. Despite that, two recent Gallup surveys indicate that the public is almost evenly divided over whether she should step into the political ring.

In a Gallup Poll taken on May 23–24, only 44% would like to see Hillary Clinton become a candidate for the U.S. Senate from New York while 47% would not like to see her run. Similarly, a Gallup survey taken a month earlier (April 30–May 2) found that, if given the opportunity to vote in New York, only 47% of the public would support Mrs. Clinton for the U.S. Senate. Nearly one-half (49%) would not vote for her.

Support for the idea of a Hillary Clinton run for the Senate is sharply divided along party lines. Democrats nationwide tend to be supportive of Mrs. Clinton's political aspirations to fill the seat being vacated by Daniel Patrick Moynihan of New York, with 65% saying that they would like to see her run, compared to only 41% of political independents and 25% of Republicans. Aside from Democrats (and blacks, who are highly likely to identify themselves as Democrats), Mrs. Clinton's biggest supporters are women and young adults. However, only one-half of even these groups favor her candidacy. Fifty percent of women, and the same percentage of adults age 18 to 29, would like to see her run. These rates of support compare with 38% of men, 45% of Baby Boom-era adults age 30–49, and 38% of adults age 50 and older.

JUNE 11
AL GORE VS. GEORGE W. BUSH/FORMER PRESIDENT BUSH

Interviewing Dates: 6/4–5/99
CNN/*USA Today*/Gallup Poll
Survey #GO 127853

Asked of registered voters: Thinking about each of the following, do you know enough about him to decide whether he would make a good president, or do you feel you need to know more:

Al Gore?

Know enough	41%
Need to know more	58
No opinion	1

	Know enough	Need to know more	No opinion
By Politics*			
Republicans	50%	48%	2%
Democrats	38	61	1
Independents	32	67	1

*Based on entire sample

George W. Bush?

Know enough	26%
Need to know more	73
No opinion	1

	Know enough	Need to know more	No opinion
By Politics			
Republicans	30%	68%	2%
Democrats	24	74	2
Independents	22	78	*

*Less than 1%

*From what you have heard, read, or remember about former President George Bush, do you approve or disapprove of the way he handled his job as president?**

Approve	71%
Disapprove	25

No opinion	4

*Based on half sample

	Approve	Dis-approve	No opinion
By Politics			
Republicans	96%	3%	1%
Democrats	56	39	5
Independents	64	29	7

Selected National Trend

	Approve	Dis-approve	No opinion
1993			
January 8–11	56%	37%	7%
1992			
December 18–20	49	41	10
December 4–6	49	47	4
November 20–22	43	46	11
October 12–14	34	56	10

*From what you have heard, read, or remember about former President George Bush, do you approve or disapprove of the way he handled the economy when he was president?**

Approve	58%
Disapprove	36
No opinion	6

*Based on half sample

	Approve	Dis-approve	No opinion
By Politics			
Republicans	80%	17%	3%
Democrats	43	54	3
Independents	58	32	10

Selected National Trend

	Approve	Dis-approve	No opinion
1992			
July 24–26	18%	76%	6%
May 7–10	20	76	4
January 3–6	24	73	3

Note: If the 2000 presidential election were held today, voters indicate that they would elect Texas Governor George W. Bush over Vice President Al Gore by a substantial margin. But most voters also say that they would need to know more about each man before judging whether or not either would make a good president, with more people saying so about Bush than about Gore. In the absence of additional information, the Texas governor is apparently being helped by retrospective perceptions about how well his father did as president—perceptions that are much more positive than they actually were at the end of Bush's presidency.

According to the latest Gallup Poll, Texas Governor Bush leads Vice President Gore in a hypothetical presidential race by 16 percentage points (56% to 40%) among all Americans, by 17 points among registered voters, and by 15 points among those who voted in the 1996 presidential election. These figures have remained fairly steady over the past several months, with Bush's lead fluctuating between 11 and 21 points. But in an indication that the numbers are not especially firm at this point, almost three-quarters of registered voters (73%) would need to know more about Bush in order to decide whether he would make a good president, and 58% say the same about Gore. Those who are most likely to say that they already know enough about Gore are Republicans, who would vote overwhelmingly for Bush. Just under one-half of Republicans (48%) say that they need to know more about Gore, compared with 61% of Democrats and 67% of independents. By contrast, two-thirds of Republicans, 78% of independents, and 74% of Democrats need to know more about Bush.

In the absence of information about the Texas governor, many Americans appear to be basing their views of George W. Bush on their positive remembrances of his father. When asked in the current poll to rate President George Bush for the way that he handled his job as president overall, and separately on how he handled the economy when he was president, respondents give the former president considerably higher ratings than they did in the closing months of his presidency. In the current poll, his overall retrospective approval rating is 71%, compared to the 56% rating right before his

leaving office. Shortly before the 1992 election, only 34% approved of his job performance. Earlier in his presidency, during the Persian Gulf War, Bush received the highest approval rating ever recorded by Gallup, at 89%. A year later, his ratings had plummeted by 50 points as the nation's attention turned to the struggling economy.

The retrospective rating that President Bush receives in the current poll for his handling of the economy (58% approval) is higher than any he ever received as president. In the last two years of his presidency, Bush's approval rating on the economy never rose above 40%, and in the summer of 1992 it fell to a low of 18%. Indeed, most observers believe that the ailing economy caused Bush's defeat by Bill Clinton, whose campaign mantra—"It's the economy, stupid!"—reflected the widespread view of what was crucial to that election.

Whatever Americans felt in 1992, they are much more positive about former President Bush today, and these positive perceptions exert a significant influence on voter preferences for the 2000 presidential election. A statistical analysis of voters' party identification and their retrospective evaluations of former President Bush show that the positive evaluations are highly related to the current vote choice among independents and Democrats. Republicans are not affected, as so few of them disapprove of the former president's overall performance or handling of the economy.

More that one-half of independents currently have positive views about the economy under former President Bush, and in the 2000 contest for the presidency, they support the younger Bush by 50 points over Gore (73% to 23%). The independents who disapprove of President Bush's handling of the economy, by contrast, support Gore over the younger Bush by 24 points (55% to 31%). Democrats are affected as well, as almost four in ten remember good economic times under the former president. Among these voters, who approve of the way that President Bush handled the economy, 44% would vote for his son. However, among Democratic voters who disapprove of the economy under President Bush, only 10% would cross party lines and vote for the younger Bush.

JUNE 21
AL GORE VS. GEORGE W. BUSH

Interviewing Dates: 6/4–5/99
CNN/*USA Today*/Gallup Poll
Survey #GO 127853

As I read some personal characteristics, please tell me if you think each one applies more to George W. Bush or more to Al Gore:

Cares about the needs of people like you?

More to G. W. Bush	44%
More to Gore	44
Neither (volunteered)	4
Both equally; same (volunteered)	2
No opinion	6

By Politics	G. W. Bush	Gore	Neither; both; same	No opinion
Republicans	81%	11%	4%	4%
Democrats	18	74	3	5
Independents	40	41	11	8

A strong and decisive leader?

More to G. W. Bush	59%
More to Gore	30
Neither (volunteered)	3
Both equally; same (volunteered)	2
No opinion	6

By Politics	G. W. Bush	Gore	Neither; both; same	No opinion
Republicans	89%	7%	2%	2%
Democrats	35	55	4	6
Independents	60	24	8	8

Is inspiring?

More to G. W. Bush	54%
More to Gore	29
Neither (volunteered)	9
Both equally; same (volunteered)	2
No opinion	6

By Politics	G. W. Bush	Gore	Neither; both; same	No opinion
Republicans	81%	10%	5%	4%
Democrats	33	50	12	5
Independents	54	25	13	8

Has the proper moral character to be president?

More to G. W. Bush	47%
More to Gore	36
Neither (volunteered)	3
Both equally; same (volunteered)	9
No opinion	5

By Politics	G. W. Bush	Gore	Neither; both; same	No opinion
Republicans	80%	7%	9%	4%
Democrats	23	62	11	4
Independents	46	34	12	8

Generally agrees with you on the issues you care about?

More to G. W. Bush	47%
More to Gore	40
Neither (volunteered)	3
Both equally; same (volunteered)	2
No opinion	8

By Politics	G. W. Bush	Gore	Neither; both; same	No opinion
Republicans	86%	9%	1%	4%
Democrats	19	72	3	6
Independents	46	35	7	12

Can keep the economy strong?

More to G. W. Bush	51%
More to Gore	37
Neither (volunteered)	3
Both equally; same (volunteered)	3
No opinion	6

	G. W. Bush	Gore	Neither; both; same	No opinion
By Politics				
Republicans.....	86%	7%	3%	4%
Democrats.......	24	65	5	6
Independents ...	50	32	10	8

Next, I am going to read some policy positions taken by George W. Bush. As I read each one, please say whether that position would make you more likely or less likely to vote for him for president next year:

As governor of Texas, George W. Bush supported a law that allows private citizens to obtain permits to carry concealed weapons. Does his position on this issue make you more likely or less likely to vote for him for president?

More likely	39%
Less likely..	55
No difference (volunteered)	4
No opinion...	2

	More likely	Less likely	No dif- ference	No opinion
By Politics				
Republicans.....	49%	42%	6%	3%
Democrats.......	24	71	3	2
Independents ...	44	51	3	2

George W. Bush has stated he is personally opposed to abortion, but would not actively work as president to outlaw abortion nationwide. Does his position on this issue make you more likely or less likely to vote for him for president?

More likely	59%
Less likely..	32
No difference (volunteered)	6
No opinion...	3

	More likely	Less likely	No dif- ference	No opinion
By Politics				
Republicans.....	72%	21%	6%	1%
Democrats.......	49	41	6	4
Independents ...	57	33	6	4

As governor of Texas, George W. Bush opposed a bill that would have increased the criminal penalties against people convicted of hate crimes against minorities. Does his position on this issue make you more likely or less likely to vote for him for president?

More likely	46%
Less likely..	45
No difference (volunteered)	4
No opinion...	5

	More likely	Less likely	No dif- ference	No opinion
By Politics				
Republicans.....	48%	37%	8%	7%
Democrats.......	44	50	3	3
Independents ...	47	46	2	5

As governor of Texas, George W. Bush supported a law requiring students to meet certain minimum academic requirements before they could advance to the next grade. Does his position on this issue make you more likely or less likely to vote for him for president?

More likely	84%
Less likely..	11
No difference (volunteered)	2
No opinion...	3

	More likely	Less likely	No dif- ference	No opinion
By Politics				
Republicans.....	93%	5%	1%	1%
Democrats.......	76	17	3	4
Independents ...	85	10	2	3

As governor of Texas, George W. Bush supported a major property tax cut for homeowners. Does his position on this issue make you more likely or less likely to vote for him for president?

More likely	81%
Less likely..	12
No difference (volunteered)	4
No opinion...	3

	More likely	Less likely	No difference	No opinion
By Politics				
Republicans.....	93%	4%	2%	1%
Democrats	73	17	5	5
Independents ...	80	13	5	2

George W. Bush believes that juveniles as young as 14 who are convicted of major crimes should be prosecuted as adults. Does his position on this issue make you more likely or less likely to vote for him for president?

More likely	69%
Less likely..	26
No difference (volunteered)	2
No opinion..	3

	More likely	Less likely	No difference	No opinion
By Politics				
Republicans.....	82%	14%	2%	2%
Democrats	55	38	2	5
Independents ...	72	25	1	2

Note: With the announcement this week by Vice President Al Gore that he is running for president in 2000, and the first trips by Texas Governor George W. Bush to Iowa and New Hampshire, it would appear as though the 2000 presidential campaign has formally begun. Both Gore and Bush are the front-runners for their respective party's presidential nomination, but until this past week they have not been officially involved in campaigning. Although the two candidates have been widely covered in the news media, the public is generally unaware of their positions on the issues. According to a Gallup Poll conducted earlier this month, 60% of Americans say that they would need to know more about Gore before they could decide whether he would make a good president, and 74% would need to know more about Bush.

Still, even now most respondents have some impressions of the candidates, and those impressions decidedly favor Bush. According to the June 4–5 Gallup Poll, when asked which candidate is better described as a strong and decisive leader, Americans choose Bush by about a 2-to-1 margin (59% to 30%). Similarly, by 54% to 29%, they find Bush more inspiring than Gore. In an ironic twist, they also rate Bush higher on having the "proper moral character to be president" by a margin of 47% to 36%. These numbers suggest that Gore, whose personal life has long been viewed as a major strength, is being hurt by his association with Bill Clinton, while the "youthful indiscretions" widely attributed to Bush are either being ignored by the public or are not generally known. Respondents also are more likely to say that Bush, rather than Gore, "generally agrees with you on the issues," by a margin of 47% to 40%, but they are evenly divided between the two candidates on which one is more likely to "care about the needs of people like you," with 44% choosing each man.

One of the areas in which Gore is most likely to stress the success of the Clinton-Gore administration is the economy. However, respondents apparently are not inclined to give credit to Gore for the improved economy over the past seven years. In the early June poll, they were more likely to say that Bush, rather than Gore, would be able to keep the economy strong, by a margin of 51% to 37%. And in the most recent Gallup Poll, conducted on June 11–13, a slightly different question shows that Bush would do a better job of handling the economy, by a margin of 55% to 35%.

Apart from his image as an uninspiring leader, Gore also must cope with the traditional problem faced by any sitting vice president: how to differentiate himself from the president while at the same time taking some credit for the positive achievements of the administration. The recent Gallup Polls show that on both counts Gore has not done well. Unlike Clinton, Gore does not receive good marks for the economy, and he appears to be tarnished by his close association with the president. In fact, according to a Gallup Poll conducted on May 23–24, if Clinton were to actively support and campaign for Gore, respondents say, by a margin of 52% to 29%, that they would be less likely to vote for the vice president.

Bush is currently leading Gore by double digits largely on the basis of name recognition, but in the long run he will have to defend his record as governor. There are potentially both positive and negative aspects of his record that could bear on the presidential race. According to the June 4–5 Gallup Poll, two issues that are particularly popular with the public are Bush's support for a law requiring students to meet minimum academic requirements before they could advance to the next grade, and his support for a property tax cut for homeowners. On both issues, at least eight in ten say that Bush's position would make them more likely to vote for him while about one in ten says less likely.

Respondents also react positively to Bush's position that juveniles as young as 14 who are convicted of major crimes should be prosecuted as adults; 69% say that position makes them more likely to vote for him, while 26% say less likely. But they are not thrilled with Bush's decision to sign a bill that allows private citizens in Texas to obtain permits to carry concealed weapons; by a margin of 55% to 39%, that action makes them less likely to vote for the Texas governor.

JUNE 27
CAMPAIGN ISSUES

Interviewing Dates: 6/4–5/99
CNN/*USA Today*/Gallup Poll
Survey #GO 127853

I'm going to read a list which includes some national issues and some problems facing Americans today. For each one, please tell me how important a candidate's position on that issue is to you personally in deciding which candidate you will support for president— would you say that it is a top priority in how you vote, a high priority in how you vote, very important but not a priority, somewhat important, or not important:

The nation's economy?

	June 4–5, 1999*	Jan. 5–7, 1997
Top priority	29%	37%
High priority	41	27
Very important	21	26
Somewhat important	6	7
Not important	2	1
No opinion	1	2

*Based on half sample

The quality of education in public schools through Grade 12?

	June 4–5, 1999*	Jan. 5–7, 1997
Top priority	42%	44%
High priority	33	23
Very important	18	25
Somewhat important	3	5
Not important	3	2
No opinion	1	1

*Based on half sample

The rate of violent crime in the United States?

	June 4–5, 1999*	Jan. 5–7, 1997
Top priority	35%	41%
High priority	32	25
Very important	24	24
Somewhat important	6	8
Not important	3	1
No opinion	**	1

*Based on half sample
**Less than 1%

Social Security and Medicare policy?

Top priority	33%
High priority	36
Very important	21
Somewhat important	7
Not important	2
No opinion	1

*Based on half sample

The situation in Kosovo?

Top priority	19%
High priority	24
Very important	29
Somewhat important	18
Not important	7
No opinion	3

*Based on half sample

Race relations?

Top priority	17%
High priority	28
Very important	29
Somewhat important	16

Not important 8
No opinion 2

*Based on half sample

*Campaign finance reform?**

Top priority 10%
High priority 14
Very important 29
Somewhat important 26
Not important 18
No opinion 3

*Based on half sample

The availability of good jobs in the United States?

	June 4–5, 1999*	Jan. 5–7, 1997
Top priority	32%	35%
High priority	31	28
Very important	26	27
Somewhat important	7	7
Not important	3	2
No opinion	1	1

*Based on half sample

The cost of health care in the United States?

	June 4–5, 1999*	Jan. 5–7, 1997
Top priority	36%	36%
High priority	32	27
Very important	22	26
Somewhat important	7	9
Not important	3	1
No opinion	**	1

*Based on half sample
**Less than 1%

The amount Americans pay in federal taxes?

	June 4–5, 1999*	Jan. 5–7, 1997
Top priority	26%	29%
High priority	28	23
Very important	28	31
Somewhat important	13	12
Not important	4	4
No opinion	1	1

*Based on half sample

*Gun laws?**

Top priority 26%
High priority 24
Very important 24
Somewhat important 13
Not important 11
No opinion 2

*Based on half sample

*The problem of raising children in today's culture?**

Top priority 41%
High priority 26
Very important 21
Somewhat important 8
Not important 2
No opinion 2

*Based on half sample

*Abortion policy?**

Top priority 17%
High priority 18
Very important 24
Somewhat important 18
Not important 21
No opinion 2

*Based on half sample

Form A. *As you may know, the federal government is currently running a budget surplus, meaning it is taking in more money than it spends. President Clinton and Republicans in Congress agree that most of the surplus money should be used for Social Security, but they disagree over what to do with the rest. How would you prefer to see the rest of the budget surplus used—to fund new retirement savings accounts as well as increase spending on education, defense, Medicare, and other programs; or to cut taxes?**

	March 5–7, 1999
Fund retirement and increase spending	59%
Cut taxes	36

Neither; other (volunteered) 5

No opinion... **

> Form B. *As you may know, the federal gov-*
> *ernment is currently running a budget sur-*
> *plus, meaning it is taking in more money than*
> *it spends. President Clinton and Republicans*
> *in Congress agree that most of the surplus*
> *money should be used for Social Security, but*
> *they disagree over what to do with the rest.*
> *How would you prefer to see the rest of the*
> *budget surplus used—to increase spending on*
> *other government programs, or to cut taxes?**

	March 5–7, 1999
Increase spending	21%
Cut taxes	74
Neither; other (volunteered)	1
No opinion	**

Note: Republican leaders in the House are now developing a major tax cut plan, which, according to press reports, will be unveiled in July and could entail as much as $778 billion in tax savings over the next ten years. A number of Republican presidential candidates are also focusing on tax cuts as major planks in their campaign platforms. Senator John McCain, for example, recently proposed a $16-billion tax cut, saying that "it's hard to defend a system that taxes your salary, your investments, your property, your expenses, your marriage, and your death."

The generic appeal of a tax cut is clear from a number of Gallup Polls conducted over the last twenty years. Each time the public is asked about a "cut in federal income taxes," the responses are overwhelmingly positive. In 1977, for example, 79% said that they favor a federal income tax cut; and earlier this year, when the same question was posed again to the public, 72% said that they favor a tax cut. In similar fashion, Gallup Polls conducted around tax time each year in April show that Americans consistently say that they pay too much in federal income taxes.

The real-world popularity of a tax cut with the voting population is tempered, however, by additional polling which shows that its generic or top-of-mind approval is moderated significantly when it is placed in context or juxtaposed against other proposals. For example, in a March Gallup Poll, respondents were given a choice for uses of the federal budget surplus after Social Security had been taken care of: either to cut taxes or to "fund new retirement savings accounts as well as increase spending on education, defense, Medicare, and other programs." With this juxtaposition of the tax cut against a litany of very popular programs the public's opinion shifts strongly, to 59% who favor the funding of the programs against only 36% who favor the tax cut. On the other hand, when the alternative to the tax cut was phrased as simply "to increase spending on other government programs," the number in favor of the tax cut zoomed to 74%, suggesting that the way in which the alternative to a tax cut is worded or explained to the public can be extremely important. Funding specific popular programs is more important than a tax cut, but the idea of a more generic increase in government spending is viewed as less important.

Recent Gallup polling also suggests that the issue of taxes is by no means the highest priority for voters who are pondering which candidate to support in the 2000 presidential race. Respondents were given a list of thirteen different issues or programs and asked to rate each one in terms of its importance to them in choosing a presidential candidate. The amount that Americans pay in federal taxes came in only eighth on that list, with 54% saying that it was a top or high priority. The highest priority issues were education, the economy, and Social Security and Medicare.

The poll data do show, however, that tax cuts are a significantly higher priority for Republicans across the country than they are for independents or Democrats, perhaps explaining why Republican candidates facing next year's early primaries are focusing on the issue. Additionally, no doubt because they pay the most in taxes, tax cuts are more important to the higher income groups in the country than they are to lower income groups.

If tax cuts are enacted, the public strongly favors an across-the-board income tax cut for all citizens rather than "targeted tax 'cuts'" for certain groups and for specific situations," by a 72%-to-26% margin. Despite this sentiment, Republicans are no doubt cautioned by the fact that their candidate Bob Dole pegged much of his campaign in 1996 on the promise of such an across-the-board income tax cut—to no avail. Apparently, the initial surface appeal of Dole's concept did not outweigh the various other considerations that voters took into account in reelecting Bill Clinton.

The 1992 Clinton campaign motto—"It's the economy, stupid!"—could be redefined for the upcoming 2000 presidential election in terms of the youth issues emanating from the Columbine High School shooting rampage in Littleton, Colorado. Of the thirteen different issues tested in the recent election survey, the quality of public education and "the problems of raising children in today's culture" rank as the two most important voting issues. Over 40% of respondents in Gallup's June 4–5 survey say that the candidates' stands on these issues will be a top priority for them in deciding whom to support for president. Women seem to be especially concerned about the quality of public education, with 47% of women rating it a top priority, compared to 38% of men. However, men and women are about equally likely to cite the problems of raising children, with 43% of men and 40% of women saying that a candidate's stand on this issue will be a top priority in their vote choice.

Interestingly, the other key issue raised by the Columbine shooting—gun laws—ranks much farther down the list of issue priorities, with just one-quarter rating it the top priority. Other issues rated more important than gun laws include the economy, Social Security and Medicare policy, healthcare costs, the rate of violent crime, the availability of good jobs, and the amount paid in federal taxes. The four issues ranked at the bottom of the list are mentioned by less than one-quarter of the public as being top priorities in their presidential vote: the situation in Kosovo, race relations, abortion policy, and last, campaign finance reform.

JUNE 30
REPUBLICAN AND DEMOCRATIC CANDIDATES/PRESIDENTIAL TRIAL HEAT

Interviewing Dates: 6/25–27/99
CNN/*USA Today*/Gallup Poll
Survey #GO 128120

Asked of Republicans and those leaning Republican: I'm going to read a list of people who may be running in the Republican primary for president in the next election. Which of those candidates would you be most likely to support for the Republican nomination for president in the year 2000?

	June 25–27, 1999*	June 4–5, 1999*
Lamar Alexander	2%	3%
Gary Bauer	2	1
Patrick Buchanan	3	6
George W. Bush	59	46
Elizabeth Dole	8	14
Steve Forbes	6	5
Orrin Hatch	2	–
John Kasich	3	1
John McCain	5	5
Dan Quayle	6	9
Bob Smith	1	1
Other (volunteered)	**	**
None; wouldn't vote	1	2
No opinion	2	7

*Margin of sampling error: ±5 percentage points
**Less than 1%

Selected National Trend
(First Mentions)

	May 23–24, 1999*	April 13–14, 1999*	March 12–14, 1999*	Jan. 8–10, 1999*
Alexander	1%	**	2%	4%
Bauer	2	2	1	2
Buchanan	6	4	4	–
G. W. Bush	46	53	52	42
E. Dole	18	16	20	22
Forbes	5	6	1	5
Hatch	–	–	–	–
Kasich	2	2	3	2
McCain	6	5	3	8
Quayle	7	7	9	6
Smith	2	**	1	1
Other	**	**	1	1

None;
wouldn't
vote.............. 1   2   1   1
No opinion 4   3   2   6

*Margin of sampling error: ±5 percentage points
**Less than 1%

Asked of Democrats and those leaning Democratic: I'm going to read a list of people who may be running in the Democratic primary for president in the next election. Which of those candidates would you be most likely to support for the Democratic nomination for president in the year 2000?

	June 25–27, 1999*	June 4–5, 1999*
On Current List		
Bill Bradley....................................	28%	28%
Al Gore	64	63
Off Current List		
Dick Gephardt................................	–	–
Jesse Jackson	–	–
Bob Kerrey	–	–
John Kerry	–	–
Paul Wellstone..............................	–	–
Other (volunteered).......................	1	**
None; wouldn't vote	3	3
No opinion....................................	4	6

*Margin of sampling error: ±5 percentage points
**Less than 1%

Selected National Trend
(First Mentions)

	May 23–24, 1999*	April 13–14, 1999*	March 12–14, 1999*	Jan. 8–10, 1999*
Bradley............	30%	34%	21%	12%
Gore	59	54	58	47
Gephardt.........	–	–	–	13
Jackson............	–	–	15	11
Kerrey	–	–	–	–
Kerry	–	–	–	5
Wellstone	–	–	–	1
Other	–	1	–	1
None; wouldn't vote..............	4	3	4	3

No opinion 7   8   2   7
*Margin of sampling error: ±5 percentage points

If Vice President Al Gore were the Democratic party's candidate and Texas Governor George W. Bush were the Republican party's candidate, whom would you be more likely to vote for—Al Gore, the Democrat, or George W. Bush, the Republican? [Those who were undecided were asked: As of today, do you lean more toward Al Gore, the Democrat, or George W. Bush, the Republican?]

	June 25–27, 1999	June 4–5, 1999
Gore	41%	40%
G. W. Bush	56	56
Neither; it depends (volunteered); no opinion	3	4

Selected National Trend

	Gore	G. W. Bush	Neither; it depends; no opinion
1999			
May 23–24...................	40%	54%	6%
April 30– May 2......................	40	56	4
April 13–14.................	38	59	3
March 12–14...............	41	56	3
March 5–7...................	41	56	3
February 19–21...........	43	54	3
January 8–10...............	47	48	5
1998			
May 8–10....................	46	50	4

Note: Texas Governor George W. Bush has expanded his commanding lead as the number one choice of Republicans for their party's nomination for president next year, and he is maintaining a comfortable lead over Vice President Al Gore in trial heat polling representing the general election. Both Bush and Gore have received a great degree of publicity over the past several weeks as they have formally announced their campaigns and have made obligatory swings through New Hampshire, Iowa, and other states with critical campaign primaries. For Bush, these weeks were the first chance that many Americans outside of Texas have had to observe the candidate who, since earlier this year, has emerged as the man to beat in next year's election.

The initial impact of the last few weeks' activities, as measured by a new Gallup Poll completed on Sunday [June 27], reveals nothing but positive news for the Texas governor. Bush's lock on Republican voters has never been stronger. His lead over his closest rival, Elizabeth Dole, has expanded from 32 points earlier this month to an impressive 51 points today. Bush currently gets the support of 59% of Republicans as their first choice for the Republican nomination, compared to only 8% for Elizabeth Dole. This represents a significant downturn for the former Red Cross president, who as recently as early May was the clear second choice behind Bush, with 24% of the vote. However, she is no longer doing better than a number of the other Republican contenders, including former Vice President Dan Quayle and businessman Steve Forbes, who come in at 6% of the vote, and Arizona Senator John McCain, with 5%.

At the bottom of the list are political commentator Pat Buchanan and Ohio Congressman John Kasich, at 3% each; former Tennessee Governor Lamar Alexander and Family Research Council Chairman Gary Bauer, at 2% each; and New Hampshire Senator Bob Smith, at 1%. This weekend's poll included for the first time newly announced candidate Orrin Hatch, but the senator from Utah has a way to go before his presence as an active candidate has an impact on the Republican field; he gets only 2% of the Republican vote. In addition, Republicans were asked in this most recent poll to name their second choice for the nomination. Here, Elizabeth Dole does somewhat better, coming in with a combined total of 35% of first- and second-choice votes, putting her ahead of Quayle, who has 16%; McCain, with 15%; and Forbes, with 13%. Bush leads with a 75% combined total.

On the Democratic side of the ledger, Vice President Al Gore overwhelms his only announced challenger for the Democratic nomination, former New Jersey Senator Bill Bradley, by a 64%-to-28% margin, essentially unchanged from previous polls taken over the past several months. When Bush and Gore are matched up among all voters in a hypothetical general election trial heat, Bush beats Gore, 56% to 41%. This margin is highly similar to that of previous Gallup election polls conducted since March, suggesting that all of the drama and publicity of recent weeks have done nothing to shake up the race and allow Gore to make gains on front-runner Bush.

The fact that both parties have established such strong front-runners this early in the election cycle is perceived as a more negative state of affairs among Democrats than among Republicans. When asked whether it would be better for their party to have a clear front-runner or for there to be a "number of strong candidates competing for the nomination," 61% of Republicans chose the former, compared to only 36% who wanted competition among candidates. Democrats, on the other hand, are slightly more likely to want a number of strong candidates rather than an early front-runner, by a 50%-to-46% margin, perhaps reflecting their dissatisfaction with Gore's lagging support in pre-election polls.

JULY 23
THIRD-PARTY MOVEMENT—AN ANALYSIS*

Americans give encouraging lip service to the concept of a third active political party in the United States, and a not insubstantial 13% say they would vote for former professional wrestler and Minnesota Governor Jesse Ventura, if he were to run for president. At the same time, a new Gallup Poll sends mixed signals about whether real support for a third-party president is waxing or waning. According to the Gallup survey conducted on July 16–18, 67% of Americans favor a strong third party that would run candidates for president, Congress, and state offices against the Republican and Democratic nominees, while just 28% are opposed.

An additional positive sign for third parties is the relatively high support received by one possible independent contender, Minnesota Governor

*This analysis was written by Lydia Saad, Managing Editor, The Gallup Poll.

Jesse Ventura. When Americans are asked whom they would support in a three-way race for president in 2000, 50% of national adults say they would vote for the Republican front-runner, Texas Governor George W. Bush; 34% would support the leader of the Democratic field, Vice President Al Gore; and 13% would back Jesse Ventura as the Reform party candidate. This level of support for Ventura is lower than the 19% of the vote Ross Perot received as an independent candidate for president in 1992, but is substantially higher than the 8% Perot received in his repeat performance in 1996. (Without Ventura on the ballot, Bush beats Gore by a 55%-to-38% margin.)

A more negative outlook for third parties is presented by the trend in public satisfaction with the major party choices for president. Roughly half of Americans, 51%, currently say they would be satisfied if Gore and Bush were the only two candidates on the presidential ballot next year. Slightly fewer, 46%, indicate they want to see a third-party candidate on the ballot as well. By comparison, in August 1995 only 40% were satisfied with the prospect of a two-man race between Bill Clinton and Bob Dole, while 55% preferred adding a third-party candidate to the field.

This increase in satisfaction with having only two candidates on the ballot is seen mostly among Americans who identify with the Republican and Democratic parties, while most political independents—perhaps not surprisingly—remain interested in having the option of a third-party candidate. In August 1995 satisfaction with a two-way race for president was 54% among Republicans, 48% among Democrats, and only 26% among independents. Today, that satisfaction has risen to 68% among Republicans and 60% among Democrats, but to only 32% among independents.

One pattern seen across both elections is widespread support among younger adults for a competitive third party. This year, 61% of those age 18–29 say they want a third-party candidate on the ballot for president in 2000, compared with only 49% of those in the 30–49 age group and just 34% of those 50 and older. Similarly, 71% of the 18–29 group favor a third national political party that runs candidates for president, Congress, and state offices, as do 77% of those age 30–49, but only 52% of those 50 and older.

JULY 31
THE PRESIDENT AND FIRST LADY'S POPULARITY—AN ANALYSIS*

President Clinton's job approval rating surged to 64% this past week, up 6 points from the previous week, according to the latest Gallup Poll, conducted on July 22–25. The poll shows that the president's favorability rating also increased last week and now stands at 57%, the highest since last January and up by 9 points over the last reading a month ago.

One possible factor in the improved ratings could be the generally favorable press coverage the president received from his press conference last week, during which—among other things—he argued that among all the presidential candidates, only Vice President Al Gore was laying out a detailed plan of what needs to be accomplished in the next presidential term. But if that press conference alone was the reason for Clinton's improved ratings, it does not explain why the First Lady's ratings also increased and why Gore's ratings remained essentially unchanged.

The poll shows that 62% of Americans now have a favorable opinion of Hillary Clinton, up 6 points from the end of June. By contrast, Gore's favorability rating is at 53%, down slightly from the 56% he received last June. However favorable the president's comments, they did not seem to help the vice president.

The other major event last week that could have had an impact on the Clintons' ratings was the national mourning following the deaths of John F. Kennedy, Jr., his wife Carolyn, and her sister Lauren Bessette, killed in an airplane crash off Martha's Vineyard in Massachusetts. In his press conference, President Clinton discussed JFK Jr.'s visit to the White House last year, and both the president and First Lady were among those who attended the memorial services. It is likely that this public demonstration of sympathy by Mr. and Mrs. Clinton is at least partly related to the surge in their popularity.

Some evidence for this hypothesis is that the increase in positive feelings for both Clintons was significantly higher among older Americans—those who were alive when President Kennedy was assas-

*This analysis was written by David W. Moore, Consulting Editor, The Gallup Poll.

sinated and remember his little son saluting his father's casket—than among younger Americans. Clinton's job approval rating was up by 5 points among Americans under the age of 50, but up 11 points among those 50 and older. Similarly, his favorability rating surged by 17 points among older Americans, but increased by just 5 points among those under 30. The increase in Hillary's favorable ratings followed a similar pattern, up by 10 points among older Americans, with essentially no change among those under the age of 30.

The general trend of Clinton's job approval ratings has been lower this year than last, when the president's approval—either despite, or because of, the Monica Lewinsky scandal and impeachment hearings—ranged in the mid to high 60s. In fact, right after the impeachment vote by the House of Representatives last December, 73% of Americans said they approved of the president's job performance, a record for Clinton's presidency. However, once the focus of national attention shifted to policy matters and the "normal" politics of Washington, the president's approval began to decline, reaching a year-low of 53% last May. In June, it bounced back to 60% and has ranged in the high 50s since then. The current 64% rating is Clinton's highest since last March.

AUGUST 7
RICHARD NIXON'S RESIGNATION—
TWENTY-FIVE YEARS LATER

Interviewing Dates: 8/3–4/99
CNN/*USA Today*/Gallup Poll
Survey #GO 907928

How familiar are you with the Watergate affair during the Nixon administration—would you say you are very familiar, somewhat familiar, not too familiar, or not at all familiar with Watergate?

Very familiar	21%
Somewhat familiar	44
Not too familiar	22
Not at all familiar	13
No opinion	*

*Less than 1%

Selected National Trend

	Very familiar	Somewhat familiar	Not too familiar	Not at all familiar*
May 30–June 1, 1997	17%	46%	25%	11%
June 4–8, 1992	18	47	24	11

*"No opinion"—at 1% or less—is omitted.

It has now been twenty-five years since Richard Nixon resigned as president over the Watergate controversy. Which of these two statements comes closer to your own point of view about Watergate—it was a very serious matter because it revealed corruption in the Nixon administration; or it was just politics, the kind of thing both parties engage in?

Very serious	51%
Just politics	46
No opinion	3

Selected National Trend

	Very serious	Just politics	No opinion
May 30–June 1, 1997	52%	44%	4%
June 4–8, 1992	49	46	5
June 1982	52	45	3

Thinking back to Watergate, do you think Nixon's actions regarding Watergate were, or were not, serious enough to warrant his resignation?

Yes, serious enough	72%
Not serious enough	23
No opinion	5

Selected National Trend

	Yes, serious enough	Not serious enough	No opinion
May 30–June 1, 1997	68%	26%	6%
June 4–8, 1992	70	21	9

May 1986* 71	24	5
June 1982 75	19	6
August 1974 65	32	3

*Gallup/*Newsweek* Poll

Finally, comparing the impeachment charges against Bill Clinton over the Lewinsky controversy with the charges against Richard Nixon in the Watergate controversy, which do you think were more serious—the charges against Richard Nixon; the charges against Bill Clinton; or do you think the charges against both men were about equally serious?

	Aug. 3–4, 1999	Oct. 6–7, 1998
Nixon charges 54%	64%
Clinton charges 14	10
Both equally serious 29	23
No opinion 3	3

Note: August 9 marks the twenty-fifth anniversary of Richard Nixon's forced resignation in the wake of the Watergate scandal. Gallup polling conducted since that time, including a just-completed early August survey, suggests that the stigma of Watergate lives on. Nixon continues to reign in the minds of Americans as the worst president of the last half-century, despite the fact that almost one-half of respondents says that the Watergate affair was "just politics."

Nixon was in bad shape in the eyes of the public just before his resignation. An early August 1974 Gallup Poll showed him with a job approval rating of only 24%, just 1 point above the all-time lowest number measured by Gallup for any president before or since—the 23% recorded for Harry Truman in the fall of 1951. Despite the temptation to ascribe all of Nixon's problems to Watergate, however, it was clear at the time that his low standing was not just Watergate-related. The U.S. economy was in terrible shape, and by early 1974 there were long gas lines in many parts of the country as a result of an energy crisis. As Gallup analysts noted in assessing Nixon in 1974 after his resignation, "By early 1973, in the grip of what was to become a 'double-digit' inflation rate, the economy and high cost of living were far and away the biggest concerns of the American people."

Still, Watergate was the obvious factor that brought Nixon down. In a Gallup Poll conducted just before his resignation, 57% said that his behavior in relation to Watergate was so egregious that it warranted his being removed from office, an action that was forestalled by his resignation on August 9. Now, some twenty-five years later, Gallup polling suggests that Nixon, for the most part, was unable to overcome the stigma of Watergate despite his best efforts in the years between 1974 and his death in 1994.

Only 22% now say that Nixon will go down in history as outstanding or above average, while 41% rate him as a below-average or poor president. Thirty-five percent think that he will be seen as average. Nixon's retrospective positive standing is significantly below that of other presidents such as Jimmy Carter (39%) and Bill Clinton (36%). Nixon's negative image exceeds that of the next higher contender in that category, Clinton, by 10 percentage points.

Additionally, in a February 1999 poll, 28% said that Nixon was the worst of the ten presidents since World War II. The results of that poll, however, were not quite as negative for Nixon as one conducted thirteen years ago, when 34% chose him as the worst president in a 1986 poll. Nixon barely edged out Carter, who got 29% of the "worst president" nod. Now, Clinton comes in second behind Nixon, with 21% of the "worst" vote.

Despite the passage of time, the Watergate scandal remains top-of-mind for the majority of the public. About two-thirds (65%) are still at least somewhat familiar with the Watergate affair. Americans 50–64 years of age, who would have been 25–39 at the time of Nixon's resignation, are most likely to be familiar with Watergate, while only 43% of young people age 18–29, the oldest of whom were only 4 years old at the time of the resignation, are familiar with the scandal.

AUGUST 19
PRESIDENTIAL RATINGS

Interviewing Dates: 8/3–4/99
CNN/*USA Today*/Gallup Poll
Survey #GO 907928

How do you think each of the following presidents will go down in history—as an out-

standing president, above average, average, below average, or poor:

Ronald Reagan?

	Aug. 3–4, 1999	Jan. 8–11, 1993
Outstanding, above average	54%	38%
Average	34	37
Below average, poor	12	24
No opinion	*	1

*Less than 1%

George Bush?

	Aug. 3–4, 1999	Jan. 8–11, 1993
Outstanding, above average	41%	36%
Average	46	51
Below average, poor	12	12
No opinion	1	1

Bill Clinton?

Outstanding, above average	36%
Average	33
Below average, poor	31
No opinion	*

*Less than 1%

Jimmy Carter?

	Aug. 3–4, 1999	Jan. 8–11, 1993
Outstanding, above average	30%	16%
Average	50	40
Below average, poor	18	41
No opinion	2	3

Richard Nixon?

Outstanding, above average	22%
Average	35
Below average, poor	41
No opinion	2

Note: Of the five men elected to the presidency in the last thirty years—Richard Nixon, Jimmy Carter, Ronald Reagan, George Bush, and Bill Clinton—Ronald Reagan will be judged most favorably in the history books, according to Americans today. In a Gallup survey taken earlier this month, a solid majority (54%) believes that the nation's fortieth president will be remembered as outstanding or above average. Another 34% think that Reagan will be regarded as average, while just 12% say that he will be remembered more negatively, as below average or poor.

Reagan fares better in the August 3–4 survey of national adults than do all other modern elected presidents rated. (Gerald Ford is excluded from the list because he assumed the office upon Nixon's resignation in 1974 and did not serve a full four-year term.) Compared to Reagan's 54%, the percentage predicting that each president will be regarded as outstanding or above average is 41% for Bush, 36% for Clinton, 30% for Carter, and 22% for Nixon.

Interestingly, current public opinion is more sharply divided about Clinton than it is about any of the other presidents measured. Thirty-six percent believe that he will go down in history as outstanding or above average, 33% as average, and 31% as below average or poor.

AUGUST 20
REPUBLICAN PRESIDENTIAL CANDIDATES—AN ANALYSIS*

Despite the high visibility given to the Iowa straw poll results this past weekend, and the beginnings of a controversy concerning Republican candidate George W. Bush's refusal to answer specific questions about past cocaine use, a new Gallup Poll indicates that not much has changed in terms of the political landscape of the 2000 presidential election. Among Republican respondents nationwide, Bush's huge lead over all GOP challengers has stayed the

*This analysis was written by Frank Newport, Editor in Chief, The Gallup Poll.

same, and he maintains a comfortable lead over Al Gore in the national general election trial heat.

Bush gets 61% of the votes of Republicans for the Republican nomination in the new poll, conducted on Monday through Wednesday, August 16–18. This is essentially unchanged from June, when Bush received 59% of the Republican vote. Bush also leads Vice President Al Gore in a nationwide general election trial heat by a 55%-to-41% margin, almost identical to the margin in a number of Gallup Polls conducted since early May.

Both Steve Forbes and Elizabeth Dole received a good deal of visibility as a result of the Iowa straw poll—based on their second- and third-place finishes. The new nationwide Gallup Poll shows that the Iowa vote may have provided a bit of a residual benefit for Dole, who now gets 13% of the Republican vote nationwide, putting her in second place behind Bush. This is up from her low point of 8% in late June, but is essentially where she was in early June. Dole has been the second-place contender, behind Bush, in every Gallup Poll conducted over the past four months. Forbes no doubt hoped that his second-place finish in Iowa would have boosted his standing among Republicans nationwide, but there is no evidence of such a bounce in the new poll. Forbes gets only 4% of the Republican vote, very similar to the 5% and 6% levels for the magazine publisher in earlier polling. While Forbes did better in Iowa than either former Vice President Dan Quayle or Arizona Senator John McCain, both of the latter candidates get slightly more of the national Republican vote than Forbes.

An analysis of a series of general election trial-heat questions pitting various Republican candidates against Democratic front-runner Al Gore provides more negative news for Forbes. As noted, Bush beats Democratic front-runner Gore by a 14% margin. Elizabeth Dole also beats Gore, although by a smaller, 6% margin. Steve Forbes loses to Gore among the general American population by a 54%-to-40% margin.

Majority of Republicans Would Like to See Bush, Dole, and Forbes Stay in Race

Former Tennessee Governor Lamar Alexander dropped out of the race after his poor showing in Iowa. The current national poll asked Republicans their views on whether a number of the remaining candidates should or should not stay in the race for the Republican party's presidential nomination. Not surprisingly, 96% of Republicans say that Bush should stay in. Seventy-seven percent say that Elizabeth Dole should stay in, and 55% say that Forbes should stay in.

There is little encouragement in the poll for the other Republican candidates. Sixty-two percent of Republicans say that Gary Bauer and Pat Buchanan should get out of the race altogether, and 66% say the same about former Vice President Dan Quayle. Fifty-three percent say that Arizona Senator John McCain should drop out.

Little Difference in Candidate Standing among Conservative Republicans

Much has been made about the race among the Republican presidential candidates to claim the allegiance of conservative Republicans. The latest poll shows that there is little difference between conservative and moderate Republicans in their presidential choices: Bush wins by about 60% among both groups. Elizabeth Dole is second among conservatives with 13%, followed by Forbes with 5% of the vote, and McCain and Quayle with 4% each. Gary Bauer gets only 2%.

SEPTEMBER 17
GEORGE W. BUSH—AN ANALYSIS*

The United States is fourteen months, numerous primaries, and at least three conventions away from the general election that will determine who will be its next president. At this early point in the process, however, Texas Governor George W. Bush seems to have cornered the market on the winning poll numbers.

A new Gallup Poll, conducted on September 10–14, finds little change in the Year 2000 electoral picture compared to previous surveys. Governor Bush maintains an imposing presence in the race for the Republican party nomination—earning 62% of the vote and leading second-place rival Elizabeth Dole, who has just 10%. The poll also shows that

*This analysis was written by Lydia Saad, Managing Editor, The Gallup Poll.

Bush would win the November election handily if it were held today, against either of the two major Democratic contenders. Bush maintains a large lead in the general election (56% vs. 39%) over the leading Democrat, Vice President Al Gore. Put former New Jersey Senator Bill Bradley on the ticket, rather than Gore, and Bush performs slightly better, winning by 57% to 37%.

Among Democrats, Bill Bradley's campaign for his party's nomination shows no signs of momentum nationally, despite some recent evidence that he is doing better in selected states, such as New Hampshire and Iowa. Today, Democrats nationwide favor Al Gore over Bradley by 63% to 30%—a slightly greater lead for Gore than last month, when his margin was 58% to 31%.

Bush Weathered Drug Controversy without Injury

The latest survey is the first conducted by Gallup since troubles emerged in August for the Bush campaign surrounding issues relating to possible past drug use by the candidate. There is no sign, however, that public support for the Texas governor or his personal image has diminished as a result. Current support for Bush among Republicans nationwide is similar to that found in Gallup surveys taken in June and August, when 59% and 61% of Republicans, respectively, favored him for the nomination. His current 17-point lead over Al Gore also represents no significant change, compared with his 14-point lead in August and a 17-point lead in June.

Beyond electoral support, George W. Bush continues to be viewed in positive personal terms by a majority of Americans. Today, 56% say the phrase "shares your values" applies to Bush. A similar proportion, 58%, felt this way in March when Gallup last asked the question. (By contrast, slightly fewer, 52%, feel that Al Gore shares their values.)

Republican "Also-Rans" Are Currently Stalled

George W. Bush's electoral appeal has left a crowded GOP field scrambling over the relatively few remaining Republican votes. Thus far, none of the eight other major Republican candidates has been able to consolidate sufficient numbers to claim a dominant second-place position. Elizabeth

Dole showed promise shortly after she announced her candidacy this spring, when she garnered the support of 24% of Republicans nationwide and cut Bush's lead in half (from 37 points to just 18 points). Dole's support quickly dwindled, however, and today, at 10%, her poll figures are barely distinguishable from those of Dan Quayle, Steve Forbes, and John McCain, each favored by just 5% of Republicans.

Further down in the Republican pack are Pat Buchanan, Gary Bauer, Orrin Hatch, and Alan Keyes. Their support levels fall in the 1%–3% range and have shown no sign of movement, either up or down, since late June.

Dole Could Be a Contender

While Dole, a former Red Cross president and well-credentialed former cabinet member, has not been able to sustain a high level of public support for the GOP nomination, there are indications in the new Gallup survey that she is well positioned to emerge as a credible alternative to Bush for the nomination —or to be an attractive vice presidential choice.

In addition to measuring candidate strength in election matchups, Gallup explored the relative strength of various candidates by asking respondents how likely they would be to vote for each if the candidate's name were to appear on the ballot in November 2000. Out of the ten candidates rated, Elizabeth Dole ranks second behind George W. Bush, but ahead of both Al Gore and Bill Bradley, as someone Americans would be "very" or "somewhat" likely to support next November. Over half the public, 54%, say they would likely vote for Dole if she were on the ballot, compared to 68% who feel this way about Bush. By contrast, 51% say they would be likely to vote for Gore and 45% for Bradley. However, all other announced and potential candidates rated, including Forbes, Quayle, McCain, Buchanan, Jesse Ventura, and Warren Beatty, receive far less support using this measure, ranging from 11% for Beatty to 33% for Forbes.

One distinguishing feature of the potential support for Elizabeth Dole is that it crosses party lines. Nearly two-thirds of Republicans, 63%, say they would likely vote for her next November if she were on the ballot, as would 55% of independents and 47% of Democrats. By contrast, support for Gore is highly partisan, with 82% of Democrats saying they would support him, compared to 45% of independents and just 23% of Republicans. Bush's support also tends to vary substantially by party, although support for him is high among all three groups: 91% among Republicans, 68% among independents, and 48% among Democrats.

Elizabeth Dole also provides the Republican party with crossover appeal to a group her party has been anxious to attract in recent elections: women. With 59% of women saying they would be likely to support her if she were on the ballot, compared to 50% of men, she is the only Republican presidential candidate rated—including Bush—who has greater support among women than among men.

SEPTEMBER 21
AL GORE VS. GEORGE W. BUSH

Interviewing Dates: 9/10–14/99
CNN/*USA Today*/Gallup Poll
Survey #GO 128526

*Please say whether you think Al Gore would do a good job or a poor job of dealing with each of the following issues:**

The economy?

Good job	58%
Poor job	32
No opinion	10

Foreign affairs?

Good job	46%
Poor job	41
No opinion	13

The gun issue?

Good job	45%
Poor job	40
No opinion	15

The environment?

Good job	67%
Poor job	24
No opinion	9

Education?

Good job	67%
Poor job	24
No opinion	9

Taxes?

Good job	47%
Poor job	41
No opinion	12

Crime?

Good job	52%
Poor job	37
No opinion	11

Health care?

Good job	57%
Poor job	32
No opinion	11

Keeping the federal budget balanced?

Good job	50%
Poor job	39
No opinion	11

The problems of raising children in today's culture?

Good job	62%
Poor job	28
No opinion	10

Social Security and Medicare?

Good job	55%
Poor job	35
No opinion	10

*Based on half sample

*Next, please say whether you think George W. Bush would do a good job or a poor job of dealing with each of the following issues:**

The economy?

Good job	63%
Poor job	22
No opinion	15

Foreign affairs?

Good job	61%
Poor job	22
No opinion	17

The gun issue?

Good job	50%
Poor job	32
No opinion	18

The environment?

Good job	55%
Poor job	29
No opinion	16

Education?

Good job	70%
Poor job	18
No opinion	12

Taxes?

Good job	54%
Poor job	30
No opinion	16

Crime?

Good job	65%
Poor job	20
No opinion	15

Health care?

Good job	57%
Poor job	26
No opinion	17

Keeping the federal budget balanced?

Good job	56%
Poor job	29
No opinion	15

The problems of raising children in today's culture?

Good job	62%
Poor job	23
No opinion	15

Social Security and Medicare?

Good job	53%
Poor job	29
No opinion	18

*Based on half sample

Thinking about each of the following characteristics and qualities, please say whether you think it applies or does not apply to Al Gore:

Shares your values?

	Sept. 10–14, 1999	March 12–14, 1999	Aug. 21–23, 1998
Applies	52%	56%	52%
Does not apply	41	37	35
No opinion	7	7	13

Cares about the needs of people like you?

	Sept. 10–14, 1999	March 12–14, 1999	Aug. 21–23, 1998
Applies	61%	63%	59%
Does not apply	33	31	31
No opinion	6	6	10

Can manage the government effectively?

	Sept. 10–14, 1999	March 12–14, 1999
Applies	53%	59%
Does not apply	40	35
No opinion	7	6

Inspiring?

	Sept. 10–14, 1999	March 12–14, 1999
Applies	38%	35%
Does not apply	56	61
No opinion	6	4

Can bring about the changes this country needs?

	Sept. 10–14, 1999	March 12–14, 1999
Applies	42%	46%
Does not apply	50	47
No opinion	8	7

Honest and trustworthy?

	Sept. 10–14, 1999	Aug. 21–23, 1998
Applies	63%	63%
Does not apply	31	25
No opinion	6	12

Tough enough for the job?

Applies	50%
Does not apply	45
No opinion	5

*Based on half sample

Thinking about each of the following characteristics and qualities, please say whether you think it applies or does not apply to George W. Bush:

Shares your values?

	Sept. 10–14, 1999	March 12–14, 1999
Applies	56%	58%
Does not apply	34	31
No opinion	10	11

Cares about the needs of people like you?

	Sept. 10–14, 1999	March 12–14, 1999
Applies	59%	59%
Does not apply	32	32
No opinion	9	9

Can manage the government effectively?

	Sept. 10–14, 1999	March 12–14, 1999
Applies	72%	77%
Does not apply	19	15
No opinion	9	8

Inspiring?

	Sept. 10–14, 1999	March 12–14, 1999
Applies	58%	55%
Does not apply	34	36
No opinion	8	9

Can bring about the changes this country needs?

	Sept. 10–14, 1999	March 12–14, 1999
Applies	58%	59%
Does not apply	33	31
No opinion	9	10

Honest and trustworthy?

Applies	62%
Does not apply	29
No opinion	9

Tough enough for the job?

Applies	76%
Does not apply	17
No opinion	7

*Based on half sample

Note: With more than a year to go before the presidential election, it may not be surprising to learn that apart from party loyalties, the most important factors dividing voters in their current preferences relate to the images of the two front-running candidates, not to their perceived abilities to handle specific issues. The latest Gallup Poll, conducted on September 10–14, shows Texas Governor George W. Bush with a 17-point advantage over Vice President Al Gore, little changed over the past six months. In the same poll, respondents were asked to rate the two front-runners on a variety of personal image characteristics and on issues of the day. An analysis of the responses shows that for Governor Bush, his image as a candidate who can "manage the government effectively" and "bring about the changes this country needs" goes a long way toward explaining why he continues to lead Vice President Gore in the polls.

Bush leads Gore by substantial margins on four of the seven image characteristics included in the poll—"can manage the government effectively," "can bring about the changes this country needs," is "inspiring," and is "tough enough for the job." On the other three characteristics—"shares your values," "cares about the needs of people like you," and is "honest and trustworthy"—the candidates are essentially tied.

In contrast to his substantial leads over Gore on the four image characteristics, Bush leads Gore by margins of 13 to 15 points in two issue areas—handling foreign affairs, and crime. Gore, on the other hand, has a 12-point lead over Bush on handling the environment. On the several other issue areas included in the poll, Bush enjoys a slight lead over Gore on four of them, while the two candidates are essentially tied on four other issues.

SEPTEMBER 28
DAN QUAYLE—AN ANALYSIS*

Despite the vastly different announcements made Monday by former Vice President Dan Quayle and Senator John McCain—with Quayle dropping out of the presidential race while McCain formally announced that he was in—neither candidate is receiving much support among Republicans nationwide. The fact that McCain is still relatively unknown to many Americans, however, suggests there is the potential for him to do better as he campaigns more vigorously in the months ahead.

Both Quayle and McCain received only 5% of the Republican vote in the latest Gallup Poll conducted on September 10–14, dwarfed by the enormous 62% of the vote received by front-runner George W. Bush. In fact, both Quayle and McCain also trail Elizabeth Dole, who has consistently run second behind Bush this year and who received 10% of the vote in the mid-September

*This analysis was written by Frank Newport, Editor in Chief, The Gallup Poll.

survey. Quayle's and McCain's poor current showing reflects a decided lack of progress for both; Quayle's high point among Republicans has been only 9% (in June), while McCain has been continually mired with 4% to 6% of the vote.

Prior to dropping out, Quayle was focusing his efforts on trying to win over conservative Republicans, but neither he nor any candidate other than Bush has been able to develop much support among this group. Quayle receives only 5% of the conservative Republican vote in the mid-September poll, exactly the same percentage he received among all Republicans. Bush wins strongly among all segments of Republicans, regardless of their ideology, and Dole comes in second among both conservative and moderate Republicans.

Quayle has long suffered from image problems, with unfavorable ratings that rose to 48% and 59% in the summer of 1992 when he was being chosen again to run with George H. Bush (at the time, it should be noted, the senior Bush's own job approval ratings were at the low point of his administration). Additionally, Gallup polling in the summer of 1992 showed that almost four out of ten Republicans thought President Bush should dump Quayle in favor of someone else. Quayle, of course, stayed on the ticket, and the Republicans lost the November election to Bill Clinton and Al Gore.

Gallup polling earlier this year found that Quayle has been unable to repair his image after leaving the White House. According to a February poll, Quayle's favorable-to-unfavorable image ratio remained anemic, at 46% favorable to 44% unfavorable. McCain's image, on the other hand, has been more positive than negative, although the largest percentage of Americans say they don't know enough about him to rate him. In fact, the relative obscurity under which McCain is currently operating may be one of his strongest selling points as he begins mounting his presidential campaign in earnest.

While Quayle is a very well-known commodity, as might be expected given his four years as vice president, McCain is not. This would seem to allow McCain to hold out some hope that he may do better against Bush as he becomes better known. For example, in the mid-September poll, 61% of Americans said it would be unlikely that they would vote for Quayle if he were to be on the November

2000 ballot, while 32% said they might vote for him. Only 7% had no opinion. When Americans were asked the same question about McCain, however, the percentage saying they might consider voting for him was 27%, with 32% saying it was unlikely, but with 41% saying they didn't know. That 41% figure is presumably McCain's best hope—that he can create a more positive image as he becomes better known in the months ahead.

OCTOBER 1
THE YEAR 2000 CAMPAIGN

Interviewing Dates: 9/10–14/99
CNN/*USA Today*/Gallup Poll
Survey #GO 128526

If each of the following candidates were on the ballot for president next November, please say how likely it is that you would vote for him or her—very likely, somewhat likely, not too likely, not at all likely, or you don't know enough about that person to say:

	Total likely to support	Total not likely	Don't know enough to say
George W. Bush	68%	27%	5%
Elizabeth Dole	54	34	12
Al Gore	51	44	5
Bill Bradley	45	31	24
Steve Forbes	33	43	24
John McCain	27	32	41
Patrick Buchanan	24	56	20
Jesse Ventura	23	56	21
Warren Beatty	11	71	18

Support for Third-Party Presidential Candidate
(By Party Identification, 1992–1999)

	Republicans	Democrats	Independents
Pat Buchanan in 1999*	10%	4%	13%
Ross Perot in 1996**	5	4	19
Ross Perot in 1992†	16	10	31

*September 23–26
**November 3–4
†November 1–2

Note: According to the latest Gallup survey, if the 2000 election for president were held today, political commentator Pat Buchanan would receive 9% of the vote as the Reform party candidate in a three-way race against the two major-party frontrunners, Al Gore and George W. Bush. This hypothetical support level for Buchanan is nearly identical to the 9% that Ross Perot received as the Reform party candidate in 1996 but is well behind the 19% share that Perot won in his first attempt at capturing the presidency, in 1992.

The new September 23–26 Gallup survey suggests that Buchanan's mix of social conservatism and national isolationism draws more votes from Republicans than Democrats. As a result, the addition of Buchanan to the ballot reduces Bush's lead over Gore from 18 points to 12 points. When voters are asked for their preference in a two-way race between Bush, the Republican, and Gore, the Democrat, Bush beats Gore by 55% to 37%, with 8% undecided. In a three-way race, Buchanan draws 9%, Gore continues to receive 37%, but support for Bush drops to 49%.

With Bush's lead over Gore quite wide, in addition to the fact that support for Buchanan is limited, Buchanan's entrance into the race as a third-party candidate would not affect the outcome of the election if it were held today. But if either of these basic factors were to change, the former aide to Ronald Reagan has the potential of playing the spoiler—throwing the election to the Democrat—in a way that Perot did not.

In both 1996 and, to a lesser degree, in 1992, Perot drew the majority of his support from political independents. According to Gallup's final 1996 pre-election survey, Perot was favored by only 4% of Democrats and 5% of Republicans, but by 19% of independents. By contrast, Buchanan is currently favored by 4% of Democrats, 10% of Republicans, and by 13% of independents. His relatively strong appeal among Republicans could explain why the GOP national chairman, Jim Nicholson, met with Buchanan recently to ask him not to mount a third-party challenge.

In order to be a spoiler, Buchanan will need to get his name on the ballot. With over $12 million available in federal matching funds and ballot status in many states, the Reform party nomination is an attractive option, but one that Buchanan has yet to formally declare he will seek. If he does, Gallup surveys taken this September suggest that he could be a credible contender for the nomination. Nationally, Buchanan's image tilts negative, with 32% saying that they have a favorable view of him and 45% an unfavorable view. In terms of voter support, just one in four (24%) would be "very" or "somewhat" likely to vote for him if he were on the ballot next November.

At the same time, none of the other major names being floated for the Reform party nomination—Donald Trump, Lowell Weicker, or Warren Beatty—enjoys clearly superior numbers to Buchanan's. Trump is viewed favorably by 41% and unfavorably by 47%, Weicker is unknown to 75% of the public. Only 11% of the nation's adults would be likely to vote for Beatty if he were on the ballot. Even Jesse Ventura, who has taken himself out of consideration (at least for the time being), has limited national appeal. While 51% have a favorable view of the Minnesota governor (according to a Gallup survey conducted prior to the release of his comments in an upcoming issue of *Playboy* magazine), only 23% would be likely to vote for him as president.

OCTOBER 8
DONALD TRUMP—AN ANALYSIS*

Businessman Donald Trump's announcement that he will form an exploratory committee to look into a possible run for the Reform party presidential nomination will apparently not create an immediate groundswell of enthusiasm among Americans. Recent polling conducted by Gallup and other organizations shows that Trump has a more negative than positive image nationwide, and that he runs significantly behind other possible Reform party candidates such as Jesse Ventura and Pat Buchanan in hypothetical election matchups.

One problem for Trump is that although he is already a well-known personality, his image is perceived as more negative than positive. In some ways this perception is worse than a situation in

*This analysis was written by Frank Newport, Editor in Chief, The Gallup Poll.

which a newly announced candidate has low existing name recognition, because this type of candidate at least has a chance to create a positive image as he or she becomes better known. The challenge for Trump, on the other hand, will be to rehabilitate an already existing negative image, which is usually a more difficult process.

In a Gallup Poll conducted on September 23–26, Trump was viewed negatively by 47%, compared to 41% who had a favorable image. These percentages are actually slightly more positive than the ratings given to Buchanan and Ross Perot, but are in sharp contrast to the much more positive opinions of such major party contenders as George W. Bush, Al Gore, and Bill Bradley.

Trump is a registered Republican, but at this point his image is not significantly different across the various partisan groups in the country. He is viewed roughly the same by Republicans, Democrats, and independents. Trump is thus in a different situation than Buchanan, whose image is more favorable among Republicans and much less so among independents and Democrats. While the current data suggest that a Buchanan Reform party candidacy would hurt a Republican candidate more than a Democratic candidate (a fact which worries the Bush campaign), a Trump candidacy at this point would not appear to have such an unequal impact on the two major parties.

Several polls in recent weeks have tested Trump against other Reform party candidates in terms of nationwide voter preference measures. A CNN/*Time* poll conducted on September 21–23 showed that Trump is a weak third-party choice when voters are asked which of four different possible Reform party candidates they might vote for. Buchanan, despite having an even more unfavorable image than Trump, wins with 28%, followed by Ventura with 24%, Trump with only 11%, and former Connecticut Governor Lowell Weicker with 8%. The fact that Trump scores only slightly more votes than Weicker is important given that Weicker has much lower name identification nationally than does Trump. In similar fashion, a recent *Newsweek* poll conducted on October 1 found that only 6% of a national registered voter sample said that Trump would be the most effective Reform party candidate, behind Buchanan with 24%, Perot with 16%, Ventura with 13%, and actor Warren Beatty, who only 10% of voters say would be the most effective Reform party candidate.

OCTOBER 12
BILL BRADLEY—AN ANALYSIS*

The latest Gallup Poll shows that what had once seemed unlikely now seems quite probable—a competitive race for the Democratic nomination for president. Conducted over the past weekend, October 8–10, the poll shows that Democrats prefer Vice President Al Gore to former New Jersey Senator Bill Bradley by a margin of only 51% to 39%. A month ago, Gore led Bradley among Democrats by more than a 2-to-1 margin, 63% to 30%. Gore's slippage nationally reflects similar results in some statewide polls, as in New Hampshire and New York, where Gore and Bradley are now within a few percentage points of each other.

The new Gallup Poll also shows an overall increase in Bradley's favorability rating nationwide, now at 53% favorable to 20% unfavorable, considerably improved over the 44% to 14% rating Bradley received last month. Most of that increase has come among Democrats, who currently give him a 60% to 17% rating, compared with a 46% to 13% rating in September.

Although Democrats who expressed preferences for either Gore or Bradley were asked their reasons for selecting one candidate over the other, no single issue emerged to explain the sudden surge in Bradley's popularity. Also, Democrats do not seem particularly concerned whether the candidate they prefer actually wins: just over two-thirds each of Bradley supporters and Gore supporters say it would be "acceptable" to them if the opposing candidate won the nomination. Perhaps the question that best correlates with Democrats' vote preferences is one that asked if respondents could describe themselves as "tired of anyone or anything associated with Bill Clinton." Only 24% of the Democrats said yes, but among this group, Bradley leads Gore by 48% to 39%. Among the

rest of the Democrats, Gore leads Bradley by 55% to 36%.

Major Income and Gender Gaps

Bradley's increased support comes only among Democrats who earn more than $30,000 a year; among lower-income Democrats, there has been no change in candidate preference from last month's poll. The new poll shows that Bradley leads Gore by 52% to 39% among Democrats whose annual income is between $30,000 and $50,000, and that Bradley ties Gore among those earning over $50,000 a year. But among Democrats earning less than $30,000 a year, Gore leads Bradley by more than a 2-to-1 margin, little changed from the previous month.

Men are considerably more likely than women to have rallied around Bradley's candidacy over the past month, with male Democrats now expressing a slight preference for the former college and professional basketball star, by 43% to 40%, compared with their overwhelming 61% to 31% support for Gore last month. Female Democrats, on the other hand, maintain a strong preference for the vice president, 56% to 33%, although that is down somewhat from the 64%-to-27% margin they gave Gore last month.

While Gore continues to draw greater support from the South than from the rest of the country, even Southern Democrats have expressed less support this month than last. In the South, Gore's support is now at 59% to Bradley's 31%, while it averages about 47% to 42% in the other parts of the country. Last month, however, Southern Democrats supported Gore over Bradley by 71% to 22%, while the rest of the country supported Gore by about a 60%-to-33% margin.

Bush Beats Both Democrats

Despite Bradley's surge among Democrats, Texas Governor George W. Bush continues to lead both Democratic candidates in the general election contest, and the margins remain similar whether Bush is pitted against Bradley or Gore. The Texas governor leads Bradley by 54% to 42%, and Gore by 56% to 40%. The margins of Bush's leads over Gore and Bradley have been roughly the same in four polls that go back to April of this year.

*This analysis was written by David W. Moore, Consulting Editor, The Gallup Poll.

OCTOBER 13
GEORGE W. BUSH AND THE
REPUBLICAN PARTY

Interviewing Dates: 10/8–10/99
CNN/*USA Today*/Gallup Poll
Survey #GO 128813

Do you agree or disagree with each of the following statements about the Republican party:

The Republican party has gone too far in its criticisms of the federal government?

Agree 51%
Disagree 45
No opinion 4

	Agree	Dis-agree	No opinion
By Politics			
Republicans	25%	72%	3%
Democrats....................	76	21	3
Independents...............	51	43	6

The Republican party has not been compassionate enough about the needs of the poor?

Agree 64%
Disagree 33
No opinion 3

	Agree	Dis-agree	No opinion
By Politics			
Republicans	38%	58%	4%
Democrats....................	82	16	2
Independents...............	70	27	3

The Republican party has been too pessimistic about moral standards in the United States?

Agree 51%
Disagree 46
No opinion 3

	Agree	Dis-agree	No opinion
By Politics			
Republicans	35%	63%	2%
Democrats....................	61	36	3
Independents...............	54	42	4

Note: In the same week that George W. Bush found fault with Republican party politics and philosophy in a major policy speech, a new Gallup Poll finds national Republicans undeterred in their support for the Texas governor. Not only does he continue to attract widespread support for the Republican nomination and to maintain a substantial lead over Democratic challengers in general election trial heats, he also enjoys high confidence levels within his party for the direction that his policies would give the nation.

According to the new poll, conducted on October 8–10, Bush maintains a firm hold on his position as the top choice of Republicans for their presidential nomination, far ahead of the seven other major candidates in the race. Bush also continues to be viewed favorably by more than nine in ten Republicans. And when asked who should have more influence over the direction that the Republican party takes in the next year, 55% of rank-and-file Republicans choose Bush, while just 35% choose the Republican leaders in Congress.

The image of Bush among Republican respondents in this survey seems to be of a party leader who can do no wrong. The poll demonstrates, paradoxically, that Republicans disagree with the specific negative sentiments about the GOP expressed by Bush but react favorably to the general fact that the Republican governor has criticized his own party.

There has been little change in Republicans' support for Bush over the past two weeks, with the new Gallup Poll finding him acceptable to at least three in four Republicans nationwide. Bush is now chosen by 60% of Republicans as the person whom they are most likely to support for the Republican presidential nomination, essentially equal to the 62% that he received in a mid-September Gallup survey. With another 15% of Republicans naming Bush as their second choice, a total of 75% of Republicans—compared with 76% three weeks ago—seem willing to see him become their party's nominee.

The only other Republican to achieve double-digit support for the nomination is Elizabeth Dole, named by 11% of Republicans as their first choice. With Dan Quayle out of the race, the remaining candidates are led by John McCain, now with 8%, up from 5% in late September. Steve Forbes, Pat

Buchanan, Gary Bauer, Orrin Hatch, and Alan Keyes all garner less than 5% of the GOP vote.

Among all national adults, Bush continues to beat Democrat Al Gore by a wide margin in a hypothetical matchup for president (56% to 40%) and leads Bill Bradley by nearly as much, 54% to 42%. There is no significant change in the public's overall view of Governor Bush. Seven in ten, including 93% of Republicans, have a favorable opinion of him, virtually unchanged since a September 23–26 Gallup survey.

Respondents in the new survey were asked about Bush's policy leadership and his criticisms of the GOP in several ways—both directly and indirectly—in an effort to detect any possible fallout from his recent critique of the party. Before any mention was made about Bush's criticisms of the Republican party, respondents indicated widespread support for his policy leadership. When asked whether his policies would lead the country in the right or wrong direction, 64% (including 91% of Republicans) believe that Bush would move the country in the right direction. Bush scores higher on this measure among the general public than either the Republicans in Congress, Bill Clinton, or Al Gore.

When asked who should exert greater influence over the direction of the Republican party during the next year, a 55% majority of Republicans choose Governor Bush, while just 35% choose the Republican leaders in Congress. Furthermore, when asked how they feel about Bush as a result of his recent comments "that were critical of the Republican party," the reaction is net positive. Thirty-eight percent feel more favorable toward him, while just 25% feel less favorable. (The remainder, 37%, express no opinion.) The reaction among Republicans is even more positive, with 45% saying that the critiques made them now feel more favorable toward Bush, while only 21% feel less favorable.

Later in the same survey, respondents were asked about some of the specific criticisms of the GOP that Bush expressed in his Manhattan Institute speech—using paraphrased statements and without attributing them to Bush. Interestingly, despite their earlier support for Bush on policy and on his criticism of the party, a majority of Republicans disagree with his specific criticisms.

Bush's first criticism concerned his perception that the GOP has failed to take sufficient notice of the social progress now being made at the state and municipal levels. According to Bush's prepared speech (see www.georgewbush.com), "Too often, on social issues, my party has painted an image of America slouching toward Gomorrah. Of course, there are challenges to the character and compassion of our nation—too many broken homes and broken lives. But many of our problems —particularly education, crime, and welfare dependence—are yielding to good sense and strength and idealism." The Gallup survey summarized these remarks by asking respondents whether "the Republican party has been too pessimistic about moral standards in the United States." Only 35% of Republicans agreed, while 63% disagreed.

Bush also charged that the party has failed to show sufficient concern for the needy in society: "Too often, my party has focused on the national economy, to the exclusion of all else—speaking a sterile language of rates and numbers, of CBO this and GNP that. Of course, we want growth and vigor in our economy. But there are human problems that persist in the shadow of affluence." Here again, just over one-third of Republicans (38%) agree with the summarized restatement that "the Republican party has not been compassionate enough about the needs of the poor," while 58% disagree.

Finally, Bush charged that the Republican party has gotten away from the Founding Fathers' concept of a small but effective government, saying: "Too often, my party has confused the need for limited government with a disdain for government itself." On this point even fewer Republicans side with the Bush perspective. Only 25% of Republicans agree with the statement that "the Republican party has gone too far in its criticisms of the federal government," while 72% disagree.

OCTOBER 15
THE YEAR 2000 CAMPAIGN

Interviewing Dates: 10/8–10/99
CNN/*USA Today*/Gallup Poll
Survey #GO 128813

Now suppose that the year 2000 presidential election were being held today, and it in-

cluded Al Gore as the Democratic candidate, George W. Bush as the Republican candidate, and political commentator Patrick Buchanan as the Reform party candidate. Would you vote for Al Gore, the Democrat; George W. Bush, the Republican; or Patrick Buchanan, the Reform party candidate? [Those who were undecided were asked: As of today, do you lean more toward Gore, the Democrat; Bush, the Republican; or Buchanan, the Reform party candidate?]

	Oct. 8–10, 1999	Sept. 23–26, 1999
Gore	38%	37%
G. W. Bush	51	49
Buchanan	9	9
None (volunteered)	*	3
Other (volunteered)	*	*
No opinion	2	2

*Less than 1%

Now suppose that the year 2000 presidential election were being held today, and it included Al Gore as the Democratic candidate, George W. Bush as the Republican candidate, and businessman Donald Trump as the Reform party candidate. Would you vote for Al Gore, the Democrat; George W. Bush, the Republican; or Donald Trump, the Reform party candidate? [Those who were undecided were asked: As of today, do you lean more toward Gore, the Democrat; Bush, the Republican; or Trump, the Reform party candidate?]

Gore	37%
G. W. Bush	51
Trump	10
None (volunteered)	*
Other (volunteered)	*
No opinion	2

*Less than 1%

The Reform party will hold a primary next year to choose its presidential nominee and currently plans to give a primary ballot to every registered voter who asks for one. How likely is it that you would participate in the Reform party's presidential primary next year—very likely, somewhat likely, not too likely, or not likely at all?

Very likely	16%
Somewhat likely	22
Not too likely	23
Not likely at all	38
No opinion	1

Asked of those who replied "very likely" or "somewhat likely": In terms of the Reform party ticket for president, which of the following two possible candidates would you prefer to see win the Reform party nomination for president—Pat Buchanan, or Donald Trump?

Buchanan	54%
Trump	33
Other (volunteered)	1
None (volunteered)	8
No opinion	4

Regardless of whether or not you would vote for the following people, please say whether you would view each as a serious candidate if he or she decided to run for president:

Pat Buchanan?

Yes	44%
No	53
No opinion	3

Donald Trump?

Yes	23%
No	74
No opinion	3

Jesse Ventura?

Yes	22%
No	74
No opinion	4

Oprah Winfrey?

Yes	16%
No	82
No opinion	2

Warren Beatty?

Yes... 13%
No 82
No opinion... 5

Cybill Shepherd?

Yes... 6%
No 90
No opinion... 4

Note: With political commentator Pat Buchanan about to announce his candidacy for the Reform party's nomination for president in 2000, and businessman Donald Trump establishing an exploratory committee to assess his presidential possibilities within the same party, a new Gallup Poll shows that almost four in ten Americans are either "very" or "somewhat" likely to participate in the Reform party's primary balloting. Among this group, Buchanan is favored over Trump by 54% to 33%, with the rest undecided. In a hypothetical general election race, with either Buchanan or Trump pitted against Vice President Al Gore and Texas Governor George W. Bush, each Reform party candidate would fare about the same, with Buchanan receiving 9% of the vote and Trump 10%.

The number of Americans who actually participate in the Reform party balloting is almost certain to be smaller than the 38% who now indicate that they would likely ask for a ballot and then send in their preference. Voter turnout models developed by Gallup and other polling organizations over the past several decades all recognize that when answering polls, respondents are more optimistic about the likelihood of their voting than is warranted by their actual turnout on Election Day. Nevertheless, even if "only" the 16% who are very likely to participate in the Reform party nomination process are counted, Buchanan still leads Trump by about the same margins as noted before, 54% to 33%.

The low level of support for both Buchanan and Trump is related to their images among the public as nonserious candidates. Despite Buchanan's having run for president twice before, less than one-half of respondents (44%) view him as a "serious" candidate for president. An even smaller number (23%) see Trump as a serious candidate. By comparison, 22% regard Jesse Ventura as a serious candidate, while 16% say the same about Oprah Winfrey, 13% about Warren Beatty, and 6% about Cybill Shepherd, all of whom have been mentioned in the news recently as possible presidential or vice-presidential candidates. Even among those who view Buchanan as a serious candidate, just 16% would vote for him in a three-way contest that includes Gore and Bush. Among those who view Trump seriously, however, 31% would vote for him in a similar three-way contest.

Most of the respondents who indicate that they might participate in the Reform party balloting process nevertheless do not intend to vote for a Reform candidate in the general election, even if their preferred candidate wins the nomination. Among self-identified Reform party voters who prefer Buchanan to Trump, just 21% would then go on to vote for Buchanan in the general election against Gore and Bush. While this number seems low, it would be even lower if Buchanan lost the nomination: only 6% of his supporters would remain loyal to the Reform party and vote for Trump in the general election. Trump's supporters are no more loyal to the party than Buchanan's. If Trump won the nomination, 41% of his supporters would then vote for him in the general election; but if he lost, just 7% of his supporters would vote for Buchanan in the general election.

Many Republicans worry about Buchanan's abandoning the Republican party to become a Reform party candidate, in the expectation that a Buchanan candidacy would draw more votes from the Republicans than from the Democrats. While much is likely to change in the next year, an analysis of the current poll suggests that either a Buchanan or Trump candidacy would draw almost equally from Republicans and Democrats. Buchanan receives 9% of the Republican, 11% of the independent, and 7% of the Democratic vote; while Trump receives 6% of the Republican, 25% of the independent, and 10% of the Democratic vote. Among those who would vote for Bush in a two-way contest with Gore, 8% say that they would vote for Buchanan in a three-way race—the same percentage of Gore voters who would choose Buchanan if he were a candidate. A similar pattern holds for a Trump candidacy—9% of Bush supporters in a two-way race would vote for Trump in a three-way contest, compared with 8% of Gore supporters who would back Trump.

While the percentages of likely defections are about equal, Bush's greater support now means that the net effect of the Reform party candidates is a slight reduction in the margin by which Bush leads Gore. In a hypothetical contest with just Bush and Gore, the Texas governor enjoys a 16-point lead, 56% to 40%. That margin is reduced by 3 percentage points if Buchanan is part of a three-way contest, to 51% to 38% (with 9% for Buchanan); and the lead is reduced by just 2 percentage points if Trump is a candidate, to 51% to 37% (with 10% for Trump).

OCTOBER 18
CONGRESS/PRESIDENT CLINTON

Interviewing Dates: 10/8–10/99
CNN/*USA Today*/Gallup Poll
Survey #GO 128813

Do you approve or disapprove of the way the following are handling their job:

The Republicans in Congress?

Approve 37%
Disapprove 55
No opinion 8

Selected National Trend

	Approve	Dis-approve	No opinion
1999			
August 16–18	36%	53%	11%
June 25–27	40	53	7

The Democrats in Congress?

Approve 48%
Disapprove 44
No opinion 8

Selected National Trend

	Approve	Dis-approve	No opinion
1999			
August 16–18	48%	41%	11%
June 25–27	46	46	8

Whom do you want to have more influence over the direction the Republican party takes over the next year—Texas Governor George W. Bush, or the Republican leaders in Congress?

G. W. Bush 50%
Republican leaders 37
Neither; other (volunteered) 7
No opinion 6

Do you think the policies being proposed by the Republican leaders in the U.S. House and Senate would move the country in the right direction or in the wrong direction?*

Right direction 54%
Wrong direction 35
No opinion 11

Selected National Trend

	Right direction	Wrong direction	No opinion
1998			
November 13–15	43%	40%	17%
October 23–25	47	33	20
July 7–8	43	28	29
1997			
December 18–21	44	36	20
April 18–20	46	39	15

*Based on half sample

Do you think the policies being proposed by Bill Clinton would move the country in the right direction or in the wrong direction?*

Right direction 60%
Wrong direction 35
No opinion 5

Selected National Trend

	Right direction	Wrong direction	No opinion
1998			
October 23–25	70%	22%	8%
1997			
April 18–20	56	33	11

*Based on half sample

When it comes to dealing with the tough choices involved in deciding on the federal budget for next year, whose approach do you prefer—the Republicans in Congress, or President Clinton's?

Republicans 38%
Clinton's 55
Neither (volunteered) 2
Both (volunteered) 1
No opinion 4

Selected National Trend

	Republicans	Clinton's	Neither	Both*
1999				
Sept. 10–14†	38%	53%	4%	**
Aug. 16–18†	36	53	4	1
July 16–18†	40	48	5	1

*"No opinion"—at 6% or less—is omitted.
**Less than 1%
†Question wording: *When it comes to dealing with the tough choices involved both in cutting taxes and still maintaining needed federal programs, whose approach do you prefer . . . ?*

*As you may know, President Clinton and the Republicans in Congress are trying to negotiate an agreement on the federal budget. Based on what you've read or heard about those negotiations, who do you think have acted more responsibly—the Republicans in Congress, or President Clinton?**

Republicans 36%
Clinton 48
Neither (volunteered) 6
Both (volunteered) .... **
No opinion 10

Selected National Trend

	Republicans	Clinton	Neither	Both†
1996				
Feb. 23–25‡	35%	44%	13%	2%
Jan. 12–15‡	38	45	12	1
Jan. 5–7‡	37	38	14	3

*Based on half sample

**Less than 1%
†"No opinion"—at 10% or less—is omitted.
‡Question wording: *Now, thinking about the budget conflict which has been going on in Washington, who do you think has acted more responsibly in the negotiations over the budget . . . ?*

Note: Only five of the thirteen spending bills needed to keep the federal government operating have been passed so far this year, and another deadline comes later this week. A continuing resolution to keep government agencies operating while Congress and the Clinton administration hash out a fiscal year 2000 spending plan expires on Thursday [October 21]. While analysts expect both sides to agree on another stopgap bill, President Bill Clinton is threatening to veto five spending bills and has chided Congress for what he calls "unconscionable" cuts in education and other programs.

A new Gallup Poll shows that the American public tends to side more with the president than with the Republican leaders in Congress when it comes to these budget issues: 55% prefer the president's approach to the tough choices relating to the budget and spending decisions, while 38% support the GOP leadership's approach. One interesting note: even 25% of those who describe themselves as Republicans side with the administration on the budget issue, while 68% support the Republican leadership on Capitol Hill. By way of comparison, 81% of Democrats back the Clinton budget plan. In addition, 48% believe that President Clinton has acted more responsibly than the Republicans in Congress in trying to negotiate a budget agreement, while 36% give the Republicans the edge.

While some analysts have speculated about Clinton's status as a "lame duck" president, the public still tends to support him. His current job approval rating stands at 56%, down from his highest point this year (70% in February) but still above average for Clinton's entire tenure in office. By comparison, the Republicans in Congress have a lower, 37% approval rating, while the Democrats in Congress have a 48% approval rating. In addition, even those who disapprove of Clinton's performance in office are split over the performance of the Republicans in Congress: 47% approve of the GOP's actions, while 46% disapprove.

OCTOBER 19
KENNETH STARR—AN ANALYSIS*

Kenneth Starr's official announcement on Monday [October 18] that he is stepping down as Independent Counsel marks the end of his formal role at the epicenter of one of the most highly publicized events in recent American history. And, despite Starr's protestations that he was only doing the job he was appointed to do, he leaves the office as one of the most negatively evaluated public figures measured in Gallup Poll annals. About two-thirds of Americans said that they had a negative opinion of Starr earlier this year, after the impeachment crisis was over, and the same number disapproved of the job that he did as Independent Counsel. Other measures taken during 1998 and early 1999 show the degree to which they distrusted both his motives and his decisions. Still, while Bill Clinton, the target of the Lewinsky investigations, was acquitted in a Senate trial, a large percentage agreed with the charges brought against the president first by Starr and then by the House. Perhaps largely as a result of Starr's efforts, the public's measure of Clinton as a person as well as his honesty and trustworthiness and moral character have fallen to low levels.

The public formed an unfavorable opinion of Independent Counsel Starr almost as soon as he was swept into the limelight as a result of the Clinton-Monica Lewinsky revelations in early 1998. Those initial impressions became more negative as the series of tumultuous events unfolded that ultimately resulted in the second impeachment of a president in American history.

Gallup first asked respondents to give their impressions of Starr in a January 23–24, 1998, poll. At that time, public opinion split down the middle: 24% had a favorable opinion of Starr, and 24% had an unfavorable one. (The rest had never heard of him or had no opinion.) Within days, however, as the Lewinsky charges became public, and as Clinton made his famous "I did not have sexual relations with that woman, Miss Lewinsky" assertion, coupled with Hillary Rodham Clinton's

claims on national television that her husband was being hounded by a "vast right-wing conspiracy," Starr's image quickly turned more negative. By mid-February, 46% had an unfavorable opinion of Starr; and by the following October, shortly after the release of the Independent Counsel's report to Congress, Starr's unfavorable image reached a high point up to that time of 60%. Immediately after the Senate vote to acquit Clinton in February of this year, Starr's negative image was up to 62%, and by March of this year it reached 66%—almost a 3-to-1 margin, negative to positive.

Additionally, 64% said in the March 1999 poll that they disapproved of the way in which Starr was handling his job as Independent Counsel, while only 28% approved. While Starr was perceived by some of his critics as being a highly partisan Republican, only a bare majority of Republicans in the March poll (52%) approved of the job that Starr was doing. By comparison only a miniscule 8% of Democrats approved. And in February 1999, when the public was asked to rate a list of individuals and groups as winners or losers in the impeachment process, 73% of those polled said that Starr was a loser, with only 20% saying that he was a winner.

Other polls conducted during 1998 and early 1999 give some indication of the reasons behind Starr's decidedly negative image. First, at one point in November 1998, when given a choice, 53% said that Starr was acting more like a "persecutor," while only 39% said that he was acting more like a "prosecutor." Second, one of his most controversial actions was his decision to send the Starr Report containing Lewinsky's explicit descriptions of her sexual encounters with Clinton to Congress, which in turn released them to the public. On September 10, 1998, 71% said that the sexual details in the report should not have been released, while only 26% said that they should have been. And third, respondents thought that Starr's motives were more political than professional. In January 1998, when Starr was first becoming widely known, 48% said that he was "mostly trying to damage President Clinton politically," while just 38% said that Starr was attempting to "find out the facts." By June 1998, 57% agreed with the "damage politically" explanation, compared to 38% who agreed with the "find out the facts" alternative.

*This analysis was written by Frank Newport, Editor in Chief, The Gallup Poll.

At the same time, it is important to remember that the charges developed by Starr's office—that Clinton obstructed justice and committed perjury —were not disregarded by the public. In a February poll conducted just before the Senate vote on impeachment, 73% believed the perjury charge and 49% believed the obstruction of justice charge. Additionally, although the public maintained its highly unfavorable opinion of Starr, it downgraded Clinton significantly during the year on measures such as his honesty and trustworthiness, its favorable opinion of him "as a person," and his moral leadership.

Finally, despite the low opinions of Starr and his motivations, the entire Lewinsky impeachment situation did not cause Americans to disparage the concept of the office of Independent Counsel. In a March poll, only 17% said that the Independent Counsel law should be totally abolished, while 32% wanted it kept as is, and another 48% said that they wanted it kept but modified.

OCTOBER 20
THE REPUBLICAN PRIMARY CONTEST— AN ANALYSIS*

Elizabeth Dole's announcement today that she is dropping out of the race for the Republican nomination for president comes at a time when neither she nor other Republican candidates has been able to make a significant dent in the extraordinary strength of front-runner George W. Bush. Despite her unique positioning as the only major female presidential candidate in either party, and the fact that she has been the number two choice among Republicans since early spring, Dole ends her quest for the White House with only 11% of the Republican vote in the latest Gallup polling, far behind Bush, who dominates with 60%. An analysis of the second choices of Dole's voters indicates that 6% of her 11% would opt for Bush, with the rest scattered among other candidates, suggesting that her withdrawal may further increase Bush's first-place dominance.

*This analysis was written by Frank Newport, Editor in Chief, The Gallup Poll.

Dole's campaign was a success to the degree that she managed to pull ahead of all other Republican challengers to Bush and consistently came in number two in trial heat polls asking Republicans for their first choice for their party's nomination. At one point, in late April and early May, almost one-quarter of Republicans nationwide said that she was their first choice for their party's nomination, putting her within 18 percentage points of front-runner Bush. Dole gradually lost her standing in the Republican trial heats from that point on, however, falling to 18% of the Republican vote in May, 14% in June, and 11% in the latest Gallup Poll conducted on October 8–10. Dole was credited with a reasonably strong showing in the Iowa straw poll conducted in August of this year, but the publicity generated by that occasion had little or no impact on her national numbers. Bush strengthened his lead among Republicans in August, September, and October polling, garnering 60% in the October 8–10 survey.

Dole's 11% in the October poll was still enough to keep her in second place, at 3 points ahead of Arizona Senator John McCain, who has 8% of the vote. Dole and McCain are followed by Steve Forbes, with 4%; Pat Buchanan (who is set to leave the Republican party and join the contest for the Reform party nomination), Gary Bauer, and Alan Keyes with 3% each; and Utah Senator Orrin Hatch with 2%.

Despite the fact that Dole is only 3 points ahead of McCain when it comes to Republicans' first choices, she has a stronger position when Republicans' second choices are taken into account. Bush wins overwhelmingly with 75% of the GOP vote when Republicans' first and second choices are combined, and Dole comes in second with 38%. McCain is considerably behind, with only 20% of combined choices.

Gallup polling conducted in recent months has also provided additional data to suggest that Dole appeared to be the strongest of the Republican candidates challenging Bush. For example, when Republicans were asked in mid-August if each of a list of seven Republican candidates should stay in the race for the nomination or withdraw, 77% said that Dole should stay in, second only to Bush (urged to stay in by 96% of Republicans). The next candidate in line was Steve

Forbes, with a 55% "stay in" vote. Indeed, Dole had a very positive image among respondents of both parties. In mid-August, only 15% said that they did not know enough about her to have an opinion, and her image broke at 69% favorable and only 16% unfavorable.

Dole was running to become the first female president in U.S. history, and many observers assumed that she would have a particular strength among women. She did slightly better among Republican women than among Republican men, but this strength was not nearly enough to enable her to challenge Bush. In the October poll, Dole received the vote of 16% of Republican women, compared to 7% of Republican men, but Bush dominated in both categories with 63% of the male vote, and 56% of the female vote. Dole also did slightly better among the youngest Republicans, age 18–29; and in the Midwest, the home of her husband, Bob Dole, the former senator from Kansas.

What will be the impact of Elizabeth Dole's decision on the Republican race? In the October poll, Republican voters were asked to name their second choice for the GOP nomination. The results show that 6% of Dole's 11% of Republican voters say that they would vote for Bush if they could not vote for her, with the rest scattered among other candidates or moving into the ranks of the undecided. These figures suggest preliminarily that Dole's exit from the campaign could strengthen Bush's dominance.

OCTOBER 21
PRESIDENT CLINTON

Interviewing Dates: 10/8–10/99
CNN/*USA Today*/Gallup Poll
Survey #GO 128813

Please tell me if the following statement describes or does not describe you personally: You are tired of anyone or anything associated with Bill Clinton.

Yes, describes 43%
Does not describe 56
No opinion 1

	Yes, describes	Does not describe	No opinion
By Sex			
Male	44%	55	1%
Female	43	56	1
By Ethnic Background			
White	47	52	1
Nonwhite	24	75	1
By Age			
18–29 Years	50	49	1
30–49 Years	41	58	1
50–64 Years	43	56	1
65 Years and Over	41	57	2
By Region			
East	31	68	1
Midwest	49	50	1
South	48	50	2
West	44	56	*
By Politics			
Republicans	69	30	1
Democrats	19	81	*
Independents	45	53	2
By Clinton Approval			
Approve	18	80	2
Disapprove	82	18	*

*Less than 1%

Apart from whether you approve or disapprove of the way Bill Clinton is handling his job as president, what do you think of Clinton as a person—would you say you approve or disapprove of him?

Approve 35%
Disapprove 62
No opinion 3

Would you like to see the next president generally continue with Bill Clinton's policies, or would you rather see the next president change direction from Clinton's policies?

Continue policies 50%
Change direction 47
No opinion 3

Do you think the policies being proposed by Bill Clinton would move the country in the right direction or in the wrong direction?*

Right direction 60%
Wrong direction... 35
No opinion... 5

*Based on half sample

Selected National Trend

	Right direction	Wrong direction	No opinion
1998			
October 23–25	70%	22%	8%
1997			
April 18–20.................	56	33	11
1996			
October 28–29*	55	33	12
April 9–10...................	55	35	10
1995			
December 15–18.........	51	39	10

*Likely voters

Next, do you think the policies being proposed by each of the following presidential candidates would move the country in the right direction or in the wrong direction:

George W. Bush?

Right direction 64%
Wrong direction... 27
No opinion... 9

Al Gore?

Right direction 52%
Wrong direction... 40
No opinion... 8

Which candidate, if elected president, do you think would do a better job of keeping the country prosperous—Al Gore, or George W. Bush?*

Gore 37%
G. W. Bush 56
No difference (volunteered) 3
No opinion... 4

*Based on half sample

Note: "Clinton fatigue," a political syndrome characterized by its proponents as causing rapid channel surfing at the sight of Bill Clinton on television and the desire to see anyone but Al Gore elected president, is emerging as an important theory in the 2000 election coverage. A search of publications in the Dow Jones news database produces 399 references to the term, and it was recently defined by the *New York Times* as "essentially a catch-all to describe a general sense that people have had enough of Bill Clinton." It is hard to find solid evidence in the latest Gallup survey, however, that Clinton fatigue pervades the electorate or, more important, that it is having a major impact on voter preferences.

References to Clinton fatigue are being fueled by the serious political problems that Vice President Gore faces in the early stages of the election process. Gore consistently trails the Republican front-runner, Texas Governor George W. Bush, in election surveys, and in the new October 8–10 poll, Gallup found Bush beating Gore by 16 percentage points, 56% to 40%. The same survey finds that Bill Bradley has gained support among Democratic voters for their party's nomination. Gore still leads Bradley among Democrats nationwide, but by just 12 points, 51% to 39%, down from a 33-point lead in mid-September.

Is it valid to attribute the weaknesses in Gore's candidacy, in whole or in part, to his association with Clinton? The president could theoretically be a liability for Gore if respondents view his presidency as unsuccessful, or if they are merely tired of him and want no future reminders. Of course, the question of whether Clinton is perceived as successful or unsuccessful is a matter of interpretation. Still tarnished by the Monica Lewinsky scandal, Clinton receives extremely low personal ratings in the new poll, but at the same time he receives majority support for his job performance and policies. These results are generally consistent with those of Gallup Polls conducted over the last two years:

- A majority (56%) currently approves of the way that Clinton is handling his job as president; just 39% disapprove.
- A slightly higher proportion (60%) thinks that the policies proposed by Clinton would move the country in the right direction, while only 35% say the wrong direction.
- When asked about their preferences for the next administration, 50% would like to see a

continuation of Clinton's policies, while 47% want a change in direction.

- At the same time, only one-third of the public (35%) say that they approve of Clinton as a person, while 62% disapprove.

Notably, this pattern is the reverse of the public's impression of Ronald Reagan a year before the 1988 election, when his vice president, George Bush, won the presidency. In 1987, with investigation of the Iran-*contra* affair ongoing, Reagan received personal approval ratings of over 70%, while his job approval rating suffered, falling below 50%. Additionally, only 36% in August 1987 wanted to see the next president continue with Reagan's policies, compared to 50% today for Clinton's. Thus, compared to Reagan, Clinton has had greater political success but much less personal success. What is the net evaluation of his presidency? When last asked early in 1999, despite his personal image problems and the impact of the impeachment crisis, 77% said that they believed Clinton's presidency had been a success.

One question included in the October 8–10 Gallup survey asked the public directly about their being fatigued with Clinton. The results are split: 43% agree that they are "tired of anyone or anything associated with Bill Clinton," while the majority (56%) disagree. An analysis of voter preferences indicates that this sentiment is driving some voters, but not large numbers, away from Gore.

Perhaps not surprisingly, the "Clinton fatigue" group—the 43% who are tired of the president—is largely composed of the standard GOP base in the electorate (including Republicans and independents who are inclined to support the Republican party). It also includes almost the same set of people who disapprove of the job that Clinton is doing as president. Importantly, this group prefers George W. Bush for president regardless of whether the Texas governor is running against Gore or Bradley, his Democratic challenger. In a head-to-head trial heat with Bush, only 24% of this group would vote for Bradley, compared to 17% who would vote for Gore. This vote translates into a loss of 2% for Gore that might be ascribed directly to "Clinton fatigue." However, if these voters who are tired of Clinton were opting for Gore rather than Bush, Gore would still trail Bush by 11 points rather than the current 15.

Within the Democratic party, the impact of "Clinton fatigue" on voter preferences is slight. Democrats who admit to being tired of Clinton favor Bradley over Gore by a 48%-to-39% margin. However, since they account for only 19% of all Democrats, their effect on the overall Democratic vote choice is small. Even among Democrats who approve of Clinton's job performance and are not tired of him, Gore receives just 55% of the vote, compared to 36% for Bradley.

Additionally, when Democrats are asked to agree or disagree with various reasons for their choice, very few Bradley voters (28%) admit that his distance from Clinton is a key reason why they favor him over Gore for the nomination. Of much greater importance is their admiration for Bradley's character, intelligence, and political independence as well as the sense that he can bring needed change to government. Conversely, many Gore voters view the vice president's ties to Clinton as a positive factor. Over one-half cite the continuation of Clinton's policies as a key reason why they support Gore for the nomination, and 42% cite their admiration for Gore's loyalty to his president.

There are several indicators in Gallup Poll data that Gore's weak performance in pre-election surveys to date is due more to the formidable appeal of Governor Bush than to voter rejection of Gore for his association with Clinton. Gore's image has remained relatively constant throughout the Clinton presidency, with just over one-half of the public having a favorable image of the vice president. While the percentage viewing Gore unfavorably has grown as he has become better known, his current rating of 54% favorable and 42% unfavorable is similar to his ratings in October 1997, months before Clinton's impeachment problems or any sense of fatigue with his presidency emerged. In sharp contrast, Bush is viewed favorably by 70% and unfavorably by only 25%.

When asked if each candidate's policies would move the country in the right or wrong direction, 64% predict that Bush's policies would take the United States in the right direction, compared with only 52% who say the same for Gore. In fact, Gore fares worse on this measure than does Clinton, whose policies are perceived as "right-headed" by 60%. And while respondents are evenly divided over whether the Republican party or the Democratic party would do a better job of keeping the country prosperous—a measure that presumably taps perceptions of Clinton's handling of the economy—a solid majority chooses Bush over Gore as the candidate who could do the better job with this important task. Thus, Gore underperforms his party on this critical measure, at least in comparison with Governor Bush.

OCTOBER 22
CAMPAIGN FINANCE REFORM

Interviewing Dates: 10/8–10/99
CNN/*USA Today*/Gallup Poll
Survey #GO 128813

As you may know, Congress will be considering several issues this fall, including tax cuts, Social Security, gun control, and campaign finance. In terms of all these issues and others that Congress will be considering, do you think campaign finance reform should be the top priority, a high priority, a low priority, or should it not be a priority at all?

Top priority.. 11%
High priority 28
Low priority... 41
Not a priority 19
No opinion.. 1

In general, which of the following statements best represents what you feel about the way federal campaigns are financed—it needs to be completely overhauled, it needs major changes, it needs minor changes, or it is basically fine the way it is?

Completely overhauled.................................. 20%
Major changes 44
Minor changes 26
Fine as is.. 8
No opinion.. 2

Note: With the defeat this week of the latest attempt to pass campaign finance reform legislation in the

U.S. Senate, a new Gallup Poll shows that most Americans probably do not care a great deal about the subject, and that the matter is unlikely to emerge as a major issue in the 2000 presidential election.The poll did not ask specifically about the campaign finance measure jointly sponsored by Senator John McCain, the Republican from Arizona (and a candidate for his party's presidential nomination in the 2000 election), and Senator Russell D. Feingold, the Democrat from Wisconsin —a bill which would have banned unlimited and unregulated donations to political parties, or "soft money" contributions. The poll instead focused generally on campaign finance and found that while almost two-thirds of respondents think that the way federal campaigns are financed needs at least major changes, less than four in ten say that Congress should make the issue a high priority.

Conducted on October 8–10, the poll shows that just 39% say that campaign finance should be treated as either a top or high priority matter compared with other issues before Congress, such as tax cuts, gun control, and Social Security. Sixty percent say that it should be a low priority or not a priority at all. Despite this relatively low priority, 20% say that the financing of federal campaigns needs a complete overhaul, and another 44% say that major changes are needed. The total of 64% who think that campaign financing needs fixing is higher than the 57% and 58% who expressed the same opinion about Medicare and Social Security in a June 1999 Gallup Poll and is almost as high as the 68% who expressed that opinion about the HMO system in a July 1999 survey. In January 1997, right after the last presidential election, at a time when questions were raised about the sources of Democratic campaign funds, an even larger percentage (70%) indicated that the way campaigns are financed needed at least major changes.

Although the Republicans and Democrats in Congress appear to be greatly opposed in their approaches to changing the way that federal campaigns are financed, the rank-and-file party identifiers show few differences on the more general question of whether campaign finance reform is needed. Among Republicans, 38% say that the issue should be of high priority, compared with 41% of Democrats. When asked how much change is necessary, 63% of the self-identified members of each party say that at least major changes are needed.

Overall, older Americans appear more concerned about campaign finance reform than younger ones, both in the priority the issue should receive and how extensively the system needs to be changed. While only 32% under the age of 30, for example, say that campaign finance should be a high priority for Congress, that proportion rises to 35% among those in the 30–49 age group, to 43% among those in the 50–64 age group, and to a clear majority (53%) among those 65 and older. Also, older people are more likely to want greater changes in the campaign finance system, although the differences are primarily between respondents under 30 and those 30 and older. In the latter group, all agree, by about 65% to 71%, that major changes are needed, while only 48% of the youngest group feel that way.

OCTOBER 26
PAT BUCHANAN

Interviewing Dates: 10/21–24/99
CNN/*USA Today*/Gallup Poll
Survey #GO 907190

Now suppose that the year 2000 presidential election were being held today, and it included Al Gore as the Democratic candidate, George W. Bush as the Republican candidate, and political commentator Patrick Buchanan as the Reform party candidate. Would you vote for Al Gore, the Democrat; George W. Bush, the Republican; or Patrick Buchanan, the Reform party candidate? [Those who were undecided were asked: As of today, do you lean more toward Gore, the Democrat; Bush, the Republican; or Buchanan, the Reform party candidate?]

	Oct. 21–24, 1999*	Oct. 8–10, 1999*	Sept. 23–26, 1999*
Gore	42%	38%	37%
G. W. Bush	48	51	49
Buchanan	5	9	9
No opinion	5	2	5

*Based on half sample

In general, how likely are you to vote for Pat Buchanan if he leaves the Republican party and runs as the Reform party's presidential candidate next November—would you definitely vote for Buchanan if he were the Reform party candidate, would you consider voting for him, or would you definitely not vote for that candidate?

Definitely vote for Buchanan	4%
Consider voting for Buchanan	26
Definitely not vote for Buchanan	65
No opinion	5

*Based on half sample

In general, how likely are you to vote for Donald Trump if he runs as the Reform party's presidential candidate next November—would you definitely vote for Trump if he were the Reform party candidate, would you consider voting for him, or would you definitely not vote for that candidate?

Definitely vote for Trump	2%
Consider voting for Trump	15
Definitely not vote for Trump	79
No opinion	4

*Based on half sample

Asked of Buchanan voters: If Pat Buchanan were not running for the Republican nomination, which one of the remaining Republican candidates would you be most likely to support for the Republican nomination for president?

	With Buchanan	Without Buchanan
George W. Bush	66%	68%
Elizabeth Dole	–	–
Dan Quayle	–	–
Steve Forbes	7	8
John McCain	11	11
Pat Buchanan	4	–
Gary Bauer	1	1
Orrin Hatch	3	3
Alan Keyes	1	2
None; other (volunteered); no opinion	7	7

Note: This week, Pat Buchanan announced his intention to leave the Republican party and become a candidate for the Reform party's 2000 presidential nomination. A new Gallup Poll suggests that his candidacy now may have little impact on the general election contest if, as still seems likely, it involves Vice President Al Gore and Texas Governor George W. Bush. If the contest should become very close, however, the slightly greater number of Bush than Gore supporters who would vote for Buchanan could give the Democratic candidate a victory that might otherwise go to Bush.

In a hypothetical two-way race between Gore and Bush, the Texas governor currently leads the vice president by 9 percentage points among all adults (52% to 43%), by 8 points among registered voters (52% to 44%), and by 7 points among "regular" voters (51% to 44%). (Regular voters are those who are registered and who voted in the last presidential election.) Each of those margins is reduced by 3 points if Buchanan is listed as a Reform party candidate, although Buchanan himself draws only 5% support, regardless of the composition of the electorate. Thus, among "regular" voters, Bush leads Gore by just 48% to 44% if Buchanan is a candidate, compared to 51% to 44% if Buchanan is not a candidate.

Despite the 3-point drop in Bush's lead if Buchanan is a candidate, the number of Democrats, independents, and Republicans who would support Buchanan is identical at 5% each, suggesting that despite his previous association with the Republican party, his appeal is not easily defined by normal partisan groupings. His appeal is greater among conservatives (7%) than among moderates (3%) and liberals (5%), but, given Buchanan's strong conservative orientation, these differences are not as stark as one might expect. His appeal is also highly related to income, as he receives only 2% support from those who earn more than $50,000 per year, but 7% from those who earn less than that amount.

Republicans are about evenly divided on whether Buchanan should leave the Republican party, with 38% saying that he should stay and 41% saying that he should leave. They are also divided on what effect he might have on the GOP's chances in the 2000 election. Although this poll suggests that Buchanan's candidacy is likely to

have only a slight influence on the presidential race, about one-third of Republicans (37%) believe that if Buchanan were to run as the Reform party's candidate, it would hurt the Republican party's chances of winning the 2000 presidential election. Another 12%, however, believe that Buchanan's candidacy would actually help the Republicans, while almost one-half (46%) say that it would have no effect.

Buchanan's nomination as the Reform party presidential candidate cannot be taken for granted, as Donald Trump announced this week that he, too, was switching his political allegiance to the Reform party and would likely be seeking its nomination for president. But the poll shows that among the 16% who consider themselves "supporters" of the Reform party, Buchanan would beat Trump by a margin of 57% to 32%, while among all respondents, Buchanan leads Trump by 48% to 29%.

When asked how likely they would be to vote for Buchanan in the general election if he were to become the Reform party's presidential candidate, 12% of the Reform party's supporters would definitely vote for him, and another 33% would consider doing so. When asked the same question about Trump, just 8% of Reform party supporters would vote for him, and another 24% would consider it.

NOVEMBER 1
AL GORE VS. BILL BRADLEY

Interviewing Date: 10/28/99*
CNN/*USA Today*/Gallup Poll
Special survey

The following questions were asked of New Hampshire voters:

*Based on telephone interviews with a randomly selected national sample of 432 New Hampshire voters who plan to vote in the 2000 New Hampshire Democratic primary. For results based on this sample, one can say with 95% confidence that the maximum error attributable to sampling and other random effects is ±5 percentage points. Polls conducted entirely in one evening, such as this one, are subject to additional error or bias not found in polls conducted over several days.

Suppose the Democratic primary election for president were being held today. If you had to choose between Bill Bradley or Al Gore, which candidate would you vote for? [Those who were undecided were asked: As of today, do you lean more toward Bill Bradley or Al Gore?]

Bradley 48%
Gore 46
Other; undecided 6

Do you support Al Gore or Bill Bradley strongly, or not so strongly?

	Gore voters	Bradley voters
Strongly	43%	49%
Not so strongly; no opinion	57	51

Next, please tell me if you have a favorable or unfavorable opinion of each of the following candidates, or if you have never heard of him:

Al Gore?

Favorable 75%
Unfavorable 21
No opinion 4
Never heard of .... *

*Less than 1%

Bill Bradley?

Favorable 75%
Unfavorable 11
No opinion 12
Never heard of 2

As you may know, Al Gore and Bill Bradley both appeared at a town meeting in Hanover, New Hampshire, last night, which was broadcast on CNN and WMUR, where they answered questions from members of the audience. How much of that town meeting did you happen to watch—all or most of it, about half of it, only some of it, or none of it?

All or most.. 18%
About half.. 5

Only some.. 16
None 61
No opinion.. –

Asked of those who watched the town meeting: Just your best impression, who do you think did a better job in that town meeting—Al Gore, or Bill Bradley?

Asked of those who did not watch: Just your best impression from what you may have heard or read, who do you think did a better job in that town meeting—Al Gore, or Bill Bradley?

	Total	Watched	Did not watch
Gore............................	26%	38%	18%
Bradley	23	39	13
Both; equally (volunteered)	11	14	9
No opinion..................	40	9	60

If George W. Bush wins the Republican nomination, who do you think would have a better chance to beat him in the presidential election in November 2000—Al Gore, or Bill Bradley?

Gore.. 51%
Bradley 35
Both equally (volunteered)............................ 3
Neither (volunteered) 3
No opinion.. 8

Regardless of which candidate you support, please tell me whether you think each of the following personal characteristics and qualities applies more to Al Gore, or Bill Bradley:

Fights for what he believes in?

Applies more to Gore 37%
Applies more to Bradley................................. 36
Both equally (volunteered)............................. 19
No opinion.. 8

Understands the nation's problems?

Applies more to Gore 49%
Applies more to Bradley................................. 27

Both equally (volunteered).............................. 17
No opinion... 7

Strong and decisive leader?

Applies more to Gore 43%
Applies more to Bradley................................. 38
Both equally (volunteered)............................. 8
No opinion... 11

Has new ideas?

Applies more to Gore 24%
Applies more to Bradley................................. 56
Both equally (volunteered)............................. 8
No opinion... 12

Not a typical politician?

Applies more to Gore 15%
Applies more to Bradley................................. 66
Both equally (volunteered)............................. 8
No opinion... 11

Inspiring?

Applies more to Gore 35%
Applies more to Bradley................................. 44
Both equally (volunteered)............................. 8
No opinion... 13

Has a vision for the country's future?

Applies more to Gore 38%
Applies more to Bradley................................. 37
Both equally (volunteered)............................. 19
No opinion... 6

Likeable?

Applies more to Gore 33%
Applies more to Bradley................................. 42
Both equally (volunteered)............................. 21
No opinion... 4

Sincere?

Applies more to Gore 30%
Applies more to Bradley................................. 41

Both equally (volunteered).............................. 21
No opinion... 8

Cares about the needs of people like you?

Applies more to Gore 35%
Applies more to Bradley................................. 38
Both equally (volunteered)............................. 19
No opinion... 8

Thoughtful?

Applies more to Gore 34%
Applies more to Bradley................................. 38
Both equally (volunteered)............................. 21
No opinion... 7

Presidential?

Applies more to Gore 51%
Applies more to Bradley................................. 34
Both equally (volunteered)............................. 9
No opinion... 6

If elected president, who do you think would do the better job of improving the health-care system in this country—Al Gore, or Bill Bradley?

Gore 41%
Bradley 40
Both equally (volunteered)............................. 6
Neither (volunteered) 3
No opinion... 10

If you had to choose, which of the following schedule of Democratic party debates would you like to see happen—a debate between Bill Bradley and Al Gore on a different issue every week between now and the primary election in February, or four debates between Bill Bradley and Al Gore between now and the primary election in February?

Every week.. 39%
Four times.. 56
No opinion... 5

Note: A special CNN/Gallup survey of New Hampshire Democratic voters finds Al Gore and Bill Bradley in a tight race for their support in the first presidential primary election in 2000. Bradley is favored by 48% of the voters surveyed, compared to 46% for Gore, with 6% undecided.

The poll was conducted on Thursday, October 28, one day after a televised forum in Hanover, New Hampshire, patterned after a town meeting, during which the two candidates answered questions from the public. The winner of New Hampshire's February 1 primary will earn only a handful of delegates to the Democratic National Convention but, more important, is likely to leave the state with valuable political momentum in the quest for the Democratic presidential nomination.

The close race in New Hampshire is markedly different from the current pattern of support nationally, where Gore leads by a substantial margin. According to the most recent Gallup national poll, conducted on October 21–24, Gore leads Bradley among Democrats by 25 points, 57% to 32%.

While the race in New Hampshire is close among all Democratic voters, Bradley performs significantly better among men, receiving 57% of the male vote, compared with 37% for Gore. Conversely, women, by a 54%-to-40% margin, favor Gore. Bradley also wins among voters with college degrees, while those with less formal education prefer Gore. This pattern could have an important impact on the outcome of the primary, perhaps giving Bradley an additional advantage if voters who are more educated disproportionately turn out to vote on the day of the primary, as is typically the case.

Who won the October 27 debate? Among the subset of New Hampshire voters in the new survey who watched all or some of the town meeting forum last Wednesday night, Bradley and Gore are tied: 39% choose Bradley, compared to 38% for Gore, while 14% think that both men performed equally well. Most of the Democratic voters who say that they watched none of the debate refrain from giving their impression of who won on the basis of news reports, but among those who did respond, perceptions are divided, with Gore chosen by 18% and Bradley by 13%.

The one issue at the town meeting that generated the most discussion was health care, with Gore and Bradley swapping criticisms about the costs of each other's plans. When asked who would do a better job of improving the nation's health-care system, New Hampshire Democratic voters split evenly, with Gore chosen by 41% and Bradley by 40%.

One perception where Gore maintains a solid lead over Bradley is his electability. One-half of the Democratic voters surveyed (51%) believe that Gore would have the better chance of winning the national election against George W. Bush as the possible Republican nominee. Only 35% believe that Bradley stands a better chance of beating Bush.

While the New Hampshire primary vote for Bradley and Gore reflected in the poll is evenly divided, both men enjoy very positive personal images among New Hampshire Democrats, with 75% saying that they have a favorable impression of each candidate. Only 21% currently have an unfavorable image of Gore, and even fewer (11%) feel negatively about Bradley.

Beyond these generally favorable impressions, however, voters make many distinctions between the qualities and characteristics that each candidate possesses. When twelve different positive qualities were tested, Gore was chosen over Bradley on just two. By a 51%-to-34% margin, he is more likely to be perceived as "presidential" and, by a slightly greater margin, as someone who "understands the nation's problems." Bradley wins on five counts: he "has new ideas," is "not a typical politician," is "inspiring," "likeable," and "sincere." Gore and Bradley are closely matched on all other qualities rated.

Interestingly, on all the personal qualities tested, Bradley tends to rate better with Democrats who watched Wednesday's town meeting than with those who did not watch. This difference in Bradley's ratings is particularly wide in terms of "caring about the needs of people like you" and "understanding the nation's problems," on which Bradley is rated 8 points higher by people who watched the forum. However, it is not clear whether these results are due to Bradley's performance at the event or are simply a result of more Bradley supporters tuning in the program.

NOVEMBER 2
GOING TO THE POLLS

Interviewing Dates: 9/10–14/99
CNN/*USA Today*/Gallup Poll
Survey #GO 128526

Do you happen to know where people who live in your neighborhood go to vote?

Yes.. 72%
No 27
No opinion.. 1

Have you ever voted in your precinct or election district?

Yes.. 70%
No 30

How often would you say you vote—always, nearly always, part of the time, seldom, or never?

Always.. 40%
Nearly always; part of the time 40
Seldom; never.. 20

	Always	Nearly always; part of the time	Seldom; never
By Politics			
Republicans	48%	41%	11%
Democrats....................	44	41	15
Independents...............	30	38	32

Note: Americans going to the polls today in elections for mayor, city council, and other local offices are likely to be in the minority, regardless of how they cast their ballots. If voter turnout in recent national elections is any indication, significantly less than one-half of the eligible public can be expected to take part in this year's races. Just 49% of eligible voters participated in the election for president in 1996, and turnout in the 1998 midterm congressional elections was just 36%.

According to a recent Gallup election survey, 72% know the location of their polling place and 70% have voted in their community before, but only 40% indicate that they always vote. Another 27% say that they nearly always vote, while 13% vote part of the time and 20% seldom or never.

Who are the Americans most likely to say that they "always" vote? The most reliable voters in the electorate are older and college educated, while the least reliable are young people, those without any college education, and political independents. Age is a particularly strong factor in voting habits, with the percentage saying that they always vote increasing from 21% among those in the 18–29 age bracket to 37% among those 30–49, 51% among those 50–64, and 59% among those age 65 and older. Conversely, the percentage saying that they seldom or never vote is 42% among young people, but then it drops off precipitously to only 19% of those age 30–49.

The turnout trend is similar, but less pronounced, based on education. One-third of those who have attained no more than a high-school diploma say that they always vote. This figure compares with 42% who have some college education, 46% among those with a college degree, and 55% among those with at least some postgraduate education. Moreover, people who identify with one of the two major parties are more likely to vote than are those who describe themselves as politically independent. Roughly one-half of Republicans (48%) always vote, as do 44% of Democrats, but only 30% of independents.

Doing a better job of letting voters know the location of their polling place on Election Day would help some of the less participatory groups overcome their inertia. For instance, 50% of young voters (age 18–29) do not know where people who live in their neighborhood go to vote. However, this excuse is most likely a symptom of larger obstacles to young people voting rather than a direct reason. In addition to the fact that some 18-to-29 year olds are just entering the eligible electorate, lack of interest in politics, low trust in the political system, and high rates of mobility among younger people could explain why so many in this generation are unaware of where to vote. By contrast, only 21% of those older than 29 lack this important information about where to vote. Political independents are the second least-informed group, with 38% saying that they do not know where to vote in their community, compared to 24% of Democrats and only 18% of Republicans.

Asked to look ahead to November 2000, 67% currently are absolutely certain that they will vote in the presidential election next year—substantially higher than the expected rate, according to past turnout patterns. This figure includes roughly one-half of young and independent voters and three-quarters of those in the high turnout groups.

NOVEMBER 8
AL GORE VS. GEORGE W. BUSH

Interviewing Dates: 10/8–10/99
CNN/*USA Today*/Gallup Poll
Survey #GO 128813

I'm going to read some qualities and characteristics. For each quality, please say how important you think it is for a president to have—very important, somewhat important, not too important, or not important at all:

Has a vision for the country's future?

	Very important
Gore voters	92%
G. W. Bush voters	91

By Party

Republicans	92
Democrats	93

Is a strong and decisive leader?

	Very important
Gore voters	87%
G. W. Bush voters	91

By Party

Republicans	94
Democrats	88

Can keep the economy strong?

	Very important
Gore voters	92%
G. W. Bush voters	87

By Party

Republicans	86
Democrats	92

Knows how to get things done in Washington?

	Very important
Gore voters	90%
G. W. Bush voters	77

By Party

Republicans	77
Democrats	87

Cares about the needs of people like you?

	Very important
Gore voters	87%
G. W. Bush voters	78

By Party

Republicans	76
Democrats	87

Cares about the needs of the poor?

	Very important
Gore voters	91%
G. W. Bush voters	74

By Party

Republicans	71
Democrats	89

Has good moral character?

	Very important
Gore voters	72%
G. W. Bush voters	86

By Party

Republicans	90
Democrats	71

Is an effective manager?

	Very important
Gore voters	79%
G. W. Bush voters	75

By Party

Republicans	75
Democrats	77

Has experience in government?

	Very important
Gore voters	74%
G. W. Bush voters	67

By Party

Republicans	66
Democrats	74

Has foreign policy experience?

	Very important
Gore voters	73%
G. W. Bush voters	60

By Party

Republicans	60
Democrats	70

Is inspiring?

	Very important
Gore voters	62%
G. W. Bush voters	53

By Party

Republicans	52
Democrats	60

Has been faithful to his spouse?

	Very important
Gore voters	38%
G. W. Bush voters	67

By Party

Republicans	66
Democrats	45

Generally agrees with you on the issues you care about?

	Very important
Gore voters	59%
G. W. Bush voters	44

By Party

Republicans	44
Democrats	57

Has experience running a business?

	Very important
Gore voters	48%
G. W. Bush voters	44

By Party

Republicans	43
Democrats	46

Attends religious services regularly?

	Very important
Gore voters	35%
G. W. Bush voters	39

By Party

Republicans	42
Democrats	35

Has never used illegal drugs?

	Very important
Gore voters	34%
G. W. Bush voters	26

By Party

Republicans	32
Democrats	31

Has served in the military?

	Very important
Gore voters	21%
G. W. Bush voters	25

By Party

Republicans	25
Democrats	21

Note: The American public overwhelmingly agrees that having a vision for the country's future, being a strong and decisive leader, and being able to keep the economy strong are the three most important characteristics that they would like in a president. At the same time, there is agreement that military service, never having used illegal drugs, and regular religious service attendance are not important. There are differences in the emphasis given these qualities between those respondents supporting Al Gore for president and those supporting George W. Bush. Bush voters place more emphasis on moral leadership and marital fidelity, while Gore voters are more concerned about caring for the poor, Washington experience, and foreign policy experience.

An October 8–10 Gallup Poll asked Americans to rate how important it is for the president to possess seventeen different qualities and characteristics. The respondents were not asked to rate individual candidates but rather to evaluate their more general importance as criteria for choosing a president. The range among those qualities judged "very important" was very wide, from 92% who rated "has a vision for the country's future" as very important, to only 23% who rated "has served in the military" as very important.

Overall, three characteristics were rated very important by about nine in ten respondents and therefore clearly rank as the top qualities that the public desires in its chief executive:

- Has a vision for the country's future
- Is a strong and decisive leader
- Can keep the economy strong

The next group was rated very important by roughly three-quarters of those polled:

- Knows how to get things done in Washington
- Cares about the needs of people like you
- Cares about the needs of the poor
- Has good moral character
- Is an effective manager

A midrange group, given a very important rating by 46% to 70%, included:

- Has experience in government
- Has foreign policy experience
- Is inspiring
- Has been faithful to his spouse
- Generally agrees with you on the issues you care about
- Has experience running a business

(One important factor in this list is the relatively low importance given to the statement, "agrees with you on the issues you care about." Some observers have considered positions on the issues to be of top importance in a race, but the public obviously considers other less specific qualities to be more important.)

Finally, three characteristics were rated very important by less than 40% of the public:

- Attends religious services regularly
- Has never used illegal drugs
- Has served in the military

We looked at the rating of the characteristics among those who planned to vote for Vice President Gore and among those who planned to vote for Texas Governor Bush. While both groups gave many of the characteristics very similar ratings, there were some important differences. First, the biggest difference is on "has been faithful to his spouse," rated very important by only 38% of Gore voters but by 67% of Bush voters, representing a difference of 29 points. One explanation for this finding is that Gore voters are those most likely to have defended Bill Clinton through the past two years of his own infidelity scandal and therefore have become inured to this presidential flaw; another explanation would be that Democrats are less interested in a president's morals than the typically more conservative Republicans. Second, there is a similar but smaller difference on "has good moral character," which is rated as very important by 86% of Bush voters but by only 72% of Gore voters. Third, the second largest difference between the candidates is on "cares about the needs of the poor"; 91% of Gore voters rate it as very important, compared to 74% of Bush voters, which may reflect traditional Democratic and Republican differences on the government's role in addressing social issues. Fourth, the third largest difference is on "generally agrees with you on the issues you care about," which is rated as very important by 59% of Gore voters but by only 44% of Bush voters. Fifth, "has foreign policy experience" is rated as very important by 73% of Gore voters, compared to 60% of Bush voters; this difference may reflect Gore supporters' recognition of the vice president's international experience, as opposed to Bush's state-level role as a governor. And sixth, a similar pattern appears in "knows how to get things done in Washington," which is rated as very important by 90% of Gore voters, compared to 77% of Bush voters.

Overall, the top-five list for each group—Bush voters and Gore voters—is similar, with one or two important exceptions:

Top Five among Gore Voters

- Has a vision for the country's future
- Can keep the economy strong
- Cares about the needs of the poor
- Knows how to get things done in Washington
- (tie) Is a strong and decisive leader
- (tie) Cares about the needs of people like you

Top Five among Bush Voters

- Has a vision for the country's future
- Is a strong and decisive leader
- Can keep the economy strong
- Has good moral character
- Cares about the needs of people like you

In this comparison, the biggest difference between the two groups is the importance attached by Gore voters to getting things done in Washington and caring about the poor, and the differentially high importance attached by Bush voters to a president's having good moral character.

NOVEMBER 11
THE YEAR 2000 CAMPAIGN—AN ANALYSIS*

Texas Governor George W. Bush and Vice President Al Gore continue to maintain very strong national leads among potential primary voters in their respective parties. Although the precise percentage of the votes that each receives has varied from poll to poll, their commanding leads have been roughly constant over the past eight months. In similar fashion, Bush continues to lead Gore in general election trial heats, and this too represents little change from polling that stretches back to February of this year.

*This analysis was written by Frank Newport, Editor in Chief, The Gallup Poll.

The biggest changes in the potential makeup of this year's race have come in the Republican party. Earlier this year, Gallup Polls asked Republicans about ten potential candidates for the nomination. That number has dwindled as Dan Quayle, Pat Buchanan, and Elizabeth Dole have left the field. Now, in the most recent poll, Republicans are asked about Bush, John McCain, Steve Forbes, Gary Bauer, Orrin Hatch, and Alan Keyes. The main impact of the narrowing of the race has been to increase the size of George W. Bush's lead, which at its low point in late April and early May was only 18 points, and which has grown to the overwhelming 56-point lead evident in Gallup's most recent November poll.

Bush's campaign has gone through three distinct phases:

- Between April and early June, Bush averaged 47% of the vote. It was during this time period that Elizabeth Dole made the strongest challenge that anyone has mounted to date, pushing her vote total up to 24% at one point, within 18 points of Bush.
- From late June through September, Bush increased his average percentage of the Republican vote to 61% as Dole's candidacy faded. This represents the time period during which Bush was being challenged by the full complement of Republican politicians, including a former vice president.
- Finally, in three Gallup Polls conducted from October through the most recent one of November 4–11, Bush has surged to an average of 65% of the vote, benefiting from the dropouts of Buchanan, Quayle, and Dole.

The bad news for the campaigns of John McCain and Steve Forbes: they have been unable to capture significant percentages of the vote totals of the candidates who dropped out of the race. Dole's, Quayle's, and Buchanan's withdrawals put into play up to 20% of the Republican vote, and the data suggest that at least half of that has gone to Bush, with McCain getting the bulk of the rest.

Still, McCain has benefited only marginally. His current 12% of the vote, against the diminished field, is his highest percentage to date, but significantly below the 24% that Elizabeth Dole obtained at one point in late spring. And, despite the narrowing of the field, wealthy magazine publisher Steve Forbes is still getting only 6% of the Republican vote in the most recent poll, exactly the same percentage he received against the full field of contenders back in April and May.

On the Democratic side, the vote choice has been much simpler all year long: Gore versus Bradley. Gore has been ahead of the former New Jersey senator in every poll taken during that time period. The margin between the two candidates has varied somewhat from poll to poll, and Bill Bradley managed to come within 12 points of the vice president in one poll in early October, but Gore quickly rebounded. In fact, across ten polls conducted from April through this past weekend, Gore has averaged 59% of the vote and Bradley 31%. In the most recent poll, Gore's 58% and Bradley's 33% of the Democratic vote are remarkably close to those averages, underscoring the essential lack of change in the race over the course of the year.

There has been a flurry of press reports discussing a putative Bradley surge. Much of this is built on the fact that Bradley has done better in certain key primary states (and on Bradley's success in fundraising). There is no national primary vote, of course. Voting will take place on a state-by-state basis, and the vote in early states can have an impact on the vote in the states whose primaries follow. Therefore, the poll results from a state such as New Hampshire—which have shown Bradley catching up with Gore—can be important despite the Granite State's small population. Nevertheless, there has been no major shift in the national polls which aggregate all Democratic voters together, suggesting that Bradley's campaign is still waiting for events which will shift him to the more competitive position he will need if he is to capture the Democratic nomination.

George W. Bush is also maintaining a healthy lead among voters when they are asked to vote in hypothetical general election ballots. In the most recent poll, Bush leads Gore by a 55%-to-40% margin. Gore's 40% now is actually smaller than the percentage he received in May 1998, when he got 47% of the vote against Bush. Gore did best in that May 1998 poll and in an early

January poll this year (he came close to tying Bush in each), but since February, Gore has dropped to roughly his current levels. Since February, Gore's high point has been only 43% of the vote, not substantially different from his low point of 37%.

NOVEMBER 19
THE REPUBLICAN FRONT-RUNNER—AN ANALYSIS*

Texas Governor George W. Bush and Vice President Al Gore continue to be dominant leaders in the races for their respective parties' presidential nominations. Bush now has an enormous lead of more than 50 percentage points over his nearest competitor, Arizona Senator John McCain, and Gore leads former New Jersey Senator Bill Bradley by over 20 points. Both Bush's and Gore's national leads have generally remained strong throughout the year.

Some polls in the early caucus and primary states of Iowa and New Hampshire, however, show that Bush and Gore could be in significantly tighter races than is the case nationally. A good deal of press coverage is being given to the challenges Bush and Gore are facing from John McCain and Bill Bradley, respectively, based on polls taken in these states. The assumption is that strong showings by competitors to Bush and Gore in early primaries can have a multiplicative domino effect, changing the voters' preferences in subsequent states, until in a cascading snowball effect, the front-runners could end up losing the nominations.

History in Many Ways Is Best Available Guide

It is worthwhile to examine the historical record in this regard. There have been twelve presidential elections from the 1950s through 1996, and most of the Gallup Polls conducted in the fall before these election years measured the same type of national sentiments being measured in the fall of 1999. By comparing these *one-year-out polls* with

*This analysis was written by Frank Newport, Editor in Chief, The Gallup Poll.

the ultimate nominee the following year, we get a sense of the nature of the relationship between what the voters say to pollsters in the fall before the election and what actually happens as the primary and convention season unfolds in the election year itself.

Eventual Republican Nominee Usually Ahead in Polls Conducted Year before Election

There is one immediately apparent conclusion. The Democrats have been much more unsettled over the past fifty years than have the Republicans. An analysis of elections since 1952 shows that in almost every case, the man to whom Republican voters were giving the highest poll total in the fall before the election ended up becoming the eventual GOP nominee, and in no situation did a strong front-runner go on to lose the nomination.

The Republicans have first and foremost been able to take advantage of the incumbency factor over the past fifty years. In each of the years 1956, 1972, 1976, 1984, and 1992, there was an incumbent Republican president running for reelection, and despite challenges in some of these years, each of the incumbents—Dwight Eisenhower, Richard Nixon, Gerald Ford, Ronald Reagan, and George Bush, respectively—easily got their party's nomination in the summer of the election year (even though Ford and Bush, of course, went down to defeat in the November general election). Additionally, in 1960 and in 1988 there were incumbent vice presidents—Nixon and Bush—who moved fairly easily on to their party's nomination.

Thus, there have actually been only relatively few elections in which there was no incumbent Republican president or vice president who was the natural heir to the nomination:

- The least predictive pre-election polls were in the fall of 1963. Barry Goldwater, the eventual winner of the Republican nomination, was very much in the thick of the race in polling conducted in 1963 but was not dominant. Goldwater led Nelson Rockefeller in the early fall polls and fell slightly behind Richard Nixon in the late fall Gallup Polls.

- In the fall of 1967, Richard Nixon—who got the Republican nomination the next year—was the leader in all polls, pulling in 40% or more of the Republican vote, way ahead of the three other contenders Gallup included in trial heat questions: Rockefeller, Ronald Reagan, and George Romney.

- In 1979 the leader in the Republican polls was Ronald Reagan, who ended up getting the nomination. Reagan had significant competition, including former President Gerald Ford, Howard Baker, John Connally, and George Bush, but Reagan led in all fall polls.

- And, in 1995, in pre-election polls leading up to the 1996 election, Bob Dole, the eventual Republican nominee, was significantly ahead in fall polls.

In short, although there have been years in which there was sharp competition for the Republican nomination, there has never been a situation in which a candidate was consistently leading in Gallup Polls one year before the election and did not go on to win the nomination. The closest to that situation occurred in 1963, when Richard Nixon was slightly ahead of Barry Goldwater in some polls, but Nixon did not have a strong, nor a consistent, lead.

This year, George W. Bush has been a consistent 50+ points ahead of his nearest competitor in the pre-election polls—competition that has included a former vice president, a popular and well-known woman, a candidate who won the New Hampshire primary in 1996, and the publisher of one of the country's best-known business magazines. Bush's continuing ability to outdistance these contenders in the national polls, and the Republicans' historical track record of sticking to the person they favor at this point one year before the election, would suggest that a scenario in which George W. Bush ultimately loses the Republican nomination would be unprecedented.

Democratic Nominee Often Not Known until Winter and Spring of Election Year

It has been a different story on the Democratic side, however. Only in 1964, 1980, and 1996 was there an incumbent Democrat in the White House seeking reelection. In all other years there was a fight for the nomination, and in many of those years the eventual nominee was still obscure and behind in fall polls conducted one year before the election:

- In 1959, John F. Kennedy was locked in a tight race with Adlai Stevenson in Gallup Polls conducted in September, October, and November and was by no means dominant in these fall polls.
- In 1971, George McGovern was a single-digit minor player in fall polling. Ted Kennedy, Edmund Muskie, and Hubert H. Humphrey all led McGovern in polls conducted in November and December.
- In 1975, Jimmy Carter was relatively unknown and low in the ranking produced by Gallup Polls. Ted Kennedy, Hubert Humphrey, and George Wallace all led the Georgia governor in fall polls.
- In 1983 the eventual Democratic nominee, Walter Mondale, had moved ahead of Ohio Senator John Glenn in fall Gallup polling but was not above 50% of the Democratic vote.
- Massachusetts Governor Michael Dukakis was beginning to show up in the polls in the fall of 1987 but was still trailing Jesse Jackson and had poll numbers only in the teens.
- And, at this point in 1991, Bill Clinton was an obscure governor of Arkansas. In fall polling in that year, five other candidates got higher totals than Clinton in the polls; the leader was former California Governor Jerry Brown.

In short, *one-year-out polls* have been of little use in predicting the eventual Democratic nominee in many of the elections in the second half of this century. At the same time, it is important to note that the Al Gore situation this year is unlike that of any of the other post-1950 elections. In none of the Democratically volatile years—1959, 1971, 1975, 1983, 1987, and 1991—was there a strong candidate who was 20 points or more ahead in the polls a year out and who went on to lose. The most similar elections were in 1975, when Ted Kennedy had an 11-point lead over his nearest competitor; and in 1991, when Jerry Brown had a 9-point lead in one Gallup Poll. Gore's lead over

Bill Bradley this year has at one stage been as low as 11 points but has averaged a much more robust 20+ points in late October and November polling. And it is important to remember that it has been very rare in the past half-century for a candidate to be above 50% of the Democratic vote at this point in time. Gore's primary challenger, Bill Bradley, can thus pin his hopes on mimicking the ultimate success of such come-from-behind candidates as George McGovern, Jimmy Carter, Michael Dukakis, and Bill Clinton, but the situation is different enough this year to suggest that this may be a difficult scenario to pull off.

NOVEMBER 24
HILLARY RODHAM CLINTON

Interviewing Dates: 11/18–21/99
CNN/*USA Today*/Gallup Poll
Survey #GO 129182

As you may know, Hillary Rodham Clinton may run for the U.S. Senate from the state of New York in the 2000 election. Regardless of whether or not you would vote for her, do you think Hillary Rodham Clinton is qualified to be a U.S. senator, or not?

	Nov. 18–21, 1999	June 25–27, 1999
Yes	62%	69%
No	34	29
No opinion	4	2

If Hillary Clinton does run for the Senate, the campaign would take place while she is still First Lady. Do you think it is appropriate for her to run while First Lady, or not?

	Nov. 18–21, 1999*	Feb. 19–21, 1999*
Yes	48%	45%
No	49	52
No opinion	3	3

*Based on half sample

Some people have suggested that if Hillary Clinton decides to run for the Senate from

New York, she should end her duties as First Lady and move to New York where she can run full time for the Senate. Do you think it would be appropriate or not appropriate for her to do this?*

Appropriate.. 62%
Not appropriate.. 33
No opinion... 5

*Based on half sample

Note: Falling just short of a formal announcement, First Lady Hillary Rodham Clinton nonetheless publicly confirmed on Tuesday [November 23] for the first time that she will be a candidate for the U.S. Senate from New York State next year. She further indicated that it would not be long before she reduces her White House role and moves into the Clintons' new home in Chappaqua, New York, in order to campaign full time.

Have the First Lady's political ambitions, her recent spate of bad press in New York, or the controversy over her visit to Israel this month caused public opinion to sour on Mrs. Clinton? According to the latest Gallup Poll, the answer seems to be "no." While some ambivalence exists about her candidacy, her job approval rating as First Lady remains high, as does the percentage of respondents who consider her qualified to be a U.S. senator.

Americans today express the same feelings that they did nine months ago about Mrs. Clinton's candidacy. Only about one-half (48%) say that it is appropriate for her to run for the Senate while she is First Lady; 49% say that it is not appropriate for her to run. At the same time, however, a large majority (62%) believe that she is qualified to be a U.S. senator—down just slightly from 69%, when the measure was last taken in June.

It seems that traditional feelings about the role of the First Lady among some Democrats are combining with Republican political opposition to Mrs. Clinton, and are working together to suppress public support for her candidacy. Specifically, only 55% of Democrats consider her run appropriate, while 41% of this group—which otherwise would be expected to support a Democratic candidate in much higher numbers—say that it is inappropriate. The views of Democrats toward her

candidacy are similar to those of political independents and only moderately more supportive than those of Republicans, among whom just 36% think that Mrs. Clinton's candidacy is appropriate.

Further evidence that nationwide support among Democrats for her candidacy may be currently suppressed by traditional feelings about the role of First Lady is found in their views toward her qualifications for office. Nearly four in five Democrats (78%) believe that Mrs. Clinton is qualified to be a U.S. senator, while only 18% think that she is not. Nevertheless, as noted, only 55% think that it is appropriate for her to run. Such a large gap between the two attitudes is not seen among independents and Republicans:

	Think she's qualified	Think it's appropriate for her to run	Point gap
Total............................	62%	48%	14
Democrats....................	78	55	23
Independents...............	62	51	11
Republicans	48	36	12

In addition to running, Mrs. Clinton has faced a secondary decision about leaving the White House in order to devote herself full time to the New York Senate bid. Indeed, she announced on Tuesday that she has made up her mind to move into the family's new home in New York as soon as possible, in order to devote more time to her campaign. Although respondents are divided over whether or not it is appropriate for her to run, they seem sympathetic to the pragmatic imperative that requires candidate Hillary Rodham Clinton to move to New York and therefore to spend less time in her official role as First Lady. A majority of Americans (62%) say that if she does decide to run, it would be appropriate for her to end her duties as First Lady and make the move to New York; just one-third say that it would not be appropriate.

The good news for Mrs. Clinton is that the ambivalence about her Senate candidacy and the negative press of the past few weeks over her official trip to the Middle East do not seem to be hurting her image as First Lady. Two-thirds currently approve of the way that she is handling her job as First Lady, while just 30% disapprove.

Her current job ratings are down from the exceptionally high approval scores that Mrs. Clinton received earlier this year, such as 80% in February. However, those high ratings were most likely inflated by the public sympathy that Americans felt for her during the close of the impeachment hearings over the Monica Lewinsky scandal. Pre-Monica, Mrs. Clinton's approval rating was just 62%. And earlier in Bill Clinton's presidency, when Mrs. Clinton was the object of criticism over health-care reform and Whitewater, her approval ratings were even lower. For instance, in January 1995, only 54% approved of the job that she was doing, while 40% disapproved. Thus, on a relative basis, Mrs. Clinton is faring quite well with the American people.

Mrs. Clinton is especially popular today with women and young adults. Nearly three-quarters of women (72%) approve of the job that she is doing, compared to 60% of men. Perhaps reflective of a generation gap over her untraditional approach to the role of First Lady, only 55% of those age 50 and older approve of her job performance, compared to 69% of those in the 30–49 age bracket, and 80% of adults under 30.

DECEMBER 2
AL GORE VS. BILL BRADLEY

Interviewing Dates: 11/18–21/99
CNN/*USA Today*/Gallup Poll
Survey #GO 129182

If you had to choose, would you describe the political views of each of the following as liberal, or as moderate:

Al Gore?

Liberal 42%
Moderate... 49
Conservative (volunteered) 1
No opinion... 8

	Liberal	Moderate	Conser-vative	No opinion
By Politics				
Republicans.....	58%	34%	1%	7%
Democrats	26	66	*	8
Independents ...	43	46	1	10

*Less than 1%

Bill Bradley?

Liberal 27%
Moderate... 48
Conservative (volunteered) 1
No opinion... 24

	Liberal	Moderate	Conser-vative	No opinion
By Politics				
Republicans.....	28%	45%	1%	26%
Democrats	25	52	1	22
Independents ...	27	46	2	25

Note: Vice President Al Gore continues to lead former New Jersey Senator Bill Bradley in the race for the 2000 Democratic nomination for president, recording a 22-point lead in the latest national Gallup Poll, conducted on November 18–21. But in the Northeast, where Bradley gained his fame—as an outstanding basketball player both at Princeton University and professionally with the New York Knicks, and later as a U.S. senator from New Jersey—the race between the two Democratic candidates is tied at 44%. Gore enjoys 25-point leads each in the Midwest and the West, and a 31-point lead in the South, where he rose to prominence as a U.S. senator from Tennessee.

These regional differences are important, since the first official primary is in the Northeast—specifically, in New Hampshire, where a Gallup Poll in late October showed Gore and Bradley in a dead heat, much like the current situation in the Northeast overall. One reason that Bradley does better in New Hampshire is that more men are attracted to his candidacy there than they are elsewhere across the country. Although Gore enjoys majority support among both male and female Democrats nationally, in New Hampshire the two groups differ, with men supporting Bradley by a 19-point margin and women supporting Gore by a 14-point margin. Bradley also receives much more support in New Hampshire than elsewhere from the college educated and from those with household incomes over $50,000 per year. Whatever the differences in their support among Democrats, in the projected general election contest each candidate fares about the same against the Republican front-runner, Texas

Governor George W. Bush. Gore trails Bush by 16 points among registered voters, while Bradley trails by 15 points.

For the past seven years, Gore has been associated with the "New Democrat" Bill Clinton, so-called because of Clinton's efforts to avoid being tagged as a "liberal" and to position himself and the Democratic party as more centrist. Many analysts have suggested that Bradley, with his self-characterized "big" solutions for "big" problems, may be more in the tradition of the old liberal Democrats and less of a moderate as projected by Clinton and Gore. But these terms are not precise, and many politicians and analysts would disagree about how much they might apply to the two candidates. The Gallup Poll shows that Americans in general apply the terms quite differently, depending on their party affiliation.

Among the national public overall, Gore is more likely to be seen as liberal than Bradley, with 42% describing Gore this way, compared to just 27% for Bradley, a reversal of what many analysts are saying. This distinction, however, is mostly driven by Republicans, 58% of whom call Gore a liberal, compared to only 28% who see Bradley that way. Democrats tend to perceive the two candidates' ideologies in similar terms, with the majority of Democrats describing Bradley and Gore as moderate, and only one-quarter saying that each is liberal.

In part, these differences may reflect the fact that it is difficult to categorize any candidate along ideological dimensions, and it is especially difficult to do so for a candidate such as Bradley, who has had little national exposure on the issues. Indeed, nearly one-quarter of the public (24%) express no opinion about Bradley's ideological orientation, compared to 8% who are unsure about Gore's.

DECEMBER 3
CONGRESSIONAL ELECTIONS

Interviewing Dates: 11/18–21/99
CNN/*USA Today*/Gallup Poll
Survey #GO 129182

If the elections for Congress were being held today, which party's candidate would you vote for in your congressional district—the Democratic party's candidate, or the Republican party's candidate? [Those who were undecided were asked: As of today, do you lean more toward the Democratic party's candidate, or toward the Republican party's candidate?]

Democratic candidate 46%
Republican candidate 43
Undecided; other
(volunteered); no opinion 11

Selected National Trend

	Demo-cratic candidate	Repub-lican candidate	Un-decided; other; no opinion
1999			
September 10–14	46%	42%	12%
February 12–13	52	39	9
1998			
October 29–November 1	48	39	13
October 23–25	45	41	14
October 9–12	46	42	12
September 23–24	50	39	11
September 14–15	47	41	12
September 11–12	50	38	12
August 21–23	48	42	10
July 7–8	46	40	14
May 8–10	49	41	10
April 17–19	46	44	10
January 16–18	50	39	11

Please tell me whether you have a favorable or unfavorable opinion of each of the following parties:

The Republican party?

Favorable 50%
Unfavorable 44
No opinion 6

Selected National Trend

	Favorable	Un-favorable	No opinion
1999			
April 30–May 2	47%	44%	9%

February 19–21.......... 45	46	9
February 12–13.......... 40	54	6
February 4–8............... 45	47	8
January 8–10.............. 40	52	8
1998		
December 19–20......... 31	57	12
December 15–16......... 43	47	10
1997		
October 27–29 50	42	8
1996		
August 30–		
September 1*.......... 50	45	5
August 16–18* 55	41	4
August 5–7* 51	44	5
April 9–10................... 52	41	7
1995		
April 17–19................. 52	42	6
1992		
July 6–8 53	39	8

*Registered voters

The Democratic party?

Favorable 51%
Unfavorable 41
No opinion 8

Selected National Trend

	Favorable	Un-favorable	No opinion
1999			
April 30–			
May 2...................... 53%	37%	10%
February 19–21........... 55	37	8
February 12–13........... 56	38	6
February 4–8............... 57	37	6
January 8–10.............. 57	35	8
1998			
December 19–20......... 57	30	13
December 15–16......... 58	32	10
1997			
October 27–29 54	39	7
1996			
August 30–			
September 1*.......... 60	36	4
August 16–18* 55	41	4
August 5–7* 57	38	5
April 9–10................... 55	38	7

1995		
April 17–19................. 51	43	6
1992		
July 6–8* 54	38	8

*Registered voters

Note: With Republicans now controlling Congress by the slimmest majority of either party in a half-century, several findings in the latest Gallup Poll suggest that the contest for control of Congress in the 2000 elections could be another highly competitive one, similar to 1998. The poll shows that Americans today are evenly divided in their support for the Republican and Democratic parties on several measures, including their voting preferences for Congress, party identification, and favorable ratings of the parties.

The past six years have been marked by increasingly close races for control of Congress, with the Republicans winning control of the U.S. House by a 26-seat margin in 1994, 19 seats in 1996, and just 12 seats in 1998. Today, because of various special elections since the 1998 contest, the Republicans hold a 10-seat lead, 222 to 212. By way of comparison, the Democratic party prevailed in Congress from 1954 to 1994 with margins generally upward of 50 seats, and in some years close to 150 seats.

Gallup measures the congressional strength of the two major parties by asking respondents whether they plan to vote for the Republican or Democratic candidate in their district. Among national adults in the new November 18–21 poll, these preferences are essentially even, with Democrats currently leading Republicans by 46% to 43%—roughly the same as when last measured in September. However, based on historical polling patterns, it is likely that the race is much closer among the subset who will actually vote in the election, with Republicans perhaps slightly ahead. It should also be noted that although the race looks close today, the congressional election picture can easily change with eleven months to go in the campaign.

The new Gallup Poll also finds the two major parties evenly matched in terms of public image and the percentage of the population that identifies with each one. Nearly equal numbers currently claim allegiance to each of the two major parties, with 44% calling themselves Democratic or leaning toward the Democratic party, and 43% calling themselves Republican or leaning Republican. This is good news for the Republicans, who had been trailing the Democrats on this measure by about 7 points for most of 1999, and by an even wider margin during the impeachment crisis of 1998. Although these figures fluctuate slightly from poll to poll, there has been a clear trend in the Republican direction throughout this year.

The public's assessments of the two parties are also very similar today, with 50% now saying that they have a favorable view of the Republican party and 51% having a favorable view of the Democratic party. At the other end of the scale, 44% have an unfavorable image of the Republicans, while 41% have an unfavorable opinion of the Democrats.

The current favorable rating of the Democrats is down slightly compared to earlier this year, but it is essentially consistent with how respondents have viewed the party over the past decade. The Republicans' image is also consistent with the long-term trend but represents a significant improvement over 1998 and early 1999, when the favorable rating of the Republican party fell into the low 40s, most probably due to public concerns about the impeachment of President Bill Clinton by Congress. The lowest favorable rating for the Republicans in this period was recorded in mid-December 1998, immediately after the U.S. House voted to impeach Clinton. At that time only 31% had a favorable view of the Republicans, and 57% had an unfavorable view.

DECEMBER 14
THE YEAR 2000 CAMPAIGN

Interviewing Dates: 12/9–12/99
CNN/*USA Today*/Gallup Poll
Survey #GO 129321

In your view, does Al Gore have the knowledge and experience necessary to be a good president, or not? And how about George W. Bush?

	Gore	Bush
Yes	57%	64%
No	41	30
No opinion	2	6

Thinking again about Al Gore, do you think he knows enough about each of the following issues to be a good president, or not:

Foreign affairs?

	Dec. 9–12, 1999	Nov. 18–21, 1999
Yes	58%	57%
No	33	33
No opinion	9	10

Economic policy?

Yes	63%
No	29
No opinion	8

Education?

Yes	70%
No	23
No opinion	7

Next, thinking again about George W. Bush, do you think he knows enough about each of the following issues to be a good president, or not:

Foreign affairs?

	Dec. 9–12, 1999	Nov. 18–21, 1999
Yes	44%	49%
No	44	40
No opinion	12	11

Economic policy?

Yes	65%
No	25
No opinion	10

Education?

Yes	69%
No	21
No opinion	10

Asked of registered Republicans and those leaning Republican: As you may know, in the first several months of next year, most states will hold a primary election for the Republican nomination for president. If John McCain defeats George W. Bush in some of the early primaries but all the current candidates remain in the race, whom would you be most likely to support for the Republican nomination at that point—former Family Research Council chairman Gary Bauer; Texas Governor George W. Bush; businessman Steve Forbes; Arizona Senator John McCain; Utah Senator Orrin Hatch; or political commentator Alan Keyes?

G. W. Bush	37%
McCain	34
Forbes	10
Hatch	4
Keyes	4
Bauer	2
None (volunteered)	1
Other (volunteered)	1
No opinion	7

Note: A new Gallup Poll suggests that Americans are just as confident in the knowledge and experience of Republican front-runner George W. Bush as they are in Democratic front-runner Al Gore, and that Bush continues to beat Gore in a trial heat preview of a possible general election ballot next November. Additionally, Bush still leads the second-place Republican challenger, John McCain, by over 40 percentage points, although the number of respondents with a favorable opinion of McCain has grown substantially over the last two months. At the same time, responses to a hypothetical question asking about the impact of possible McCain victories in the early Republican primaries suggest the possibility that Bush's support may be soft, and that McCain may yet gain in the race for the nomination if such a scenario plays out next January and February.

In recent weeks, several news stories have focused on whether Texas Governor Bush has the experience and knowledge necessary to be president. Some of the stories have been generated by reporters covering the election, but others have reflected criticisms of Bush by the other Republican candidates. Whatever their source the latest Gallup Poll finds that the public expresses as much confidence in Bush as it does in Vice President Gore for overall levels of experience and knowledge, although Gore is seen as more knowledgeable in foreign affairs. And in the general election contest, the Texas governor continues to have a double-digit lead over the vice president.

When asked whether each candidate, Gore and Bush, has the knowledge and experience to be a good president, 64% say that Bush does, and 57% say that Gore does. But when asked about the knowledge of the two candidates in each of three separate issue areas—foreign affairs, economic policy, and education—respondents see a clear difference in foreign affairs, although they see virtually no differences between the candidates in the other two areas. Overall, 63% see Gore as knowing enough about economic policy to make a good president, compared with 65% who say the same about Bush. Similarly, on education, 70% say that Gore knows enough, while 69% say that Bush knows enough. However, in the area of foreign affairs, 58% say that Gore knows enough to be a good president, while only 44% say the same about Bush.

Despite this clear difference in perception about Bush's foreign policy knowledge, the Texas governor continues to lead the vice president among registered voters, 55% to 42%, essentially unchanged from last month. In a hypothetical contest with Bill Bradley, Bush's lead among registered voters is somewhat smaller, at 51% to 45%. Among all Americans, Bush leads Bradley, 52% to 44%, compared with a similar lead of 54% to 39% last October—representing a slight improvement for Bradley over the past two months.

Senator John McCain has gained significant name recognition over the past two months. In October, about one-half of the public did not know enough about the former prisoner of war to rate him; that number has now fallen to 32%, and those who have an opinion of McCain are overwhelmingly positive, by a 57%-to-11% margin. This increased name recognition, however, has not translated into a significant increase in the number of Republicans who would vote for him nationally.

What would happen if Bush falters as the primary season opens next January and he begins to lose primaries to McCain? A hypothetical question included in this weekend's poll asked Republicans that question, and, given those circumstances, 37% of Republicans would vote for Bush, and 34% for McCain, a dramatic narrowing of the race. When the same type of question is asked of Democrats about a situation in which front-runner Al Gore would lose the first primaries to challenger Bill Bradley, the vote remains roughly the same. These responses suggest the possibility that support for Bush could erode rapidly if McCain wins in New Hampshire and continues to win in the primaries that follow.

DECEMBER 27
PRESIDENTIAL PRIMARY TRIAL HEATS

Interviewing Dates: 12/20–21/99
CNN/*USA Today*/Gallup Poll
Survey #GO 129385

Asked of registered Democrats: I'm going to read a list of people who may be running in the Democratic primary for president in the next election. After I read all the names, please tell me which of those candidates you would be most likely to support for the Democratic nomination for president in the year 2000—Bill Bradley, or Al Gore?

	Dec. 20–21, 1999	Dec. 9–12, 1999	Nov. 18–21, 1999
Gore	52%	54%	56%
Bradley	38	39	34
Other (volunteered)	1	*	*
No opinion	9	7	10

*Less than 1%

Selected National Trend
(All Democrats)

	Gore	Bradley	Other	No opinion
1999				
Nov. 18–21	54%	35%	*	11%
Nov. 4–7	58	33	*	9
Oct. 21–24	57	32	*	11

Oct. 8–10	51	39	1	9
Sept. 10–14	63	30	*	7
Aug. 16–18	58	31	1	10
June 25–27	64	28	1	7
June 4–5	63	28	–	9
May 23–24	59	30	–	11
April 30– May 2	66	23	1	10
April 13–14	54	34	1	11

*Less than 1%

Asked of registered Republicans: I'm going to read a list of people who may be running in the Republican primary for president in the next election. After I read all the names, please tell me which of those candidates you would be most likely to support for the Republican nomination for president in the year 2000—former Family Research Council chairman Gary Bauer; Texas Governor George W. Bush; businessman Steve Forbes; Arizona Senator John McCain; Utah Senator Orrin Hatch; or political commentator Alan Keyes?

	Dec. 20–21, 1999	Dec. 9–12, 1999	Nov. 18–21, 1999
G. W. Bush	60%	64%	63%
McCain	17	18	16
Forbes	9	7	6
Keyes	4	4	2
Bauer	2	2	3
Hatch	1	2	4
Other; no opinion	7	3	6

Selected National Trend
(All Republicans)

	G. W. Bush	Mc-Cain	Forbes	Keyes	Bauer*
1999					
Nov. 18–21	63%	16%	6%	1%	4%
Nov. 4–7	68	12	6	2	2
Oct. 21–24	68	11	8	2	1
Oct. 8–10	60	8	4	3	3
Sept. 10–14	62	5	5	1	2
Aug. 16–18	61	5	4	1	2
June 25–27	59	5	6	–	2
June 4–5	46	5	5	–	1
May 23–24	46	6	5	–	2

April 30–

May 2 42   4   6   –   3
April 13–14... 53   5   6   –   2

*Hatch ranges from 1–4 points, June–December; Elizabeth Dole, 8–24 points, April–October; Dan Quayle, 5–9 points, April–September; Pat Buchanan, 3–6 points, April–October; "none," "other," "no opinion"—at 8% or less—are omitted.

Asked of registered voters: If Vice President Al Gore were the Democratic party's candidate and Texas Governor George W. Bush were the Republican party's candidate, whom would you be more likely to vote for— Al Gore, the Democrat, or George W. Bush, the Republican? [Those who were undecided were asked: As of today, do you lean more toward Gore, the Democrat, or Bush, the Republican?]

	Dec. 20–21, 1999	Dec. 9–12, 1999	Nov. 18–21, 1999
Gore	42%	42%	40%
G. W. Bush	53	55	56
Other (volunteered)	*	*	*
No opinion	5	3	4

*Less than 1%

Selected National Trend
(Total Sample)

	Gore	G. W. Bush	Other	No opinion
1999				
Nov. 18–21	39%	56%	*	5%
Nov. 4–7	40	55	*	5
Oct. 21–24	43	52	*	5
Oct. 8–10	40	56	*	4
Sept. 23–26	37	55	*	8
Sept. 10–14	39	56	*	5
Aug. 16–18	41	55	*	4
July 16–18	38	55	*	7
June 25–27	41	56	*	3
June 4–5	40	56	*	4
May 23–24	40	54	*	6
April 30–				
May 2	40	56	*	4
April 13–14	38	59	*	3

March 12–14 ... 41	56	*	3
March 5–7 41	56	*	3
Feb. 19–21 43	54	*	3
Jan. 8–10 47	48	*	5
1998			
May 8–10 46	50	*	4

*Less than 1%

Also asked of registered voters: If former New Jersey Senator Bill Bradley were the Democratic party's candidate and Texas Governor George W. Bush were the Republican party's candidate, whom would you be more likely to vote for—Bill Bradley, the Democrat, or George W. Bush, the Republican? [Those who were undecided were asked: As of today, do you lean more toward Bill Bradley, the Democrat, or George W. Bush, the Republican?]

	Dec. 20–21, 1999	Dec. 9–12, 1999
Bradley	45%	45%
G. W. Bush	50	51
Other (volunteered)	*	1
No opinion	5	3

*Less than 1%

Selected National Trend
(Total Sample)

	Bradley	G. W. Bush	Other	No opinion
1999				
Oct. 21–24	39%	54%	*	7%
Oct. 8–10	42	54	*	4
Sept. 10–14	37	57	*	6
Aug. 16–18	40	55	*	5
April 13–14	34	61	*	5

*Less than 1%

Also asked of registered voters: If Vice President Al Gore were the Democratic party's candidate and Arizona Senator John McCain were the Republican party's candidate, whom would you be more likely to vote for—Vice President Al Gore, the Democrat, or Arizona Senator John McCain, the Republican?

	Dec. 20–21, 1999	Dec. 9–12, 1999
Gore	47%	44%
McCain	47	52
Other (volunteered)	*	*
No opinion	6	4

*Less than 1%

Also asked of registered voters: If former New Jersey Senator Bill Bradley were the Democratic party's candidate and Arizona Senator John McCain were the Republican party's candidate, whom would you be more likely to vote for—former New Jersey Senator Bill Bradley, the Democrat, or Arizona Senator John McCain, the Republican? [Those who were undecided were asked: As of today, do you lean more toward former New Jersey Senator Bill Bradley, or Arizona Senator John McCain?]

Bradley	52%
McCain	39
Other (volunteered)	*
No opinion	9

*Less than 1%

Note: Among registered Democrats across the country, Vice President Al Gore continues to lead former New Jersey Senator Bill Bradley for the presidential nomination by more than a dozen points, but in the general election contest, Bradley fares better than Gore against both Texas Governor George W. Bush and Arizona Senator John McCain. According to a recent Gallup Poll, conducted on December 20–21, Gore receives the support of 52% of registered Democrats for his party's nomination, while Bradley garners 38%. These results are very similar to the support that each candidate received in a Gallup Poll earlier this month but are better for Bradley than in a late November survey, when Gore led by 56% to 34%.

In the past three months, Gore's lead has varied from a low of 12 percentage points (in early October) to a high of 25 points (in late October and early November).

While Gore leads Bradley among Democrats for the nomination, Bradley shows greater electoral strength than Gore in the general election contest. In a hypothetical matchup between Gore and Bush among registered voters nationwide, the Texas governor beats the vice president by 11 points, 53% to 42%. A Bush-Bradley contest, by contrast, shows Bush with a smaller lead of 5 points, 50% to 45%. Against McCain, the difference in the electoral strength between Bradley and Gore is even more pronounced: Gore ties McCain at 47%, while Bradley beats McCain by a 13-point margin, 52% to 39%.

The poll shows that among Republicans, Bush leads McCain by 60% to 17% for their party's nomination, essentially unchanged over the past month. Since Elizabeth Dole dropped out of the race in mid-October, McCain's support has about doubled from the 8% he received then. Bush's support has remained fairly constant, although it surged to 68% in late October and early November, before dropping back to its current level.

Compared with Gore, Bradley fares much better against Bush among younger voters and to a lesser extent among independents, males, Republicans, and voters in the East and Midwest, while performing about as well as Gore among other groups of voters. Among those in the 18–29 age range, Bush beats Gore by a 26-point margin, while Bradley beats Bush by 2 points among the same group of voters—a stunning 28-point swing in support. Bradley also draws somewhat more support than Gore among the 50–64 age group, leading Bush by 5 points (50% to 45%), while Bush beats Gore by 2 points, 48% to 46%. Among the other two age groups, voters who are 30–49 years old and 65 and older, Bradley and Gore fare about the same against Bush, each losing to the Republican candidate by 14 points in the younger group and essentially tying Bush among the older group.

These results also show that while both candidates enjoy about the same electoral support among women, Bradley's electoral strength among men is greater than Gore's. In the Gore-Bush contest, a major gender gap is evident, with

Bush leading Gore among men by 19 points but among women by only 5 points. That gender gap disappears in the Bradley-Bush contest, as Bradley trails among men by 6 points and among women by 4 points. Bradley's relative strength among men may reflect his fame as a professional basketball player earlier in his career.

Similar results are found among independents and voters in the East and Midwest, where Bradley's electoral strength is from 10 points to 14 points greater than Gore's. Among independents, Gore trails Bush by 21 points, while Bradley trails by just 7 points, a pattern that is very similar among southern voters. The same net result, with a somewhat different pattern, is found in the East, where Bradley beats Bush by 11 points, while Gore beats Bush by just 1 point.

Against Bush, Bradley enjoys a net electoral advantage over Gore of just 6 points, trailing Bush by 5 points compared with Gore's 11-point deficit. Against McCain, however, Bradley's net electoral advantage over Gore is 13 points—as Bradley beats McCain by 13 points, while Gore ties the Arizona senator. Bradley's greater electoral strength is found about equally among men and women, and also, although unequally, among all party identifiers, among three of the four age groups, and in all regions of the country.

The groups showing the largest differences in Bradley's and Gore's electoral strength against McCain are the 18–29-year-old voters, Republicans, and eastern voters. Young voters split evenly between Gore and McCain at 47%, but they give Bradley a 24-point lead, 58% to 34%. Similarly, eastern voters support Gore over McCain by 4 points, 49% to 45%, but they support Bradley over McCain by 33 points, 63% to 30%. Bradley even appeals to a substantial number of Republicans, with 24% voting for him over McCain, while Gore draws only 14% of the Republican vote. The net effect is a McCain lead among Republicans of 70 points over Gore, but just 46 points over Bradley. The former New Jersey senator also fares better than Gore against McCain among independents and among Democrats, although the margins are not as substantial.

Business and the Economy

APRIL 15
INCOME TAX

Interviewing Dates: 4/6–7/99
CNN/*USA Today*/Gallup Poll
Survey #GO 127360

Do you consider the amount of federal income tax you have to pay as too high, about right, or too low?

Too high	65%
About right	29
Too low	2
No opinion	4

	Too high	About right	Too low	No opinion
By Politics				
Republicans	72%	25%	1%	2%
Democrats	60	33	2	5
Independents	64	29	3	4

Do you regard the income tax which you will have to pay this year as fair?

Yes, fair	45%
Not fair	49
No opinion	6

	Yes, fair	Not fair	No opinion
By Politics			
Republicans	36%	59%	5%
Democrats	52	42	6
Independents	45	48	7

As I read off some different groups, please tell me if you think they are paying their fair share in federal taxes, paying too much, or paying too little:

Lower-income people?

Fair share	34%
Too much	51
Too little	11
No opinion	4

	Fair share	Too much	Too little	No opinion
By Politics				
Republicans	36%	44%	15%	5%
Democrats	33	57	7	3
Independents	33	51	13	3

Middle-income people?

Fair share	35%
Too much	59
Too little	4
No opinion	2

	Fair share	Too much	Too little	No opinion
By Politics				
Republicans.....	32%	62%	4%	2%
Democrats.......	37	55	5	3
Independents ...	35	60	2	3

Upper-income people?

Fair share	19%
Too much...	10
Too little	66
No opinion...	5

	Fair share	Too much	Too little	No opinion
By Politics				
Republicans.....	19%	20%	58%	3%
Democrats.......	17	3	75	5
Independents ...	19	9	66	6

Did or will you or your family pay for the help of an outside tax specialist or firm this year to do your taxes, or not?

Yes..	56%
No	39
Doesn't apply (volunteered)............................	3
No opinion..	2

Are you planning to or did you already send your tax return to the IRS by mail, or electronically by computer?

Mail	66%
Electronically..	20
Not sure (volunteered)....................................	4
Other (volunteered); no opinion	10

Note: A Gallup Poll conducted in advance of this year's April 15 tax due day finds two in three Americans harboring concerns that the federal income tax that they have to pay is too high. Overall, 65% say that their tax bill is too high compared to just 2% who say that it is too low, and 29% who consider it about right. The sentiment that taxes are too high is largely uniform across all income groups in American society, ex-

cept that those in low-income households are somewhat less likely to feel overtaxed. However, even a majority of those making less than $20,000 per year consider their taxes too high.

Despite the widespread sentiment that their tax burden is too high, respondents are almost evenly divided over whether or not the income taxes they will pay this year are fair. While two-thirds indicate that they pay too much in taxes, barely one-half (49%) think that the amount they have to pay this year is unfair, while nearly as many (45%) say fair.

The issue of fairness clearly divides income groups. The perception that the amount of taxes one pays is not fair generally increases along with household income; agreement with this statement ranges from 44% of those in households earning less than $20,000 to 63% among Americans with annual incomes of $75,000 or more. Only 36% of those in this high-income group believe that their taxes are fair. At the same time, when Gallup asks whether people in each of three income groups are paying their fair share in taxes, "upper-income" Americans are charged by two-thirds of the public with paying too little. By contrast, a majority of respondents thinks that lower-income as well as middle-income Americans are paying too much in taxes.

Interestingly, the data suggest that most people earning $75,000 or more per year do not consider themselves to be in the upper-income group, even though their income puts them into the top 15% of those polled. While roughly two-thirds of this group say that the amount of their own income taxes is too high and unfair, more than one-half (55%) believe that "upper-income people" pay too little in taxes, thus suggesting that they think the question must be referring to people making more than themselves.

APRIL 23
INVESTORS AND SOCIAL SECURITY

Interviewing Dates: 3/1–17/99
CNN/*USA Today*/Gallup Poll
Special survey*

The following questions were asked of investors with at least $10,000 in investable assets:

*PaineWebber/Gallup Index of Investor Optimism

Based on what you know about the Social Security system today, what would you like Congress and the president to do during this next year—completely overhaul the system, make some major changes, make some minor adjustments, or leave the system the way it is now?

Overhaul system 19%
Make major changes 39
Make minor adjustments 30
Leave system the way it is now 11
No opinion 1

One proposal for Social Security is to take about a third of the Social Security tax now paid by a worker and employer and put that money into an individual savings account for retirement. Would you favor or oppose such a proposal?

Favor 68%
Oppose 28
No opinion 4

Let us suppose for a moment that part of the Social Security tax is put into an individual savings account for each worker, with the money invested in the stock market. Which of the following would you most like to see happen—all workers would have the funds managed by the federal government, or all workers would manage their own funds?

Managed by government 21%
Would manage own funds 73
Other (volunteered) 5
No opinion 1

If individual savings accounts are created by the federal government, using part of the Social Security taxes as just described, what would you, personally, prefer—to manage your own individual savings account, or to have your individual savings account managed by the federal government?

Manage your own account 89%
Have account managed by government 10
Other (volunteered); no opinion 1

If individual savings accounts are created, what comes closer to your point of view about how the money can be used—workers should be allowed to use the money for home mortgages and education, as well as retirement; or workers should be allowed to use the money only for retirement?

For mortgages and education 32%
Only for retirement 65
Other (volunteered) 2
No opinion 1

Note: Most investors are concerned about the current state of the Social Security system and would support a proposal to divert some of their Social Security taxes into a private retirement account, according to the March PaineWebber/Gallup Index of Investor Optimism, a monthly poll of investors with at least $10,000 in investable assets. The poll also indicates that if personal retirement accounts are established, most investors would prefer to personally manage them rather than have them managed by the federal government. And they would restrict use of the account funds to retirement only, not allowing the money to be used for mortgages and education expenses.

Overall, 58% of all investors say either that the Social Security system should be completely overhauled or that it should be changed in a major way, while only 41% say that no more than minor changes are needed. These views vary considerably by age, with investors under 30 much more critical of the Social Security system than are older investors. More than eight in ten (81%) of the youngest group of investors, age 18 to 29, say that at least major changes are needed, compared with 67% who think that way among investors in the 30-to-49 age group, 51% among investors 50 to 64, and just 39% among those 65 and older.

Younger investors are also more likely to support a proposal that would take one-third of the Social Security taxes now paid by workers and employers and invest these funds into individual savings accounts for retirement. Among all investors, 68% favor such a proposal; among the youngest group, however, support is much higher (84%) than among the oldest group (52%).

MAY 18
INVESTORS AND THE INTERNET

Interviewing Dates: 3/1–17/99
CNN/*USA Today*/Gallup Poll
Special survey*

The following questions were asked of investors with at least $10,000 in investable assets:

Do you ever get onto the Internet through a computer or Web TV?

Yes.. 59%
No 41

Have you ever bought anything on the Internet?

	All investors	Internet users
Yes	28%	47%
No	31	53
Don't use the Internet	41	–

Have you ever used the Internet to look for any type of financial or investing information?

	All investors	Internet users
Yes	37%	63%
No	22	37
Don't use the Internet	41	–

Have you ever used the Internet to conduct any trading in the financial markets?

	All investors	Internet users
Yes	8%	13%
No	51	87
Don't use the Internet	41	–

Have you ever invested in any Internet companies?

Yes.. 15%
No 82
No opinion.. 3

*PaineWebber/Gallup Index of Investor Optimism

Asked of those who have ever invested in Internet companies: In what year did you first invest in an Internet company?

Before 1995 .... 12%
1995 6
1996 13
1997 19
1998 36
1999 14

Also asked of those who have ever invested in Internet companies: Are you currently invested in one or more Internet companies?

Yes.. 88%
No 11
No opinion.. 1

Also asked of those who have ever invested in Internet companies: Did you invest in Internet companies as part of a long-term or a short-term strategy?

Long-term.. 62%
Short-term.. 30
Other (volunteered) 8

Also asked of those who have ever invested in Internet companies: Compared to most investments, how well have your investments in Internet companies done—would you say much higher than average, somewhat higher than average, about average, somewhat lower than average, or much lower than average?

Much higher than average 40%
Somewhat higher than average....................... 23
About average... 24
Somewhat lower than average....................... 5
Much lower than average 6
No opinion.. 2

Asked of those who have ever invested in Internet companies but are not currently invested: How likely are you to invest in Internet companies in the future—very likely, moderately likely, slightly likely, not at all likely, or are you unsure at this time?

Very likely	8%
Moderately likely	13
Slightly likely	22
Not at all likely	40
Unsure	17

Asked of those who have ever invested in Internet companies: Overall, compared to investing in other common stocks, do you think that investing in selected Internet companies is much more risky, somewhat more risky, about the same risk, somewhat less risky, or much less risky?

Much more risky	25%
Somewhat more risky	37
About the same risk	23
Somewhat less risky	8
Much less risky	1
Don't know	6

Also asked of those who have ever invested in Internet companies: Again, compared to the return one can get from investing in other common stocks, do you think that the percentage return from investing in selected Internet companies is much higher, somewhat higher, about the same, somewhat lower, or much lower?

Much higher	16%
Somewhat higher	30
About the same	30
Somewhat lower	10
Much lower	3
Don't know	11

Asked of those currently invested in Internet companies: Approximately what percentage of your portfolio is invested in Internet stocks?

0 to 4%	12%
5 to 9%	18
10 to 14%	19
15 to 19%	5
20 to 24%	9
25 to 29%	7
30% or more	17
Don't know	13

Here are some reasons why some people invest in Internet companies. Please tell me if that is a reason why you invested in such companies—you expected a much higher return than what you might have gotten from other investments; you knew about the companies whose stocks you bought; you had read or heard a lot about the companies in the news media; or someone recommended that you invest in Internet companies?

	Yes
Expected higher return	78%
Knew about companies	81
Read or heard about companies	70
Recommended to you	58

Asked of those who received a recommendation: Who recommended that you invest in Internet companies—was it a financial advisor, a family member or relative, a colleague at work, or a friend but not at work?

	Yes
Financial advisor	59%
Family member or relative	37
Colleague at work	28
Friend but not at work	40

Note: About six in ten investors (59%) have ever accessed the Internet, but only about one in four (28%) have ever bought anything on the Internet, and fewer still (8%) have ever used it to conduct trades. Given the little experience and familiarity that investors have with companies that sell over the Internet, it is not surprising that only 15% have invested in stocks of Internet companies. Among investors who have traded on the Internet, 4% have invested in stocks of Internet companies.

As might be expected, younger investors are much more likely to have used the Internet than are older ones: eight in ten investors (79%) under the age of 50, and just over one-half (54%) in the preretirement years of 51 to 64, but only one in six (17%) age 65 or older have used the Internet. The poll also shows that better-educated investors are much more likely to have used the Internet than are other investors: about three in four investors who are college graduates (72%) and six in seven who have done postgraduate work (86%); almost half (47%) who have done some college work have used the Internet, and only one-third (33%) who have a high-school education or less have used it.

JUNE 2
MICROSOFT ANTITRUST TRIAL

Interviewing Dates: 3/30–31/99
CNN/*USA Today*/Gallup Poll
Survey #GO 127287

Thinking about Microsoft, the computer software company that produces Windows 95 and other products, do you have a favorable or unfavorable opinion of the Microsoft Corporation?

Favorable	60%
Unfavorable	14
Other (volunteered); no opinion	26

By Politics	Favorable	Un-favorable	Other; no opinion
Republicans	70%	10%	20%
Democrats	55	16	29
Independents	59	14	27

Selected National Trend

	Favorable	Un-favorable	Other; no opinion
1999			
February 26–28	58%	16%	26%
February 8–9	66	16	18

Now thinking about Bill Gates, the founder and CEO of Microsoft, do you have a favorable or unfavorable opinion of Bill Gates?

Favorable	59%
Unfavorable	18
Other (volunteered); no opinion	23

By Politics	Favorable	Un-favorable	Other; no opinion
Republicans	65%	14%	21%
Democrats	53	21	26
Independents	61	17	22

Selected National Trend

	Favorable	Un-favorable	Other; no opinion
1999			
February 26–28	62%	16%	22%
February 8–9	66	18	16

As you may know, a lawsuit by the Justice Department against Microsoft is currently being tried in court. Based on what you know about the case, do you side more with the Justice Department, or with the Microsoft Corporation?

Justice Department	26%
Microsoft Corporation	42
Both; mixed (volunteered)	2
Neither (volunteered)	4
No opinion	26

By Politics	Justice Department	Microsoft Corporation	Both; mixed; neither; no opinion
Republicans	28%	47%	25%
Democrats	28	35	37
Independents	23	44	33

Interviewing Dates: 2/26–28/99
CNN/*USA Today*/Gallup Poll
Survey #GO 126888

Overall, do you think that Microsoft has had more of a positive impact on the computer industry, or more of a negative impact on the computer industry?

	Feb. 26–28, 1999	March 6–9, 1998
More of a positive impact	80%	75%

More of a negative impact............	8	8
Neither (volunteered)....................	3	3
No opinion	9	14

Just your opinion, is Microsoft a monopoly, or not?

	Feb. 26–28, 1999	March 6–9, 1998
Yes..	49%	43%
No	38	41
No opinion	13	16

Note: While many computer industry leaders and the U.S. Justice Department would like to see the power and dominance of computer software giant Microsoft curtailed, a majority of Americans believe that Microsoft's clout has been good for the computer industry, and a plurality take Microsoft's side in its highly publicized lawsuit with the Department.

That trial has resumed in U.S. District Court in Washington, DC, after a thirteen-week recess, during which attorneys for both sides were unable to reach a settlement. To the extent that they have an opinion, Gallup polling over the last several months has shown that the public tends to side with the Microsoft Corporation in the case. Only about one in four takes the government's side, while 42% take Microsoft's position that it has not tried to unfairly drive competitors out of business. Among computer users, 47% agree with Microsoft's position. Support for that position generally runs consistently along age, race, and political lines, with slight increases shown for the government's case among blacks, liberals, and women. Despite the fact that Microsoft has been embroiled in the case for more than a year, there was no sign that the trial had affected the image of the company among the public up to the time when the trial was put on hold in March.

JUNE 16
THE ECONOMY

Interviewing Dates: 6/4–5/99
CNN/*USA Today*/Gallup Poll
Survey #GO 127853

How would you rate economic conditions in this country today—as excellent, good, only fair, or poor?

Excellent...	18%
Good	56
Only fair	21
Poor	5
No opinion	*

*Less than 1%

	Excellent	Good	Only fair	Poor*
By Sex				
Male	22%	56%	17%	5%
Female.............	13	57	24	6
By Ethnic Background				
White..............	18	57	20	5
Nonwhite.........	16	50	26	8
Black	14	50	28	8
By Education				
Postgraduate....	29	56	10	5
College Graduate......	25	62	10	3
College Incomplete...	19	58	20	3
No College	12	54	26	7
By Region				
East.................	14	62	16	8
Midwest	20	58	20	2
South	18	52	22	7
West	20	53	24	3
By Age				
18–29 Years	16	58	21	5
30–49 Years	14	57	23	6
50–64 Years	28	52	18	2
65 Years and Over......	18	58	16	7
By Household Income				
$75,000 and Over......	31	58	9	2
$50,000 and Over......	26	60	12	2

	Excellent	Good	Only fair	Poor*
$30,000–$49,999	17	59	20	4
$20,000–$29,999	11	60	22	6
Under $20,000	9	45	35	11

By Politics

Republicans	17	55	23	5
Democrats	22	59	14	4
Independents	14	55	24	7

By Political Ideology

Conservative	17	54	23	6
Moderate	18	58	20	4
Liberal	21	60	13	6

*"No opinion"—at 1% or less—is omitted.

Selected National Trend

	Excellent	Good	Only fair	Poor*
1999				
Jan. 15–17	14%	55%	27%	4%
1998				
Dec. 4–6	13	52	27	8
Oct. 29–Nov. 1	13	53	27	6
Sept. 1	11	54	25	9
Mar. 20–22	20	46	27	7
1997				
Dec. 18–21	7	41	38	12
Nov. 6–9	10	48	33	9
Aug. 22–25**	8	41	38	13
May 6–7	7	39	38	15
Jan. 31–Feb. 2	4	38	43	15
1996				
Oct. 26–29	5	42	39	13
Aug. 30–Sept. 1	3	34	46	16
July 18–21	5	38	43	14
May 9–12	3	27	50	19
April 9–10	1	26	52	20
Mar. 15–17	2	31	48	18
Jan. 5–7	1	28	47	23
1995				
Nov. 6–8	2	28	47	22
May 11–14	2	27	50	20
1994				
Dec. 16–18	2	25	52	21
Nov. 2–6	2	28	49	20
Oct. 22–25	1	25	52	21
July 15–17	1	26	52	21
April 22–24	1	23	49	26
Jan. 15–17	†	22	54	24
1993				
Dec. 4–6	1	20	57	21
Nov. 2–4	1	16	50	33
Aug. 8–10	†	10	49	40
June 29–30	1	14	52	32
Feb. 12–14	†	14	46	39
1992				
Dec. 18–20	2	16	34	47
Dec. 4–6	1	14	41	43
Oct. 23–25	†	11	45	43
Sept. 11–15	1	10	37	51
Aug. 31–Sept. 2‡	1	9	37	53
June 12–14‡	1	11	47	41
April 9–12‡	1	11	40	48
Jan. 3–6	†	12	46	41

*"No opinion"—at 2% or less—is omitted.
**Based on half sample
†Less than 1%
‡Asked of registered voters

Note: According to a new Gallup Poll, Americans are feeling more positive today about the state of the U.S. economy than they have in the eight years that Gallup's economic confidence measure has been tracked. Three-quarters (74%) now say that economic conditions in the United States are excellent or good, up 5 points from January of this year. The latest rise represents a continuation of the "good times" economic trends that Gallup has seen since March of last year when the percentage giving the economy high ratings reached 66%. In all Gallup Polls prior to that, with one exception, less than one-half of the public viewed the economy in positive terms.

Just as most Americans feel that the economy is now doing well, they also express highly optimistic sentiments about their own finances. More than one-half of the public (57%) say that they are financially better off today than they were a year ago, and an even higher proportion (67%) expect to be better off next year. By contrast, less than one quarter (22%) are worse off this year compared to 1998, and only 17% think that they will be worse off next year.

Gallup computes a personal finances confidence score; the June 1999 score is 85 points, out of a possible high score of 200. The score is computed by adding the percentage who rate their finances as "better" on each of the two personal finances questions and subtracting the percentage who say "worse."

The current score of 85 is close to the highest score ever achieved on this measure, which was 97 points in March 1998. The lowest scores (ranging from –8 to –13) were recorded in 1979 and the early 1980s, during an economic recession that spanned Jimmy Carter's final year as president and the first half of Ronald Reagan's first term. Public perceptions of personal finances rebounded in the mid-1980s, and the score reached 55 in 1984. In 1988, shortly before George Bush was elected to succeed Reagan, the score soared to 77. While high throughout most of Bush's presidency, personal financial confidence plummeted in January 1992 to 10. At the same time, public confidence in the economy was extremely low, with only 12% rating it excellent or good, and 87% considering it only fair or poor.

These positive feelings about the economy and personal finances seem to be shared by most major groups in American society, including men and women, young and old, white and nonwhite. Even a majority of respondents living in households with relatively low incomes give the economy high marks and are optimistic about their finances, saying that they expect to be financially better off next year.

JULY 21
TAX CUTS VS. MEDICARE AND SOCIAL SECURITY

Interviewing Dates: 7/16–18/99
CNN/*USA Today*/Gallup Poll
Survey #GO 128287

> As I read a list of issues being discussed today, please tell me how important each of the following is to your vote for Congress in

November—is it extremely important to your vote for Congress, very important, somewhat important, or not important:

Health care, including HMOs?

	July 16–18, 1999	Sept. 23–24, 1998
Extremely important	32%	28%
Very important	47	43
Somewhat important	15	21
Not important	5	5
No opinion	1	3

July 16–18, 1999

	Extremely important	Very important	Somewhat important	Not important*
By Politics				
Republicans	26%	41%	26%	7%
Democrats	38	47	10	3
Independents	31	51	12	5

*"No opinion"—at 2% or less—is omitted.

Tax cuts?

	July 16–18, 1999	Sept. 23–24, 1998
Extremely important	22%	21%
Very important	38	39
Somewhat important	30	29
Not important	9	9
No opinion	1	2

July 16–18, 1999

	Extremely important	Very important	Somewhat important	Not important*
By Politics				
Republicans	23%	38%	34%	5%
Democrats	22	38	27	11
Independents	22	39	29	10

*"No opinion"—at 2% or less—is omitted.

Social Security?

	July 16–18, 1999	Sept. 23–24, 1998
Extremely important	33%	33%
Very important	51	42

Somewhat important...................... 12	20
Not important................................. 3	4
No opinion.................................... 1	1

July 16–18, 1999

	Extremely important	Very important	Somewhat important	Not important*
By Politics				
Republicans.....	30%	49%	18%	3%
Democrats.......	38	53	6	3
Independents...	32	50	12	4

*"No opinion"—at 2% or less—is omitted.

Medicare?

Extremely important....................................... 31%
Very important 47
Somewhat important...................................... 19
Not important 2
No opinion.. 1

	Extremely important	Very important	Somewhat important	Not important*
By Politics				
Republicans.....	25%	43%	29%	3%
Democrats.......	37	50	11	1
Independents...	31	48	17	3

*"No opinion"—at 1% or less—is omitted.

Gun control?

Extremely important....................................... 29%
Very important 32
Somewhat important...................................... 20
Not important 18
No opinion.. 1

	Extremely important	Very important	Somewhat important	Not important*
By Politics				
Republicans.....	24%	31%	23%	22%
Democrats.......	40	33	15	11
Independents...	25	32	21	20

*"No opinion"—at 2% or less—is omitted.

Campaign finance reform?

Extremely important....................................... 15%
Very important 25
Somewhat important....................................... 36
Not important 20
No opinion.. 4

	Extremely important	Very important	Somewhat important	Not important*
By Politics				
Republicans.....	14%	25%	39%	20%
Democrats.......	16	28	40	14
Independents...	16	22	32	24

*"No opinion"—at 6% or less—is omitted.

When it comes to dealing with the tough choices involved both in cutting taxes and still maintaining needed federal programs, whose approach do you prefer—the Republicans in Congress or President Clinton's?

Republicans 40%
President Clinton's 48
Neither (volunteered) 5
Both (volunteered)... 1
No opinion.. 6

	Republicans	President Clinton's	Neither	Both*
By Politics				
Republicans.....	82%	12%	1%	1%
Democrats.......	6	86	2	1
Independents...	35	46	10	1

*"No opinion"—at 8% or less—is omitted.

Form A. As you may know, the federal government is currently running a budget surplus, meaning it is taking in more money than it spends. President Clinton and the Republicans in Congress both plan to use much of the surplus money for Social Security, but they disagree over what to do with the rest. How would you prefer to see the rest of the budget surplus used—to increase spending on education, defense, Medicare, and other programs; or to cut taxes?

Increase spending 61%
Cut taxes 33
Neither; other (volunteered) 5
No opinion 1

	Increase spending	Cut taxes	Neither; other	No opinion
By Politics				
Republicans.....	47%	47%	5%	1%
Democrats	74	22	2	2
Independents ...	60	32	8	*

*Less than 1%

Form B. *As you may know, the federal government is currently running a budget surplus, meaning it is taking in more money than it spends. President Clinton and the Republicans in Congress both plan to use much of the surplus money for Social Security, but they disagree over what to do with the rest. How would you prefer to see the rest of the budget surplus used—to increase spending on other government programs, or to cut taxes?*

Increase spending 28%
Cut taxes 64
Neither; other (volunteered) 7
No opinion 1

	Increase spending	Cut taxes	Neither; other	No opinion
By Politics				
Republicans.....	17%	75%	7%	1%
Democrats	34	59	6	1
Independents ...	31	60	8	1

Form A. *As you may know, Congress and Clinton are debating the amount of money to use for tax cuts and funding necessary to preserve current Medicare programs. If you had to choose, which combination would you prefer—a larger tax cut and smaller increases in spending on Medicare, or a smaller tax cut and larger increases in spending on Medicare?*

Larger tax cut, smaller increases
  in Medicare 28%
Smaller tax cut, larger increases in
  Medicare 69
Other (volunteered) 2
No opinion 1

	Larger tax cut	Smaller tax cut	Other	No opinion
By Politics				
Republicans.....	39%	56%	1%	4%
Democrats	17	82	1	*
Independents ...	29	68	2	1

*Less than 1%

Form B. *As you may know, Congress and Clinton are debating over the amount of money to use for tax cuts and funding to create new Medicare programs. If you had to choose, which combination would you prefer—a larger tax cut and smaller increases in spending on Medicare, or a smaller tax cut and larger increases in spending on Medicare?*

Larger tax cut, smaller increases
  in Medicare 32%
Smaller tax cut, larger increases
  in Medicare 66
Other (volunteered) 1
No opinion 1

	Larger tax cut	Smaller tax cut	Other	No opinion
By Politics				
Republicans.....	50%	47%	2%	1%
Democrats	15	83	1	1
Independents ...	30	66	2	2

Whom do you think the Republicans in Congress are most interested in benefiting with their proposed tax cuts—the rich, the middle class, or both about equally?

Rich 51%
Middle class.. 13
Both equally 30
Neither (volunteered) 1
No opinion 5

	Rich	Middle class	Both equally	Neither*
By Politics				
Republicans.....	27%	22%	44%	2%
Democrats.......	73	5	19	**
Independents...	51	13	29	1

*"No opinion"—at 6% or less—is omitted.
**Less than 1%

Whom do you think the Democrats in Congress are most interested in benefiting with their proposed tax cuts—the rich, the middle class, or both about equally?

Rich	26%
Middle class..	33
Both equally	32
Neither (volunteered)	3
No opinion..	6

	Rich	Middle class	Both equally	Neither*
By Politics				
Republicans.....	29%	32%	26%	7%
Democrats.......	16	44	37	1
Independents...	32	26	31	2

*"No opinion"—at 9% or less—is omitted.

Note: In the current congressional debate over the federal budget, both Republicans and Democrats have agreed to use much of the anticipated budget surplus to keep the Social Security program solvent, but the two parties disagree on how to spend the rest. A new Gallup Poll suggests that the public is more likely to prefer the general approach of President Bill Clinton and the Democrats over the approach of the Republicans for spending the excess surplus.

While Republican leaders in Congress are calling for substantial tax cuts, Clinton is proposing new spending on Medicare and much smaller tax cuts. When asked what they prefer—to increase spending on education, defense, Medicare, and other programs or to cut taxes—respondents choose increased spending on those programs by a 61%-to-33% margin. Still, there is substantial support for tax cuts if the alternative is just "to increase spending on other government programs," with no mention in the question wording of any specific program. In this situation, respondents choose the tax cuts over increased spending by 64% to 28%. When Medicare, education, and defense are specifically mentioned, as noted above, the percentages are essentially reversed.

A slightly different question in the poll focused just on Medicare versus tax cuts, asking whether respondents would prefer a larger tax cut and smaller increases in spending on Medicare, or smaller tax cuts and larger increases in spending on Medicare. By about a 2-to-1 majority, they choose the latter approach. It is noteworthy that this 2-to-1 margin holds true whether the option is for increased spending either to *preserve current* Medicare programs, or to *create new* Medicare programs. In both cases, the public widely prefers the larger increases in spending accompanied by smaller tax cuts, rather than the larger tax cuts and smaller increases in spending.

These results are consistent with the priority that respondents assign to several issues before Congress. When they are asked to rate the importance of the issues to their next vote for Congress, 84% rate Social Security as very/extremely important, followed closely by health care (79%) and Medicare (78%). Farther down the priority list are gun control and tax cuts, each considered important by about six in ten, while last among the six issues rated is campaign finance reform (40%).

AUGUST 26
INCOME/PAY RAISES

Interviewing Dates: 8/16–18/99
CNN/*USA Today*/Gallup Poll
Survey #GO 128524

During the next twelve months, do you expect your income to go up more than prices go up, about the same, or less than prices go up?

More	20%
Same	43
Less..	34
No opinion..	3

Selected National Trend

	More	Same	Less	No opinion
May 1994	14%	45%	39%	2%
November 1984	17	41	35	7
November 1983	14	46	33	7
December 1982	12	37	44	7
December 1981	11	32	50	7
May 1980	7	30	55	8
April 1978	9	32	54	5

Asked of workers who are not self-employed: Do you expect to receive a pay raise from your employer in the next twelve months?

Yes..	75%
No	22
No opinion	3

Asked of those who replied in the affirmative: Do you think the pay raise you receive in the next twelve months will be larger, about the same, or smaller than the last pay raise you received?

Larger	26%
About the same	56
Smaller..	17
No opinion	1

Pay Raise Summary

Larger than last year	26%
About the same as last year	49
Smaller than last year	24
No opinion	1

Note: This week the Federal Reserve Board raised two short-term interest rates, the federal funds rate and the discount rate, in a reported effort to "diminish the risk of inflation." One fear was that in the current robust labor market with workers in short supply, the demand for higher wages could push up inflation. But a new Gallup Poll, which asked workers themselves what level of raises they expect to receive, suggests that overall wage increases this year may be about the same as last year.

Among those workers employed either part-time or full-time (excluding all self-employed), 26% expect to receive higher raises this year than they received last year, while almost the same number (24%) expect to receive lower raises. Another 49% of workers expect to receive raises that are about the same as last year's. This number includes those who received no raises last year and expect none this year as well.

The pattern of these expectations is similar for both full-time and part-time workers. In both cases, the percentage expecting a higher raise than last year is roughly equal to the percentage expecting a lower raise. Among full-time workers, 28% expect higher raises and 25% lower raises, with 46% expecting no change. Among part-time workers, 14% expect higher raises and 16% lower raises, while 69% expect no change. These results suggest that, at least from the workers' perspective, there is on balance no anticipation of significant salary or wage increases this year.

It should be noted that these results do not address the size of the wage increases, just the proportion of workers who expect such increases. Still, workers with family incomes greater than $50,000 per year are no more likely to expect higher raises this year compared to last year than are workers with family incomes in the $20,000 to $50,000 range. However, workers with family incomes of less than $20,000 per year are considerably less likely to expect higher raises. In the highest income category, 28% of all workers expect a higher raise this year than last, while 23% expect a lower raise. In the middle income category, the comparable figures are 28% higher and 24% lower. However, in the under $20,000 per year category, the numbers show only 18% expecting higher raises, with 25% expecting lower raises.

SEPTEMBER 3
JOB SATISFACTION

Interviewing Dates: 8/24–26/99
CNN/*USA Today*/Gallup Poll
Survey #GO 907169

Which of the following best describes your current situation—employed full-time, employed part-time, retired, a homemaker, a student, unemployed but looking for work, or unemployed and not looking for work?

Employed full-time.. 54%
Employed part-time.. 7
Retired 20
Homemaker 8
Student... 4
Unemployed but looking for work 4
Unemployed and not looking for work 2
Disabled (volunteered) 1
No opinion.. *

*Less than 1%

Asked of those employed full-time or part-time: How satisfied or dissatisfied are you with your job—would you say you are completely satisfied, somewhat satisfied, somewhat dissatisfied, or completely dissatisfied with your job?

	Aug. 24–26, 1999	Aug. 22–25, 1997	July 18-21, 1989
Completely satisfied...	39%	35%	28%
Somewhat satisfied.....	47	51	61
Somewhat dissatisfied..............	12	10	8
Completely dissatisfied..............	2	3	3
No opinion..................	*	1	*

*Less than 1%

Also asked of those employed full-time or part-time: Now I'll read a list of job characteristics. For each one, please tell me how satisfied or dissatisfied you are with your current job in this regard—are you completely satisfied, somewhat satisfied, somewhat dissatisfied, or completely dissatisfied with:

Your relations with co-workers?

Completely satisfied....................................... 67%
Somewhat satisfied... 27
Not satisfied.. 3
No opinion... 3

Physical safety conditions of your workplace?

Completely satisfied....................................... 63%
Somewhat satisfied... 28
Not satisfied.. 8
No opinion... 1

Flexibility of your hours?

Completely satisfied....................................... 56%
Somewhat satisfied... 31
Not satisfied.. 13
No opinion... *

*Less than 1%

Amount of vacation time you receive?

Completely satisfied....................................... 50%
Somewhat satisfied... 30
Not satisfied.. 18
No opinion... 2

Your job security?

Completely satisfied....................................... 48%
Somewhat satisfied... 33
Not satisfied.. 18
No opinion... 1

Your boss or immediate supervisor?

Completely satisfied....................................... 47%
Somewhat satisfied... 35
Not satisfied.. 11
No opinion... 7

Amount of work required of you?

Completely satisfied....................................... 46%
Somewhat satisfied... 35
Not satisfied.. 18
No opinion... 1

Opportunity you have to learn and grow?

Completely satisfied....................................... 43%
Somewhat satisfied... 38
Not satisfied.. 18
No opinion... 1

Recognition you receive at work for your accomplishments?

Completely satisfied	38%
Somewhat satisfied	35
Not satisfied	25
No opinion	2

Family and medical leave benefits your employer provides?

Completely satisfied	38%
Somewhat satisfied	32
Not satisfied	19
No opinion	11

Health insurance benefits your employer offers?

Completely satisfied	33%
Somewhat satisfied	30
Not satisfied	28
No opinion	9

Your chances for promotion?

Completely satisfied	32%
Somewhat satisfied	32
Not satisfied	27
No opinion	9

Retirement plan your employer offers?

Completely satisfied	31%
Somewhat satisfied	30
Not satisfied	29
No opinion	10

Amount of money you earn?

Completely satisfied	23%
Somewhat satisfied	47
Not satisfied	30
No opinion	*

*Less than 1%

Amount of on-the-job stress you have?

Completely satisfied	21%
Somewhat satisfied	44
Not satisfied	34
No opinion	1

Also asked of those employed full-time or part-time: Which of the following best describes your job—are you an employee of a private company or business, a government employee, or self-employed in your own business or professional practice?

	Aug. 24–26, 1999	July 18–21, 1989
Private employee	66%	62%
Government employee	16	23
Self-employed	17	14
Other (volunteered)	1	–
No opinion	*	1

*Less than 1%

Also asked of those employed full-time or part-time: Overall, which of the following descriptions best fits the way you see yourself at work—a high achiever, workaholic, a solid performer who does what is expected of you, or an underachiever who gets by with the minimum necessary to keep your job?

High achiever, workaholic	44%
Solid performer	56
Underachiever	*
No opinion	*

*Less than 1%

Note: American workers will likely be enjoying their time off for the Labor Day holiday, but not because they dislike their jobs. According to a new Gallup survey conducted on August 24–26, nearly nine in ten employed adults age 18 and older are generally satisfied with their current jobs. However, workers fall short of expressing total enthusiasm. Only 39% are completely satisfied with their jobs, while another 47% are somewhat satisfied, and 14% indicate that they are dissatisfied.

The Gallup survey provides some clues as to why workers are less than fully satisfied. When probed about specific aspects of their jobs, respondents seem to consider themselves hardworking, stressed, underpaid, and underappreciated. Forty-four percent of workers describe themselves as "workaholics," and another 56% as "solid performers," but fewer than four in ten are completely satisfied with their pay, the degree of recognition that they receive at work, or the amount of on-the-job stress that they endure.

Not surprisingly, then, the poll finds that most full-time and part-time employees (77%) enjoy the time that they spend away from their jobs more than the hours spent working. This is particularly true among high-income workers who, presumably, have greater financial means to do the things that they enjoy most when not at their jobs.

The most satisfied workers are those who are self-employed in their own business or professional practice. Nearly three in five in this group (58%) say that they are completely satisfied with their jobs. Satisfaction also correlates with age, rising from 29% among 18–29-year-old workers, to 39% among those 30–49 years, and 49% among the 50-years-and-older group.

The impact of income on job satisfaction is mostly seen at the lower end of the income spectrum. The percentage of workers in households earning $75,000 per year or more who are completely satisfied with their jobs is 47%. That figure is 42% among those making $30,000–$74,999, but just 24% among those earning less than $30,000.

Beyond overall job satisfaction, Gallup focused on fifteen specific aspects of employment in the new Labor Day survey that covered a variety of work conditions, human interrelations, and financial benefits. A majority of workers are at least somewhat satisfied with all of the items measured, but the percentage who are completely satisfied falls short of a majority in most cases. Of all the items rated, employees are most satisfied with their relations with their co-workers; 67% say that they are completely satisfied with this aspect of their jobs. More than half of all workers also report high satisfaction with the physical safety of their workplace, the flexibility of their hours, and the amount of vacation time. The general satisfaction in these areas could be driven either by good working conditions or by relatively low (or perhaps reasonable) expectations.

By contrast, workers are the least satisfied with the amount of on-the-job stress they face, their salaries, and various financial benefit issues.

The percentage who are completely satisfied ranges from 21% for stress and 23% for their pay, to 31% for the retirement plan offered by their employers, 32% for promotion opportunities, 33% for health insurance benefits, and 38% for family and medical leave benefits. Recognition for a job well done also ranks fairly low, with just 38% of workers saying that they are completely satisfied with recognition at work for their accomplishments.

In addition to rating job satisfaction, the new Gallup survey records a variety of interesting statistics about the American work force:

- Fifty-four percent work full-time and another 7% work part-time.
- The average number of hours worked per week by full-time employees is 46 hours, compared to 26 hours among part-timers. More than half of full-time employees (54%) indicate that they put in over 40 hours in a typical week.
- Two-thirds of all workers are employees of a private company or business, while another 17% are self-employed, and 16% work for the government.
- Thirteen percent of workers belong to a labor union; another 6% work in a bargaining unit but are not unionized.
- Eighty-five percent of workers hold one job, while 13% hold two jobs and 2% hold three or more jobs.
- Self-employment appears to be a benefit procured over time. Only 8% of workers age 18–29 are self-employed in their own businesses or professional practices. This figure rises to 15% among 30–49-year-old workers and reaches 29% among workers age 50 and older. Men are only slightly more likely to be self-employed than women, 19% vs. 14%.

When asked to characterize their work habits, 44% choose the description "high achiever/workaholic," while the majority (56%) call themselves "solid performer[s]." Virtually all workers reject labeling themselves as "an underachiever who gets by with the minimum necessary" to keep their jobs. Workaholics are found in big numbers across all segments of the work force. For instance, more than 40% in every age category describe themselves as workaholics, as do nearly equal percentages of men and women. Those who are self-employed are most likely to consider themselves workaholics, with 60% describing themselves this way, compared to 44% of government workers and 40% of private-sector employees.

SEPTEMBER 13
AIRLINE PASSENGERS

Interviewing Dates: 8/3–4; 24–26/99
CNN/*USA Today*/Gallup Poll
Survey #GO 907928; 907169

How many air trips, if any, have you taken on a commercial airliner in the past twelve months, counting each round trip as one trip?

None 56%
One 16
Two to four 21
Five or more 7

Asked of those who have flown within the past year: Compared to a few years ago, do you enjoy flying today more, less, or about the same as you did in the past?

More 10%
Less... 29
About the same... 58
Doesn't apply; only flown this year
  (volunteered) 2
No opinion.. 1

Also asked of those who have flown within the past year: Overall, would you say you are satisfied or dissatisfied with the job the nation's major airlines are doing?

Satisfied... 65%
Dissatisfied... 32
No opinion.. 3

Also asked of those who have flown within the past year: Now, thinking about some specific aspects of flying today, please say whether you are generally satisfied or dissatisfied with each one:

(Percent Satisfied)

	Total	One flight	Two to four flights	Five or more flights
Width of airplane seats.............	46%	47%	45%	45%
Legroom between rows of airplane seats.............	25	27	26	17
Courtesy of flight attendants	88	93	88	80
Courtesy of check-in and gate agents	87	85	89	85
In-flight food...	37	46	33	28
Number of restrooms on airplanes......	73	74	68	85
Airlines' on-time performance	67	72	69	50
Ticketing process	82	84	82	78
Overhead storage room on airplanes......	72	73	73	69
Price you pay for tickets..........	45	47	44	46
Schedules	75	80	69	80
Layout and usability of airports in which you travel	81	84	82	72
Parking at airports	58	61	56	57
Speed and reliability of luggage systems at airports	67	70	66	64

Also asked of those who have flown within the past year: How often, if ever, have you personally felt a sense of rage at the airlines or airline employees when you are flying?

	Total	One flight	Two to four flights	Five or more flights
Frequently	7%	6%	7%	9%
Occasionally	27	19	29	37
Never	66	75	64	54

Note: The majority of American commercial airline passengers say that they are satisfied with the job the country's major airlines are doing, and only about one-third say that they are enjoying flying less today than in the past. Passengers' biggest complaints focus on the practical aspects of flying, including legroom and seat width, inflight food, and the price of tickets, in particular. At the same time, about one-third of passengers at least occasionally have felt a sense of rage at the airlines or airline employees, including almost one-half of passengers who fly five times per year or more.

Forty-four percent of the nation's adults have flown on at least one commercial airline trip during the past year, and these fliers were asked a series of questions about their overall perceptions today in an August Gallup Poll. In general, passengers have somewhat mixed, but on balance positive, attitudes about the airline industry. Two-thirds are satisfied, while about one-third say that they are dissatisfied with the job the airlines are doing. Very frequent fliers, defined as those who have flown five or more times over the past year, are a little more negative than are less frequent fliers, but not by much. Forty percent of the very frequent group are dissatisfied, compared to 29% of the one-time-only fliers.

There has been a good deal of discussion about the perception that flying has become much less pleasurable in recent years. During this time, flight loads have increased and airlines have cut back on food service and have attempted to squeeze more people into already crowded cabins in order to raise profitability. But the majority of passengers say that their flying experiences either are no different in recent years from what they have been in the past, or have actually gotten better. Only 29% of fliers say that they are enjoying flying less than they did a few years ago (10% are actually enjoying it more). Frequent fliers are somewhat more likely than less frequent fliers to say that they are enjoying flying less.

SEPTEMBER 24
FAMILY'S FINANCIAL SITUATION

Interviewing Dates: 9/10–14/99
CNN/*USA Today*/Gallup Poll
Survey #GO 128526

Thinking about the past three years, has your family's own financial situation gotten better or gotten worse?

	Sept. 10–14, 1999	Jan. 8–10, 1999
Gotten better	64%	63%
Gotten worse	18	15
Same (volunteered)	16	20
No opinion	2	2

September 10–14, 1999

	Gotten better	Gotten worse	Same	No opinion
By Age				
18–29 Years	78%	13%	8%	1%
30–49 Years	69	19	11	1
50–64 Years	63	20	15	2
65 Years and Over	43	19	36	2
By Income				
$10,000 and Less	48	36	12	4
$10,000–$14,999	48	29	22	1
$15,000–$19,999	58	26	15	1
$20,000–$29,999	59	21	20	*
$30,000–$49,999	68	19	13	*

$50,000– $74,999 76	11	13	*
$75,000 and Over...... 85	7	8	*

By Marital Status

Married............ 66	17	16	1
Living with Partner......... 78	10	12	*
Widowed......... 48	18	31	3
Divorced.......... 59	25	14	2
Single, Never Married........ 71	17	11	1

*Less than 1%

Note: Almost two-thirds of all Americans (64%) say that over the past three years, their personal financial situation has gotten better, while just 18% say that it has gotten worse. But this assessment of upward mobility is not universal across all segments of society; it varies substantially by how much people earn. Among those whose annual household income is more than $75,000 per year, 85% say that their personal financial situation has improved, while just 7% say that it has gotten worse, a net improvement of 78 percentage points. But that positive ratio declines as income declines, so that among respondents earning less than $10,000 per year, about an equal number say that their financial situation has improved (39%) as say that it has gotten worse (36%), a net improvement of just 3 points.

These numbers suggest that the positive impact of the booming U.S. economy has not necessarily trickled down to all sectors of society, and they tend to underscore the perception of some observers that over the past two decades there has been a growing financial disparity between low- and high-income Americans. Still, the ratio of improvement to decline increases sharply above the lowest income group. While the net improvement is just 3 points among those earning less than $10,000 per year, it is about 20 points among those earning between $10,000 and $20,000 per year, about 30 points among those earning between $20,000 and $30,000 per year, and 40 points among those earning between $30,000 and $50,000 per year.

Younger people are more likely than older people to report improvement in their financial situation, with 78% of those under 30 saying that their financial situation has gotten better, compared with 69% of those in the 30–49 age group, 63% in the 50–64 age group, and just 43% in the 65+ age group. The much lower percentage among older people, however, does not mean that this group has experienced more of a decline in their financial situation: just 19% say that their situation has gotten worse, about the same as the two middle age groups, and only 6 points higher than the youngest group. Older respondents are more likely to say that there has been no change for them in the past three years than are other age groups, perhaps because they tend to be on fixed retirement incomes.

SEPTEMBER 30
FEDERAL BUDGET

Interviewing Dates: 9/23–26/99
CNN/*USA Today*/Gallup Poll
Survey #GO 128808

As you may know, the federal government's fiscal year ends next week, on September 30, and so far Congress has not passed the budget for the new fiscal year. How confident are you that Congress and the president will pass a budget in time to avoid a shutdown of the federal government—very confident, somewhat confident, not too confident, or not at all confident?

Very confident.................................	17%
Somewhat confident........................	43
Not too confident............................	27
Not at all confident.........................	11
No opinion......................................	2

	Very confi- dent	Some- what confi- dent	Not too confi- dent	Not at all confi- dent*
By Politics				
Republicans.....	15%	44%	27%	12%
Democrats.......	19	44	27	8
Independents ...	17	40	27	14

*"No opinion"—at 2% or less—is omitted.

How confident are you that Congress and the president will pass a budget that stays within the spending limits imposed by the 1997 budget bill—very confident, somewhat confident, not too confident, or not at all confident?

Very confident	9%
Somewhat confident	36
Not too confident	34
Not at all confident	19
No opinion	2

	Very confident	Some- what confi- dent	Not too confi- dent	Not at all confi- dent*
By Politics				
Republicans	7%	31%	39%	21%
Democrats	14	43	28	13
Independents	6	35	35	23

*"No opinion"—at 2% or less—is omitted.

How confident are you that Congress and the president will pass a budget that you, personally, approve of—very confident, somewhat confident, not too confident, or not at all confident?

Very confident	5%
Somewhat confident	30
Not too confident	36
Not at all confident	27
No opinion	2

	Very confi- dent	Some- what confi- dent	Not too confi- dent	Not at all confi- dent*
By Politics				
Republicans	3%	23%	43%	29%
Democrats	8	36	33	21
Independents	5	29	31	33

*"No opinion"—at 2% or less—is omitted.

Note: Earlier this year, Republican leaders in Congress promised to keep the overall federal budget expenditures within the spending limits they imposed in 1997. But according to a recent Gallup Poll, the American public is skeptical: only 45% feel confident that Congress and the president will pass a budget that stays within the spending limits, while 53% are not so confident. These views are strongly correlated with party affiliation, as Democrats seem generally confident that the budget will remain within the spending limits, by a margin of 57% to 41%, while both independents and Republicans disagree, by margins of 58% to 41%, and 60% to 38%, respectively.

Most respondents do not appear concerned, however, that a congressional impasse will lead to a government shutdown, as happened in December 1995. Sixty percent are either very or somewhat confident that such a shutdown will not occur, compared with 38% who are not too or not at all confident that a shutdown can be avoided. These views are shared about equally among Republicans, independents, and Democrats.

Whatever their views about the size of the budget and the budget process, strong majorities of all partisan groups express doubt that the final budget passed by Congress and the president will be acceptable. Overall, only 35% are confident that the final budget will be one they approve of, while 63% are not so confident. Among the partisan groups, Democrats are most optimistic, but even most of them are skeptical: 54% are not confident that the budget will be one they want, while just 44% are confident that it will be. By comparison, 64% of independents and 72% of Republicans express skepticism, while only 34% of independents and 26% of Republicans are confident that the budget will be acceptable.

OCTOBER 29
STOCK MARKET

Interviewing Dates: 10/21–24/99
CNN/*USA Today*/Gallup Poll
Survey #GO 907190

Do you personally, or jointly with a spouse, have any money invested in the stock market right now either in an individual stock, a stock mutual fund, or in a self-directed 401(k) or IRA?

Yes	60%
No; don't know	40

	Yes	No; don't know
By Age		
18–29 Years	42%	58%
30–49 Years	69	31
50–64 Years	60	40
65 Years and Over	55	45

Selected National Trend

	Yes	No; don't know
1999		
September 10–14	57%	43%
June 4–5	57	43
April 30– May 2	58	42
March 12–14	61	39

If you had a thousand dollars to spend, do you think investing it in the stock market would be a good or bad idea?

	Total	Stock-holders
Good idea	51%	63%
Bad idea	44	35
It depends (volunteered)	2	1
No opinion	3	1

	Good idea	Bad idea	It depends	No opinion
By Age*				
18–29 Years	51%	44%	3%	2%
30–49 Years	57	40	2	1
50–64 Years	48	47	2	3
65 Years and Over	37	53	3	7

*Based on national sample

Selected National Trend*

	Good idea	Bad idea	It depends	No opinion
1999				
Sept. 10–14	60%	33%	3%	4%

June 4–5	60	34	3	3
March 12–14	59	35	3	3

*Based on national sample

Thinking about the U.S. stock market, do you think stock prices will go higher or lower in the next six months?

	Oct. 21–24, 1999	March 12–14, 1999
Higher	50%	61%
Lower	37	29
Stay the same (volunteered)	3	3
No opinion	10	7

October 21–24, 1999

	Higher	Lower	Stay the same	No opinion
By Age				
18–29 Years	60%	29%	3%	8%
30–49 Years	52	40	1	7
50–64 Years	45	42	5	8
65 Years and Over	40	31	6	23

Note: Seventy years ago today the stock market plummeted, signaling the onset of the Great Depression, the worst financial crisis that this country has ever experienced. By the early 1950s, more than twenty years after the crash, only 8% of Americans reported having some investments in the stock market, but according to a recent Gallup Poll, 60% of American households are now invested in the stock market, a number that has remained stable in Gallup surveys conducted over the past two years.

The stock market used to be considered the financial haven of the very rich, but today—mostly because of the growth of retirement funds such as 401(k) and Individual Retirement Accounts—people of even modest incomes report stock market investments. Among middle-income respondents, for example, those with annual family incomes in the $30,000-to-$50,000 range, almost two-thirds (65%) report that they have money invested in the stock market. Many families with even lower incomes also report such investments. Of those in the $20,000-to-$30,000 range, 43% are invested in the stock market, as are one-third of families in the $15,000-to-$20,000 range. At the other end of the spectrum, 84% of families with annual incomes of $50,000 to $75,000 report stock market investments, as do 86% of families earning over $75,000 per year.

Baby Boomers age 35–53 (born in the years 1946–1964) report the highest rate of stock market investment (66%), only a little higher than the rate of investment (62%) among those age 54–64 but significantly higher than the 53% and 55% rates among the youngest (18–34) and oldest (65+), respectively. These lower rates of stock market investments, however, appear to be more related to the lower income levels reported by these groups. Among respondents with similar levels of income, rates of investment are also similar. For example, while the overall investment rate of young people is lower than that of the Baby Boomers, the rate is identical (85%) among both age groups who earn at least $50,000 per year, which is similar to the rate within the 54–64 age group (88%) and only slightly higher than the 80% reported by the 65+ age group.

With the recent wild swings in the stock market, Americans have become somewhat less bullish, although they remain more positive than negative. When asked in the latest poll whether it would be a good or bad idea to invest $1,000 in the stock market now, the optimists win by the margin of 51% to 44%, but that is down significantly from the 60%-to-33% margin recorded in a poll six weeks earlier. Gallup first asked this question in July 1997, when 62% said that it would be a good idea to invest $1,000 and 33% said a bad idea. On September 1, 1998, the day after the more than 500-point drop in the stock market, the public was evenly divided on the wisdom of investing in the market, with 48% saying that it would be a bad idea and 46% a good idea. But by March of this year, optimism had recovered, and it remained high in polls conducted in June and September as well.

NOVEMBER 4
NEW VEHICLE PURCHASES

Interviewing Dates: 8/1–9/5/99
CNN/*USA Today*/Gallup Poll
Special survey

When you buy or lease your next new vehicle, are you more likely to buy or lease a new car or truck, one not previously owned; or a used or pre-owned car or truck?

	August 1999	March 1999
New car, truck	51%	51%
Used, pre-owned car, truck	41	43
Neither (volunteered)	8	6

Note: A newly released Gallup survey of the public's vehicle-purchasing plans shows that intentions to buy a new car remain strong, with 51% saying that the next car or truck they buy or lease will be a new, rather than a used or "pre-owned," vehicle. The results from Gallup's latest AutoPoll are similar to those found last spring but higher than those found a year ago, when only 42% expected their next car or truck to be a new one. Those planning on purchasing within the next year are more likely (51%) to purchase a sport utility vehicle (SUV) than are those planning to purchase a new vehicle more than a year from now (39%). These figures suggest that the demand for SUVs will remain quite strong, at least in the short run.

Another indicator of the strength of the SUV market is the high level of repurchase intentions. Almost three in four (73%) of SUV owners say that their next vehicle will also be an SUV, similar to the repurchase intent expressed by owners of pickup trucks (71%) and sedans (69%). Although the potential market for SUVs is strong, the actual number of households currently owning SUVs is just 23%, compared to 63% of households with sedans and 40% with pickup trucks. In addition, 20% of households own sports cars, 14% minivans, and 9% full-size vans.

The preference for American vehicles continues to be more than twice as high as that for Japanese vehicles and three times as high as the preference for European vehicles. Over three-quarters of the public (78%) say that they would definitely or probably consider buying an American vehicle, compared with just 37% mentioning a Japanese brand and 25% a European brand. This pattern has remained constant since Gallup's first AutoPoll in January 1997, but the numbers have fluctuated over the years. Americans' preference for domestic brands has varied from 78% to 85%, compared with a range of 30% to 41% preferring Japanese brands, and 19% to 26% saying that they would consider European brands. Although about one-quarter of Americans may consider buying European-brand vehicles, just 10% currently own them, compared with 83% who own American vehicles, and 34% who own Japanese vehicles.

NOVEMBER 8
MICROSOFT ANTITRUST TRIAL

Interviewing Dates: 11/4–7/99
CNN/*USA Today*/Gallup Poll
Survey #GO 907193

Do you use a personal computer on a regular basis either at home, work, or school, or not?

	Nov. 4–7, 1999	Nov. 13–15, 1998
Yes	60%	56%
No	40	44

Thinking about Microsoft, the computer software company that produces Windows 95 and other products, do you have a favorable or unfavorable opinion of the Microsoft Corporation?

	Nov. 4–7, 1999*	Feb. 8–9, 1999
Favorable	67%	66%
Unfavorable	16	16
No opinion	17	18

*Computer users only: "favorable," 78%; "unfavorable," 16%; "no opinion," 6%

As you may know, a lawsuit by the Justice Department against Microsoft is currently being tried in court. Based on what you know about the case, do you side more with the Justice Department, or with the Microsoft Corporation?

	Nov. 4–7, 1999*	Feb. 8–9, 1999
Justice Department	33%	28%
Microsoft Corporation	45	45
Other (volunteered)	3	6
No opinion	19	21

*Computer users only: "Justice Department," 35%; "Microsoft Corporation," 49%; "other," 3%; "no opinion," 13%

Would you favor or oppose actions by the federal government which would require Microsoft to break up into several smaller companies?

	Total	Computer users
Favor	35%	35%
Oppose	54	59
No opinion	11	6

Note: As a result of months of hearings in the lawsuit filed by the Justice Department against the Microsoft Corporation, Federal Judge Thomas Penfield Jackson last Friday [November 5] issued his "findings of fact," which asserted that the giant software company is a monopoly that uses its power illegally to constrain competition. According to several Gallup Polls conducted over the past two years, in which the general public was asked its views about Microsoft and the lawsuit, respondents expressed mostly a favorable view of the company and its founder, Bill Gates, but were divided over whether Microsoft was a monopoly. Nevertheless, earlier this year the public rejected the notion that the company used illegal sales and business tactics to market its software, and in a survey completed this past weekend sided with the company rather than with the Justice Department in the lawsuit and also opposed any breakup of Microsoft into smaller companies.

The latest Gallup Poll to include questions about Microsoft was conducted on November 4–7 (with most interviews completed prior to the court's announcement), and it shows that two-thirds have a favorable view of both the company and Gates. The positive feelings are even more pronounced among the six in ten who are computer users, with 78% of this group expressing a favorable view of Microsoft and 72% a favorable view of Gates.

When asked specifically about the lawsuit, the public sides with Microsoft rather than with the Justice Department by a margin of 45% to 33%, with 22% expressing no opinion. In three previous polls asking the same question—in November 1998, and February and March of this year—the responses were similar. An analysis of the data from the most recent survey indicates that opinion may have shifted somewhat toward the Justice Department's side of the case as this past weekend wore on, suggesting that polling over the next several weeks might reflect some change in this position as the publicity over the case sinks into the public's consciousness. There is, however, no apparent change in attitudes toward Gates and Microsoft over the weekend's interviewing.

NOVEMBER 12
AIRLINE SAFETY

Interviewing Dates: 11/4–7/99
CNN/*USA Today*/Gallup Poll
Survey #GO 907193

Asked of those who have ever flown: When you fly, how often, if ever, are you frightened— always, most of the time, sometimes, or never?

	Nov. 4–7, 1999	July 13–14, 1999
Always	14%	12%
Most of the time	7	6
Sometimes	31	31
Never	47	50
No opinion	1	1

Asked of the entire sample: How much confidence do you have in each of the following to do all they can to maintain air safety—a great deal, a fair amount, not too much, or none at all:

Ground maintenance crews?

	Nov. 4–7, 1999	July 13–14, 1999
Great deal	27%	24%
Fair amount	52	56
Not too much	15	14
None at all	4	4
No opinion	2	2

Federal government agencies?

	Nov. 4–7, 1999	July 13–14, 1999
Great deal	18%	15%
Fair amount	50	49
Not too much	22	25
None at all	7	8
No opinion	3	3

Regional and commuter commercial airlines?

	Nov. 4–7, 1999	July 13–14, 1999
Great deal	19%	14%
Fair amount	53	58
Not too much	18	16
None at all	6	5
No opinion	4	7

Commercial airline companies that fly across the country?

	Nov. 4–7, 1999	July 13–14, 1999
Great deal	29%	26%
Fair amount	52	58
Not too much	12	10
None at all	5	4
No opinion	2	2

Commercial airline companies that fly internationally?

Great deal	27%
Fair amount	51
Not too much	13
None at all	4
No opinion	5

Air traffic controllers?

	Nov. 4–7, 1999	July 13–14, 1999
Great deal	42%	37%
Fair amount	44	50
Not too much	9	8
None at all	3	3
No opinion	2	2

Pilots?

	Nov. 4–7, 1999	July 13–14, 1999
Great deal	53%	46%
Fair amount	39	45
Not too much	5	5
None at all	2	2
No opinion	1	2

The companies that manufacture commercial airplanes?

Great deal	29%
Fair amount	49
Not too much	14
None at all	6
No opinion	2

How confident do you feel about the safety standards of the major commercial airlines, in general—very confident, somewhat confident, not too confident, or not confident at all?

	Total	Those who have ever flown
Very confident	29%	33%
Somewhat confident	51	52
Not too confident	15	12
Not confident at all	5	3
No opinion	*	*

*Less than 1%

As you may know, an EgyptAir jet crashed off the Massachusetts coast last weekend. As a result of this crash, are you less likely to fly on major commercial airlines, or not?

	Total	Those who have ever flown
Yes, less likely	23%	19%
No	76	80
No opinion	1	1

Selected National Trend*

	Yes, less likely	No	No opinion
1996			
July 18–19**	17%	79%	4%
May 14†	46	42	12

*Based on those who have ever flown
**Question wording: *As you may know, a TWA jet crashed near Long Island last Wednesday night . . .*
†Question wording: *As you may have heard, an airplane operated by ValuJet Airlines crashed in the Florida Everglades . . .*

Note: Reaction to the crash of EgyptAir Flight 990, in which 217 people were killed off the Massachusetts coast, varies by the amount of time that a person has spent in the air. A new Gallup Poll conducted on the weekend after the disaster (November 4–7) finds that 43% of those who have never flown on a commercial airliner (17% of the population) report that they are less likely to fly as a result of this accident. For these nonfliers, the crash apparently reinforced their decision to avoid air transportation altogether. However, the percentage drops significantly with experience as an airline passenger: just 15% of those who have flown within the last year report that they are less likely to fly again as a result of the crash, compared to 4% of those who have flown more than five times in the past year.

Overall, 23% of the total population would be less likely to fly on a major commercial airline. By way of comparison, a Gallup Poll conducted in July 1996 found that 17% said that they would be less likely to fly on TWA as a result of the Flight 800 crash off Long Island. In another case that year where a specific airline was mentioned, 46% said that they would be less likely to fly ValuJet (now known as AirTran) following the May 1996 crash of one of its planes in the Florida Everglades.

In addition, Gallup trends on the "fear of flying" show a slight increase in the number who say that they are frightened "always" or "most of the time" when flying. In 1989 that percentage was 16%; now, it is only slightly higher, at 21%.

NOVEMBER 16
HONESTY AND ETHICAL STANDARDS

Interviewing Dates: 11/4–7/99
CNN/*USA Today*/Gallup Poll
Survey #GO 907193

*Please tell me how you would rate the honesty and ethical standards of people in these different fields—very high, high, average, low, or very low?**

		Very high, high
1.	Nurses	73%
2.	Druggists, pharmacists**	69
3.	Veterinarians	63
4.	Medical doctors**	58
5.	Grade- and high-school teachers	57
6.	Clergy	56
7.	Judges	53
8.	Policemen	52
9.	Dentists	52
10.	College teachers	52
11.	Engineers	50
12.	Day care providers	41
13.	Funeral directors	35
14.	Computer industry executives	35
15.	Bankers	30
16.	Home repair (plumbers, carpenters, electricians)	29
17.	Chiropractors	26
18.	State governors	24
19.	Journalists	24
20.	Auto mechanics	24
21.	Business executives**	23
22.	Store salespeople	22
23.	Nursing home operators	22
24.	Computer salesmen	20
25.	Television reporters, commentators	20
26.	Local officeholders	20
27.	Jewelers	20
28.	Newspaper reporters	19
29.	Building contractors	18
30.	Labor union leaders	17
31.	U.S. Senators	17
32.	Stockbrokers	16
33.	State officeholders	16
34.	Entertainment industry executives	15
35.	Real estate developers	15
36.	Real estate agents	14
37.	Lawyers	13
38.	Gun salesmen	12
39.	U.S. Congressmen	11
40.	Journalists who publish only on Internet	10
41.	Insurance salesmen	10
42.	HMO managers	10
43.	Advertising practitioners	9
44.	Telemarketers	9
45.	Car salesmen**	8

*Based on half sample
**Based on full sample

Note: A century and one-half after Florence Nightingale's heroic efforts in the Crimean War first brought attention and adulation to the nursing profession, public esteem for this group is extremely high. In Gallup's annual Honesty and Ethics poll, expanded this year to include nurses and nineteen additional occupations (for a total of forty-five) not previously rated, nearly three-quarters of respondents (73%) deem nurses' honesty and ethics as either very high or high, putting them at the top of the list. Pharmacists remain the top-rated profession among occupations previously measured over the past twenty-two years; however, with a combined high/very high rating of 69%, they trail nurses on the expanded list by 4 percentage points.

Four professions among those asked for the first time break into the top ten: nurses, veterinarians, grade- and high-school teachers, and judges. Americans who consider their pets as family members will be happy to learn that the public finds veterinarians superior to medical doctors: 63% rate vets' honesty and ethics as very high or high, compared with 58% for doctors.

One political group, state governors, was added this year to round out the four preexisting political categories. Twenty-four percent give governors a high or very high rating—which may seem low, but it is higher than those of local and state officeholders and U.S. senators and representatives, whose positive ratings range from 20% to only 11%.

Two professions have gained the most over the last ten years: pharmacists, whose high/very high rating has gone from 62% in 1990 to 69% today; and medical doctors, whose high/very high rating has gone from 52% to 58%. On the other hand, the three professions that have lost the most in ratings over the last ten years are television reporters, down from 32% to 20%; lawyers, down from 22% to 13%; and U.S. congressmen, down from 20% to 11%.

NOVEMBER 26
CHRISTMAS SHOPPING

Interviewing Dates: 11/18–21/99
CNN/*USA Today*/Gallup Poll
Survey #GO 129182

Roughly how much money do you think you personally will spend on Christmas gifts this year?

	Nov. 18–21, 1999	Dec. 4–6, 1998
$1,000 or more	35%	24%
$500–$999	27	25
$250–$499	14	22
$100–$249	13	14
Under $100	6	8
No opinion	5	7

Median:	$500	$561
Mean:	$857	$702

Asked of those who will be spending money for Christmas: How likely are you to use each of the following to do your Christmas shopping—very likely, somewhat likely, not too likely, or not at all likely:

Television, such as the Home Shopping Page?

	Nov. 18–21, 1999	Dec. 4–6, 1998
Very likely	2%	3%
Somewhat likely	4	3
Not too likely	10	8
Not at all likely	84	85
No opinion	*	1

*Less than 1%

Catalogs?

	Nov. 18–21, 1999	Dec. 4–6, 1998
Very likely	17%	14%
Somewhat likely	28	21
Not too likely	17	15
Not at all likely	38	50
No opinion	*	*

*Less than 1%

Discount stores?

	Nov. 18–21, 1999	Dec. 4–6, 1998
Very likely	45%	48%
Somewhat likely	34	32
Not too likely	11	9
Not at all likely	10	11
No opinion	*	*

*Less than 1%

Department stores?

	Nov. 18–21, 1999	Dec. 4–6, 1998
Very likely	60%	60%
Somewhat likely	31	27
Not too likely	5	6
Not at all likely	4	6
No opinion	*	1

*Less than 1%

Specialty stores, such as stores that sell only toys or clothes or jewelry, for example?

	Nov. 18–21, 1999	Dec. 4–6, 1998
Very likely	37%	37%
Somewhat likely	33	28

Not too likely	11	14
Not at all likely	19	20
No opinion	*	1

*Less than 1%

On-line shopping on the Internet?

	Nov. 18–21, 1999	Dec. 4–6, 1998
Very likely	8%	4%
Somewhat likely	11	6
Not too likely	14	7
Not at all likely	67	82
No opinion	*	1

*Less than 1%

Note: Americans expect to spend much more on Christmas shopping this year than last, according to a recent Gallup Poll, and they are much more likely to be buying from catalogs and from the Internet than they were last year. On average, they intend to spend $857 for Christmas, up from $702 last year, which represents a 22% increase. One-half of all respondents, however, expect to spend no more than $500, a bit lower than the comparable figure from last year, when 50% expected to spend no more than $561. These numbers suggest that the overall increase in spending is coming mostly from shoppers who were already relatively high spenders.

Nevertheless, the increase in spending comes across the income spectrum. Overall, people earning less than $20,000 per year say that they expect to spend on average $451 for Christmas, up from $336 last year—an increase of $115, representing a 34% jump over last year. People earning between $20,000 and $50,000 per year report a smaller dollar and percentage increase but a higher amount overall, as they expect to spend an average of $748—an increase of $98 (and 15%) over last year's projection of $652. Finally, those earning over $50,000 per year expect to spend an average of $1,233 this year, an increase of $184 over the $1,049 projected last year—an 18% increase.

Most shoppers will continue to rely principally on department, discount, and specialty stores for their Christmas gifts, but an increasing number intend to shop at home by using catalogs and the Internet. This year, 45% of all shoppers say that they will be using catalogs, up from 35% last year. And shopping on the Internet may be double what it was last year, as 19% of shoppers expect to order gifts on-line, compared with just 10% last year. Using the shopping networks on television continues to appeal to only about 6% of all consumers.

NOVEMBER 30
CHINA TRADE AGREEMENT

Interviewing Dates: 11/18–21/99
CNN/*USA Today*/Gallup Poll
Survey #GO 129182

Do you favor or oppose the recent agreement between China and the United States that would allow China to join the World Trade Organization?

Favor	54%
Oppose	33
No opinion	13

	Favor	Oppose	No opinion
By Politics			
Republicans	50%	36%	14%
Democrats	55	30	15
Independents	56	33	11

*Based on half sample

Which of the following statements comes closer to your view—the United States should increase trade with China now, because doing so will promote more economic, political, and religious freedoms in that country; or the United States should not increase trade with China until the Chinese government gives more economic, political, and religious freedom to its citizens?

Increase trade now	35%
Wait for Chinese reforms	61
No opinion	4

	Increase trade now	Wait for reforms	No opinion
By Politics			
Republicans	28%	67%	5%
Democrats...................	39	57	4
Independents...............	37	59	4

*Based on half sample

*In your view, would more foreign trade between the United States and China increase or decrease the number of jobs available for American workers in the United States?**

Increase..	41%
Decrease	49
Have no effect (volunteered).........................	3
No opinion......................................	7

	Increase	Decrease	Have no effect	No opinion
By Politics				
Republicans.....	40%	51%	2%	7%
Democrats	46	47	2	5
Independents ...	38	49	4	9

*Based on half sample

Note: Tens of thousands of protesters are in Seattle this week for the World Trade Organization meetings, arguing that increased foreign trade with China and other countries will have a multitude of injurious effects on the U.S. and the world's economy and workers, and on the environment. A new Gallup Poll suggests that while the American public may agree with some of these negative predictions, on balance it favors the recent U.S. trade agreement with China in about the same way that Americans ultimately came to favor NAFTA after its passage by the House of Representatives in 1993.

The agreement between the United States and China, signed by the Clinton administration on November 15, opens the way for China to become a member of the World Trade Organization. When asked directly, the public favors the agreement by a 54%-to-33% margin. About the same percentage favored NAFTA in early 1994, after its final approval by the House in November 1993.

Like NAFTA, the China agreement will need to be approved by the House, but unlike many high-visibility issues that come before Congress, there is very little partisan difference in public attitudes toward it. Fifty percent of Republicans favor the agreement, a little below the 56% of independents and 55% of Democrats who favor it. There is a stronger split by ideology; only 43% of conservatives favor the agreement, compared to 62% of liberals and 60% of moderates.

One of the reasons why the agreement may be favored is that most respondents (56%) believe that increased trade between the United States and foreign countries will help U.S. companies, compared with only 39% who believe that it would hurt them. The majority support for the China trade agreement does not mean, however, that Americans totally disregard the arguments put forth by labor unions and others that increased trade will hurt the average worker. When they are asked directly about the impact of such trade on workers, their answers are a mirror image of their responses regarding the potential impact of increased foreign trade on companies. Fifty-nine percent say that increased trade between the United States and other countries will mostly hurt American workers, while only 35% say that it would help them. Additionally, in response to a different question asked specifically about increased trade with China, 49% say that more foreign trade would decrease the number of American jobs, while 41% said that it would increase them.

A more complex question included in the poll suggests that human rights may also have some potential to change Americans' opinions. Is increased trade with China warranted because it would "promote more economic, political, and religious freedoms in that country," or should the United States not increase trade until the Chinese government "gives more economic, political, and religious freedom to its citizens"? Given these two arguments about the impact of trade on freedoms, the public comes down on the side of the latter position by a 61%-to-35% margin.

Social Issues and Policy

JANUARY 30
DEFENSE SPENDING

Interviewing Dates: 11/20–22/98
CNN/*USA Today*/Gallup Poll
Survey #GO 124977

There is much discussion as to the amount of money the government in Washington should spend for national defense and military purposes. How do you feel about this—do you think we are spending too little, about the right amount, or too much?

Too little 26%
About right 45
Too much... 22
No opinion.. 7

Selected National Trend

	Too little	About right	Too much	No opinion
1993	17%	38%	42%	3%
1981	51	22	15	12
1969	8	31	52	9

Which branch of the armed services do you think should be built up to a greater extent— the Army, the Air Force, or the Navy?

Army.. 20%
Air Force... 43
Navy 17
Other; none (volunteered) 11
No opinion... 9

Note: As U.S. forces square off against Iraq in the Persian Gulf and prepare for possible action in Kosovo, the American public appears more ready to support President Bill Clinton's proposed budget increase in defense spending than it has in recent years. When Gallup interviewers asked about defense spending in November 1998, 26% replied that the United States needs to spend more. That figure compares with 17% who gave the same response in 1993 and corresponds to a drop in the number who believe that too much money is being spent on defense, from 42% in 1993 to 22% today (45% now say that defense spending should stay the same).

The president's proposed budget plan for fiscal year 2000 includes the largest increase in defense spending since the boom years of the Reagan administration. The budget just submitted to Congress calls for a $4.6-billion increase in funding for the Department of Defense, with more increases over the next five years. Part of the administration's request will help fund the missions in Iraq and Kosovo, with much of the rest targeted at improving pay and benefits for soldiers.

Public support for this type of increase in military spending, as historical trends show, is highly variable. In 1969, during the height of the Vietnam War, a Gallup Poll found that 52% believed too much was being spent on defense, while only 8% thought that the military effort was underfunded. By 1981, when Ronald Reagan took over the White House and American hostages in Iran had been freed, the situation had reversed. With 51% of the public believing that too little was being spent on defense and only 15% believing that the Pentagon received too much support, President Reagan and Congress had the backing necessary for a massive defense buildup through the 1980s.

In the decade that followed, the fall of communism took away the biggest impetus to maintaining a large military, and U.S. forces led a coalition effort to drive Iraq out of Kuwait in Operation Desert Storm. By 1993, when Clinton was starting his first term in office, support for defense spending had again flipped, with 42% believing that too much was being spent on defense and 17% believing too little. In the five years since that poll was taken, support for increased defense spending has risen to 26%, while the number of the public believing that too much is being spent has dropped to 22%.

If defense spending is to be increased, where should the money go? In 1952, during the Korean conflict, Gallup interviewers asked the public which branch of the military should be built up. In that poll, 55% supported increases in funding for the Air Force, with 12% in favor of increased Army funding and 8% favoring an increase in the Navy's budget. When the same question was asked in late 1998, support for both the Army and the Navy increased, while the Air Force's backing dropped slightly—perhaps in the belief that the end of the Cold War meant a reduced need for the Air Force's mission of maintaining a fleet of bombers capable of delivering nuclear weapons. Still, the 1998 poll shows that the Air Force still "wins": 43% favor increased funding for the Air Force, while the figures for the Army and Navy rise to 20% and 17%, respectively.

FEBRUARY 23
HATE CRIME LAWS

Interviewing Dates: 2/19–21/99
CNN/*USA Today*/Gallup Poll
Survey #GO 126799

Some states have special laws that provide harsher penalties for crimes motivated by hate of certain groups than the penalties for the same crimes if they are not motivated by this kind of hate. Would you favor or oppose this type of hate crime law in your state?

Favor	70%
Oppose	25
No opinion	5

Do you personally know anyone you think is capable of committing a hate crime?

Yes	13%
No	86
No opinion	1

What about you, personally—are you worried about being the victim of a hate crime, or not?

Yes, worried	13%
No	86
No opinion	1

If a hate crime law were enacted in your state, which of the following groups do you think should be covered:

Racial minorities?

Yes, covered	85%
Should not be	11
No opinion	4

Women?

Yes, covered	83%
Should not be	13
No opinion	4

Homosexuals?

Yes, covered	75%
Should not be	20
No opinion	5

Religious and ethnic minorities?

Yes, covered	84%
Should not be	12
No opinion	4

Note: About one in eight Americans worries that he himself may be the victim of a hate crime, a figure that rises to one in four among nonwhites. At the same time, there is strong majority support among all Americans for the idea of enacting a hate crime law in their state. The issue is particularly germane this week, given the trial and conviction of John William King in Jasper, Texas, for the murder of James Byrd, Jr.

The latest Gallup Poll shows that 70% of the U.S. public favor having a hate crime law in their state, while 25% are opposed. A hate crime law is defined as one that provides "harsher penalties for crimes motivated by hate of certain groups than the penalties for the same crimes if they are not motivated by this kind of hate." A majority of every population segment favors such laws, although support is somewhat lower among conservatives and Republicans than it is among liberals and Democrats.

Who should be covered under such hate crime laws if they are enacted? The poll gave respondents four choices: racial minorities, religious and ethnic minorities, women, and homosexuals. The public is overwhelmingly in favor of all four groups being included, with a slightly lower number in favor of including homosexuals (75%) than the other three, all of whom are favored to be included by 83% or higher.

The poll makes it clear that certain groups in society feel threatened by hate crimes more than others. Overall, 13% worry that they could be the victims of a hate crime. There are almost no differences in this respect between men and women, but 28% of nonwhites—more than one in four—say that they worry about being such a victim. The poll additionally shows that 13% personally know someone who they feel is capable of committing a hate crime.

FEBRUARY 24
DEATH PENALTY

Interviewing Dates: 2/8–9/99
CNN/*USA Today*/Gallup Poll
Survey #GO 126651

Are you in favor of the death penalty for a person convicted of murder?*

Favor	71%
Oppose	22
No opinion	7

*Based on half sample

Selected National Trend

	Favor	Oppose	No opinion
1995	77%	13%	10%
1994	80	16	4
1991	76	18	6
1988	79	16	5
1986	70	22	8
1985	72	20	8

What do you think should be the penalty for murder—the death penalty, or life imprisonment with absolutely no possibility of parole?*

Death penalty	56%
Life imprisonment	38
Other; neither; it depends (volunteered); no opinion	6

*Based on half sample

Selected National Trend

	Death penalty	Life imprisonment	Other; neither; it depends; no opinion
1997*	61%	29%	10%
1994	50	32	18
1993	59	29	12
1992	50	37	13
1991	53	35	12
1986	55	35	10
1985	56	34	10

*Based on half sample

In your opinion, is the death penalty imposed too often today, or not often enough?

Too often	25%
Not often enough	64
About right amount (volunteered)	4
No opinion	7

Note: Seven in ten respondents support the death penalty for a person convicted of murder, even though many of those same people believe that America's minorities and the poor are more likely to receive a death sentence. In the latest Gallup

Poll, 71% favor capital punishment, while 22% oppose it and 7% have no opinion. However, when Gallup interviewers asked whether the penalty for murder should be execution or life in prison with no possibility of parole, support for capital punishment drops. Fifty-six percent of those polled support the death penalty in those circumstances, while 38% prefer the option of life imprisonment without parole.

Historically, support for capital punishment has been strong for over two decades. In 1978, a year after capital punishment resumed in the United States with the execution of Gary Gilmore in Utah, 62% supported the death penalty. That support rose consistently through the 1980s before peaking in 1994, when 80% favored the death penalty in murder cases.

Critics of capital punishment contend that it unfairly targets minorities and the poor, and the public tends to agree. When asked whether a poor person is more likely than a person of average or above-average income to receive the death penalty for the same crime, 65% agree, compared to 32% who disagree. It is perhaps not surprising to see that opposition to the death penalty among minorities is higher than among whites: 41% of nonwhites say that the death penalty is imposed too often, while only 22% of whites agree. Fifty-two percent of nonwhites say that capital punishment is not used often enough, while 66% of whites agree with that statement.

MARCH 15
Y2K COMPUTER PROBLEM

Interviewing Dates: 3/5–7/99
CNN/*USA Today*/Gallup Poll
Survey #GO 127004

As you may know, most computer systems around the world have to be reprogrammed so that they can accurately recognize the date once we reach the year 2000. Do you think that computer mistakes due to the year 2000 issue will cause major problems, minor problems, or no problems at all?

	March 5–7, 1999	Dec. 9–13, 1998
Major problems	21%	34%
Minor problems	65	51
No problems at all	12	10
No opinion	2	5

Do you think that computer mistakes due to the year 2000 issue will cause major problems, minor problems, or no problems at all for you personally?

	March 5–7, 1999	Dec. 9–13, 1998
Major problems	9%	14%
Minor problems	56	53
No problems at all	32	30
No opinion	3	3

How much have you seen or heard about the year 2000 computer bug problem, sometimes called the Millennium Bug or the Y2K Bug, before now—a great deal, some, not much, or nothing at all?

	March 5–7, 1999	Dec. 9–13, 1998
Great deal	56%	39%
Some	30	40
Not much	11	13
Nothing at all	3	8
No opinion	*	*

*Less than 1%

To the extent that Y2K computer problems occur, how long do you think they will last— for only a few days around January 1, 2000; for several weeks; for several months to a year; or for more than a year?

	March 5–7, 1999	Dec. 9–13, 1998
Few days	23%	15%
Several weeks	30	30
Several months to year	37	38
More than year	7	11
No opinion	3	6

Form A. *Do you or does your household plan to take any steps to prepare or protect yourself from problems that might result from the Y2K computer bug? If "Yes," what specific* actions or precautions are you planning to take as January 1, 2000, approaches?*

Stocking up on food 22%
Stocking up on water....................................... 12
Having more cash on hand 11
Keeping better financial records; closer
   monitoring of financial records 9
Stocking up on household supplies
   (candles, radio, firewood, etc.) 6
Stocking up on gasoline 5
Purchasing a generator, heater....................... 4
Updating computer... 4
Withdrawing cash from various accounts 4
Saving more money.. 2
Making sure everything is Y2K compliant 1
No air travel.. 1
Other (miscellaneous).................................... 7
No, do not plan to take any steps.................... 44
No opinion.. 7

*Based on half sample. Total adds to more than 100% due to multiple replies.

Form B. *For each of the following, please say whether that is something you probably will or will not do in order to protect yourself against problems associated with the Y2K computer bug:*

Obtain special confirmation or documentation of your bank account balances, retirement funds, or other financial records?

	March 5–7, 1999	Dec. 9–13, 1998
Yes	66%	65%
No	33	33
No opinion	1	2

*Based on half sample

Stockpile food and water?

	March 5–7, 1999	Dec. 9–13, 1998
Yes	39%	26%
No	60	72
No opinion	1	2

*Based on half sample

Buy a generator or wood stove?

	March 5–7, 1999	Dec. 9–13, 1998
Yes	24%	17%
No	75	81
No opinion	1	2

*Based on half sample

Withdraw all your money from the bank?

	March 5–7, 1999	Dec. 9–13, 1998
Yes	15%	16%
No	84	82
No opinion	1	2

*Based on half sample

Withdraw and set aside a large amount of cash?

	March 5–7, 1999	Dec. 9–13, 1998
Yes	30%	31%
No	70	66
No opinion	**	3

*Based on half sample
**Less than 1%

Avoid traveling on airplanes on or around January 1, 2000?

	March 5–7, 1999	Dec. 9–13, 1998
Yes	54%	47%
No	44	50
No opinion	2	3

*Based on half sample

Next, I'm going to read some specific problems. As I read each one, please say whether you think it likely or unlikely to occur as a result of Y2K:

Air traffic control systems will fail, putting air travel in jeopardy?

	March 5–7, 1999	Dec. 9–13, 1998
Likely	43%	46%

	March 5–7, 1999	Dec. 9–13, 1998
Unlikely	55	52
No opinion	2	2

Banking and accounting systems will fail, possibly causing errors in employee paychecks, government payments, and other automated financial transactions?

	March 5–7, 1999	Dec. 9–13, 1998
Likely	55%	63%
Unlikely	43	36
No opinion	2	1

Food and retail distribution systems will fail, possibly causing grocery and other store shortages?

	March 5–7, 1999	Dec. 9–13, 1998
Likely	40%	37%
Unlikely	58	61
No opinion	2	2

Hospital equipment and services will fail, putting patients at risk?

	March 5–7, 1999	Dec. 9–13, 1998
Likely	32%	33%
Unlikely	66	65
No opinion	2	2

City or county emergency "911" communication systems will fail, putting citizens at risk?

	March 5–7, 1999	Dec. 9–13, 1998
Likely	32%	36%
Unlikely	66	62
No opinion	2	2

Nuclear power or defense systems could fail, causing a major accident?

	March 5–7, 1999	Dec. 9–13, 1998
Likely	27%	30%
Unlikely	69	67
No opinion	4	3

As you may know, efforts are currently under way throughout the country to upgrade computer systems in order to correct the Y2K computer problem. We'd like to know whether you are generally confident or not confident that each of the following levels of government and business will have upgraded their computer systems before any Y2K problems can occur:

The U.S. government, including all federal offices and agencies?

	March 5–7, 1999	Dec. 9–13, 1998
Yes, confident	73%	68%
Not confident	26	29
No opinion	1	3

Your state government?

	March 5–7, 1999	Dec. 9–13, 1998
Yes, confident	77%	73%
Not confident	21	25
No opinion	2	2

Your local government?

	March 5–7, 1999	Dec. 9–13, 1998
Yes, confident	71%	68%
Not confident	27	30
No opinion	2	2

U.S. corporations and large businesses?

	March 5–7, 1999	Dec. 9–13, 1998
Yes, confident	85%	82%
Not confident	13	16
No opinion	2	2

Small U.S. businesses?

	March 5–7, 1999	Dec. 9–13, 1998
Yes, confident	54%	56%
Not confident	43	41
No opinion	3	3

Foreign governments of other developed and industrialized countries?

	March 5–7, 1999	Dec. 9–13, 1998
Yes, confident	44%	48%
Not confident	51	46
No opinion	5	6

Foreign governments of Third World and other less-developed countries?

	March 5–7, 1999	Dec. 9–13, 1998
Yes, confident	15%	18%
Not confident	81	76
No opinion	4	6

Note: Americans have grown much more cognizant in recent months of the computer-based booby trap set for January 1, 2000, commonly known as Y2K or the Millennium Bug. However, rather than lead to widespread alarm or panic, this awareness has been accompanied by a marked decrease in public concern. The reaction to the Y2K issue is being tracked this year in a series of surveys conducted by the Gallup Poll in partnership with the National Science Foundation. The latest survey of national adults was conducted on March 5–7 and updates benchmark trends established in December 1998.

Today, 56% of respondents, up from 39% in December, have seen or heard a great deal about the glitch in computer programming, which, if not fixed, will cause computer errors in comprehending the correct date and could potentially set off much worse problems. At the same time, the number of those who think that Y2K-related computer mistakes around the world will cause major problems dropped to 21%, down from 34% in December. Similarly, the number who expect personally to experience major problems as a result of Y2K fell from 14% to 9%. While they clearly do not see catastrophic consequences looming around January 1, 2000, most Americans do expect the Y2K Bug to spawn minor problems: a little over one-half anticipate minor problems in their personal lives, and two-thirds expect that minor problems will occur in society.

MARCH 16
IMMIGRATION

Interviewing Dates: 2/26–28/99
CNN/*USA Today*/Gallup Poll
Survey #GO 126888

In your view, should immigration be kept at its present level, increased, or decreased?*

Present level	41%
Increased	10
Decreased	44
No opinion	5

*Based on half sample

	Present level	In- creased	De- creased	No opinion
By Politics				
Republicans	41%	7%	48%	4%
Democrats	40	9	47	4
Independents	42	12	39	7

Selected National Trend

	Present level	In- creased	De- creased	No opinion
1995	24%	7%	65%	4%
1993	27	6	65	2
1986	35	7	49	9
1977	37	7	42	14
1965	39	7	33	21

Which comes closer to your point of view—immigrants in the long run become productive citizens and pay their fair share of taxes, or immigrants cost the taxpayers too much by using government services like public education and medical services?

Pay their share	47%
Cost taxpayers	45
No opinion	8

	Pay their share	Cost taxpayers	No opinion
By Politics			
Republicans	47%	48%	5%
Democrats	47	44	9
Independents	48	42	10

Selected National Trend

	Pay their share	Cost taxpayers	No opinion
1994	36%	57%	7%
1993	37	56	7

Which of the following statements comes closer to your view—immigrants mostly take jobs that American workers want, or immigrants mostly take low-paying jobs that Americans don't want?

	Feb. 26–28, 1999	July 9–11, 1993
Take jobs that Americans want	16%	23%
Take jobs that Americans don't want	71	67
Both; neither (volunteered)	8	8
No opinion	5	2

February 26–28, 1999

	Take jobs that Americans want	Take jobs that Americans don't want	Both; neither; no opinion
By Politics			
Republicans	16%	71%	13%
Democrats	14	72	14
Independents	18	68	14

Do you think immigrants mostly help the economy by providing low-cost labor, or mostly hurt the economy by driving wages down for many Americans?

	Feb. 26–28, 1999	July 9–11, 1993
Mostly help	42%	28%
Mostly hurt	48	64
Neither (volunteered)	3	2
Both (volunteered)	1	2
No opinion	6	4

February 26–28, 1999

	Mostly help	Mostly hurt	Neither; both; no opinion
By Politics			
Republicans	45%	45%	10%
Democrats	40	50	10
Independents	42	48	10

How many recent immigrants would you say live in your area—many, some, only a few, or none?

	Feb. 26–28, 1999	July 9–11, 1993
Many	34%	27%
Some	23	25
Only a few	29	34
None	10	12
No opinion	4	2

February 26–28, 1999

	Many	Some	Only a few; none	No opinion
By Politics				
Republicans	32%	23%	42%	3%
Democrats	33	24	39	4
Independents	37	22	35	6

Note: As President Bill Clinton discusses immigration issues during his trip this week to four Central American countries, the public at home appears to be more positive about immigration than it has been at any time in this decade. A Gallup Poll conducted during the weekend of February 26–28, 1999, comes days after Republican Patrick Buchanan announced his candidacy for the GOP presidential nomination in the 2000 election. Immigration cuts have been part of the Buchanan platform in each of his two previous bids for the White House, and he has already called for a moratorium on legal immigration as part of his 2000 campaign.

While Buchanan's message was attractive to a plurality of Americans in his last campaign, the tide has shifted as the 2000 campaign begins. Fifty-eight percent of those polled oppose a five-year moratorium on legal immigration, compared to 39% in favor of it. Only three years ago, in 1996, 50% supported such a moratorium, compared to 46% who were in opposition to it.

Additionally, 51% of those polled support keeping immigration at the current level or increasing it, compared to 44% who favor lowering immigration levels. This is the first time that a Gallup Poll on this issue has shown at least plurality support for increased immigration since March 1977, when 44% supported increasing immigration or keeping it at current levels and 42% wanted a cut. In 1993 and 1995, when NAFTA and other trade issues were in the headlines, two in three Americans favored cuts in legal immigration.

The public is split on whether immigration helps the U.S. economy by providing low-cost labor or hurts it by driving wages down for many Americans. Forty-two percent of those polled believe that it helps, compared to 28% when Gallup last asked the question in 1993. At that time, 64% of those polled believed that immigrants hurt the economy, a position whose support has fallen to 48% today.

Who is most likely to say that immigration hurts the economy? One of the most significant correlates of this perception is socioeconomic status. Those in lower-income categories tend to be most likely to say that immigration hurts the economy, with 58% of those making less than $30,000 annually in this "hurts" category. However, this perception changes as income levels rise, with 58% of those making more than $50,000 annually saying that immigration helps the economy. According to the public, as is shown in the latest Gallup Poll, immigrants tend to take low-paying jobs that Americans don't want. Seven in ten respondents agree with that statement, compared to 16% who believe that immigrants take jobs that most American workers want. These attitudes, unlike others measured in the most recent poll, have not changed substantially over the past six years.

MARCH 19
PHYSICIAN-ASSISTED SUICIDE

Interviewing Dates: 3/12–14/99
CNN/*USA Today*/Gallup Poll
Survey #GO 127085

When a person has a disease that cannot be cured and is living in severe pain, do you think doctors should be allowed by law to assist the patient to commit suicide if the patient requests it, or not?

Yes	61%
No	35
No opinion	4

	Yes	No	No opinion
By Sex			
Male	66%	30%	4%
Female	57	40	3
By Ethnic Background			
White	63	34	3
Nonwhite	53	45	2
Black	46	51	3
By Education			
Postgraduate	59	38	3
College Graduate	66	31	3
College Incomplete	66	29	5
No College	58	40	2
By Region			
East	66	30	4
Midwest	58	38	4
South	54	44	2
West	70	24	6
By Age			
18–29 Years	62	36	2
30–49 Years	67	30	3
50–64 Years	59	35	6
65 Years and Over	51	46	3

Selected National Trend

	Yes	No	No opinion
June 5–7, 1998	59%	39%	2%
June 23–24, 1997	57	35	8
Jan. 3–5, 1997	58	37	5

Now, just a hypothetical question—if you personally had a disease that could not be cured and were living in severe pain, would you consider committing suicide, or not?

	March 12–14, 1999	Jan. 3–5, 1997*
Yes	40%	40%
No	51	48
Other (volunteered)	8	11
No opinion	1	1

*Based on half sample

March 12–14, 1999

	Yes	No	Other	No opinion
By Sex				
Male	45%	45%	9%	1%
Female.............	36	56	8	*
By Ethnic Background				
White..............	43	48	8	1
Nonwhite.........	27	64	9	*
Black	21	70	9	*
By Education				
Postgraduate....	46	45	8	1
College Graduate......	40	53	7	*
College Incomplete...	45	45	9	1
No College	37	56	7	*
By Region				
East..................	45	46	8	1
Midwest	36	53	11	*
South	35	60	5	*
West	49	41	9	1
By Age				
18–29 Years	47	49	4	*
30–49 Years	42	47	10	1
50–64 Years	39	53	8	*
65 Years and Over......	32	61	6	1

*Less than 1%

How closely have you followed the news story about Dr. Jack Kevorkian, who assists terminally ill people to commit suicide—very closely, somewhat closely, not too closely, or not at all?

	March 12–14, 1999	Dec. 4–6, 1993
Very closely...................................	18%	24%
Somewhat closely	54	53
Not too closely..............................	22	17
Not at all	5	6
No opinion	1	*

*Less than 1%

Do you approve or disapprove of the actions taken by Dr. Kevorkian?

	March 12–14, 1999	Dec. 4–6, 1993
Approve	52%	43%
Disapprove....................................	43	47
No opinion	5	10

Note: As a Michigan jury prepares to consider whether Dr. Jack Kevorkian should go to prison for helping to end the life of a terminally ill patient last fall, Americans remain divided over the question of physician-assisted suicide. Dr. Kevorkian's belief that physicians should be allowed to assist in the suicide of those suffering from amyotrophic lateral sclerosis (known as Lou Gehrig's disease), cancer, and other terminal illnesses has placed the issue in the spotlight, along with the debate over Oregon's so-called Right-to-Die Law. Oregon voters approved the referendum in 1994 and again in 1997 following court challenges, and the first legal physician-assisted suicides took place in March 1998.

The results of the second Oregon vote closely mirror current American attitudes on physician-assisted suicide. That referendum passed with support from 60% of Oregon voters, and a new Gallup Poll conducted during the weekend of March 12–14 shows that 61% of Americans believe that doctors should be allowed to help a terminally ill patient living in severe pain to commit suicide. Thirty-five percent oppose the practice. These results are consistent with Gallup Poll trends over the last two years, in which six in ten approved of the concept of physician-assisted suicide.

However, when the question becomes a personal matter, respondents are far more reluctant to consider the idea of suicide as a way to end the pain from a terminal illness. Forty percent of those polled would consider committing suicide in that case, but 51% would not. The results are similar to those obtained in a Gallup Poll conducted in January 1997, in which 40% would consider suicide and 48% rejected the idea.

As might be expected, support for the concept of physician-assisted suicide diminishes with age. Sixty-two percent of those age 18 to 29 support the idea of letting doctors help terminally ill patients in severe pain end their lives, but only 51% of those over 65 do. Additionally, when asked if they would consider suicide if faced with an incurable, painful disease, 47% of those age 18 to 29 say that they would consider it, while only 32% of those over 65 would.

Turning to Dr. Kevorkian, who was shown in a nationally televised videotape as he ended the life of a terminally ill Michigan man last fall, 52% approve of his actions, while 43% disapprove. A similar Gallup Poll conducted in December 1993 indicates that there has been a gain in support for Dr. Kevorkian's stand over the last five and one-half years. At that time, 43% approved of his actions, while 47% opposed them. Support for Dr. Kevorkian varies significantly by ideology: 63% of those who label themselves as liberal and 61% of moderates approve of Dr. Kevorkian's actions, while only 39% of conservatives do.

While Americans may approve of physician-assisted suicide and, to a lesser extent, Dr. Kevorkian's position on the issue, they have a far less favorable view of him as a person. In a Gallup Poll conducted during the weekend of December 28–29, 1998, only 40% of those polled viewed him favorably, while 47% had an unfavorable opinion.

MARCH 22
POLICE OFFICERS

Interviewing Dates: 3/5–7/99
CNN/*USA Today*/Gallup Poll
Survey #GO 127004

How much respect do you have for the police in your area—a great deal, some, or hardly any?

Great deal	64%
Some	29
Hardly any	7
No opinion	*

*Less than 1%

	Great deal	Some	Hardly any	No opinion
By Ethnic Background				
White	66%	28%	6%	*
Nonwhite	54	34	12	*
Black	50	35	15	*
By Politics				
Republicans	72	26	2	*
Democrats	61	33	6	*
Independents	60	28	11	1

*Less than 1%

Selected National Trend

	Great deal	Some	Hardly any	No opinion
1991	60%	32%	7%	1%
1967	77	17	4	2
1965	70	22	4	4

How much confidence do you have in the ability of the police to protect you from violent crime—a great deal, quite a lot, not very much, or none at all?

Great deal	29%
Quite a lot	41
Not very much	25
None at all	4
No opinion	1

	Great deal	Quite a lot	Not very much	None at all*
By Ethnic Background				
White	30%	42%	23%	4%
Nonwhite	23	32	37	7
Black	20	33	37	10
By Politics				
Republicans	38	40	20	2
Democrats	25	42	29	3
Independents	26	39	27	7

*"No opinion"—at 1% or less—is omitted.

Selected National Trend

	Great deal	Quite a lot	Not very much	None at all*
1995	20%	30%	39%	9%
1993	14	31	45	9
1989	14	34	42	8

1985 15	37	39	6
1981 15	34	42	8

*"No opinion"—at 3% or less—is omitted.

In general, how would you rate the job the police in your city are doing in dealing with crime—excellent, good, or only fair?

Excellent... 30%
Good 48
Only fair 21
No opinion 1

	Excellent	Good	Only fair	No opinion
By Ethnic Background				
White...............	32%	49%	18%	1%
Nonwhite.........	20	39	40	1
Black	17	34	49	*
By Politics				
Republicans.....	36	49	15	*
Democrats	27	51	21	1
Independents ...	28	44	27	1

*Less than 1%

Have you personally ever felt treated unfairly by the police or by a police officer?

Yes.. 27%
No 73

	Yes	No
By Ethnic Background		
White	24%	76%
Nonwhite	39	61
Black...	43	57
By Politics		
Republicans	19	81
Democrats.....................................	28	72
Independents.................................	31	69

In some places in the nation, there have been charges of police brutality. Do you think there is any police brutality in your area, or not?

Yes.. 38%
No 57
No opinion...................................... 5

	Yes	No	No opinion
By Ethnic Background			
White 35%		60%	5%
Nonwhite 58		36	6
Black........................... 66		28	6
By Politics			
Republicans 33		63	4
Democrats.................. 44		53	3
Independents.............. 37		55	8

Selected National Trend

	Yes	No	No opinion
July 11–14, 1991 .... 39%		56%	5%
March 14–17, 1991..... 35		60	5
1967 6		81	13
1965 9		79	12

Some people feel that the job police officers perform is so difficult and important that it is wrong to second-guess them by prosecuting or punishing them for wrongdoing which occurs in the course of their job performance. Would you agree or disagree that it is wrong to prosecute and punish police officers?

Agree 17%
Disagree.. 80
No opinion 3

	Agree	Disagree	No opinion
By Ethnic Background			
White 16%		80%	4%
Nonwhite 19		78	3
Black........................... 21		78	1
By Politics			
Republicans 18		79	3
Democrats.................. 15		83	2
Independents.............. 17		77	6

Note: As New York prosecutors prepare to put four police officers on trial for the 1997 beating of a Haitian immigrant, a new Gallup Poll finds that about one-third of Americans believe police brutality exists in their local area, and that about one in four has personally felt treated unfairly by the police. At the same time, the public's confidence in the police to protect citizens against crime has gone up significantly over the past four years.

The March poll shows that 38% believe that there have been incidents of police brutality in their area, while 57% disagree. That compares with a similar Gallup Poll conducted in March 1991, in which roughly the same number (35%) said that police brutality existed in their area. The poll also underscores perceptions that minorities feel unfairly targeted by police officers. Fifty-eight percent of nonwhites believe that police brutality takes place in their area, compared to only 35% of whites.

When asked, "Have you personally ever felt treated unfairly by the police or by a police officer," 27% say yes. Again, the answers differ along racial lines, with 39% of nonwhites saying yes, compared to just 24% of whites. Police brutality is also more likely to be reported in urban areas (57% compared to 35% in rural areas) and in the West and the South (43% and 41%, respectively).

Almost all respondents indicate that they have at least some respect for the police in their local area, with 64% saying that they have a great deal of respect, and another 29% saying some respect. This is roughly the same percentage that Gallup found in March 1991, when the question was last asked, but lower than twenty-two years ago, in 1967. Sixty-six percent of whites now have a great deal of respect for the police compared to 54% of nonwhites.

The poll reflects generally positive attitudes about the ability of the police to combat crime—attitudes which may, in part, be due to the lower crime rates that have been reported in the United States in recent years. Seventy percent are confident in the ability of police officers to protect them from violent crime, up from 50% in a Gallup Poll conducted in September 1995. Thirty percent say that the police in their city are doing an excellent job in dealing with crime, up from 19% in a 1993 Gallup Poll. Additionally, at a time when police officers are being criticized for shootings such as the one in the Amadou Diallo case in New York City, 80% believe that the police officers in their area use their guns with about the right frequency,

while the rest split equally in terms of saying that guns are used too frequently or not frequently enough. Here again, however, there are differences by race. Only 5% of whites say that police officers use their guns too frequently in their local area, compared to 21% of nonwhites. Interestingly, nonwhites are also slightly more likely to say that police in their area do not use their guns frequently enough.

The Diallo case, in which New York City police officers fired forty-one shots at an unarmed African immigrant, is now being investigated by the U.S. Justice Department and a Bronx grand jury. When Gallup interviewers posed the question, ". . . the job police officers perform is so difficult and important that it is wrong to second-guess them by prosecuting or punishing them for wrongdoing which occurs in the course of their job performance," 80% disagreed. Only 17% said that officers should not be held responsible for their actions.

MARCH 25
THE ENVIRONMENT

Interviewing Dates: 3/12–14/99
CNN/*USA Today*/Gallup Poll
Survey #GO 127085

I'm going to read a list of environmental problems. As I read each one, please tell me if you personally worry about this environmental problem a great deal, a fair amount, only a little, or not at all:

Ocean and beach pollution?

Great deal	43%
Fair amount	32
Only a little	17
Not at all	7
No opinion	1

Pollution of rivers, lakes, and reservoirs?

Great deal	55%
Fair amount	30
Only a little	12

Not at all 3
No opinion .... *

*Less than 1%

Air pollution?

Great deal 47%
Fair amount.. 33
Only a little.. 16
Not at all 4
No opinion .... *

*Less than 1%

The greenhouse effect or global warming?

Great deal 28%
Fair amount.. 31
Only a little.. 23
Not at all 16
No opinion 2

Contamination of soil and water by toxic waste?

Great deal 55%
Fair amount.. 29
Only a little.. 11
Not at all 5
No opinion .... *

*Less than 1%

The threat of nuclear power accidents?

Great deal 39%
Fair amount.. 23
Only a little.. 25
Not at all 12
No opinion 1

All in all, from what you have heard or read, how safe are nuclear power plants that produce electric power—very safe, somewhat safe, or not so safe?

Very safe.. 24%
Somewhat safe.. 57
Not so safe 17
No opinion 2

Interviewing Dates: 3/19–21/99
CNN/*USA Today*/Gallup Poll
Survey #GO 127182

About ten years ago, in 1989, there was a very large oil spill involving an oil tanker in Alaska. Would you happen to remember the name of the oil company that owned the tanker?

Exxon... 62%
Yes, other.. 7
No, don't remember 24
No opinion 7

Just from what you know and have read, has the 1989 Exxon Valdez *oil spill in Alaska mostly been cleaned up, or is there still oil left in the water and on the beaches in that part of Alaska?*

Cleaned up... 21%
Oil still left.. 66
No opinion 13

Do you think a situation such as this is, or is not, likely to happen again?

Yes, likely.. 91%
Not likely 7
No opinion 2

In 1979, about twenty years ago, there was a nuclear power plant breakdown near Harrisburg, Pennsylvania. Would you happen to remember the name of that nuclear plant, or not?

Three Mile Island 38%
Yes, other.. 3
No, don't remember 47
No opinion 12

Do you think a situation such as this is, or is not, likely to happen again?

Yes, likely.. 72%
Not likely 24
No opinion 4

Note: The United States marks the anniversaries this week of two of the nation's most highly publicized environmental disasters. Ten years ago, the *Exxon Valdez* spilled more than 11 million gallons of Alaskan North Slope crude oil into Prince William Sound in Alaska. Twenty years ago (March 28), an accident at the Three Mile Island nuclear power plant near Harrisburg, Pennsylvania, sent a plume of radiation into the air.

While both are considered among the worst environmental accidents on record, Americans appear to be more concerned today about routine dumping of industrial waste and polluting of the nation's inland waterways than the types of problems engendered by either the *Exxon Valdez* or Three Mile Island. Eighty-five percent now say that they personally worry about the pollution of rivers, lakes, and reservoirs, while 84% are concerned about the contamination of soil and water by toxic waste. A somewhat smaller percentage (75%) worry about the end result of the *Exxon Valdez* accident, ocean and beach pollution, while a still smaller percentage (62%) fear the threat of nuclear power accidents.

In addition, when asked to name the number one environmental problem facing the world today, respondents are most likely to mention air pollution, water pollution, destruction of the rain forests, and global warming, with oil spills mentioned by only 1% and nuclear waste by only 2%. Thus, despite the high visibility of the 1989 and 1979 incidents, more routine environmental problems are the specific objects of higher levels of concern today.

APRIL 6
GUN OWNERSHIP

Interviewing Dates: 2/8–9/99
CNN/*USA Today*/Gallup Poll
Survey #GO 126651

Do you have a gun in your home?

Yes	36%
No	62
No opinion	2

	Yes	No	No opinion
By Sex			
Male	47%	51%	2%
Female	27	71	2
By Ethnic Background			
White	40	59	1
Nonwhite	19	79	2
Black	18	80	2
By Education			
Postgraduate	28	70	2
College Graduate	31	66	3
College Incomplete	38	61	1
No College	39	59	2
By Region			
East	26	73	1
Midwest	39	60	1
South	46	52	2
West	33	65	2
By Age			
18–29 Years	28	71	1
30–49 Years	37	62	1
50–64 Years	46	53	1
65 Years and Over	36	61	3
By Household Income			
$75,000 and Over	37	62	1
$50,000 and Over	42	57	1
$30,000–$49,999	45	54	1
$20,000–$29,999	38	61	1
Under $20,000	23	76	1
By Politics			
Republicans	44	55	1
Democrats	33	67	*
Independents	35	62	3
By Political Ideology			
Conservative	44	54	2
Moderate	37	61	2
Liberal	22	77	1

*Less than 1%

Have you ever fired a gun?

Yes... 67%
No 33

Not including military combat, has anyone close to you, such as a friend or relative, ever been shot by a gun?

Yes... 31%
No 69

Note: Gun ownership in the United States appears to be on the decline, according to Gallup Polls surveying American attitudes on the issue. Thirty-six percent of those responding to a February Gallup Poll said that they keep a gun in their home—the lowest percentage in forty years of polling, reinforcing a trend evident across several recent Gallup surveys. Additionally, the percentage who say that they have personally fired a gun has also dropped to 67%, down from 74% in a 1993 Gallup Poll.

The specific percentage of Americans who report having a gun in the home has varied from survey to survey over the past forty years, but the general trend has been a decline. Gallup surveys taken between 1959 and 1975 showed a 47% average rate of gun ownership. The rate fell to 44% between 1980 and 1989 but rose to 48% in the period between 1990 and 1993. The overall average for the period between 1996 and 1999 stands at 40%, including Gallup's most recent poll conducted on February 8–9, with 36% gun ownership.

The Gallup replies paint a distinct picture of the average American gun owner: he is likely to be white, middle-aged, conservative, to live in a rural area, and to be a resident of the South or Midwest. For example, 47% of men report having a gun at home, compared to 27% of women, and 40% of whites have a gun at home, compared to 19% of nonwhites. Gun ownership is most likely to be found among middle-aged Americans: 46% of those age 50 to 64 own a gun, compared to 28% of those age 18 to 29, 37% of those between the ages of 30 and 49, and 36% of those 65 or over. Gun ownership is highest in the South (46%) and Midwest (39%), and lowest in the East (26%) and West (33%). Perhaps not surprisingly, guns are much more likely to be found in rural homes than they are in urban or suburban dwellings; 52% of

rural Americans admit to keeping a gun at home, compared to 25% of urban residents and 36% of suburbanites. Finally, gun owners tend to be politically conservative and Republican.

While about two-thirds of respondents have fired a gun in their lifetime, the percentage is much higher among men than among women (86% of men have fired a gun compared to 51% of women). Additionally, and perhaps a harbinger of things to come, only 55% of those age 18 to 29 have ever fired a gun, compared to significantly higher percentages among those who are older.

Two different Gallup surveys conducted over the past six years have shown that a surprisingly high number of Americans—about one-third—say that someone close to them has been shot by a gun in circumstances other than military combat. The exact percentage in Gallup's March survey is 31%, down slightly from 36% in 1993.

The probability of knowing someone who has been shot follows significantly different patterns among population subgroups than does the pattern of gun ownership. Although gun ownership is much lower among nonwhites, the percentage of this group that knows someone who has been shot is much higher than it is among whites. In fact, 47% of nonwhites have a friend or relative who has been shot by a gun, compared to only 28% among whites. Younger people are also more likely to know someone who has been shot than are those who are older. And, even though gun ownership is much lower in urban areas than it is in rural areas, the percentage of urban dwellers that knows someone who has been shot is at 36%, compared to 31% among those living in rural areas.

APRIL 7
HOMOSEXUALS

Interviewing Dates: 2/8–9/99
CNN/*USA Today*/Gallup Poll
Survey #GO 126651

Do you think homosexual relations between consenting adults should or should not be legal?

Should.. 50%
Should not 43
No opinion... 7

	Should	Should not	No opinion
By Politics			
Republicans	43%	52%	5%
Democrats	52	41	7
Independents	53	38	9

As you may know, there has been considerable discussion in the news regarding the rights of homosexual men and women. In general, do you think homosexuals should or should not have equal rights in terms of job opportunities?

Should	83%
Should not	13
Other (volunteered); no opinion	4

	Should	Should not	Other; no opinion
By Politics			
Republicans	80%	16%	4%
Democrats	86	9	5
Independents	83	13	4

Do you think homosexuals should or should not be hired for each of the following occupations:

Salespersons?

Should	90%
Should not	8
It depends (volunteered)	1
No opinion	1

Members of the armed forces?

Should	70%
Should not	26
It depends (volunteered)	2
No opinion	2

Doctors?

Should	75%
Should not	21
It depends (volunteered)	2
No opinion	2

The clergy?

Should	54%
Should not	40
It depends (volunteered)	2
No opinion	4

Elementary-school teachers?

Should	54%
Should not	42
It depends (volunteered)	2
No opinion	2

High-school teachers?

Should	61%
Should not	36
It depends (volunteered)	2
No opinion	1

Members of the president's cabinet?

Should	74%
Should not	23
It depends (volunteered)	1
No opinion	2

Do you feel that homosexual behavior should be considered an acceptable life-style, or not?*

Yes, acceptable	52%
Not acceptable	44
No opinion	4

*Based on half sample

	Yes, acceptable	Not acceptable	No opinion
By Politics			
Republicans	40%	58%	2%
Democrats	56	37	7
Independents	56	40	4

Note: A Wyoming man has received two life sentences in prison for his part in the abduction and beating death last fall of Matthew Shepard, a gay student at the University of Wyoming. Russell Henderson avoided the likelihood of a death sentence by agreeing to a plea bargain with prosecutors just as his trial was scheduled to begin on kidnapping and felony murder charges. He has agreed to testify in the August trial of Aaron McKinney, the other suspect in the Shepard case, and will never be eligible for parole.

The Shepard case and last year's brutal dragging death of an African-American man in Jasper, Texas, have ignited the national debate over hate crime legislation. President Bill Clinton has endorsed a national hate crime bill now pending in Congress that would expand current federal antidiscrimination laws to include gender, sexual orientation, and disability.

Seven in ten Americans favor hate crime legislation at the state level, according to a February Gallup Poll. Support for the concept is highest among minorities and younger people, but it also receives strong support from senior citizens and those who describe themselves as politically conservative. Three in four believe that gay men and lesbians should be included in state hate crime laws, although this is a lower percentage than for other protected groups such as religious and ethnic minorities, women, and racial minorities.

Gallup has been tracking American attitudes on the gay rights issue for more than twenty years, and the poll results continue to show that the public is divided on the acceptability of homosexual behavior and life-style. In the latest Gallup survey on the issue, taken earlier this year, just over one-half of all those polled believe that homosexuality should be considered an acceptable alternative life-style, while 44% consider it unacceptable. The same poll also found that 50% believe that homosexual relations between consenting adults should be legal; this figure marks the highest level of support in response to this question in this decade: 43% oppose consenting sexual relations between adults of the same gender, while 7% offer no opinion. Historically, the strongest level of support for consenting homosexual relations came in 1987, when 55% approved. However, that level of support fell to 36% in 1989 before starting a steady climb over the last ten years.

APRIL 9
LEGALIZATION OF MARIJUANA

Interviewing Dates: 3/19–21/99
CNN/*USA Today*/Gallup Poll
Survey #GO 127182

Suppose that on Election Day this year you could vote on key issues as well as candidates. Please tell me whether you would vote for or against each one of the following propositions:

The legalization of marijuana?

For	29%
Against	69
No opinion	2

	For	Against	No opinion
By Age			
18–29 Years	44%	54%	2%
30–49 Years	30	68	2
50–64 Years	21	78	1
65 Years and Over	11	85	4
By Politics			
Republicans	22	77	1
Democrats	27	71	2
Independents	37	60	3

Making marijuana legally available for doctors to prescribe in order to reduce pain and suffering?

For	73%
Against	25
No opinion	2

	For	Against	No opinion
By Age			
18–29 Years	77%	22%	1%
30–49 Years	75	24	1
50–64 Years	72	25	3
65 Years and Over	63	35	2
By Politics			
Republicans	63	36	1
Democrats	76	23	1
Independents	79	19	2

Note: By a large majority, Americans continue to oppose the general legalization of marijuana, but by an even larger majority they would support the drug's use for medicinal purposes. These findings, from a Gallup Poll conducted on March 19–21, followed the announcement several days earlier from the Institute of Medicine, an affiliate of the National Academy of Sciences, that marijuana's active ingredients can ease the pain, nausea, and vomiting caused by cancer and AIDS.

According to the poll, 29% of respondents support general legalization of marijuana, while 69% are opposed. These figures represent a slight gain for the proposal, with support higher than last year by 5 percentage points. In four previous polls dating back to 1979, support has varied from 23% to 28%. The earliest poll asking about this issue was conducted in 1969, when only 12% supported legalization.

Despite this opposition to the general legalization of the drug, by a 3-to-1 margin, respondents would support making marijuana available to doctors so that it could be prescribed to reduce pain and suffering. In six states, voters have already approved marijuana for medicinal use, although the drug remains banned by federal law. With the replies to both questions taken into account, the poll shows that 28% support legalization of marijuana for whatever reason, 25% oppose it even for medicinal purposes, and 43% support it for medicinal purposes but not for general use.

APRIL 22
THE ENVIRONMENT

Interviewing Dates: 4/13–14/99
CNN/*USA Today*/Gallup Poll
Survey #GO 127414

How would you rate your satisfaction with the state of the nation in terms of protection of the environment—are you very satisfied, somewhat satisfied, not too satisfied, or not at all satisfied?

Very satisfied.................................. 10%
Somewhat satisfied........................ 59
Not too satisfied............................ 22
Not at all satisfied......................... 8
No opinion..................................... 1

For each of the following, please say whether you think it is too worried about the environment, not worried enough, or expresses about the right amount of concern about the environment:

The American public?

Too worried.................................... 10%
Not worried enough........................ 57
Right amount 31
No opinion..................................... 2

The government?

Too worried.................................... 14%
Not worried enough........................ 57
Right amount 27
No opinion..................................... 2

American business and industry?

Too worried.................................... 4%
Not worried enough........................ 74
Right amount 19
No opinion..................................... 3

How much progress have we made in dealing with environmental problems in this country in the past few decades, say, since 1970— would you say we have made a great deal of progress, only some progress, or hardly any progress at all?

Great deal 36%
Only some...................................... 55
Hardly any 8
No opinion..................................... 1

Here are two statements which people sometimes make when discussing the environment and economic growth. Which of these statements comes closer to your own point of view—protection of the environment should be given priority, even at the risk of curbing economic growth; or economic growth should be given priority, even if the environment suffers to some extent?

	April 13–14, 1999	March 12–14, 1999
Protection of the environment	67%	65%
Economic growth...........................	28	30
No opinion	5	5

Do you consider yourself to be an environmentalist, or not?

Yes 50%
No 48
No opinion 2

	Yes	No	No opinion
By Politics			
Republicans	43%	56%	1%
Democrats...................	54	45	1
Independents..............	52	45	3

Note: On the eve of the thirtieth annual celebration of Earth Day, a new Gallup Poll finds that Americans have grown increasingly satisfied this decade with the nation's environmental protection efforts. A majority still sees room for improvement, but there is a growing perception that there has been progress in dealing with environmental problems and that society—particularly government and the public—expresses a sufficient amount of concern for the issue. Perhaps most striking, two-thirds today say that they are generally satisfied with the state of environmental protection in the United States, up from barely one-half who felt this positively six years ago.

The relative contentment with the environment seen today could be a considered response by the public to real improvements in this area, but it could also be viewed in the larger context of respondents' satisfaction with the state of the nation. In 1993, when only 52% were satisfied with environmental protection, overall satisfaction with the way things were going in the United States stood at just 29%. The 69% who are satisfied with the environment today should be viewed in the framework of today's 58% overall satisfaction with the country.

APRIL 23
LITTLETON, COLORADO, SHOOTING/TEEN VIOLENCE

Interviewing Date: 4/21/99
CNN/*USA Today*/Gallup Poll
Survey #GO 127494

Which of the following statements comes closer to your view of shootings like the one in Colorado—they are indications that there is something seriously wrong in the country today, or they are isolated incidents that do not indicate anything about the country in general?

Something seriously wrong 79%
Isolated incidents 17
Other (volunteered) 1
No opinion 3

In your opinion, how likely is it that these kinds of shootings could happen in your community—very likely, somewhat likely, somewhat unlikely, or very unlikely?

	April 21, 1999	April 18–20, 1998*
Very likely	30%	37%
Somewhat likely	38	34
Somewhat unlikely	14	15
Very unlikely	15	12
No opinion	3	2

*NBC/Wall Street Journal question wording: *As you may know, two young boys recently shot and killed several people at a school in Jonesboro, Arkansas. In your opinion, how likely is it that these kinds of shootings could happen in your community . . . ?*

In your view, how effective is each of the following as a way to stop violence in high schools and middle schools—very effective, somewhat effective, not too effective, or not effective at all:

Metal detectors in schools?

Very effective 53%
Somewhat effective 33
Not too effective 8
Not effective at all 4
No opinion 2

Random body searches of students?

Very effective 34%
Somewhat effective 36
Not too effective 13
Not effective at all 15
No opinion 2

Stricter gun control laws for teenagers?

Very effective	62%
Somewhat effective	18
Not too effective	6
Not effective at all	12
No opinion	2

Stricter regulation of violence on television and in movies?

Very effective	52%
Somewhat effective	29
Not too effective	10
Not effective at all	9
No opinion	*

*Less than 1%

School dress codes?

Very effective	36%
Somewhat effective	30
Not too effective	15
Not effective at all	17
No opinion	2

Restrictions on what is available to teenagers on the Internet?

Very effective	50%
Somewhat effective	27
Not too effective	10
Not effective at all	8
No opinion	5

Increased counseling for teenagers?

Very effective	60%
Somewhat effective	28
Not too effective	5
Not effective at all	5
No opinion	2

Stiffer penalties for parents whose children commit crimes?

Very effective	34%
Somewhat effective	28
Not too effective	16
Not effective at all	20
No opinion	2

Holding parents legally responsible for crimes their children commit with their parents' guns?

Very effective	47%
Somewhat effective	28
Not too effective	12
Not effective at all	12
No opinion	1

Which of the following statements comes closer to your overall view—government and society can take action that will be effective in preventing shootings like the one in Colorado from happening again, or shootings like the one in Colorado will happen again regardless of what action is taken by government and society?

Can take action	53%
Will happen again	43
No opinion	4

Note: In the aftermath of the tragic events in Littleton, Colorado, a Gallup Poll taken on Wednesday evening [April 21] found that most Americans believe that the shooting rampage at Columbine High School by two students is evidence of deeper problems in the United States. Seventy-nine percent of those surveyed say that the attack, which left a teacher and fourteen students—including the two gunmen—dead, is an indication of serious problems, compared to only 17% who see the event as an isolated incident. At the same time, only a bare majority of the public (53%) expresses confidence that government and society can do anything to prevent similar acts of violence in the future. Two-thirds consider it likely that a similar incident could happen in their own community.

The public's skepticism about acts of teen violence similar to the one that occurred in Littleton may not be surprising given that the attack at Columbine High School is, according to Associated Press reports, the seventh fatal shooting at a U.S. high school in less than two years. However, when presented with several specific proposals, respondents appear somewhat more optimistic that there are effective ways to curtail the problem of violence in schools. In particular, they indicate significant confidence in the potential impact of stricter gun control laws and teen counseling with roughly three in five (62% and 60%, respectively) saying that each of these measures would be a "very effective" way to stop violence in high schools and middle schools. About one-half of those interviewed also believe that metal detectors at schools, stricter regulation of violence on television and in movies, and restricting teenagers' access to certain material on the Internet would be very effective measures. Student dress codes and random body searches, two remedies that sometimes raise civil libertarian objections, are considered very effective by only one-third of the public.

APRIL 28
TEEN VIOLENCE—AN ANALYSIS*

In some respects, today's teens live in a world of fear and uncertainty. Many do not feel safe on the streets or even in their own homes, according to Gallup Youth Surveys carried out in the months prior to the tragic events at Columbine High School in Littleton, Colorado. At the same time, student perceptions that their schools are safe—perhaps ironically—were more positive in a survey taken just before the Littleton shootings than they were three years earlier.

The Gallup Youth Survey (conducted through The George H. Gallup International Institute) has been asking questions of teenagers in the United States for twenty-two years. A review of recent results suggests that teens are worried about becoming the victims of violence. As many as four in ten teenagers, for example, think that at some point in their lifetimes, someone is likely to fire a gun at them. Four in ten teens are fearful of walking alone at night in certain areas within a mile of their homes. Half say they will at some point be mugged.

Teens also reveal angst and are apparently becoming cynical about the world around them. Two-thirds, for example, say there are too many rules and sometimes one has to break them. Seven in ten say the world is becoming too complicated.

*This analysis was written by George Gallup, Jr., Co-Chairman, The Gallup Organization.

And more than half of teenagers (54%) say that one usually cannot trust people who are in power.

Our nation's youth are apprehensive about the future and believe the quality of life for children in the future will be worse than it is today. They are uneasy about a host of problems: the threat of AIDS; the availability of potentially deadly drugs; the ease of purchasing deadly assault weapons; random death and violence.

School Fear Had Subsided Prior to Littleton

At the same time that young people hold these more negative perceptions, a Gallup Youth Survey completed just before the tragedy in Littleton revealed that the percentage of teens that consider school an unsafe place was actually significantly lower than in earlier years. In the early part of this year, 15% of teens said that they sometimes fear for their physical safety at school. In 1996, however, the percentage was nearly double this figure—28%. A Gallup Youth Survey now in the field, after the widespread publicity surrounding the Littleton events, may reveal an increase in this percentage over the current 15%.

Even in the early 1999 pre-Littleton survey, teens named the following as "very" or "fairly" big problems: vandalism and destruction of personal or school property (44%); theft of personal property (42%); students bringing weapons such as guns or knives to school (17%, up from 13% recorded in 1998); students attacking teachers (8%).

Learning Modern Survival Skills

Many young people, concerned about the violent world around them today, feel it is important to learn modern survival skills. Virtually every teen interviewed (96%) says it is very or somewhat important to "know how to keep safe in a big city"; 82% hold these views about "knowing self-defense skills" such as karate; 46% say it is very or somewhat important to know how to shoot a gun, while 6% indicate it is very or somewhat important to belong to a "gang" or "posse."

Possible Factors Contributing to Violence

Gallup Youth Surveys shed light not only on the extent of the problem of violence in the world of young people, but also on the factors that may contribute to this violence, as well as possible strategies to deal with this situation. More than half of U.S. teens believe that television shows, movies, or news programs containing violence may play a role in violent behavior by teens, such as gang warfare or shootings at schools.

Teens are also likely to perceive an influence by the media and Internet in terms of life-styles. More than six in ten say they have noticed changes in their friends, such as the way they talk, dress, or act, because of something they saw or heard in the media or on the Internet.

Possible Causes?

There are many factors that may contribute to a climate of violence or acts of violence. Here, on the basis of interviews of teens, are some possible causes:

- *Peer Pressure.* One-third of teens (35%) say they are under a "great deal" or "some" pressure from their peers to "break rules." Many report being teased about their appearance and clothes.
- *Attitudes of Adults.* Half of teens say they receive "too little" respect from adults, and many feel that they are misunderstood.
- *Physical Abuse.* One teen in eight reports that he or she has been physically abused—that is, intentionally harmed by beating, hitting, kicking, and so on, out of anger rather than play.
- *Community to Blame.* Many teens fault their communities for not doing more to provide counseling and mentoring for young people.
- *Missing Parents.* One-third of teens cannot talk about "life with Father." When asked what relatives live at home with them, although 91% say their mother, only 67% say their father.
- *Alienated.* One in five teens falls into the category of "alienated," as determined by a Gallup Youth Survey scale. As many as one teen in ten is willing to admit that they are not happy with "the way they are."
- *Spiritual Vacuum.* Only 13% of teens say people their age are influenced a "great deal" by religion. Twice as many turn to themselves to answer the problems of life as turn to God.
- *Too Much TV.* Seven in ten teens admit that they watch too much television.

- *Dangerous Music.* Six in ten teenagers believe "gangsta rap" encourages violence.
- *Living Dangerously.* Four in ten teens say they "like to live dangerously"; 48% say they like to "shock people"; one-third (36%) "worry a lot about death."

What Can Be Done?

What are some of the things that teens say they would be willing to do or want society to do that could, either directly or indirectly, reduce the climate of violence?

1. Six in ten say that laws governing the sale of firearms should be more strict; 54% would favor a total ban on assault rifles; 70% say Americans should not have the right to own large quantities of ammunition.
2. Seven in ten in the pre-Littleton survey say they would report someone who brought a weapon to school, yet three in ten would not.
3. Many teens say that there should be a reduction in violence on television, in movies, and on the Internet.
4. Seven in ten say there should be a greater number of positive role models on television, in movies, and in song lyrics.
5. Teens overwhelmingly favor the teaching of values in schools, such as honesty, caring for a friend or family member, moral courage, patriotism, democracy, and the Golden Rule.
6. In terms of national service, half of all teens say they are very interested in working to "keep kids out of gangs and off drugs." Six in ten would like to be tutors and mentors to younger students.
7. There is support for the idea of undergirding life with spiritual moorings. The nearer a person feels to God, surveys reveal, the better they feel about themselves and others.

APRIL 30
TEEN VIOLENCE/LITTLETON, COLORADO, SHOOTING

Interviewing Dates: 4/26–27/99
CNN/*USA Today*/Gallup Poll
Survey #GO 127538

Do you have any children now attending school, Kindergarten through Grade 12?

Yes 30%
No 70

Asked of those who replied in the affirmative: Thinking about your oldest child, when he or she is at school, do you fear for his or her physical safety?*

	April 26–27, 1999	April 21, 1999
Yes, fear	49%	55%
Do not	51	45

*Margin of sampling error: ±6 percentage points

Also asked of those who replied in the affirmative: Now, thinking about your school-age child or children, have you:

Talked with a child about their concerns and fears at their school?

Yes, have 78%
Have not 22

Talked with a child about the Littleton shootings?

Yes, have 81%
Have not 19

Cautioned a child to take safety precautions at their school?

Yes, have 72%
Have not 28

Cautioned a child not to get involved in confrontations with other students?

Yes, have 81%
Have not 19

Contacted a child's school to discuss safety issues?

Yes, have 23%
Have not 77

Also asked of those who replied in the affirmative: Have any of your school-age children expressed any worry or concern about feeling unsafe at their school since the Littleton shootings, or not?

Yes, have 17%
Have not 82
No opinion 1

In your opinion, do you think criminal charges should or should not be filed against the parents of the students involved in the Littleton deaths, or are you unsure?

Should 25%
Should not 26
Unsure 48
No opinion 1

Overall, do you feel the news media have acted responsibly or irresponsibly in this situation?

Responsibly 67%
Irresponsibly 29
No opinion 4

In general, do you think the amount of coverage the news media have given to the Littleton situation has been too much, not enough, or is the coverage about right?

Too much 47%
Not enough 2
About right 50
No opinion 1

Note: As police in Littleton, Colorado, try to figure out just what provoked last week's shooting spree that claimed the lives of twelve students, a teacher, and the teenage gunmen, a new Gallup Poll finds that one-quarter of the U.S. public thinks that the parents of gunmen Dylan Klebold and Eric Harris should face criminal charges, although one-half of those interviewed say that it is too early to tell. Similarly, when asked to offer their explanation for why this tragedy occurred, most Americans place blame on a wide combination of different factors, although parents are the most prominent single cause mentioned.

On April 26 and 27, Gallup interviewers asked the public an open-ended question about what caused the shootings. About one-half of the respondents said that a variety of many different factors were responsible, rather than any one issue. Twenty percent placed the blame solely on poor parenting or family breakdown generally, or lack of parental discipline specifically. By comparison, just 6% put the blame solely on the mental or psychological state of the teen gunmen, 3% blamed the teasing from other students that made the gunmen outcasts, while 2% cited the entertainment industry. Other factors were mentioned by 1% to 2% of respondents, such as lack of school security and a decline in religious values.

Americans are split on the question of whether the parents of Klebold and Harris should face criminal charges in the shootings. That issue is still being debated by Colorado prosecutors and police, but 25% already believe that some form of prosecution should take place. About the same number (26%) say that charges should not be filed, while 48% remain unsure. There is a slight difference in the replies of parents and nonparents to this question, with 30% of parents of school-age children favoring prosecution, compared to 23% of nonparents.

The Columbine High shootings have again forced parents to confront the issue of safety in the nation's schools. However, fear appears to affect parents more than it does students. In the latest Gallup Poll, 49% of parents fear for their oldest child's safety at school, significantly higher than the 37% who expressed such fears last summer. When those parents were asked whether their children have expressed any concerns about their safety after the Columbine High shootings, only 17% of parents responded yes. Eight in ten parents have talked with their children about the shootings, and the same percentage have urged their children to avoid confrontations with other students, but only 23% have contacted their child's school to discuss safety issues.

While the media have been quick to report so-called copycat cases at other schools since the shootings, only 11% of parents have heard of an actual copycat threat at their child's school.

However, the media get high marks for their coverage of the shootings: two in three respondents (67%) say that the media have acted responsibly in their coverage, and 50% say that the amount of media coverage has been about right.

MAY 3
GUN CONTROL/THE NRA

Interviewing Dates: 4/26–27/99
CNN/*USA Today*/Gallup Poll
Survey #GO 127538

Which of the following statements comes closest to your view—there should be no restrictions on owning guns; there should be minor restrictions, such as a five-day waiting period to buy a gun, and gun registrations; there should be major restrictions that would also ban ownership of some guns altogether, such as handguns and certain semiautomatic rifles; or all guns should be illegal for everyone except police and authorized persons?

	April 26–27, 1999	Feb. 8–9, 1999
No restrictions	4%	5%
Minor restrictions	30	37
Major restrictions	38	36
All guns illegal except for police	22	18
Some restrictions (volunteered)	4	–
No opinion	2	4

April 26–27, 1999

	No restrictions	Minor, major, some restrictions	All guns illegal	No opinion
By Politics				
Republicans	6%	76%	17%	1%
Democrats	5	68	26	1
Independents	3	74	22	1

Next, what is your overall opinion of the National Rifle Association, also known as the NRA—very favorable, mostly favorable, mostly unfavorable, or very unfavorable?

Very favorable 14%

Mostly favorable.. 37
Mostly unfavorable... 22
Very unfavorable.. 18
No opinion.. 9

Do you have a favorable or unfavorable opinion of Charlton Heston, the movie actor who is president of the National Rifle Association?

Favorable 43%
Unfavorable.. 28
Heard of, no opinion (volunteered)................ 22
Never heard of (volunteered) 5
No opinion.. 2

Note: One result of the Littleton, Colorado, high-school shooting tragedy has been the increased focus on laws governing gun sales and gun possession in this country. President Bill Clinton has proposed new and more rigid gun control measures, and other proponents of gun control at the national and state levels have used the Columbine High School shootings as a platform for advocacy of stricter gun control legislation. In fact, a Gallup Poll taken on April 21, immediately after the shootings, shows that the availability of guns is seen as the number one cause of the deaths (among a list of potential causes read to respondents) and that making guns less available to teens is seen as the most effective potential remedy.

In the most general terms, and perhaps not surprisingly in light of these views, Gallup Poll data suggest that the public is highly receptive to gun control measures. Two-thirds say that the United States needs gun control laws that are more strict, and six in ten say either that there should be a total ban on guns or that there should be major restrictions on their availability.

More than one-half of the public has indicated throughout this decade that gun laws should be more strict, although the prevalence of this attitude was declining prior to the Littleton events. In 1990, 78% said that gun laws should be more strict, a percentage that had fallen to 60% in February of this year. In the aftermath of the Columbine High School deaths, however, the percentage choosing the "more strict" alternative has gone back up to 66%, most likely in direct response to these events.

Another question included in the April 26–27 Gallup Poll asked respondents to place themselves in one of four categories in relation to gun control: in favor of a total ban on guns, in favor of major gun restrictions, in favor of minor gun restrictions, or in favor of no restrictions whatsoever. The results show that 22% of those interviewed favor the total ban and another 38% favor major restrictions, meaning that a total of 60% are in favor of fairly strong gun control measures. Another 30% favor minor restrictions, while only 4% say that there should be no restrictions at all. In short, about 90% of the public favors at least minor restrictions on gun purchases and gun possession.

These attitudes are exemplified in the reaction of the public to one of the gun control measures proposed by President Clinton, which would require a background check on purchasers of weapons at gun shows. This is an important question in the current environment, given that authorities believe that at least one of the weapons used in Littleton may have been purchased at a show. The reaction of the public is overwhelmingly in favor of such a law, with 83% of those interviewed in a February 1999 poll saying that they approve.

The National Rifle Association has been in the center of the debate on gun control, particularly given the publicity surrounding the fact that the NRA's annual meeting was scheduled for Denver, near Littleton, this past weekend. (The NRA shortened the convention to a business meeting only.) Despite the strong desire for new and stricter gun control measures, the public's opinion of the NRA is actually higher now than it was in 1995, with 51% now having a favorable opinion, compared to 40% who have an unfavorable one. The NRA's highly visible president, actor Charlton Heston, also gets a more favorable than unfavorable rating from the public, by 43% to 28%; the rest could not or would not rate him.

MAY 10
TEEN VIOLENCE

Interviewing Dates: 4/30–5/2/99
CNN/*USA Today*/Gallup Poll
Survey #GO 127557

Do you think any of the blame for teenage crimes can be placed on television and movie violence? If "Yes," how much of the blame should be put on television and movies—a great deal, some, or only a little?

A great deal	31%
Some	34
Only a little	8
None	26
No opinion	1

For each of the following, please say whether you think the federal government should do more to regulate violence in that area, whether it should do less, or if it is doing the right amount:

On television?

More	56%
Less	15
Right amount	28
No opinion	1

In movies?

More	49%
Less	15
Right amount	34
No opinion	2

In popular music?

More	48%
Less	17
Right amount	31
No opinion	4

On the Internet?

More	65%
Less	12
Right amount	17
No opinion	6

In video games?

More	58%
Less	15
Right amount	22
No opinion	5

Interviewing Date: 4/21/99
CNN/*USA Today*/Gallup Poll
Survey #GO 127494

How much do you blame each of the following for causing shootings like the one in Littleton, Colorado—a great deal, a moderate amount, not much, or not at all:

The Internet?

Great deal	34%
Moderate amount	30
Not much	18
Not at all	11
No opinion	7

Parents?

Great deal	51%
Moderate amount	33
Not much	10
Not at all	4
No opinion	2

Schools?

Great deal	11%
Moderate amount	35
Not much	30
Not at all	22
No opinion	2

Television programs, movies, and music?

Great deal	49%
Moderate amount	30
Not much	14
Not at all	6
No opinion	1

Availability of guns?

Great deal	60%
Moderate amount	19
Not much	9
Not at all	9
No opinion	3

Social pressures on youth?

Great deal	43%
Moderate amount	36

Not much 13
Not at all 5
No opinion 3

Media coverage of similar incidents?

Great deal 34%
Moderate amount 40
Not much 14
Not at all 9
No opinion 3

Note: The Littleton, Colorado, tragedy has focused renewed attention on the impact of violence on television, in movies, in video games, and on the Internet. While Gallup polling suggests that Americans did not immediately think of such media portrayals as causes of the Columbine High School shooting deaths, media violence is considered one of the major causes of school violence and teenage crimes more generally. Additionally, a substantial percentage endorses increased government regulation of media and Internet violence and thinks that it would be effective in preventing such incidents in the future.

A Gallup Poll conducted in late April asked Americans to describe in their own words why they thought that the Littleton tragedy occurred. Only 5% explicitly mentioned entertainment, television, movies, music, the Internet, or video games in reply to this question. The cause most frequently mentioned—named by 40% of those interviewed—was the breakdown of the family and poor parenting. The situation was somewhat different, however, when respondents were read a list of possible causes for the violent events in Colorado in an April 21 poll, conducted immediately after the Littleton tragedy had occurred. "Television programs, movies, and music" was the third most-highly-blamed cause out of seven read to respondents, with 49% of those polled saying that it should be given a great deal of blame for causing shootings such as the one in Littleton. The highest degree of blame was assigned to the availability of guns (60%) and to parents (51%).

And, in another recent poll, 31% placed a great deal of blame on television and movies for teenage crimes, with another 34% saying that these media merit some blame. Interestingly, in 1954, when Gallup asked a similar question, 24% said that "mystery and crime TV and radio shows" had a great deal of blame for teenage crimes, with another 32% saying that they deserved some blame. The impact of comic books on teenage crime was rated almost the same. In short, it does not appear that blaming the media for teenage deviance is a new phenomenon.

How effective would the regulation of violence on television, in movies, and on the Internet be in curbing violence in schools? Out of nine possible remedies suggested in an April poll, stricter regulation of violence on television and in movies was seen as potentially very effective by 52% of those surveyed, about the same percentage as thought that restrictions on the Internet would be very effective. On a relative basis, both of these actions were perceived as being potentially somewhat less effective than stricter gun control laws and increased counseling for teenagers, but they were given about the same level of potential effectiveness as metal detectors in schools and holding parents legally responsible for crimes committed by children with their parents' guns.

There is increased discussion of the value of possible government regulation of the content of television, movies, and the Internet—a subject to be reviewed in detail at a youth violence summit at the White House. The survey results suggest that substantial numbers are in favor of such regulation. Sixty-five percent favor more government regulation of violence on the Internet, 58% favor increased government regulation of violence in video games, and 56% favor increased government regulation of violence on television. Slightly smaller percentages (about one-half) favor more government regulation of violence in movies and in popular music.

MAY 13
SCHOOL VIOLENCE—AN ANALYSIS*

An enormous amount of energy has been expended since the tragic events of April 20 in Littleton, Colorado, in attempting to disentangle

*This analysis was written by Frank Newport, Editor in Chief, The Gallup Poll.

both the tragedy's causes and ways in which similar events can be prevented in the future. The White House youth violence summit held this past Monday [May 10] laid a foundation for a national campaign against youth violence, and plans were made to conduct a study of the causes of such violence. Representatives at the meeting discussed a wide variety of possible causes, including guns, violence in movies, lack of parental responsibility, lack of religious faith, the Internet, and so forth.

The American public, as an analysis of Gallup Poll data suggests, has similar tendencies to recognize that there are a number of causes of youth violence and therefore a number of possible remedies that will be necessary to avoid a repetition of such events in the future. A Gallup Poll conducted this past weekend, for example, included a question that asked Americans to identify, in their own words, the single most important thing that could be done to prevent another incident of school shootings by students. The responses varied widely. The top three responses were:

- More parental involvement and parental responsibility: 32% of Americans chose this, making it the number one response
- More security at schools, chosen by 16% of Americans
- Better gun control, mentioned by 12% of Americans

Additionally, 6% of the public mentioned hiring more counselors and an additional 6% mentioned the lifting of laws on disciplining children, while controlling media violence and better communication among parents, students, and teachers were each mentioned by 4%.

There are interesting differences in these answers based on the ages of the respondents. Almost no 18-to-29 year olds, the youngest group included in the survey, mentioned the lifting of laws preventing discipline of children as a remedy, compared to 11% of those 65 and older. On the other hand, young people were much more likely to mention better security at schools (as many, in fact, as mentioned parental responsibility).

Coming at the issue in a slightly different way, this past weekend's Gallup Poll also asked Americans to rate the importance of each of thirteen specific possible causes of increased violence in the nation's public schools. The items had originally been rated in a poll conducted by Gallup for Phi Delta Kappa, the national educational society, in 1994. The survey revealed the following rank order of the thirteen potential causes:

Very im-portant

1. Breakdown of the American family 76%
2. Increased use of drugs and alcohol among school-age youth......................... 74
3. Easy availability of weapons, including guns and knives 72
4. Growth of youth gangs........................... 71
5. Schools not having the authority to discipline that they once had 69
6. Inability of school staff to resolve conflicts between students...................... 64
7. Increased portrayal of violence in media (especially in movies and on television)... 62
8. Trying to deal with troubled or emotionally disturbed students in the regular classroom instead of in special classes or schools 61
9. Shortages of school personnel................ 55
10. Cutbacks in many school support programs.. 54
11. A school curriculum that is out of touch with the needs of today's students.. 50
12. Increased cultural, racial, and ethnic diversity among the public-school student population 41
13. Increased poverty among parents........... 39

One notable factor in this list is the relatively low priority given by Americans to the portrayal of violence in the media. Previous Gallup polling has indicated that Americans are quite willing to agree that such media portrayals may lead to real-life violence, but this measure shows that other factors are considered even more important as causes of school violence. For example, although six out of ten Americans agreed that media violence may be an important cause of events such as Littleton, up to three-quarters of those interviewed agreed that the breakdown in the American family is a very important cause.

Americans who are 18 to 29 are closest in age to high-school students, and in some ways may have the best perspective on the causes of school violence. The table below compares 18-to-29 year olds' ratings of these causes with the ratings of the oldest group in the survey, those 65 and older:

| | Very important | | |
	18–29	65+	Difference
Shortages of school personnel	56%	50%	+6
Cutbacks in school support programs	55	51	+4
Increased diversity among students	41	42	−1
Increased poverty among parents	34	36	−2
Easy availability of weapons	74	79	−5
Breakdown of family	75	81	−6
Out-of-touch school curriculum	52	59	−7
Mainstreaming troubled students	58	68	−10
Inability of schools to resolve conflicts	59	72	−13
Growth of youth gangs	64	78	−14
Increased use of drugs and alcohol	65	83	−18
Schools don't have authority to discipline	56	86	−30
Violence in media	45	77	−32

The biggest differences occur in terms of two of the causes in the list—the impact of violence in the media, and schools not having the authority to discipline. Young people are much less likely than older Americans to feel that these are important causes of incidents such as Littleton. On the other hand, those most recently in high school are more likely than those 65 and over to blame two dimensions related to the schools themselves: shortages of school personnel, and cutbacks in school support programs.

A separate question included in this past weekend's survey asked directly if the depiction of violence in popular entertainment is a cause of violence among young people. Although 62% of all Americans agreed, there were again enormous differences between young and old: only 43% of those 18 to 29 agreed, a percentage that jumps to 63% among those 30 to 49 and 79% among those 65 and above.

Some of the controversy surrounding media portrayals of violence concerns what should be done about it. Vice presidential spouse Tipper Gore, for example, has argued that voluntary attempts to control the content of media will work better than official government regulation. Media moguls in Hollywood, as well, tend to resist any thought of government regulation. The public's response to this issue depends on the way in which it is framed. Gallup Poll questioning that asks only about the need for government regulation as a way of controlling violence finds majority support for such regulation of the Internet, video games, and television. This past weekend, on the other hand, a question was asked of the public that juxtaposed two alternatives: increased protests, including boycotts and other voluntary actions by citizens, versus increased government regulation. Given this choice, the public comes down in favor of voluntary actions by a 55%-to-36% margin.

MAY 14
RUSSIA

Interviewing Dates: 5/7–9/99
CNN/*USA Today*/Gallup Poll
Survey #GO 127652

Is your overall opinion of Russia very favorable, mostly favorable, mostly unfavorable, or very unfavorable?

	May 7–9, 1999	April 13–14, 1999	Feb. 8–9, 1999
Very favorable	4%	3%	6%
Mostly favorable	42	30	38
Mostly unfavorable	36	45	34
Very unfavorable	13	14	10
No opinion	5	8	12

May 7–9, 1999

	Very favorable	Mostly favorable	Mostly unfavorable	Very unfavorable*
By Politics				
Republicans.....	4%	42%	38%	12%
Democrats	2	44	34	15
Independents ...	5	41	35	12

*"No opinion"—at 7% or less—is omitted.

Interviewing Dates: 4/13–14/99
CNN/*USA Today*/Gallup Poll
Survey #GO 127414

In your view, should the United States continue to support Russian President Boris Yeltsin, or don't you think so?

	April 13–14, 1999	March 19–21, 1999
Yes, continue to support	48%	59%
Don't think so	42	32
No opinion	10	9

April 13–14, 1999

	Yes, continue to support	Don't think so	No opinion
By Politics			
Republicans	52%	40%	8%
Democrats..................	50	40	10
Independents...............	45	44	11

In your view, is Russia a significant military threat to the United States today, or don't you think so?

	April 13–14, 1999	March 19–21, 1999
Yes, significant threat	48%	42%
Don't think so	48	54
No opinion	4	4

April 13–14, 1999

	Yes, significant threat	Don't think so	No opinion
By Politics			
Republicans	47%	52%	1%
Democrats..................	49	46	5
Independents..............	49	46	5

As a result of the disagreements between NATO countries and Russia on the NATO military action in Yugoslavia, do you think that it is likely that a new Cold War will break out between Russia and the Western nations, or not?

Yes, likely..	33%
No	59
No opinion..	8

	Yes, likely	No	No opinion
By Politics			
Republicans	33%	64%	3%
Democrats..................	32	56	12
Independents...............	32	59	9

Interviewing Dates: 3/19–21/99
CNN/*USA Today*/Gallup Poll
Survey #GO 127182

Would you favor or oppose the United States increasing economic aid to Russia?

Favor...	43%
Oppose..	53
No opinion.......................................	4

	Favor	Oppose	No opinion
By Politics			
Republicans	41%	57%	2%
Democrats..................	40	54	6
Independents...............	47	49	4

Note: The American public continues to maintain a cautiously skeptical view of Russia, with less than one-half holding a favorable view of the country. Sentiments about Russian President Boris Yeltsin are similarly mixed, and there is concern on the part of the American people that Russia could still constitute a significant military threat to the United States. Additionally, a majority of Americans oppose increasing economic aid to the beleaguered nation.

Gallup Poll assessments of Russia go back more than forty-five years. Not surprisingly, almost nine in ten Americans in 1954 had an unfavorable opinion of Russia, a view that moderated only slightly as the Cold War progressed through the 1970s and 1980s. But the end of the Soviet Union at the beginning of this decade did not totally change the public's perception. In a poll conducted on May 7–9, only 46% of Americans had a favorable opinion of Russia, with 49% having an unfavorable one. This result puts Russia in a midrange position in terms of Americans' perceptions of other countries, below such traditional allies as Great Britain and Israel but more favorably evaluated than such countries as China or Iraq. Older Americans, who have the longest memory, have a more unfavorable opinion of Russia than do those who are younger, but there are not large differences in opinion between Republicans and Democrats or between conservatives and liberals.

The American opinion of Boris Yeltsin has gone up and down throughout this decade. Recently, in Gallup's December 1998 poll, just 47% had a favorable opinion of the Russian president, and 48% in an April 13–14, 1999, poll say that the United States should continue to support him. Both of these percentages are lower than measurements earlier in the decade.

There is no question that the Soviet Union constituted the number one military threat to the United States during the days of the Cold War. The American public has apparently still not gotten over its perception of Russia's military power as a possible problem for our country. Almost one-half of Americans interviewed in an April Gallup Poll said that Russia continues to constitute a significant military threat to the United States, up slightly from a previous poll that asked the same question in 1994. The increase may be due to concerns about uncertain Russian leadership as well as the widespread publicity given to the fact that there are still huge numbers of nuclear weapons in former Soviet Union territory.

About one-third of the American public says that the differences in opinion between Russia and the United States over the current Kosovo situation could lead to a renewal of the Cold War. Although an actual resumption of the Cold War may be unlikely, the fact that one-third of respondents thinks that it could happen suggests the degree to which the public continues to worry about

Russian intentions and future Russian behavior. Thus, perhaps as a result of all of the unsettledness in Russia, the American public is leery of expanding the U.S. role in propping up the country economically: in a March poll 53% were opposed to increasing economic aid to Russia.

MAY 17
ISRAEL

Interviewing Dates: 5/7–9/99
CNN/*USA Today*/Gallup Poll
Survey #GO 127652

How important do you feel the outcome of the Israeli elections is to the interests of the United States—very important, somewhat important, not too important, or not important at all?

Very important	44%
Somewhat important	39
Not too important	10
Not important at all	5
No opinion	2

	Very important	Some what important	Not too important	Not important at all*
By Politics				
Republicans	47%	38%	9%	4%
Democrats	48	41	6	3
Independents	39	38	12	8

*"No opinion"—at 3% or less—is omitted.

As you may know, elections for prime minister are coming up in Israel later this month. Would you prefer to see current Prime Minister Benjamin Netanyahu of Israel reelected, or see current Prime Minister Benjamin Netanyahu of Israel replaced by someone else?

Reelected	42%
Replaced	31
No opinion	27

	Re-elected	Re-placed	No opinion
By Politics			
Republicans	52%	26%	22%
Democrats	36	38	26
Independents	41	30	29

Is your overall opinion of Israel very favorable, mostly favorable, mostly unfavorable, or very unfavorable?

Very favorable	15%
Mostly favorable	53
Mostly unfavorable	19
Very unfavorable	6
No opinion	7

	Very favorable	Mostly favorable	Mostly unfavorable	Very unfavorable*
By Politics				
Republicans	16%	57%	15%	4%
Democrats	16	49	23	5
Independents	14	55	18	6

*"No opinion"—at 8% or less—is omitted.

Do you favor or oppose the establishment of an independent Palestinian state on the West Bank and the Gaza Strip?

Favor	53%
Oppose	26
No opinion	21

	Favor	Oppose	No opinion
By Politics			
Republicans	54%	27%	19%
Democrats	52	27	21
Independents	54	23	23

Note: With Israeli elections scheduled for May 17 and the future of Prime Minister Benjamin Netanyahu on the line, the Gallup Poll recently probed American attitudes about Israeli politics. The May 7–9 Gallup survey finds that most Americans believe that U.S. interests are at stake in the Israeli elections for prime minister. A majority also has a favorable view of the Jewish state. But in the three years since Netanyahu took office, he has not made a strong impression on the American people, although his reelection is favored by a plurality who have an opinion on the issue.

More than anything, Americans seem to be ambivalent about the Israeli leader, who was elected prime minister in 1996 shortly after the as-sassination of Yitzhak Rabin. Asked how they prefer to see the elections turn out, less than one-half of the U.S. public (42%) wants to see Netanyahu reelected, while one-third (31%) thinks that he should be replaced; the remaining 27% have no preference. Similarly mixed views are expressed by Americans when asked about their overall view of Netanyahu. Close to one-half either have not heard of the Israeli leader or have no opinion of him. Among the remainder who have a view, opinion is more positive than negative but not widely so, with 34% holding a favorable view of Netanyahu and 20% holding an unfavorable one. While Americans express some ambivalence about Netanyahu, he clearly enjoys a more positive image in the United States than does longtime Palestinian leader Yasser Arafat, who is viewed favorably by only one-quarter of Americans but unfavorably by close to one-half—a 26%-to-44% margin, with 30% unfamiliar or having no opinion.

One of the key issues in Israeli politics is Palestinian control of the West Bank and the Gaza Strip, territories currently occupied by Israel. Despite Americans' favorable view of Israel, their generally unfavorable view of Arafat, and separate Gallup polling showing that American sympathies in the Middle East lie more with the Israelis than with the Palestinian Arabs, a 53% majority of the U.S. public favors the establishment of a Palestinian state on the West Bank and Gaza, with only 26% opposed. Public support for this position is roughly equal in two forms of the question, including one that does and one that does not mention that these territories are currently occupied by Israel. Support for Palestinian sovereignty in the new poll is particularly high among men and older Americans, with 61% of both groups favoring statehood.

MAY 18
ABORTION

Interviewing Dates: 4/30–5/2/99
CNN/*USA Today*/Gallup Poll
Survey #GO 127557

Do you think abortions should be legal under any circumstances, legal only under certain circumstances, or illegal in all circumstances?

Legal, any circumstances	27%
Legal, certain circumstances	55

Illegal, all circumstances 16
No opinion 2

	Legal, any circum-stances	Legal, certain circum-stances	Illegal, all circum-stances	No opinion
By Sex				
Male	23%	57%	15%	5%
Female.............	31	50	17	2
By Ethnic Background				
White...............	27	55	15	3
Nonwhite.........	29	49	19	3
Black	28	46	22	4
By Education				
Postgraduate....	35	53	8	4
College Graduate......	35	48	14	3
College Incomplete...	32	48	17	3
No College	19	60	18	3
By Region				
East.................	36	47	14	3
Midwest	24	56	17	3
South	18	59	19	4
West	36	50	12	2
By Age				
18–29 Years	29	50	18	3
30–49 Years	32	53	12	3
50–64 Years	24	58	14	4
65 Years and Over......	16	55	25	4
By Household Income				
$75,000 and Over......	41	47	10	2
$50,000 and Over......	34	51	13	2
$30,000– $49,999	28	59	11	2
$20,000– $29,999	22	55	19	4
Under $20,000	17	55	24	4

By Politics

Republicans.....	16	59	24	1
Democrats	31	49	15	5
Independents ...	31	54	12	3

By Political Ideology

Conservative ...	15	58	24	3
Moderate	32	54	11	3
Liberal............	45	45	9	1

Asked of those who replied "legal only under certain circumstances": Do you think abortion should be legal in most circumstances or only in a few circumstances?

Legal, most circumstances 12%
Legal, few circumstances 42
No opinion... 1
                                                                    55%

With respect to the abortion issue, would you consider yourself to be pro-choice or pro-life?

Pro-choice... 48%
Pro-life.. 42
Don't know what terms mean (volunteered)... 4
Other (volunteered) 3
No opinion... 3

Thinking about how the abortion issue might affect your vote for major offices, would you only vote for a candidate who shares your views on abortion, consider a candidate's position on abortion as just one of many important factors when voting, or would you not see abortion as a major issue?

Shares your views... 19%
One of many factors 51
Not a major issue... 27
No opinion... 3

	Shares your views	One of many factors	Not a major issue	No opinion
By Politics				
Republicans.....	17%	53%	27%	3%
Democrats	21	46	29	4
Independents ...	18	54	27	1

Note: Three decades of extensive polling on the abortion issue have shown that Americans hold a complex set of opinions about the morality and legality of terminating a woman's pregnancy. However, when asked in a new Gallup Poll to sum up their abortion views according to the labels favored by activists on each side, members of the public are almost evenly split on the issue, with 48% currently calling themselves pro-choice and 42% identifying themselves as pro-life. More than one-half in each group feel very strongly about their position, but just 19% insist that they will support only candidates for major offices who share their abortion views.

While adherence to the abortion labels tilts slightly in the pro-choice direction, a followup question in the latest Gallup Poll finds greater intensity of feeling on the part of pro-life respondents. Two-thirds of those who hold the pro-life view feel very strongly about it, compared to just over one-half of pro-choice adherents. The net result of these patterns is a nearly even division of those who feel very strongly on the sides of the issue, with a slight tilt in the pro-life direction: 29% are very strongly pro-life, while nearly as many (26%) are very strongly pro-choice. Taken together, 55% hold a very strong view on abortion, while the rest indicate that they feel less strongly about their position or have no opinion at all.

The new Gallup Poll suggests that while feelings may run strong for many people, abortion is not a key electoral issue for most Americans. Just 19% would vote only for a candidate who shares their views on the issue, while 51% would consider a candidate's position as just one of many important factors; the rest (27%) say that abortion is not a major voting issue for them at all. Again, however, intensity on the issue favors the pro-life side, with 24% of pro-lifers saying that abortion is a critical issue for them in supporting candidates, compared to only 16% of those in the pro-choice camp.

There has been little change in Americans' views about abortion since Gallup last studied them over a year ago. In January 1998, on the twenty-fifth anniversary of the landmark abortion case of *Roe versus Wade*, Gallup found 48% identifying as pro-choice and 45% as pro-life (compared to 48% and 42% today). Moreover, in addition to the pro-choice and pro-life labels,

Gallup has polled the public's views on the legality of abortion for twenty-four years. In the latest survey, 27% favor abortion being legal in any circumstances, 16% favor it being illegal in all circumstances, with the majority (55%) saying that it should be legal only under certain circumstances. Most of those in the middle group say that abortion should be legal in only a few circumstances, meaning that about four in ten (39%) say that abortion should be legal in all or most circumstances, while 58% would restrict abortion to only a few or no circumstances. This pattern has also shown little change from 1998, when the overall split on legality of abortion was 39% versus 59%.

Abortion is often considered a women's issue, but the latest Gallup Poll finds few gender differences in public opinion or voting behavior on this topic. There is no significant difference in the percentage of men and women identifying with the two abortion labels. The pro-choice label is preferred by a plurality of both groups, including 49% of women and 47% of men. The percentage calling themselves pro-life is also very similar: 42% among women and 43% among men. In terms of their specific views about the legality of abortion, women tend to be slightly more liberal, with 41% of women, compared to 35% of men, saying that abortion should be legal under all or most circumstances. However, the majority of both groups favors the more conservative set of positions, with 57% of women and 60% of men saying that abortion should be restricted to few or no circumstances.

While their basic attitudes toward abortion are similar, women do express somewhat greater intensity about the issue than do men. Overall, 60% of women, compared with 47% of men, feel very strongly about their abortion views. (Interestingly, women are equally divided, at 30% each, between those who are very strongly pro-choice and those who are very strongly pro-life.) However, women are only slightly more likely than are men (21% versus 17%) to vote only for candidates who share their views on the issue.

Where Gallup does find significant differences on abortion is between people belonging to different political parties, and between those who hold different levels of religious commitment. Democrats and independents are much more likely than are Republicans to consider themselves pro-choice, with slightly more than one-half of Democrats and independents calling themselves pro-choice, compared to only 38% of Republicans. The differences are even stronger according to the religious commitment of respondents. Among those who say that religion is very important in their lives, more than one-half identify themselves as pro-life. However, among those for whom religion is only fairly important or not important at all, the pro-choice position is the dominant view.

MAY 20
SCHOOL VIOLENCE

Interviewing Dates: 5/5–17/99
CNN/*USA Today*/Gallup Poll
Gallup Youth Survey

The following questions were asked of students age 13 to 17:

Are there any groups at your school who you think are violent or capable of violence based on what they do, what they say, or what they claim they will do?

Yes.. 46%
No 54
Don't know.. *

*Less than 1%

Are there any groups at your own school which remind you in any way of the so-called Trenchcoat Mafia at Columbine High School?

Yes.. 30%
No 69
Don't know.. 1

When you are in school, do you ever fear for your physical safety, or not?

Yes.. 20%
No 80

Because of the violence such as occurred at Columbine High School in Littleton, Colorado, *or at other schools, did you stay home from school on any day, or consider staying home?*

Yes.. 18%
No 82

Have your heard of any students at your school making "copycat" threats—that is, students threatening to do similar things to what happened at Columbine High School, or not?

Yes.. 37%
No 63

Was the school evacuated because of a bomb threat?

Yes.. 20%
No 80

Are there any individual students at your school who you think are potentially violent enough to cause a situation such as the one that occurred at Columbine High School?

Yes.. 36%
No 64

The following questions were asked of students familiar with groups at school who are violent or capable of violence.

Do you think any members of these (violent) groups in your school could be dangerous or potentially dangerous to the following, or not:

Every student in your school?

Yes.. 47%
No 53

Your friends?

Yes.. 47%
No 53

You, personally?

Yes.. 29%
No 71

Blacks, Hispanics, or other minority students?

Yes.. 51%
No 49

Gay students?

Yes.. 58%
No 42

Based on what you hear at school, have members of these (violent) groups ever done the following:

Beaten up other students, teachers, or school staff?

Yes.. 68%
No 32

Physical or sexually abused girls?

Yes.. 18%
No 82

Also based on what you hear at school, do members of these groups ever threaten to kill other students or members of the school staff?

Yes.. 35%
No 65

Also based on what you hear at school, do members of these groups talk about any of the following:

Satanism or devil worship?

Yes.. 55%
No 45

Hatred of gays?

Yes.. 50%
No 50

Hatred of blacks, Hispanics, or other minorities?

Yes.. 42%
No 58

Admiration for Hitler and the Nazis?

Yes.. 28%
No 72

Also based on what you hear at school, do members of these groups have guns or knives, or other weapons, at school?

Yes.. 38%
No 62

Are you able to tell who these groups are by what they wear, by their appearance, or by their manner?

Yes.. 81%
No 19

Have members of any of these groups ever done the following to you, or your friends:

Made fun of or insulted you or your friends?

Yes.. 55%
No 45

Threatened to physically assault you or your friends?

Yes.. 32%
No 68

Physically assaulted you or your friends?

Yes.. 14%
No 86

Threatened to kill you or your friends?

Yes.. 11%
No 89

Just your impression, how many students in your school generally admire these groups or think they are "cool"—most, quite a few, hardly any, or none?

Most 8%
Quite a few 21
Hardly any 57
None 13
Don't know 1

How about yourself—do you generally admire these groups a great deal, quite a lot, not much, or not at all?

A great deal 1%
Quite a lot 2
Not much 13
Not at all 84

Do you happen to have any friends who are members of these groups, or not?

Yes 31%
No 69

How about yourself—do you, yourself, happen to be a member of any of these groups?

Yes 5%
No 95

Do any students at your school ever do any of the following things to members of these groups that you think has either caused them to become violent or could provoke violence in the future:

Made fun of or insulted them?

Yes 83%
No 17

Abused or physically assaulted them?

Yes 26%
No 74

Threatened to kill them?

Yes 18%
No 82

Note: With school districts across America struggling to deal with copycat threats in the aftermath of the April 20th Columbine High School massacre, a new Gallup Youth Survey finds that 37% of teens nationwide know of similar threats at their own school since Columbine and 20% have experienced a copycat-related evacuation. Nearly as many (18%) report being frightened enough in the wake of the Littleton, Colorado, tragedy to stay home from school, although just 5% say that their school actually closed for a day or more as a result.

These rates of student concern may not be surprising, given the high proportion of teen survey respondents who report the presence of violent or violence-prone groups in their schools. According to the new survey of a national sample of students age 13 to 17, close to one-half of junior and senior high-school-age students (46%) say that their school has groups of students who are violent or capable of violence. Even more disturbing, 30% of all students interviewed by Gallup say that there are groups at their schools that remind them of the infamous Trenchcoat Mafia at Columbine High School, two of whose members were responsible for the shooting.

While the copycat measures indicate that the Littleton shooting has sent a shock wave through schools, Gallup trends concerning students' fear of physical safety provide no clear evidence of a significant increase in fundamental feelings of safety at school. Currently, 20% are fearful, including 15% of boys and 25% of girls. This figure is substantially higher than the 13% recorded in a pre-Littleton Gallup Youth Survey last year, but it is very similar to the levels of fear recorded from 1977 through 1994. The high point of student fear for their physical safety (28%) was recorded in 1996.

Several follow-up questions of teens who are cognizant of potentially violent groups in their schools indicate that the perceived threat of violence by these students is significant. Roughly one-half of students aware of such groups, ranging from 47% to 58% of all students, believe that the violence-prone groups represent a threat to minority students and gay students specifically as well as to every student in their school more generally. A somewhat lower percentage (29%) perceives a threat to themselves personally, and there is apparently solid cause for their fears. Among the subset of students who are aware of violence-prone groups in their schools, seven in ten (68%) say, based on what they have heard at school, that these groups have beaten up students, teachers, or school staff, while one in five (18%) reports that adherents of these violence-prone groups have physically or sexually abused female students. About one-third say that members of these groups have even threatened to kill students or school staff.

What are the distinguishing marks or characteristics of these groups? More than one half of high-school students who say that such groups exist within their schools claim that the members talk about Satanism or worship of the devil, and almost the same proportion of students say that these group members profess hatred of racial and ethnic minorities and gays. Also, more than one-quarter (28%) say that a key characteristic of members of these groups is admiration for Hitler and the Nazis. About four in ten teens who know of such groups believe that the members also have guns, knives, or other weapons at school. Moreover, eight in ten students in this special survey who say that violent groups exist in their high schools have no trouble in spotting the members by what they wear, by their appearance, or by their manner. Names of such groups reportedly include the Crypts KKK, the Goths, the Trenchcoat Gang, and the Southside Sedenos.

Among teens who are aware of violent or violence-prone groups in their schools, more than one-half of these (55%) have fallen victim to such groups, saying that they or their friends have been made fun of or harassed. Others report threats of physical assault (32%) and actual assaults (14%). Most disturbing of all, 11% of the teens with violent groups present in their schools say that there have been threats against their own lives or the lives of their friends.

At the same time that America's young people describe various threats posed by violent groups in their schools, the vast majority report that jokes or insults have been directed against these groups by other students. More than eight in ten survey respondents who are familiar with violent groups in their schools say that students have made fun of or insulted gang members in a way

that has caused them to become violent or could provoke violence in the future. One quarter (26%) say that students have physically assaulted gang members, while 18% report that there have been threats against the lives of members of these groups.

Despite the widespread fear of these groups, with many reporting frightening experiences, almost one-third of teens (29%) venture the opinion that "most" or "quite a few" of the students in their schools admire them or find them "cool." The survey respondent himself or herself, however, is far less likely to regard these groups in favorable terms. Only 3% admire them a great deal or quite a lot. Presumably, a high proportion of those who admire these violence-prone groups are among the 5% who admit that they themselves are members.

MAY 21
LITTLETON, COLORADO, SHOOTING

Interviewing Dates: 5/5–17/99
CNN/*USA Today*/Gallup Poll
Gallup Youth Survey

Asked of young people age 13 to 17: In your opinion, why did the shooting tragedy at Columbine High School in Littleton, Colorado, happen?

Peer issues	40%
Personal problems	16
Warning signs ignored	7
Parents, family	4
Other; no opinion	33

Also asked of young people age 13 to 17: In your opinion, what could be done to reduce the likelihood of a situation like this happening at your own school? [open-ended]

Better security	24%
Counseling and communication	18
Getting along, tolerance	18
Awareness	10
Other; no opinion	30

Interviewing Dates: 5/7–9/99
CNN/*USA Today*/Gallup Poll
Survey #GO 127652

We have some questions about the shooting at the Littleton, Colorado, high school where two students killed twelve of their classmates and one teacher. In your opinion, what is the single most important thing that could be done to prevent another incident of school shootings by students like the one in Littleton? [open-ended]

Parental involvement, responsibility 32%
More security at schools 16
Better gun control; laws; issues 12
More counselors, counseling, teachers 6
Lift laws on disciplining children 6
Control media violence, video games,
    Internet 4
Better communication with students,
    parents, teachers 4
Raise morals, people's standards 3
Better education, students, parents 3
Put prayer back in school, home 3
Stricter punishment of children; laws 2
Dress codes, uniforms 1
Other 4
None 1
No opinion 3

Interviewing Dates: 4/26–27/99
CNN/*USA Today*/Gallup Poll
Survey #GO 127538

We have some questions about the shooting at the Littleton, Colorado, high school where fifteen [twelve] students were killed by two of their classmates.* In your opinion, why did this happen? [open-ended]

Breakdown of family; poor parenting;
    lack of discipline; parents not
    involved with kids 20%
Mental problems; anger; hatred; bad
    kids; wanted attention 6
Teasing from other kids; outcasts 3
Entertainment industry; television;
    movies; music 2

*Question wording should read: twelve students and a teacher were killed by two student gunmen

Lack of morals; societal values; moral
    decline of country 2
Not enough attention paid to kids;
    negligence 1
Guns 1
Lost touch with God, religion; religion
    taken out of schools 1
Lack of supervision (general) 1
Not enough supervision at school 1
Not enough security at school 1
Violence in society; too much exposure
    to violence 1
Internet; computer .... *
Other 51
No opinion 9

*Less than 1%

Note: A new Gallup Poll shows that America's teenagers put the blame for tragedies such as Columbine High School and the Thursday [May 20] shooting outside of Atlanta directly on themselves rather than on parents, gun laws, or media violence. The country's young people also suggest that one of the best ways to prevent such occurrences in the future is to foster better communication among students and to break down the barriers that apparently create hostility between groups in today's high schools.

The findings of a new Gallup Youth Survey, conducted among a random sample of teenagers age 13 to 17 on May 5–17, show first and foremost that teens think that the blame for school violence lies within the social structure that dominates today's school scene. When asked directly to explain why they think that the Columbine tragedy occurred, 40% of teenagers focus on problems of peer relations and peer pressures. The types of replies grouped in this category include the observations that students are taunted by other students, are picked on, are made to feel like outcasts, feel left out, have been pushed too far, and are lonely.

The second category of explanations for Columbine, used by 16% of teenagers in the survey, includes comments focused on the perpetrators themselves: that they had personal problems, that they were sick, angry, confused, jealous, or "stupid." Another 7% of teenagers talk about the fact that warning signs were ignored by those involved, while 4% mention factors relating to the parents. In short, about two-thirds of the students, when asked to explain the tragedy at Littleton, focus directly on students themselves, with these explanations more likely to be directed at the behavior around the youths who did the shooting than at the shooters per se.

A Gallup Poll of adults conducted several weeks ago included the same questions about the primary cause of the Columbine shootings. The replies given by the grownups are significantly different from those given by the students. Adults first and foremost blame parents and families for the tragedy, according to 45% of the adults interviewed. Only 11% of parents mention personal problems relating to the teenagers themselves, followed by 8% who mention the lack of morals and religion in society, and another 6% who cite the prevalence of violence in the media. In other words, students tend to look within themselves and at their peers, while adults tend to place blame on other adults and on society at large.

The recent polling of both adults and young people also included a question asking these groups what can be done to prevent a future Columbine. The question of preventive steps is, of course, the key issue to come out of the Littleton incident and one that has preoccupied Congress, pundits, and experts in the month since the Littleton shooting occurred. These replies also have an increased urgency given the school shooting outside of Atlanta, Georgia.

Mirroring their views on the causes of the tragedy, the number one strategy suggested by adults for preventing such events in the future is to focus on the parents themselves, mentioned by 32% of those interviewed. Adults next mention tightened security at schools, cited by 16%, stricter gun control (12%), and increased counseling and communication.

There is agreement among teens on the importance of school security. Twenty-four percent of teenagers, the largest single category of replies, think that better security would be the best way to prevent future incidents. Following school security in terms of teenagers' suggestions are better communication and counseling (18%), trying to compel teenagers to get along, stop name-calling,

and be nice to one another (18%). The importance of these preventive measures, underscored by the Georgia shooting, is apparent in the finding from the Gallup Youth Survey that 36% of all teenagers interviewed felt that there were young people in their schools capable of Littleton-type violence. Almost one-half said that there were gangs in their schools capable of perpetrating violent acts.

MAY 24
CUBA

Interviewing Dates: 5/7–9/99
CNN/*USA Today*/Gallup Poll
Survey #GO 127652

Is your overall opinion of Cuba very favorable, mostly favorable, mostly unfavorable, or very unfavorable?

	May 7–9, 1999	March 19–21, 1999
Very favorable	4%	4%
Mostly favorable	20	28
Mostly unfavorable	45	48
Very unfavorable	24	13
No opinion	7	7

May 7–9, 1999

	Very favorable	Mostly favorable	Mostly unfavorable	Very unfavorable*
By Politics				
Republicans	1%	15%	49%	28%
Democrats	5	25	41	23
Independents	5	20	46	23

*"No opinion"—at 7% or less—is omitted.

Suppose that on Election Day this year you could vote on key issues as well as candidates. Please tell me whether you would vote for or against each one of the following propositions:

For or against reestablishing U.S. diplomatic relations with Cuba?

	May 7–9, 1999	March 19–21, 1999
For	71%	67%

Against	25	27
No opinion	4	6

May 7–9, 1999

	For	Against	No opinion
By Politics			
Republicans	68%	32%	3%
Democrats	73	23	4
Independents	73	22	5

For or against ending the U.S. trade embargo with Cuba?

	May 7–9, 1999	March 19–21, 1999
For	51%	51%
Against	42	39
No opinion	7	10

May 7–9, 1999

	For	Against	No opinion
By Politics			
Republicans	46%	48%	6%
Democrats	50	43	7
Independents	55	36	9

Note: Most Americans favor reestablishing diplomatic relations between the United States and Cuba, according to a new Gallup Poll conducted on May 7–9, and a bare majority would also end the U.S. trade embargo against Cuba. But in spite of these more favorable views about U.S. relations with Fidel Castro's Communist island nation, Americans still express an unfavorable opinion of Cuba by close to a 3-to-1 margin.

The poll shows that 71% of Americans support reestablishment of U.S. diplomatic relations with Cuba, while just 25% are opposed—the largest margin of support in the past quarter-century. The question was first asked by Gallup in October 1974, when Americans supported renewing diplomatic ties with Cuba by a margin of 63% to 37%. In 1977 the margin fell to a bare majority (53% to 32%), and in April 1996 more people were opposed (49%) than were in favor (40%). However, in March of this year, Americans supported reopening diplomatic relations with Cuba

by a 67%-to-27% margin, only slightly lower than the figures reported in the current poll.

A bare majority also supports ending the U.S. trade embargo with Cuba, by 51% to 42%. These figures are essentially unchanged from those found in the March Gallup Poll, but they do represent a major movement toward accommodation with Cuba from the sentiments expressed by Americans five years ago. A poll in September 1994 by Time/CNN found that only 35% of Americans said that the United States should end its embargo against Cuba, while 51% said that we should not do so.

With these positive sentiments expressed by the public, it is not surprising that the overall views that Americans have of Cuba are better today than in the past. Still, a majority expresses negative sentiments: today, 69% have an unfavorable opinion of Cuba, while just 24% have a favorable one—somewhat worse than the 61%-to-32% margin found in the poll two months ago, but much better than the opinion expressed three years ago in March 1996, when 81% had an unfavorable opinion and just 10% a favorable one.

MAY 28
MOST IMPORTANT PROBLEM/ GUN CONTROL

Interviewing Dates: 5/23–24/99
CNN/*USA Today*/Gallup Poll
Survey #GO 127701

*What do you think is the most important problem facing this country today?**

Economic problems

Unemployment; jobs	4%
Taxes	3
Economy in general	3
Federal budget deficit	1
Trade relations; trade deficit	1
High cost of living; inflation	**
Other	2

Noneconomic problems

Ethics; moral decline; family decline; children not raised right	18
Crime; violence	17

Education.. 11
Guns; gun control 10
Kosovo; Serbia; Yugoslavia; Milosevic 10
Poverty; homelessness.................................... 7
School shootings; school violence 7
Youth; teen pregnancy.................................... 7
Dissatisfaction with government, Clinton,
    Republicans 5
Drugs; drug abuse... 5
Health care.. 5
Foreign aid; focus overseas 3
International issues; foreign affairs 3
Medicare; Social Security 3
Racism; race relations 3
War; peace... 2
Welfare 2
Environment 2
Immigration; illegal aliens............................. 1
Media; television 1
Parental rights taken away.............................. 1
Y2K computer problem................................... **
Becoming socialistic; taking away rights .... **
Iraq; Saddam Hussein..................................... **
Terrorism; national security .... **
Abortion... **
AIDS.. **
Lewinsky controversy; impeachment............. –
Other.. 12

*Total adds to more than 100% due to multiple replies. Respondents may name up to three problems.
**Less than 1%

Selected National Trend

Economic problems

	Jan. 15–17, 1999	Sept. 14–15, 1998	April 17–19, 1998
Unemployment; jobs...	6%	4%	5%
Taxes	4	4	6
Economy in general....	6	12	6
Federal budget deficit......................	2	2	5
Trade relations; trade deficit......................	1	1	1
High cost of living; inflation	1	1	1
Other...........................	3	4	3

Noneconomic problems

	Jan. 15–17, 1999	Sept. 14–15, 1998	April 17–19, 1998
Ethics; moral decline; family decline; children not raised right.............	13	15	16
Crime; violence	13	10	20
Education....................	13	13	13
Guns; gun control	*	*	1
Kosovo; Serbia; Yugoslavia; Milosevic...............	–	–	–
Poverty; homelessness	11	6	10
School shootings; school violence.......	–	–	–
Youth; teen pregnancy	1	3	6
Dissatisfaction with government, Clinton, Republicans	9	14	8
Drugs; drug abuse.......	6	9	12
Health care.................	7	6	6
Foreign aid; focus overseas	1	2	2
International issues; foreign affairs	6	6	4
Medicare; Social Security..................	6	3	8
Racism; race relations	2	2	2
War; peace.................	2	–	–
Welfare	3	2	8
Environment	2	1	2
Immigration; illegal aliens......................	1	1	2
Media; television	*	1	1
Parental rights taken away......................	–	–	–
Y2K computer problem...................	1	–	–
Becoming socialistic; taking away rights.....................	–	–	–
Iraq; Saddam Hussein...................	8	–	–
Terrorism; national security...................	1	2	–
Abortion.....................	*	*	1

AIDS	*	*	1
Lewinsky controversy; impeachment	2	2	–
Other	12	7	9

*Less than 1%

In general, do you feel that the laws covering the sale of firearms should be made more strict, less strict, or kept as they are now?

	May 23–24, 1999	April 26–27, 1999	Feb. 8–9, 1999
More strict	65%	66%	60%
Less strict	5	7	9
Kept as now	28	25	29
No opinion	2	2	2

May 23–24, 1999

	More strict	Less strict	Kept as now	No opinion
By Politics				
Republicans	49%	8%	42%	1%
Democrats	80	2	16	2
Independents	64	6	27	3

Thinking about how the gun issue might affect your vote for major offices, would you only vote for a candidate who shares your views on gun control, consider a candidate's position on gun control as just one of many important factors when voting, or would you not consider gun control as a major issue?

Shares your views	15%
One of many factors	64
Not a major issue	19
No opinion	2

	Shares your views	One of many factors	Not a major issue	No opinion
By Politics				
Republicans	9%	68%	21%	2%
Democrats	19	64	15	2
Independents	16	62	19	3

Which party do you think can do a better job of reflecting your views about gun control—

the Republican party, or the Democratic party?

Republican party	39%
Democratic party	42
Neither (volunteered)	8
No opinion	11

	Republican party	Democratic party	Neither	No opinion
By Politics				
Republicans	77%	11%	4%	8%
Democrats	8	77	6	9
Independents	36	37	11	16

Interviewing Dates: 2/8–9/99
CNN/*USA Today*/Gallup Poll
Survey #GO 126651

Do you favor or oppose a law which would require background checks before people, including gun dealers, could buy guns at gun shows?

Favor	83%
Oppose	16
No opinion	1

	Favor	Oppose	No opinion
By Politics			
Republicans	81%	16%	3%
Democrats	86	14	*
Independents	82	16	2

*Less than 1%

Note: While members of Congress debate the need for new gun control legislation to prevent future school massacres such as the Columbine High School shootings in Colorado, nearly two in three Americans say that a politician's stance on gun control will be just one of many issues they look at when deciding how to vote. A new Gallup Poll conducted on May 23–24 shows that just 15% of respondents will only support candidates who share their views on gun control, while 64% will look at gun control as well as other issues when evaluating a candidate. Nineteen percent say that gun control will not be an important issue in determining how they vote.

These findings may reflect the fact that, despite the recent wave of school shootings, the public does not generally consider school violence and the gun control debate as the country's most urgent problems. When Gallup interviewers asked Americans to list the most important problems facing the United States today (respondents could give up to three answers), just 7% cited school shootings and violence, while 6% cited the availability of guns—the first time that this reply has come in significant numbers in the last thirteen months. However, the general category of crime and violence reached the high figure of 17%. Another 4% named gun control, but their replies were mixed between those who consider current gun laws too strict and those who consider them too weak.

There is widespread support for the idea of stronger federal gun control legislation. Two in three respondents believe that the laws covering the sale of firearms should be made stricter, while 28% say that the current standards are strict enough and should be left alone. The results are similar to a poll conducted in late April, just after the Columbine shootings, and reflect an increase in support from February, when 60% supported stricter legislation on firearms sales. As might be expected, support for tougher laws breaks sharply along party lines, with 80% of Democrats favoring tougher laws, compared to just 49% of Republicans.

Support for stricter legislation had been on the decline for several years after peaking in March 1993 when 70% favored tougher standards on firearms sales. However, the Columbine tragedy appears to have reversed that downward trend. Moreover, one key issue where public support appears to be overwhelmingly in favor of a tougher federal law concerns background checks for sales at gun shows. A Senate bill passed the same day as a school shooting in Georgia would require those checks. A Gallup Poll conducted in February found that 83% liked the idea, while just 16% opposed it. But the public strongly disagrees with another new trend—that of local governments suing gun manufacturers to recover damages for the cost of gun-related violence. Sixty-one percent oppose those lawsuits, while 36% favor them.

The shootings in late April have also sparked a political debate that could carry into the 2000 presidential race. That debate reflects traditional stereotypes, with Democrats generally favoring tougher gun laws and Republicans favoring minimal restrictions. The May 23–24 poll shows that voters believe those stereotypes. When those who supported stricter legislation were asked which party better reflects their views, 55% picked the Democratic party, while 27% favored the Republicans. When those who opposed tougher gun laws were asked the same questions, 65% picked the Republicans and just 17% chose the Democrats.

JUNE 3
CHINA

Interviewing Dates: 5/21–23/99
CNN/*USA Today*/Gallup Poll
Survey #GO 127701

How would you rate the job the government of China does in respecting the human rights of its citizens—very good, mostly good, mostly bad, or very bad?

	May 21–23, 1999	May 30– June 1, 1997
Very good	3%	3%
Mostly good	18	17
Mostly bad	35	35
Very bad	34	34
No opinion	10	11

May 21–23, 1999

	Very good	Mostly good	Mostly bad	Very bad*
By Politics				
Republicans	2%	17%	31%	44%
Democrats	3	19	35	28
Independents	3	17	40	32

*"No opinion"—at 15% or less—is omitted.

Which of the following statements comes closer to your view—the United States should link human rights issues in China with U.S.-China trade policy, even if doing so hurts U.S. economic interests; or the United States should not link human rights issues in China with U.S.-China trade policy because doing so might hurt U.S. economic interests?

	May 21–23, 1999	June 22–23, 1998	Oct. 27–29, 1997
Should link rights, trade	46%	47%	55%
Should not link rights, trade	45	45	36
No opinion	9	8	9

May 21–23, 1999

	Should link rights, trade	Should not link rights, trade	No opinion
By Politics			
Republicans	49%	44%	7%
Democrats	40	48	12
Independents	49	43	8

Interviewing Dates: 5/7–9/99
CNN/*USA Today*/Gallup Poll
Survey #GO 127652

Is your overall opinion of China very favorable, mostly favorable, mostly unfavorable, or very unfavorable?

	May 7–9, 1999	August 10–13, 1989
Very favorable	5%	5%
Mostly favorable	33	26
Mostly unfavorable	38	35
Very unfavorable	18	23
No opinion	6	11

May 7–9, 1999

	Very favorable	Mostly favorable	Mostly unfavorable	Very unfavorable*
By Politics				
Republicans	4%	29%	39%	22%
Democrats	7	36	38	12
Independents	6	33	38	19

*"No opinion"—at 7% or less—is omitted.

Note: On the tenth anniversary of the Chinese military crackdown on pro-democracy protests in Tiananmen Square in Beijing, American public opinion remains negative toward China. At the same time, there is sharp disagreement on whether or not its internal human rights actions should be reflected in U.S.-China trade relations policy. While the public's attitudes toward China have undergone an enormous amount of change over the last thirty years, these attitudes, in the final analysis, are very little different today than they were ten years ago after the Tiananmen Square events took place.

Americans' views toward China were consistently unfavorable in Gallup Polls conducted in 1967 and in the 1970s, reflecting the dominant Cold War thought of that time. During the 1980s, however, as China underwent significant social and political reforms, Americans' attitudes became progressively more positive, culminating in an extraordinary 72% who indicated in a February 1989 Gallup Poll that they had a favorable opinion of the country. Then the Tiananmen Square crackdowns occurred in June 1989, and by August of that year, favorable attitudes had fallen precipitously, to only 34%. There has been some slight movement up and down in the intervening years, but in a recent Gallup Poll conducted in early May of this year, favorable attitudes were at 38%, almost exactly the same as ten years ago. In short, the decade that has transpired since Tiananmen Square has witnessed very little change in the American public's majority negative views toward the world's most populous country. The current 38% favorable rating puts China at the lower end of the spectrum of countries that Gallup measures—above Cuba and Iraq, but rated more negatively than Russia and traditional U.S. allies such as Great Britain and Israel.

Gallup's latest survey on China was conducted in May, just before Congressman Christopher Cox's report on alleged Chinese stealing of U.S. nuclear secrets was formally released. Since many of the report's accusations have been public for a number of months, it may well be that the Chinese nuclear secrets issue is at least partially responsible for the unfavorable attitudes toward China measured in the May poll. Still, it is clear that continuing doubts about how China handles the human rights of its citizens also play a big part in constituting Americans' opinions of the country. When asked directly in Gallup's most recent poll to rate "the job the government of China does in respecting the human rights of its citizens," the American public, by more than a 3-to-1 margin, gives China a "bad job" rating. Specifically, 34% say that China does a very bad job, with another 35% saying a mostly bad job; only 21% say that China does a mostly or very good job of respecting these human rights. These results are essentially unchanged from two years ago, when Gallup last asked the question.

Despite these strongly negative perceptions, opinion is split on the issue of whether or not U.S.-China trade policies ought to be curtailed as a result of China's human rights record—an important consideration, given that the Clinton administration is slated to ask Congress to renew China's trading privileges on June 3. When asked if the United States should link human rights issues to trade policy "even if doing so hurts U.S. economic interests," the public is evenly divided: 46% say that the two should be linked, while 45% say that they should not. (These results, though similar to those obtained last year, are somewhat less in favor of a specific linkage policy than was the case in October 1997.)

Perhaps not surprisingly, Republicans and conservatives are somewhat more likely to want the linkage, while Democrats and liberals are less so. There is also a strong relationship between socioeconomic status and the desire to see human rights linked to U.S.-China trade policies—the higher the level of education and income, the more likely the respondent is to favor explicit linkage. In March, a similar Gallup Poll question asked the public to assess whether or not the Clinton administration had acted appropriately in "attempting to maintain a constructive working relationship with China." The results were very similar to those of the linkage question: 46% said yes, while 47% said no.

It is also clear from the polling data that Americans, while holding unfavorable opinions of China, do not necessarily consider the country to be an enemy of the United States. A March poll asked the public to rate the U.S.-China relationship with one of four labels: ally, friendly, unfriendly, or an enemy. While almost no one rated China as an ally, 28% said that it was friendly, 26% said unfriendly, and only 10% said that China was an enemy. One-third did not know enough about it to reply.

JUNE 14
O. J. SIMPSON: FIFTH ANNIVERSARY

Interviewing Dates: 2/26–28/99
CNN/*USA Today*/Gallup Poll
Survey #GO 126888

Do you personally believe the charges that O. J. Simpson murdered Nicole Brown Simpson and Ronald Goldman are definitely true, probably true, probably not true, or definitely not true?

Definitely true	36%
Probably true	38
Probably not true	15
Definitely not true	6
No opinion	5

In your opinion, should O. J. Simpson continue to be given legal custody of his two children, or be denied legal custody of his two children?

Given custody	40%
Denied custody	51
No opinion	9

Based on what you know and have seen in the news, how do you feel toward O. J. Simpson— very sympathetic, somewhat sympathetic, somewhat unsympathetic, or very unsympathetic?

Very sympathetic	6%
Somewhat sympathetic	16
Somewhat unsympathetic	21
Very unsympathetic	54
No opinion	3

Note: Has there been any change in the perceptions of Americans that O. J. Simpson is guilty of the murders of Nicole Brown Simpson and Ron

Goldman, five years ago on June 12, 1994? Respondents still say that O. J. Simpson committed the murders, as they have almost since the beginning of the tragic saga in 1994. A majority (66%) said that the accusation against Simpson was probably or definitely true in June 1994, right after the celebrated car chase and his arrest. That percentage has stayed at about that level or higher ever since, with a gradual shift from the "probably true" category to "definitely true." In Gallup's most recent poll, conducted in February of this year, 74% said that the charges were true.

Americans' convictions on this issue have stayed remarkably stable over the last five years, even after Simpson's innocent verdict in the famous criminal trial, on October 3, 1995. A poll conducted shortly after the verdict, on October 5–7, found that 67% of the public thought that the charges were true, including 30% who said definitely true and another 37% who said probably true. Similarly, the February 1997 civil trial verdict of guilty induced hardly any change in these percentages.

The highest percentage to think that the charges were not true (25%) came in the October 1995 poll conducted after Simpson's acquittal in the criminal trial. In this year's February poll, 21% said that the charges that Simpson committed the murders were probably or definitely not true. In short, respondents reached their decisions on Simpson's guilt soon after the murders, and all of the events since that time have not changed their opinions.

Race continues to be a sharply differentiating factor in perceptions of Simpson's guilt or innocence. Gallup polling has consistently shown major differences in the views of whites and blacks on Simpson's guilt, and these differences have remained. In the poll conducted immediately after the criminal verdict of innocence, in October 1995, only 27% of blacks said that the murder charges against Simpson were true, compared to 73% of whites. In this year's February poll, not much has changed: 79% of whites said that the charges were true, compared to 35% of blacks.

There was some sympathy for Simpson among the public shortly after his arrest, when 49% of those interviewed felt very or somewhat sympathetic toward him, and only 41% were at least somewhat unsympathetic. These levels evaporated fairly quickly, however, dropping to only

about 30% who were sympathetic in the summer of 1995. In Gallup's February 1999 poll, 22% of the public were sympathetic toward Simpson, 6% very sympathetic, and 16% somewhat sympathetic. The rest (75%) were unsympathetic, including a majority of 54% who said that they were very unsympathetic toward the former NFL star. Not surprisingly, there are differences by race in terms of this sympathy question: 59% of blacks were sympathetic toward Simpson, compared to only 16% of whites.

Finally, one of the recurring issues relating to O. J. Simpson has been the custody of his two children, whose mother, Nicole Brown Simpson, was one of the two murder victims. Do Americans feel comfortable with the idea of his retaining custody of his two children? When asked in February about the issue, 51% said that Simpson should be denied legal custody of his children, while 40% said that he should continue to be given legal custody.

JUNE 16
GUN CONTROL

Interviewing Dates: 6/11–13/99
CNN/*USA Today*/Gallup Poll
Survey #GO 127916

Please tell me whether you would generally favor or oppose each of the following proposals which some people have made to reduce the amount of gun violence:

Mandatory prison sentences for felons who commit crimes with guns?

Favor... 89%
Oppose.. 9
No opinion.. 2

	Favor	Oppose	No opinion
By Politics			
Republicans	92%	7%	1%
Democrats...................	88	10	2
Independents...............	89	9	2

Mandatory background checks before people, including gun dealers, could buy guns at gun shows?

Favor.. 87%
Oppose... 12
No opinion... 1

	Favor	Oppose	No opinion
By Politics			
Republicans	84%	15%	1%
Democrats	92	7	1
Independents	86	14	*

*Less than 1%

Require safety locks or trigger guards to be included with all new handgun purchases?

Favor.. 85%
Oppose... 14
No opinion... 1

	Favor	Oppose	No opinion
By Politics			
Republicans	84%	15%	1%
Democrats	90	9	1
Independents	83	16	1

Raise the minimum age for handgun possession to 21 years of age?

Favor.. 82%
Oppose... 17
No opinion... 1

	Favor	Oppose	No opinion
By Politics			
Republicans	77%	22%	1%
Democrats	87	12	1
Independents	81	18	1

Registration of all firearms?

Favor.. 79%
Oppose... 20
No opinion... 1

	Favor	Oppose	No opinion
By Politics			
Republicans	71%	28%	1%
Democrats	88	11	1
Independents	78	21	1

Impose a lifetime ban on gun ownership for any juvenile convicted of a felony?

Favor.. 77%
Oppose... 21
No opinion... 2

	Favor	Oppose	No opinion
By Politics			
Republicans	75%	22%	3%
Democrats	80	19	1
Independents	75	23	2

Ban the importing of high-capacity ammunition clips?

Favor.. 68%
Oppose... 29
No opinion... 3

	Favor	Oppose	No opinion
By Politics			
Republicans	59%	39%	2%
Democrats	74	22	4
Independents	69	27	4

Hold parents legally responsible if their children commit crimes with the parents' guns?

Favor.. 57%
Oppose... 39
No opinion... 4

	Favor	Oppose	No opinion
By Politics			
Republicans	58%	37%	5%
Democrats	62	33	5
Independents	51	44	5

Note: Motivated in part by the tragic school shootings in Colorado and Georgia this spring, the idea of instituting new and more stringent gun control laws has become one of the most hotly debated issues on the current national agenda. A new Gallup Poll shows that Americans strongly support most of the specific types of gun control measures now being debated in Congress, and that support for the idea of a general requirement that all firearms be registered is now higher than it was as recently as last fall. A Gallup Poll conducted in May after the Columbine High School shootings indicated that almost two-thirds of respondents favored the idea of stricter gun control laws in this country, with most of the rest saying that the laws should be kept as they are, rather than made less strict.

A new Gallup Poll conducted on June 11–13 asked the public more explicitly about eight specific gun control proposals that in one way or the other have been discussed or debated in recent weeks. The "registration of all firearms" proposition now receives somewhat stronger support than in the past. In 1975, and as recently as last fall, 67% favored this type of broad-based measure; the current higher level of support (79%) may reflect the influence of this spring's tragic school shootings in Colorado and in Georgia. There are some differences by party in support for the measure, but even among Republicans, support is strong at 71%, compared to 88% of Democrats. Women are also somewhat more likely than men to support registration of all firearms by an 88%-to-69% margin. Interestingly, more than sixty years ago, in 1938, Gallup asked Americans about their support for registration of all "pistols and revolvers" and found 84% approval, suggesting that the current sentiment in favor of many of these gun measures does not necessarily represent a wholesale change in the attitudes of the public over the previous decades.

JUNE 23
CHILDREN'S EXPOSURE TO
MEDIA VIOLENCE

Interviewing Dates: 6/11–13/99
CNN/*USA Today*/Gallup Poll
Survey #GO 127916

*How serious a problem is the amount of violence that children are exposed to in each of the following forms of entertainment—extremely serious, very serious, moderately serious, not too serious, or not at all serious:**

Movies?

Extremely serious	30%
Very serious	32
Moderately serious	24
Not too serious	9
Not at all serious	4
No opinion	1

Video or computer games?

Extremely serious	30%
Very serious	31
Moderately serious	24
Not too serious	8
Not at all serious	5
No opinion	2

Lyrics to popular music on CDs, tapes, or radio?

Extremely serious	25%
Very serious	23
Moderately serious	36
Not too serious	10
Not at all serious	3
No opinion	3

Television programming?

Extremely serious	23%
Very serious	29
Moderately serious	33
Not too serious	10
Not at all serious	4
No opinion	1

*Based on half sample

*Do you believe that the producers of the following entertainment media do or do not provide adults with enough information about the violence content to make decisions about what is appropriate for children:**

Movies?

Do provide	40%
Do not	58
No opinion	2

Video or computer games?

Do provide 20%
Do not 74
No opinion 6

Lyrics to popular music on CDs, tapes, or radio?

Do provide 22%
Do not 74
No opinion 4

Television programming?

Do provide 39%
Do not 59
No opinion 2

*Based on half sample

Form A. *As a general rule, in order to control the exposure of children to violent entertainment, do you think that it is sufficient that the industry just provide information to the public about the violence content of movies, music CDs, and video games, or do you think that there should also be restrictions on the sales of such violent materials to children under 18?*

Form B. *As a general rule, in order to control the exposure of children to violent entertainment, do you think that there should be restrictions on the sales of movies, music CDs, and video games to children under 18; or do you think that it is sufficient that the industry just provide information to the public about the violence content of such materials?*

Sufficient to provide information 26%*
Restrictions on sales 73
No opinion 1

*Margin of sampling error: ±5 percentage points. Results for Form A and Form B are combined.

Finally, for each of the following, please indicate how much responsibility you think they should have for restricting children's access to violent entertainment—the most responsibility, a major responsibility along with others, little responsibility, or no responsibility:

Children under 18 themselves?

Most responsibility 21%
Major responsibility along with others 47
Little responsibility 27
No responsibility 4
No opinion 1

Parents of children under 18?

Most responsibility 59%
Major responsibility along with others 35
Little responsibility 3
No responsibility 1
No opinion 2

The entertainment industry?

Most responsibility 23%
Major responsibility along with others 54
Little responsibility 18
No responsibility 4
No opinion 1

Local governments?

Most responsibility 14%
Major responsibility along with others 38
Little responsibility 33
No responsibility 13
No opinion 2

The federal government?

Most responsibility 14%
Major responsibility along with others 38
Little responsibility 32
No responsibility 14
No opinion 2

*Based on half sample

Note: As Congress debates how best to deal with the content of entertainment offered to children, a new Gallup Poll shows that the public views the potential impact of violence in movies, video games, television, and recorded music as a very serious problem, while the current efforts to control children's exposure to such violence are inadequate. According to the poll, conducted on June 11–13, Americans are most concerned about violence in movies and video/computer games, with more than six in ten saying that both these forms of entertainment pose at least a very serious problem: 30% say that the problem of violence in movies and in video/computer games is extremely serious, while another 31% to 32% say very serious. About one-half of the public (52%) also find the violence in television programming to be very or extremely serious, while 48% say that the violence content in the lyrics to popular music is at least a very serious issue.

Although the entertainment industry has adopted ratings systems for some forms of entertainment—most notably movies, television programs, and music—the public does not think that those ratings systems provide the information needed by adults to make decisions about what is appropriate for children. Three in four adults (74%) say that the information about violence in lyrics and, separately, in video/computer games is not sufficient. In addition, almost six in ten indicate that the information about violence in movies and television programming is inadequate for judging the appropriateness for children of such entertainment.

Even if the information provided by the ratings systems were more comprehensive, respondents believe that more needs to be done to control children's exposure to violent material. The voluntary ratings systems rely on parents themselves to exercise restraint, but most adults (73%) believe that an additional step should be taken: the sales of violent movies, music CDs, and video games to children under age 18 should be restricted. Only 26% say that it is sufficient for the industry to provide information to the public about the violence content of such materials.

Despite these views, Americans have not shifted responsibility for restricting children's access to violent entertainment from the parents to others. Instead, they believe that the responsibility is shared among many people and groups, particularly those within the entertainment industry. The poll shows that 94% believe that parents still have either the most responsibility (59%) or at least "major responsibility along with others" (35%) for restricting children's access to violent entertainment. But the poll also shows that 77% believe that the entertainment industry also has at least a major responsibility to restrict such access. And, in a sign that the public is willing to have some form of government regulation of the industry, just over one-half (52%) say that both the local government and the federal government have at least a major responsibility along with others to control children's exposure to violence in the entertainment media.

JUNE 30
MEDICARE

Interviewing Dates: 6/25–27/99
CNN/*USA Today*/Gallup Poll
Survey #GO 128120

Whom do you have more confidence in when it comes to handling Medicare—President Clinton, or the Republicans in Congress?

Clinton 55%
Republicans 38
Same; both (volunteered) 1
Neither (volunteered) 3
No opinion 3

	Clinton	Repub-licans	Some; both; neither	No opinion
By Politics				
Republicans.....	18%	75%	4%	3%
Democrats	88	9	2	1
Independents ...	53	36	7	4

Selected National Trend

	Clinton	Repub-licans	Same; both; neither	No opinion
March 1998.....	54%	33%	6%	7%
June 1997	49	35	9	7

Jan. 1997 54	37	6	3
Nov. 1996........ 53	34	8	5
Aug. 1995........ 45	38	9	8
May 1995 49	36	8	7

Which of the following statements best represents how you feel about Medicare—it needs to be completely overhauled, it needs major changes, it needs minor changes, or it is basically fine the way it is?

Needs complete overhaul 16%
Needs major changes...................................... 41
Needs minor changes...................................... 31
Basically fine... 10
No opinion... 2

	Needs complete overhaul	Needs major changes	Needs minor changes	Basically fine*
By Politics				
Republicans.....	18%	38%	27%	13%
Democrats	13	41	31	13
Independents ...	17	42	32	8

*"No opinion"—at 4% or less—is omitted.

Note: The public is generally receptive to the idea of reforming Medicare and has more trust in President Bill Clinton than in the Republican leadership in Congress to modernize the thirty-four-year-old program. At the same time, there are indications that the group of Americans currently most affected by Medicare, those age 65 and older, are much less interested in reforms and also less likely to trust Clinton himself than is the younger generation, whose experience with the program looms in the future.

A new Gallup Poll conducted on June 25–27 shows that the majority says that Medicare needs significant reform: 16% think that Medicare is in need of a total overhaul, and another 41% say that it needs major changes. Thirty-one percent say that it needs minor changes, while only 10% believe that it needs no changes at all.

Other Gallup polling conducted this year has consistently shown that Medicare, along with Social Security, has a high priority position in the views of the public. In that polling, Medicare consistently shows up near the top of the list when respondents are asked to rate issues on which Congress or presidential candidates should focus. Thus, overall, Clinton's White House speech on Tuesday [June 22] announcing proposed reforms in the program most likely fell on generally receptive ears.

The clamor for change in the system, however, varies significantly by age group. Those most likely to want major changes are between 30 and 64 years of age, most of whom are not enjoying Medicare benefits yet but who face the prospect of a switch to Medicare for medical benefits in the years ahead. This group includes the Baby Boom generation, the huge numbers of which have led to warnings of pending catastrophe in 2011, when they first begin to turn 65. On the other hand, only 37% of those 65 and older want major changes in Medicare. This group for the most part is already using Medicare, and their reluctance to endorse reform may be based on their fears that changes would result in either increased costs or decreased benefits.

Although Clinton's proposed reforms are sure to form the basis of the usual political and partisan wrangling in the weeks and months ahead, there are relatively few differences in basic desire for change between rank-and-file Republicans and Democrats nationally. Fifty-six percent of those who call themselves Republicans want at least major changes, almost the same as the 54% of Democrats who want such changes.

Overall, the general public is more likely to trust President Clinton than the Republican leadership in Congress to deal with Medicare, by a 55%-to-38% margin. This tilt toward Clinton has been consistent over the past several years for both Medicare and Social Security. Perhaps not surprisingly, given that older people are least likely to desire changes in Medicare, those 50 and up are also less likely to trust Clinton and more likely to trust Republicans than are younger Americans.

JULY 2
PATRIOTISM

Interviewing Dates: 6/25–27/99
CNN/*USA Today*/Gallup Poll
Survey #GO 128120

How patriotic are you—would you say extremely patriotic, very patriotic, somewhat patriotic, or not especially patriotic?

	June 25–27, 1999	June 17–19, 1994
Extremely patriotic	19%	21%
Very patriotic	46	44
Somewhat patriotic	28	28
Not especially patriotic	5	6
No opinion	2	1

As far as you know, what specific historical event is celebrated on July 4th?

Signing of the Declaration of Independence; day it was signed	55%
Independence Day	32
Birth of United States	1
Other	6
No opinion	6

As far as you know, from what country did America gain its independence following the Revolutionary War?

England; Great Britain; United Kingdom	76%
France	2
Other	3
No opinion	19

If the signers of the Declaration of Independence were alive today, do you think they would generally agree or disagree with the way in which the Constitution is being followed in the United States today?

Agree	31%
Disagree	67
No opinion	2

Overall, do you think the signers of the Declaration of Independence would be pleased or disappointed by the way the United States has turned out?

Pleased	44%
Disappointed	55
No opinion	1

Note: On the eve of Independence Day, most Americans claim a strong sense of patriotism toward the United States. They also do fairly well answering questions about the historical facts surrounding the holiday. At the same time, they express significant doubts that the signers of the Declaration of Independence would agree with the way in which the Constitution is being followed today, and one-half think that the Founding Fathers would be disappointed with the way the country has turned out.

In response to the new poll, 65% indicate that they are extremely or very patriotic, while 28% are somewhat patriotic, with 5% not especially so. While expressed patriotism seems high, it appears that neither the military events surrounding U.S. involvement in Kosovo nor the strong economy has triggered newfound pride in the country. The current results are nearly identical to those found in 1994.

Levels of self-reported patriotism vary significantly according to certain demographic categories. The most notable differences are by race: 69% of whites claim to be extremely or very patriotic, as opposed to 40% of nonwhites. Age is also a factor, with Generation X members lagging behind their elders in patriotism; only 40% of those age 18–29 claim a strong sense of patriotism, compared to 65% of those age 30–49 and 77% of those 50 and older. Moreover, there is also a substantial gap between those who identify with the two major political parties, with 79% of Republicans saying that they are extremely or very patriotic, compared with 63% of independents and 56% of Democrats.

JULY 9
PRAYER IN PUBLIC SCHOOLS

Interviewing Dates: 6/25–27/99
CNN/*USA Today*/Gallup Poll
Survey #GO 128120

I'm going to read a variety of proposals concerning religion and public schools. For each one, please tell me whether you would generally favor or oppose it:

Making public school facilities available after school hours for use by student religious groups?

Favor.. 78%

Oppose.. 21

No opinion...................................... 1

Allowing public schools to display the Ten Commandments?

Favor.. 74%

Oppose.. 24

No opinion...................................... 2

Allowing students to say prayers at graduation ceremonies as part of the official program?

Favor.. 83%

Oppose.. 17

No opinion...................................... *

*Less than 1%

Using the Bible in literature, history, and social studies classes?

Favor.. 71%

Oppose.. 28

No opinion...................................... 1

Allowing daily prayer to be spoken in the classroom?

Favor.. 70%

Oppose.. 28

No opinion...................................... 2

Teaching creationism along with evolution in public schools?

Favor.. 68%

Oppose.. 29

No opinion...................................... 3

Teaching creationism instead of evolution in public schools?

Favor.. 40%

Oppose.. 55

No opinion...................................... 5

Note: In the aftermath of the recent shootings in the nation's schools, more people are calling for a re-turn to traditional family values, including prayer in the classroom. Once a daily staple for many schools, prayer in the public schools was banned by court decisions in the early 1960s on the grounds that it violated constitutional protections guaranteeing the separation of church and state. Returning prayer to the schools has become a rallying cry for conservatives in the wake of the Columbine High School tragedy in Colorado, and it is also a key part of the platforms of conservative presidential candidates such as Dan Quayle and Gary Bauer.

According to a new Gallup Poll conducted on the weekend of June 25–27, seven in ten Americans favor allowing daily spoken prayers in the nation's classrooms, and a somewhat greater percentage (74%) supports a proposal allowing schools to display the Ten Commandments. As might be expected, there are partisan differences, with 81% of those who describe themselves as politically conservative supporting school prayer, compared with 58% of liberals. In addition, blacks are more likely to support school prayer (85%) than are whites (69%), and older people—those 50 and over—are more likely to support prayer in schools (76%) than are those 18–29 (62%).

In Maryland this spring, a high-school senior was refused re-entry into his commencement ceremony and was detained and threatened with arrest after he walked out in protest against an unofficial prayer in which community leaders participated. The student had previously won his fight to keep prayer from being an official part of the ceremony. Respondents do not appear highly sympathetic to this minority concern, with 83% in favor of allowing students to say prayers as an official part of the graduation program. In addition, 78% support the use of public school facilities after hours by student religious groups (such as Bible clubs and the Fellowship of Christian Athletes).

JULY 13
GUN CONTROL

Interviewing Dates: 2/26–28; 6/11–13/99
CNN/*USA Today*/Gallup Poll
Survey #GO 126888; 127916

A recent court case found that gun manufacturers were liable for shootings committed with weapons they had manufactured and that they had allowed to flow illegally into certain states with strict antigun laws. What is your opinion—should gun manufacturers be held liable when their weapons are used in this manner, or not?

Yes.. 41%
No 58
No opinion.. 1

More generally, would you favor or oppose allowing local governments to sue gun manufacturers in order to recover the costs incurred because of gun violence in their areas?

Favor.. 36%
Oppose.. 61
No opinion.. 3

Please tell me whether you would generally favor or oppose the following proposal which some people have made to reduce the amount of gun violence:

Ban the importing of high-capacity ammunition clips?

Favor.. 79%
Oppose.. 20
Mixed (volunteered)....................................... 1
No opinion.. *

*Less than 1%

Note: The handgun industry is under fire again on both the political front and the legal front. In the wake of a series of shootings at American high schools, the U.S. Senate passed gun control legislation designed to keep guns out of the hands of juveniles. While the bill has apparently died in the House, handguns are also a popular target for candidates in the year 2000 presidential election, primarily Democrats Al Gore and former New Jersey Senator Bill Bradley. Finally, the National Association for the Advancement of Colored People (NAACP) announced plans on Monday [July 12] to sue gun manufacturers in the hopes of curbing street violence by limiting the distribution of handguns.

Overall, a majority of Americans appears to be opposed to this type of large lawsuit filed against major companies or industries. While Gallup has not polled on the public's support for lawsuits by specific advocacy groups such as the NAACP, a Gallup survey conducted on February 26–28 found 61% opposed to the idea of lawsuits filed by local governments to recover the costs that result from gun violence in their areas. However, it should be noted that among blacks, the NAACP's core constituency, 53% supported the lawsuits, with 44% in opposition. The general opposition to these lawsuits is further explained by a belief among respondents that gun manufacturers should not be held liable for the illegal use of their products. In the same February poll, 58% believed that gun makers should not be held responsible when their products are sold illegally in states with strict antigun laws. Along similar lines, by way of comparison, a 1996 Gallup Poll found only 30% believing that cigarette manufacturers should be held responsible for deaths brought on by smoking-related causes.

JULY 14
CONFIDENCE IN INSTITUTIONS

Interviewing Dates: 6/25–27/99
CNN/*USA Today*/Gallup Poll
Survey #GO 128120

I am going to read you a list of institutions in American society. Please tell me how much confidence you, yourself, have in each one—a great deal, quite a lot, some, or very little:

The church or organized religion?

Great deal 32%
Quite a lot 26
Some.. 28
Very little... 12
None (volunteered)....................................... 1
No opinion.. 1

The military?

Great deal 34%
Quite a lot 34
Some.. 26

Very little.. 6
None (volunteered)...................................... *
No opinion.. *

*Less than 1%

The U.S. Supreme Court?

Great deal 20%
Quite a lot 29
Some... 35
Very little.. 13
None (volunteered)...................................... 1
No opinion.. 2

Banks?

Great deal 16%
Quite a lot 27
Some... 40
Very little.. 15
None (volunteered)...................................... 1
No opinion.. 1

Public schools?

Great deal 14%
Quite a lot 22
Some... 37
Very little.. 24
None (volunteered)...................................... 2
No opinion.. 1

Newspapers?

Great deal 12%
Quite a lot 21
Some... 44
Very little.. 21
None (volunteered)...................................... 1
No opinion.. 1

Congress?

Great deal 9%
Quite a lot 17
Some... 51
Very little.. 21
None (volunteered)...................................... 1
No opinion.. 1

Television news?

Great deal 14%
Quite a lot 20
Some... 41
Very little.. 24
None (volunteered)...................................... 1
No opinion.. *

*Less than 1%

Organized labor?

Great deal 13%
Quite a lot 15
Some... 44
Very little.. 24
None (volunteered)...................................... 2
No opinion.. 2

The presidency?

Great deal 23%
Quite a lot 26
Some... 30
Very little.. 19
None (volunteered)...................................... 1
No opinion.. 1

The police?

Great deal 24%
Quite a lot 33
Some... 33
Very little.. 10
None (volunteered)...................................... *
No opinion.. *

*Less than 1%

The medical system?

Great deal 17%
Quite a lot 23
Some... 36
Very little.. 22
None (volunteered)...................................... 1
No opinion.. 1

The criminal justice system?

Great deal 8%

Quite a lot 15
Some.. 40
Very little... 34
None (volunteered)....................................... 3
No opinion.. *

*Less than 1%

Big business?

Great deal 11%
Quite a lot 19
Some.. 44
Very little... 24
None (volunteered)....................................... 1
No opinion.. 1

News on the Internet?

Great deal 8%
Quite a lot 13
Some.. 35
Very little... 22
None (volunteered)....................................... 3
No opinion.. 19

The computer industry?

Great deal 20%
Quite a lot 30
Some.. 34
Very little... 10
None (volunteered)....................................... 1
No opinion.. 5

Health maintenance organizations, also known as HMOs?

Great deal 8%
Quite a lot 9
Some.. 34
Very little... 42
None (volunteered)....................................... 4
No opinion.. 3

Note: The Gallup Poll's annual rating of Americans' confidence in the country's major institutions shows that the public has more confidence in the military than in any other institution tested,

followed by organized religion and the police. At the other end of the spectrum, HMOs suffer from the lowest level of public confidence of any of the seventeen institutions included in the June 25–27 survey. Additionally, respondents have significantly more confidence in the presidency and the U.S. Supreme Court than they do in the third branch of government, Congress; and the computer industry generates more confidence than does big business in general.

This year, the Gallup Poll added three institutions that did not exist when the initial Confidence in Institutions survey first appeared in 1973. On the list of seventeen institutions (ranked by combining the responses of those expressing "a great deal" or "quite a lot" of confidence), the computer industry fares very well, debuting in fourth place. The second new entry, news on the Internet, finishes next to last behind both television news and newspapers, but it remains an unknown quantity to nearly one in five respondents. The third, health maintenance organizations (known as HMOs), makes a disastrous debut. No doubt reflecting the unrelentingly bad press they have lately received, HMOs find not only a mere 17% rating them worthy of a great deal or quite a lot of confidence, but 46% express very little or no confidence whatever in these modern purveyors of health care.

Meanwhile, the military, enjoying both a scandal-free year and a strong performance in Yugoslavia, receives high confidence marks from nearly seven in ten (68%), finishing comfortably ahead of the church or organized religion, in second place at 58%. Other highly rated institutions include the police (57%), the presidency (49%), and the U.S. Supreme Court (49%). (The public's assessment of the presidency did not change as a result of the Clinton/Lewinsky controversy and resulting impeachment last year.) Congress continues to have low ratings, with only 26%. Other institutions with low levels of public confidence include the criminal justice system (23%) and organized labor (28%).

JULY 18
MANAGED HEALTH CARE

Interviewing Dates: 7/13–14/99
CNN/*USA Today*/Gallup Poll
Survey #GO 128278

Which of the following statements best represents the way you feel about managed health-care plans, such as HMOs—they need to be completely overhauled, they need major changes, they need minor changes, or they are basically fine the way they are?

Needs complete overhaul	26%
Needs major changes	41
Needs minor changes	20
Basically fine	7
No opinion	6

	Needs complete overhaul	Needs major changes	Needs minor changes	Basically fine*
By Politics				
Republicans	25%	41%	22%	8%
Democrats	33	43	15	4
Independents	23	39	23	8

*"No opinion"—at 7% or less—is omitted.

Which party's approach to government regulation of how managed care organizations treat their patients comes closer to your own—the Republican party, or the Democratic party?

Republican party	34%
Democratic party	41
Neither (volunteered)	10
No opinion	15

How concerned are you that the Republicans' plan to reform managed care would not go far enough in regulating the industry and, as a result, fail to give enough protection to patients— very concerned, somewhat concerned, not too concerned, or not at all concerned?

Very concerned	40%
Somewhat concerned	37
Not too concerned	12
Not at all concerned	7
No opinion	4

How concerned are you that the Democrats' plan to reform managed care would go too far in regulating the industry and, as a result,

increase health-care costs for patients—very concerned, somewhat concerned, not too concerned, or not at all concerned?

Very concerned	38%
Somewhat concerned	38
Not too concerned	12
Not at all concerned	8
No opinion	4

Note: The American public is strongly in favor of reforming the system of managed care in this country and has low levels of confidence in the medical system, and in HMOs in particular. At the same time, despite the extensive partisan debate that accompanied this week's Senate deliberations on a new Patients' Bill of Rights, neither political party in Congress seems to have grabbed a position of superiority in the eyes of the public based on its approach to the health-care problem.

About two-thirds of the public says that the system of managed care in this country, including HMOs, needs either major changes or a complete overhaul. This response puts HMOs in the same general category as the off-maligned federal income tax system, which 73%, in a 1997 Gallup Poll, said is in need of major changes or an overhaul. On the other hand, by way of comparison, the desire for changes in managed care and HMOs is higher than the same feelings about two programs that have occupied a great deal of congressional thought and debate in recent years: the Social Security and Medicare systems. Only 58% say that Social Security needs at least major changes, and only 57% say the same about Medicare.

One does not have to look far to come up with reasons for this strong desire for change in the managed care system. Only 17% have a great deal or quite a lot of confidence in HMOs, according to a recent Gallup Confidence in Institutions update, which puts HMOs at the very bottom of the list of seventeen institutions tested. The public's evaluation of the more generic "medical system" is somewhat better, with a 40% confidence rating, suggesting that the specific specter of HMOs and managed care at this point in time carries particularly onerous perceptual baggage. (By way of comparison, the military comes in at the top of the list, with a 68% confidence rating from the public.)

The health-care reform bill debate this past week in the Republican-controlled Senate was highly partisan, with the final plan passing by an almost purely partisan margin, 53 to 47. Attempts at compromise failed, and Democrats, including Vice President and presidential contender Al Gore, lined up to criticize the bill, with the subtext that the Republican Senate's failure to pass a more stringent bill would become a major political plus for the Democrats going into next year's congressional and presidential campaigns.

The evidence from a Gallup Poll conducted this week, however, suggests that the public has yet to form the impression that one party's position is significantly better than the other's on this issue. Forty-one percent say that the Democrats' position on managed care is closer to their own, compared to 34% who choose the Republicans' position. Although this represents a slight advantage for the Democrats, it is not nearly as high as the Democrats' edge on other issues in recent months.

The July 13–14 poll also asked about the two parties' positions. Forty percent are very concerned that the Republican plan on managed care reform would not go far enough in regulating HMOs, which is the Democrats' argument. But almost as many respondents (38%) are very concerned that the Democrats' reform plan would go too far, which is the Republican position. Thus, the public has yet to move strongly to one side of the partisan aisle or the other on this issue, despite the fact that both parties are essentially claiming victory out of Thursday night's [July 8] Senate vote.

JULY 20
SPACE EXPLORATION AND NASA—AN ANALYSIS*

How well do Americans remember the Apollo 11 mission from thirty years ago?

About seven out of ten Americans who are 35 years of age or older say they watched the moon landing on television in July 1969.

*This analysis was written by Frank Newport, Editor in Chief, The Gallup Poll, based on a series of interviews conducted on July 13–14, 1999.

Do Americans remember the Apollo program with the same type of glowing terms being used to describe its historical significance today?

It appears that some of the hyperbole surrounding the moon effort is not necessarily endorsed by the average American. A July 13–14 poll asked Americans if they agreed with a statement, based on an assertion appearing on the NASA web site, that "the human race accomplished its single greatest technological achievement of all time by landing a man on the moon." Only 39% agree with this statement; 59% don't. Presumably, technological developments that have occurred since 1969, including in particular the computer, have stolen some of the moon program's luster.

Neil Armstrong has been very reclusive in the thirty years since his historic first step on the surface of the moon. How well is he remembered?

Not nearly as well as one might think for someone who may go down in history on the same page as Christopher Columbus. In the Gallup Poll conducted last Tuesday and Wednesday nights, only 50% of the public correctly named Armstrong as the first person to walk on the moon. The second most prevalent guess was John Glenn, named by 13%, followed by Alan Shepard (who was the first American into space), and Buzz Aldrin, who was the second man on the moon. About 3% named someone else, while 28% couldn't come up with any name at all.

One assumes that it is young Americans who are least likely to remember Armstrong, since they were not alive at the time of the historic mission. Is this true?

No, exactly the opposite is true. Those who are now 18–29 years old, and thus who were not yet born in 1969, are most likely to be able to name Neil Armstrong. The older one gets, the less likely he or she is to name Armstrong, culminating in the fact that only 29% of those 65 and older can name him. It can be assumed that the youngest Americans are most likely to have run across the Armstrong name in their history classes, while older Americans, who may have watched on television, have fading memories when it comes to specifics. And by the way, Armstrong is better known now than he was ten years ago, when in a similar Gallup Poll only 39% could name him as the first man to walk on the moon.

Do Americans know how many astronauts walked on the moon before the Apollo program was shut down?

As is often the case when it comes to numerical matters, most Americans are pretty wide of the mark in their attempts to answer this question. The correct answer—twelve—is given by only 5% of Americans, most of whom guess a number that is substantially lower than the right total. Perhaps because of the recent emphasis on the Apollo 11 mission, which was manned by three astronauts (only two of whom actually walked on the moon, of course), about a third of Americans guess that only one, two, or three men have ever walked on the moon. Another third guess between four and seven, meaning that about two-thirds of Americans feel that seven or fewer humans have been on the lunar surface. The median response is five, meaning that about half guess less than five, while about half guess more than five. Only 11% overestimate the correct total and say that thirteen or more men have walked on the moon.

Have the billions spent on the space program been worth it?

Americans have gradually become more likely to say that the space program has brought enough benefits to this country to justify its costs. Back in 1979, ten years after Apollo 11, an NBC/AP poll showed that only 41% of Americans said the benefits of the space program outweighed its costs. By 1994, twenty-five years after Apollo 11, that number had risen to 47%. Now, at the thirty-year mark, 55% are positive about the benefits outweighing the costs, perhaps in part due to the publicity in the last year or two given to John Glenn's historic senior citizen voyage on the space shuttle.

Looking ahead, do Americans want more money to be spent on space exploration, or less?

Americans have mixed feelings. Since 1984, Gallup has been asking a question which empha-

sizes that all government programs have to be paid for out of taxes and then asks if specific programs should be increased, kept at the present level, decreased, or ended altogether. In most years, the plurality of Americans say that the NASA budget should be kept the same, although the rest have usually tilted toward a view that it should be reduced or ended.

In 1986, a high water mark for NASA, 26% said that its budget should be increased, only 14% said that it should be reduced, 5% said that it should be ended, while 50% said that it should remain the same. In September 1993, on the other hand, only 9% wanted it increased, 37% said it should be kept the same, 41% said it should be reduced, and 10% said it should be ended, meaning that a majority of Americans wanted NASA's budget cut or totally terminated. In the most recent poll, 45% say that NASA's budget should remain the same. Of the rest, however, there is a more negative tilt, with 26% saying that it should be reduced, and another 8% saying that it should be ended altogether; only 18% want NASA's budget to be increased.

One possible next target for manned exploration is Mars. How do Americans feel about the investment of billions to put a live human on the Red Planet?

Interestingly, Gallup asked Americans back in 1969—within a few days of the successful Apollo 11 mission—if they favored "the United States setting aside money" for an attempt to land an astronaut on the planet Mars. Despite the extraordinary success of the just-completed mission to the moon, Americans were less than enthusiastic about extending the effort to Mars. Only 39% of those interviewed favored such an attempt, while 53% opposed it. Gallup recently re-asked the same question and found much the same results thirty years later. Forty-three percent favor the Mars project today, while 54% now oppose it.

Are Americans themselves interested in going to the moon if they could?

About a fourth (27%) say they would like to go to the moon. That number, by the way, is double what Gallup found back in 1965, when the question was last asked.

Was there strong support for the Apollo program during the 1960s in the time between JFK's 1961 pledge to put a man on the moon before the decade was out, and the eventual landing on the moon in 1969?

Not nearly as much as might be imagined. In most polls conducted by Gallup during the 1960s, less than a majority of Americans said that the investment in getting a man to the moon was worth the cost. For example, a 1965 poll found that only 39% of Americans thought that the United States should do everything possible, regardless of cost, to be the first nation on the moon.

A number of years ago there was a movie, **Capricorn One,** *whose premise was that the U.S. government was faking the televised landings of astronauts on other planetary bodies. From time to time, one hears that people still don't believe the moon landings really happened. Is that belief widespread?*

No. According to the July 1999 Gallup Poll, only about 6% of the American public buys into that conspiracy theory, exactly the same number as did in a *Time*/CNN poll of four years ago. Although, if taken literally, 6% translates into millions of individuals, it is not unusual to find about that many people in the typical poll agreeing with almost any question that is asked of them, so the best interpretation is that this particular conspiracy theory is not widespread.

AUGUST 2
MIDDLE EAST SITUATION

Interviewing Dates: 7/22–25/99
CNN/*USA Today*/Gallup Poll
Survey #GO 128335

As you may know, last year President Clinton helped to negotiate a peace agreement between the Israelis and Palestinian Arabs, known as the Wye River peace accords. The terms of that agreement have yet to be implemented because of disagreements on both sides. Do you think that the United States should put pressure on Israel and the Arabs to implement the terms of that peace agreement, or do you think that the United States

should leave it up to Israel and the Arabs to settle the peace process on their own?

Put pressure on Israel and Arabs 31%
Leave it to Israel and Arabs 66
No opinion 3

	Put pressure on Israel and Arabs	Leave it to Israel and Arabs	No opinion
By Politics			
Republicans	26%	71%	3%
Democrats....................	37	59	4
Independents...............	28	70	2

As far as you are concerned, should the development of a peaceful solution to each of the following be a very important foreign policy goal of the United States, a somewhat important goal, not too important, or not an important goal at all:

The Palestinian/Israeli situation in the Middle East?

Very important 41%
Somewhat important....................................... 41
Not too important 9
Not important at all.. 6
No opinion 3

The situation in Kosovo?

Very important 44%
Somewhat important....................................... 38
Not too important 9
Not important at all.. 6
No opinion 3

The situation in Northern Ireland?

Very important 23%
Somewhat important....................................... 46
Not too important 16
Not important at all.. 8
No opinion 7

In the Middle East situation, are your sympathies more with the Israelis or more with the Palestinian Arabs?

Israelis 43%
Palestinian Arabs.. 12
Both; neither (volunteered) 30
No opinion.. 15

Do you think there will or will not come a time when Israel and the Arab nations will be able to settle their differences and live in peace?

Will.. 49%
Will not.. 47
No opinion.. 4

Thinking about the financial aid the United States provides Israel for economic purposes, do you think U.S. economic aid to Israel should be increased, kept the same, or decreased?

Increased.. 8%
Kept the same 45
Decreased 41
Eliminated (volunteered).............................. 1
No opinion.. 5

Thinking about the financial aid the United States provides Israel for military purposes, do you think U.S. military aid to Israel should be increased, kept the same, or decreased?

Increased.. 10%
Kept the same 42
Decreased 44
Eliminated (volunteered).............................. *
No opinion.. 4

*Less than 1%

Note: Despite the substantial involvement of the Clinton administration in brokering peace accords between the Israelis and Palestinians last year, Americans are inclined to leave the peace process to the parties directly involved. The agreement between the two groups is known as the Wye River peace accords, and, among other points, it calls for greater autonomy for the Palestinians. However, the terms of the agreement have not yet been car-

ried out, and in the meantime an election in Israel earlier this year produced a new prime minister, Ehud Barak. While Barak has expressed determination to achieve peace, some observers have argued that the United States should take a more active role in pressuring the Israelis and Palestinians to implement the agreement that they signed last year. But according to the latest Gallup Poll, Americans disagree by a 2-to-1 majority: just 31% say that the United States should pressure the two parties, while 66% say that it should let the Israelis and Arabs settle the peace process on their own.

Americans seem somewhat more optimistic than they have been in the past that eventually Israel and the Arab nations will be able to settle their differences and live in peace. The latest poll shows about an even split, with 49% saying that peace will eventually come and 47% saying that it will not. But this response is more positive than the one given in a Gallup Poll last December, when only 40% expected peace to someday be achieved, and 56% said not.

Although Americans may not want the United States to pressure the parties involved, an overwhelming majority (82%) still believe that achieving a peaceful solution to the conflict between the Palestinians and Israelis should be an important foreign policy goal of the United States. Forty-one percent say that it should be a very important goal, and another 41% say a somewhat important one; just 15% say that achieving peace between the Israelis and Palestinians is not too or not at all important. By comparison, 82% of Americans also believe that achieving peace in Kosovo should be an important foreign policy goal of the United States, while 69% say so about the conflict in Northern Ireland.

However important the goal of achieving peace in the Middle East might be, about four in ten Americans seem inclined to reduce the amount of aid that the United States currently gives to Israel, whether it is intended for economic or military purposes. One in ten think that aid to Israel should be increased, while another four in ten say that it should remain the same. These views on aid do not suggest that Americans are becoming less pro-Israel than they have been over the past decade. By a margin of 43% to 12%, they say that their sympathies are with the Israelis rather than with the Palestinian Arabs, a ratio that has generally been reflected in the Gallup Polls conducted over the past eleven years. The widest margin occurred in February 1991 during the Gulf War, when 64% expressed their sympathies for the Israelis and just 7% for the Palestinian Arabs, but by the end of 1993 the margin was 42% to 15%, about what it is now. The last previous reading, in December 1998, showed a similar margin of 46% to 13%.

Typically, foreign policy matters are not of great interest to most Americans, and the recent election of Israeli Prime Minister Ehud Barak is no exception. About six in ten are not familiar enough with the new prime minister to say whether they have either a favorable or unfavorable impression of him—about one-half of those because they have never heard of him, and the other half because they have not heard enough to form an opinion. Among the rest, Barak's rating is about 2-to-1 positive, with 26% having a favorable opinion of him and 12% an unfavorable one. The rating of the former prime minister of Israel, Benjamin Netanyahu, was also about 2-to-1 positive when it was last measured this past May. However, more people were able to make a rating, as 39% said that they had a favorable opinion of him and 20% an unfavorable one.

AUGUST 6
VIOLENCE IN THE WORKPLACE

Interviewing Dates: 8/3–4/99
CNN/*USA Today*/Gallup Poll
Survey #GO 907928

In general, do you feel that the laws covering the sale of firearms should be made more strict, less strict, or kept as they are now?

More strict	66%
Less strict	6
Kept as now	27
No opinion	1

	More strict	Less strict	Kept as now	No opinion
By Politics				
Republicans	57%	8%	35%	*
Democrats	81	3	15	1
Independents	62	7	30	1

*Less than 1%

Selected National Trend

	More strict	Less strict	Kept as now	No opinion
1999				
June 25–27	62%	6%	31%	1%
May 23–24	65	5	28	2
April 26–27	66	7	25	2
Feb. 8–9	60	9	29	2

Asked of those who are employed outside the home: How worried are you about possible violence in your workplace by a co-worker or other employee—very worried, somewhat worried, not too worried, or not worried at all?

Very worried	7%
Somewhat worried	13
Not too worried	27
Not worried at all	53
No opinion	*

*Less than 1%

Also asked of those who are employed outside the home: Do you personally know anyone who you think is capable of committing an act of violence at your place of work?

Yes	18%
No	82

Note: Despite highly publicized acts of workplace violence, such as last week's deadly shootings at two Atlanta brokerage firms and Thursday's fatal shootings at two Alabama businesses, a new Gallup Poll finds that most Americans generally feel safe at the office. The poll conducted on August 3–4 found that 80% of those who work outside the home are not worried about a coworker committing an act of violence; only 7% are very worried, and another 13% are somewhat worried. However, 18% of American workers personally know someone capable of committing such an act at their workplace.

When broken down by regions, Americans living in the West tend to have the highest level of concern about possible violence in their workplace (28%), compared to the East and South (20% each) and the Midwest (16%). In addition, the Gallup survey found that workers living in suburban areas are more likely to fear an act of violence (23%) than those who live in urban (20%) or rural (15%) areas. Moreover, although the victims of the Atlanta shootings were primarily white, African Americans and other minority groups have a higher level of concern regarding workplace violence: 28% of nonwhites polled were worried about the potential for violence in their workplace, compared to 18% of whites.

AUGUST 10
WEATHER CONDITIONS

Interviewing Dates: 8/3–4/99
CNN/*USA Today*/Gallup Poll
Survey #GO 907928

Compared to previous summers in your part of the country, has the weather where you live been especially hot this summer, or not?*

Yes... 76%
No 24

	Yes	No
By Region		
East	96%	4%
Midwest	90	10
South...	80	20
West..	27	73

*Based on half sample

Thinking about the weather, have you ever known a summer as hot as this one?*

Yes... 49%
No 49
No opinion... 2

	Yes	No	No opinion
By Region			
East	30%	68%	2%
Midwest......................	52	46	2
South...........................	49	50	1
West............................	67	31	2

*Based on half sample

Do you have any air conditioning in the house or apartment where you live? [Those who replied in the negative were asked: Do you wish you had air conditioning in the house or apartment where you live, or not?]

Yes, have air conditioning............................... 81%
No, but want it 8
No, but don't want it.. 11
No opinion.. *

*Less than 1%

Is your local area experiencing a drought— that is, a serious shortage of rainfall—this year, or not?

Yes... 50%
No 49
No opinion... 1

	Yes	No	No opinion
By Region			
East	88%	11%	1%
Midwest......................	44	56	*
South...........................	47	52	1
West............................	16	83	1

*Less than 1%

Note: A new Gallup Poll shows that one-half of all Americans report suffering from drought conditions in their local area, and that about one in five is already taking active steps to conserve water. The impact of drought conditions is especially high in the East, where one-half of all residents are conserving water. Additionally, three-quarters of respondents report that this summer has been especially hot in their area.

Several Eastern states have been forced to impose restrictions on water use as reservoir and underground water table levels drop during the drought. Not surprisingly, Gallup's findings show that people living in the East are most likely to report drought conditions, with 88% reporting serious shortages of rainfall in their area this summer. A little less than one-half of those in the Midwest and South are experiencing drought conditions, compared to only 16% in the West.

Correspondingly, 49% of Easterners are taking active steps to conserve water, including refraining from watering their lawns, filling their swimming pools, and taking long showers. Such steps are much rarer elsewhere around the country, where relatively few residents report that weather conditions have forced them to change their life-styles: 5% in the West, 16% in the South, and 11% in the Midwest.

What are Eastern residents doing? When they are asked to name some examples of life-style changes that they have made as a result of the drought, 24% mention that they have cut back on watering their lawns, now banned or severely restricted in several states. Another 12% have quit washing their cars, also banned or restricted to commercial car washes. And interestingly, just 6% are cutting back on water use in the shower, mostly by taking shorter showers.

AUGUST 12
TAX CUTS

Interviewing Dates: 8/3–4/99
CNN/*USA Today*/Gallup Poll
Survey #GO 128335

If the member of Congress from your district were to vote for a bill which cuts taxes by approximately $800 billion over the next ten years, would this make you more likely to vote for your representative in the election, less likely to vote for your representative, or would it not make much difference one way or the other?

More likely 46%
Less likely.. 13
No difference 39
No opinion.. 2

If the member of Congress from your district were to vote against a bill which cuts taxes by approximately $800 billion over the next ten years, would this make you more likely to vote for your representative in the election, less likely to vote for your representative, or would it not make much difference one way or the other?

More likely 19%
Less likely.. 37
No difference 41
No opinion.. 3

If Congress passes a Republican-sponsored bill to cut taxes by approximately $800 billion over the next ten years, do you think President Clinton should sign that bill into law, or should he veto the bill so it does not become law?*

Sign bill into law 63%
Veto bill... 30
No opinion.. 7

*Based on half sample

If Congress passes a Democrat-sponsored bill to cut taxes by approximately $300 billion over the next ten years, do you think President Clinton should sign that bill into law, or should he veto the bill so it does not become law?*

Sign bill into law 65%
Veto bill... 26
No opinion.. 9

*Based on half sample

Next, if Congress passes a Democrat-sponsored bill to expand Medicare coverage to include prescription drugs for Medicare recipients, do you think President Clinton should sign that bill into law, or should he veto the bill so it does not become law?

Sign bill into law 87%
Veto bill... 10
No opinion.. 3

Note: Republicans in Congress are reportedly using the current August recess to garner public support for their $792 billion tax-cut bill, amid criticism from President Bill Clinton and congressional Democrats that the plan jeopardizes funding for Medicare and other government programs. Recent Gallup polling, including a new survey taken on August 3–4, reveals that the public favors the major elements in both parties' budget agendas, creating an opening for political gain by either side.

The bottom line seems to be that, when it comes to tax cuts and Medicare, Americans want it all. When each is presented as a distinct proposal, most respondents favor a federal income tax cut as well as increased spending on Medicare: 63% would like to see President Clinton sign the Republicans' $800 billion tax-cut bill, while 87% support the Democratic initiative to expand Medicare coverage to include prescription drugs. However, when they are confronted with a choice between having tax cuts or expanding Medicare, their concern for Medicare takes precedence over their desire to cut taxes. By a 66%-to-32% margin, most respondents prefer the Democratic approach of smaller tax cuts and greater spending on Medicare over the Republican approach of larger tax cuts and smaller increases in Medicare. Thus, Republicans enter the budget debate armed with a popular proposal—tax cuts. Democrats enter armed with a persuasive idea—that, when forced to choose, most Americans say that Medicare funding should take priority over tax cuts. Building on this basic finding, Gallup polling reveals advantages and disadvantages for each political party in the brewing budget battle.

Tax cuts are certainly popular. According to Gallup polling conducted during tax-filing season this year, two-thirds (65%) consider the amount that they pay in federal income taxes to be too high. Additionally, three-quarters said in a poll in February that they would favor a 10% cut in federal income taxes. And, as noted, 63% today want to see Clinton sign the Republican plan into law. Moreover, the Democratic argument that the Republicans' $800 billion tax cut is irresponsible does not seem to have taken hold. Without providing any details about the budgetary implications of either proposal, Gallup survey respondents were asked whether Clinton should sign or veto each of the following bills: a Republican-sponsored bill to cut taxes by approximately $800 billion; and a Democrat-sponsored bill to cut taxes by approximately $300 billion. (The national sample of respondents was divided for this question, with one-half being asked about each proposal.)

The answers to the two tax questions are remarkably similar, with 63% saying that Clinton should sign the Republican $800 billion tax cut and 65% saying that he should sign the Democratic $300 billion tax cut. The similarity suggests that respondents are not informed about the details of each proposal, particularly those related to Medicare. Roughly two-thirds simply favor tax cuts and thus willingly support either proposal. Furthermore, Americans seem poised to reward members of Congress who support the Republican bill and punish those who oppose it. Nearly one-half of all respondents would be more likely to support the member of Congress from their district for reelection if he or she voted for the $800 billion tax-cut bill; only 13% would be less likely to support that person, while 39% say that the tax vote would make no difference. Theoretically this result gives incumbents supporting the bill a 33-point advantage among voters.

Reaction to members of Congress who vote against the bill tilts negative. Only 19% would be more likely to vote for their member of Congress if that person opposed the $800 billion tax-cut bill, while 37% would be less likely to support that person—an 18-point disadvantage for incumbents opposing the bill.

AUGUST 24
BEST UNIVERSITIES

Interviewing Dates: 8/3–4/99
CNN/*USA Today*/Gallup Poll
Survey #GO 128335

What university do you recognize as the best in the United States, all things taken into consideration?

Harvard	16%
Stanford	4
MIT	3
Princeton	3

Yale	2
Notre Dame	2
Duke	2
UCLA	2
Penn State	2
Other	40
No opinion	24

Note: Harvard is chosen by more Americans than any other school as the best university in the country. Over three-quarters of the American public name a college when they are asked to identify the best university in the United States, but the responses are widely divided between dozens of different schools, with only Harvard getting more than 5% of the total mentions. Perceptions about the top colleges vary significantly by region of the country.

The views of the average citizen can be contrasted with the annual Best College rankings just released by *U.S. News & World Report*. The *U.S. News* rankings are based on a complex statistical formula, including such factors as academic reputation, retention of students, faculty resources, student selectivity, financial resources, graduation rate, and alumni giving rate. The academic reputation component of the *U.S. News* formula is based on the perceptions of the academic elite: college presidents, deans of admissions, and provosts. The August 3–4 Gallup Poll, by contrast, was much simpler: it asked a random sample to name the best university in the United States. The responses give a good sense of the degree to which a group of elite universities dominates the perceptions of Americans.

The poll makes it clear that there is one school that stands out above all others using this top-of-mind questioning technique: Harvard. The Cambridge, Massachusetts, university is mentioned by about one in six (16%) as the best university, and as such it dwarfs all other colleges. Stanford is second in the list of colleges, but with only 4% of all mentions, followed by MIT and Princeton with 3% each. Five other schools were nominated by 2% of respondents: Yale, Notre Dame, Duke, the University of California at Los Angeles (UCLA), and Penn State, while all others receive only 1% of mentions or fewer.

The biggest contrast between the perceptions of the public and the *U.S. News* list is the

California Institute of Technology (Caltech), which this year comes in number one on the *U.S. News* list. Less than 1% of those polled by Gallup mention the Pasadena, California, college, suggesting that its excellence and academic reputation have not been translated to the population at large. The rest of the top five on the *U.S. News* list—Harvard, MIT, Princeton, and Yale—all draw at least 2% of all mentions on the Gallup Poll list.

SEPTEMBER 7
SCHOOL VIOLENCE

Interviewing Dates: 8/24–26/99
CNN/*USA Today*/Gallup Poll
Survey #GO 907169

The following questions were asked of parents who have children in Kindergarten through Grade 12.

Thinking about your oldest child, when he or she is at school, do you fear for his or her physical safety?

	Aug. 24–26, 1999	May 21–23, 1999
Yes, fear	47%	52%
Do not	53	47
No opinion	*	1

*Less than 1%

Have any of your school-age children expressed any worry or concern about feeling unsafe at their school when they go back to school this fall?

| Yes | 18% |
| No | 82 |

How serious a problem are each of the following at the school your oldest child attends—very serious, somewhat serious, not too serious, or not serious at all:

Violence?

Very serious	13%
Somewhat serious	15
Not too serious	38

Not serious at all.. 33
No opinion.. 1

Gangs?

Very serious... 11%
Somewhat serious... 16
Not too serious... 26
Not serious at all.. 45
No opinion.. 2

Drugs?

Very serious... 17%
Somewhat serious... 26
Not too serious... 28
Not serious at all.. 27
No opinion.. 2

Sex?

Very serious... 14%
Somewhat serious... 26
Not too serious... 30
Not serious at all.. 28
No opinion.. 2

Discipline in the classroom?

Very serious... 17%
Somewhat serious... 22
Not too serious... 34
Not serious at all.. 26
No opinion.. 1

Social pressure among students to be popular?

Very serious... 25%
Somewhat serious... 39
Not too serious... 21
Not serious at all.. 14
No opinion.. 1

Note: Students at Columbine High School in Littleton, Colorado—the site of the worst school shooting spree in U.S. history last April—are slowly returning to normal. The school reopened on August 16 for the first time since thirteen people were killed in a rampage by two students who later took their own lives.

The shootings generated fear among parents nationwide and, as many schools reopen their doors for a new school year this week, a Gallup Poll on education issues finds nearly one-half of all parents (47%) fearing for their children's safety at school. The percentages have fallen slightly since the end of the school year last May, when a Gallup Poll found that 52% of parents feared for their children's safety at school. Rural parents are more likely to be afraid (54%) than are parents in urban or suburban school districts (46% and 44%, respectively), and parents in the South are more likely to be afraid (56%) than are those in any other region.

SEPTEMBER 8
QUALITY OF EDUCATION

Interviewing Dates: 8/24–26/99
CNN/*USA Today*/Gallup Poll
Survey #GO 907169

Do you think salaries for teachers in your community are too high, too low, or just about right?

Too high 6%
Too low... 53
About right 37
No opinion.. 4

Overall, how satisfied are you with the quality of education students receive in Kindergarten through Grade 12 in the United States today—would you say completely satisfied, somewhat satisfied, somewhat dissatisfied, or completely dissatisfied?

Completely satisfied..................................... 8%
Somewhat satisfied....................................... 39
Somewhat dissatisfied.................................. 38
Completely dissatisfied 13
No opinion.. 2

Asked of parents with children in Kindergarten through Grade 12: How satisfied are you with the quality of education your oldest child is receiving—would you say completely satisfied, somewhat satisfied, somewhat dissatisfied, or completely dissatisfied?

Completely satisfied 37%
Somewhat satisfied 46
Somewhat dissatisfied 12
Completely dissatisfied 2
Just starting school (volunteered)................... 2
No opinion.. 1

Note: As the bell rings on a new school year, a Gallup Poll on education issues shows that parents give their local education system high marks, although the perspective on the nationwide status of schools is much less positive. The poll, conducted on August 24–26, finds that 83% of parents are pleased with the education their children receive in their school. There are only minor differences by region: residents of the South are the most satisfied, with 90% of parents expressing satisfaction with their children's schools. In the East, 82% are satisfied, compared to 81% of those living in the West and 78% in the Midwest.

However, the nationwide perception of the country's education system is far less optimistic. When asked to rate their satisfaction with the system nationwide, just 47% are satisfied, compared to 51% who express levels of dissatisfaction. In contrast, 81% are satisfied with the quality of the education that they themselves received when they went to school. Gallup's findings on these questions are very similar to other broad-based topics in which the public is asked to rate a group on both a local and a national level. For instance, Congress as a whole tends to receive much lower ratings than the performance of the individual respondent's own representative in Congress.

SEPTEMBER 17
GUN CONTROL—AN ANALYSIS*

The tragic shooting incident at the Wedgwood Baptist Church in Fort Worth, Texas, this week has again underscored the salience of pending

*This analysis was written by Frank Newport, Editor in Chief, The Gallup Poll.

congressional gun control legislation. Here are questions and answers about the key gun control issues from the perspective of the American public, based on recent Gallup polling:

Do Americans want Congress to pass stricter gun control laws?

Yes. This has been true for some time. In 1990, Gallup began asking a very basic question: "In general, do you feel that the laws covering the sale of firearms should be made more strict, less strict, or kept as they are now?" A majority of Americans have responded "yes" to the question each time it has been asked, although the percentages have changed some. In 1990, 78% said yes. That number began to drop through the decade, and by February of this year, a smaller majority (60%) said yes. After the events of Columbine, the percentage favoring stricter gun control laws went back up to 66%, and in the most recent asking in August remained at 66%.

How high a priority, politically speaking, is gun control for Americans?

A majority of Americans say that it is important that Congress pass gun control legislation, but—at least through this past summer—it has not been the highest priority. An August poll asked about the importance that the public placed on Congress passing four different forms of legislation before the end of the year. The results:

	Extremely, very important
HMO reform	83%
Increased funding for Medicare	77
Federal income tax cut	68
Gun control	65

Another poll conducted in July asked how important a variety of issues were to the respondent's congressional vote, with the following results:

	Extremely, very important
Social Security	84%
Health care, including HMOs	79

Medicare 78
Gun control 61
Tax cuts 60
Campaign finance reform 40

In both situations, as can be seen, a majority of Americans say that gun control is important, but that other issues—including Social Security, HMO reform, and Medicare—are more important.

Do Republicans differ from Democrats in the perceived need for gun control?

Yes. Although a majority of all Americans say that passing gun control legislation is important, there are clear differences based on party identification. Only 52% of Republicans say that passing gun control legislation is extremely or very important (in the August Gallup Poll), compared to 62% of independents and 80% of Democrats.

Similarly, 57% of Republicans say that gun control laws should be made more strict, while 62% of independents and 81% of Democrats agree with this stricter alternative. It should be noted that the rest of the Republicans in the sample did not want the laws to be made less strict, but rather kept as they are.

Do Americans differ on which party they think can do the best job on gun control issues?

Despite the partisan differences in the perceived importance of passing gun control legislation, there are not substantial differences in the perception of which party can do the better job on gun control, perhaps suggesting that each party's members are happy with the way in which their party is approaching the topic. A late June poll showed that 41% of those interviewed said that the Republican party could do the better job of reflecting their views about gun control, while 44% said that the Democratic party could do the better job.

What exactly do Americans favor in terms of gun control measures?

Americans pretty much favor most gun control proposals put in front of them. A June Gallup Poll listed eight different proposals, and a majority —and in most instances a substantial majority— said that they favored each:

Those in favor

Mandatory prison for felons who
  commit crimes with guns 89%
Mandatory gun show background
  checks, including gun dealers 87
Require safety locks or trigger guards 85
Raise minimum age for hand gun
  possession to 21 82
Registration of all firearms 79
Lifetime ban on gun ownership
  for juveniles convicted of a felony 77
Ban importing high-capacity
  ammunition clips 68
Hold parents legally responsible
  when children commit crimes
  with parents' guns 57

What about the most draconian measure, banning of all guns?

Americans do not seem to favor a total ban on gun ownership. A Gallup Poll conducted in 1994 asked respondents to choose between three alternatives: no restrictions whatsoever on gun ownership, some restrictions, or making it illegal "for everyone except police and authorized persons" to own guns. The "some restrictions" alternative was the overwhelming favorite, with 73% of all choices, while only 20% chose the total ban option.

SEPTEMBER 22
PUERTO RICAN NATIONALISTS

Interviewing Dates: 9/10–14/99
CNN/*USA Today*/Gallup Poll
Survey #GO 128526

As you may know, President Clinton has offered clemency to several members of a group who used violence in the 1970s to support political independence for Puerto Rico. Clinton has said that these Puerto Ricans can be released from jail if they agree to certain conditions. How closely have you followed the news about this clemency offer—very closely, somewhat closely, not too closely, or not at all?*

Very closely.. 12%
Somewhat closely... 25
Not too closely.. 26
Not at all 36
No opinion... 1

*Based on half sample

*From what you know about the matter, do you agree or disagree with President Clinton's decision to offer clemency to these people?**

Agree 19%
Disagree... 61
No opinion... 20

*Based on half sample

*Which of the following statements do you think is the main reason why Bill Clinton made this clemency offer—because religious and international leaders asked him to do so, and he decided it was the right thing to do; or because he was attempting to win political support for Hillary Clinton among Hispanics in New York, where she may run for the U.S. Senate?**

Right thing to do... 25%
Win support for Hillary Clinton 60
Other (volunteered) 2
No opinion... 13

	Right thing to do	Win support for Hillary Clinton	Other	No opinion
By Politics				
Republicans.....	10%	76%	2%	12%
Democrats	40	43	1	16
Independents ...	25	60	2	13

*Based on half sample

Note: The House Government Reform Committee has opened hearings on President Bill Clinton's decision to offer clemency to sixteen Puerto Rican nationalists, many of whom were members of the Armed Forces of National Liberation (known by its Spanish acronym FALN), a group responsible for bombings of U.S. military and civilian targets

in the late 1970s and early 1980s. A Gallup Poll finds that a relatively low level of attention is being paid to the controversy, but that the majority of Americans disagree with the president's decision and think that it was motivated by a desire to help Hillary Rodham Clinton's campaign for the U.S. Senate seat from New York.

The poll, conducted on September 10–14—after the clemency decision was announced but before the White House invoked executive privilege in refusing to turn over documents on the case to the House committee—shows that 61% oppose the president's decision; just 19% agree with his clemency offer, while 20% express no opinion on the matter. There are differences along party lines, with 70% of Republicans opposing the decision compared to 51% of Democrats; and also along racial lines, with 64% of whites in opposition compared to 42% of nonwhites.

The poll found that 37% of the public has been following the clemency controversy closely. This is a fairly low level of attention, about on a par with such news stories as the Clinton race initiative in 1998, the ethics investigation of Senator Bob Packwood of Oregon in 1993, or consideration of the GATT trade agreement in Congress in 1994. Those who are following the situation closely are stronger in their opposition to Clinton's decision than the general population, with a 78%-disagree to 19%-agree ratio.

OCTOBER 4
EAST TIMOR

Interviewing Dates: 9/23–26/99
CNN/*USA Today*/Gallup Poll
Survey #GO 128808

How closely have you followed the news about the conflict in East Timor—very closely, somewhat closely, not too closely, or not at all?

Very closely 5%
Somewhat closely... 24
Not too closely... 29
Not at all 41
No opinion... 1

As far as you are concerned, should the development of a peaceful solution to the conflict in East Timor be a very important foreign policy goal of the United States, a somewhat important goal, not too important, or not an important goal at all?

Very important	14%
Somewhat important	42
Not too important	20
Not important at all	13
No opinion	11

Would you favor or oppose the United States sending in military troops as part of the international peacekeeping force in East Timor?

Favor	34%
Oppose	59
No opinion	7

Note: The American public is paying relatively little attention to the conflict in East Timor and to date has little inclination to support the involvement of U.S. military troops there as part of the international peacekeeping force. Only about two in ten are aware that the conflict involves Indonesia, but those who are following the situation closely are most likely to feel that the peaceful resolution of the conflict is an important foreign policy goal of the United States.

About 30% are following the news about the conflict in East Timor closely, which puts it almost at the bottom of a list of news events that Gallup has tracked over the past decade using this measure. Such high-profile news stories as the death of Princess Diana or the fatal plane crash involving John F. Kennedy, Jr., receive "closely following" scores in the 80% range. The East Timor situation, at 29%, is currently above only one other news event that Gallup has tested: the Japanese political reforms in 1994. Still, it is instructive to note that the public's reaction to the East Timor situation is closely approximating the attention paid to the situation in Kosovo last February, before the massive Allied bombing attacks began. Only 30% of Americans were following that situation closely in February, but after the

active U.S. involvement began, the attention rating jumped to 78% by the end of March. Thus, the East Timor situation has the potential to push its way into the American public's consciousness in the weeks or months ahead if the situation deteriorates or if the United States becomes more directly involved.

Most Americans, given the low overall levels of attention being paid to the conflict, do not have a great deal of practical knowledge about the situation in East Timor. Over two-thirds of those interviewed had no answer when asked, "With what country is East Timor currently having a dispute?" Of the 30% who did venture a response, 20% correctly said Indonesia, a few said China, a few Australia, and 2% said that the conflict was internal. Not surprisingly, there are very large differences in responses to this question by such variables as age and income: 46% of those with postcollege educations named Indonesia, compared to only 10% of those with high-school educations.

Despite their general lack of knowledge about, or interest in, East Timor at this point, Americans are not willing to dismiss the importance of the situation there out of hand. Fourteen percent say that achieving a peaceful solution to the conflict is a very important foreign policy goal of the United States, while another 42% say that it is a somewhat important goal; only 33% say that such a solution is not important. Still, on a relative basis, this is the lowest "importance" rating that Americans have given when asked about international situations in the 1990s. It contrasts with the higher ratings given by Americans when asked about the importance to the United States of four other situations: in Kosovo, in Bosnia, in Northern Ireland, and in the Middle East between the Palestinians and Israelis. Those who are following the East Timor situation most closely are also most likely to say that it has importance for the United States, although those who are not following it at all are more likely not to have an opinion about its importance.

Only a very small number of U.S. military forces are currently in East Timor, but 59% of Americans oppose sending in "military troops as part of the international peacekeeping force in East Timor." As is often the case, men are slightly more likely than women to favor sending in the troops. Politically speaking, 40% of Democrats favor sending in U.S. troops, compared to 28% of Republicans and 35% of independents.

OCTOBER 5
FOOD SAFETY AND BIOTECHNOLOGY

Interviewing Dates: 9/23–26/99
CNN/*USA Today*/Gallup Poll
Survey #GO 128808

Do you feel confident or not confident that the food available at most grocery stores is safe to eat?

Yes	80%
No	19
No opinion	1

Do you feel confident or not confident that the food served at most restaurants is safe to eat?

Yes	69%
No	30
No opinion	1

How much confidence do you have in the federal government to ensure the safety of the food supply in the United States—would you say you have a great deal, a fair amount, not much, or none at all?

Great deal	15%
Fair amount	61
Not much	19
None at all	5
No opinion	*

*Less than 1%

As you may know, some food products and medicines are being developed using new scientific techniques. The general area is called "biotechnology" and includes tools such as genetic engineering and genetic modification of food. How much have you heard or read about this issue—a great deal, some, not much, or nothing at all?

Great deal	10%
Some	40
Not much	32
Nothing at all	18
No opinion	*

*Less than 1%

Overall, would you say you strongly support, moderately support, moderately oppose, or strongly oppose the use of biotechnology in agriculture and food production?

Strongly support	9%
Moderately support	42
Moderately oppose	25
Strongly oppose	16
No opinion	8

Some people say that all food should be labeled by the manufacturer to indicate whether the food contains products which have been produced using biotechnology. However, such labeling would require special handling that would raise the price of food. Would you, personally, be willing to pay more for your food in order to have new labels that would indicate the presence of foods produced using biotechnology?

Yes	68%
No	29
It depends (volunteered)	1
No opinion	2

From what you know or have heard, do you believe that foods that have been produced using biotechnology pose a serious health hazard to consumers, or not?

Yes	27%
No	53
No opinion	20

Note: U.S. public concern about genetically modified foods barely registers a ripple in a new Gallup Poll survey. While Europe is reportedly in an uproar over biotechnology-related food safety and environmental concerns—fraught with boycotts, vandalism, and charges of "Frankenfood"— only 10% of Americans report having heard a great deal about the issue, and just one-quarter (27%) currently believe that it poses a serious health hazard to consumers.

The biotech controversy focuses on concerns that specialized strains of corn, soybeans, and other agricultural products may not be safe for human consumption when they utilize genetic manipulation rather than traditional cross-pollination methods The debate encompasses food-testing issues that could eventually try the trust that Americans have in the U.S. Food and Drug Administration's ability to guarantee the safety of the food supply.

According to the September 23–26 Gallup survey, Americans today seem relaxed about food safety issues. Without reference to any specific hazard, 80% feel confident that the food available in most grocery stores is safe to eat; 69% feel confident about the safety of restaurant food. This conviction stands in stark contrast to the situation in Europe, where consumer concerns and boycotts have forced a mounting number of food producers and grocery chains to take a "biotech-free" pledge.

When asked specifically about the use of biotechnology in food production, Americans express a fair amount of uncertainty but nevertheless come down on the side of biotechnology. Only 27% of the public currently believe that biotechnology poses a serious health hazard to consumers; 53% think that it does not pose a hazard, and the rest (20%) are unsure. These levels of doubt and concern are reflected in the public's responses to an additional question, one that measures overall support for the use of biotechnology in food production. A bare majority (51%) support such a use of biotechnology, while 41% are opposed.

Even though Americans' overall reaction favors the biotech industry, the Gallup survey, which allowed respondents to register their intensity of feeling on the issue, reveals that its harshest critics outnumber its fervent advocates by close to 2 to 1. Overall, 9% strongly support biotech methods, 42% moderately support them, 25% moderately oppose them, and 16% strongly oppose them. The strongest opposition is levied by lower-income and less-educated persons, while those with college degrees and high incomes are most likely to be strong supporters. For instance, 21% of those with no college experience strongly oppose the technology, compared with only 8% of those with a college or postgraduate degree.

Low public awareness of the biotech issue in the United States could be one explanation for Americans' widespread confidence in the food supply. Only 10% of those surveyed in the September 23–26 poll claim to have heard a great deal about the issue—defined in the survey as new scientific techniques such as genetic engineering and genetic modification for producing food and medicines. Another 40% have heard or read "some," while one-half indicate that they have heard little to nothing about it. However, at this early stage of public awareness, those most familiar with the issue are also the most supportive. Two-thirds of those who have heard a great deal about biotechnology (66%) support its use in food production, compared to 63% among those who have heard some information, 42% of those who have heard not much, and 30% of those who have heard nothing.

OCTOBER 11
POPULATION GROWTH

Interviewing Dates: 9/23–26/99
CNN/*USA Today*/Gallup Poll
Survey #GO 128808

Have you heard or read about the great increase in population which is predicted for the world during the next few decades?

Yes... 58%
No 42%

Asked of those who replied in the affirmative: Are you worried or not worried about this population increase?

Worried.. 48%
Not worried.. 51
No opinion.. 1

How serious a problem for the country do you think population growth in the United

States is—would you say it is a major problem now, not a problem now but likely to be a problem in the future, or not a problem now and you don't expect it to become a problem?

Major problem now 18%
Likely in future 59
Don't expect problem 22
No opinion 1

Selected National Trend

	Major problem now	Likely in future	Don't expect problem*
April 9–12, 1992.........	29%	44%	34%
Jan. 8–11, 1971...........	41	46	13

*"No opinion"—at 3% or less—is omitted.

How serious a problem for the world do you think population growth internationally is— would you say it is a major problem now, not a problem now but likely to be a problem in the future, or not a problem now and you don't expect it to become a problem?

Major problem now 47%
Likely in future 41
Don't expect problem 11
No opinion 1

Note: The United Nations has declared Tuesday, October 12, as the "Day of 6 Billion"—the day when the Earth's population is expected to reach 6 billion people. Concern over a coming overpopulation crisis stretches at least back to the 1960s, when environmentalists and futurists claimed that the Earth's resources would soon be strained and unable to support the growing number of people. They predicted massive famine, disease, and chaos worldwide.

The warnings at that time apparently did not go unheeded. In 1963 a Gallup Poll showed that two-thirds of Americans had read or heard about the population crisis. By 1992, however, the percentage who had heard about it was down to 51%. Now, in Gallup's most recent poll, the percentage of the population who have heard or read about

the situation is back up slightly to 58% but still below the 68% of the early 1960s.

Concern over the issue is also down. Even as recently as 1992, 68% of those who had heard about the population crisis said that they were worried about it. Now, even as the world's population has continued to multiply, only 48% of those who have heard about it are worried about its possible impact.

OCTOBER 27
FEDERAL BUDGET—AN ANALYSIS*

President Bill Clinton and the Republicans in Congress continue to do battle over the provisions of the remaining spending bills which will be necessary to approve in order to complete the federal budget process for this year. The government continues to operate, despite the fact that the new fiscal year began October 1, thanks to stopgap continuing resolutions. However, the threat of a government shutdown still hangs over the proceedings if the budget cannot be resolved. Here are the major questions and answers about the budget process, based on recent Gallup polling:

Are Americans paying close attention as Congress and the president attempt to settle on a budget for the fiscal year that has already begun?

No. Only 41% say that they are following the "news about the budget negotiations between President Clinton and Congress" very or somewhat closely. This is below the 49% that were following the Congress and Clinton budget agreement in May 1997 closely, and far below the attention being paid to such news stories as NAFTA in 1993 or the Clinton health-care plan announced in 1993. (In contrast, the highest "closely following" measure of the decade, of those stories measured, was the death of Princess Diana, which was followed closely by 85% of those interviewed.)

*This analysis was written by Frank Newport, Editor in Chief, The Gallup Poll, based on a series of interviews conducted on October 21–24, 1999.

Are Americans optimistic that they will like the final form of this year's budget?

While Americans are not wildly positive about the outcome of the budget process this year, they are now more optimistic than they were a month ago. In a September 23–26 poll, only 35% said that they were either very or somewhat confident that Congress and the president would pass a budget that they would personally approve. Now, in the most recent October 21–24 poll, that number has risen to 46%.

Who is more likely to think that the eventual outcome will be a budget they like—Republicans or Democrats?

Perhaps surprisingly, it is Democrats who are more optimistic about the budget process this year. Only 39% of Republicans say that they are confident that a budget they personally approve of will be passed, compared to 59% of Democrats. This may be the result of the fact that Clinton's veto power has stymied previous Republican budget plans.

As in 1995, it appears that this budget is coming down to a head-to-head battle between President Clinton and the Republicans in Congress. Who's winning?

President Clinton continues to own a perceptual edge over the Republicans in Congress on budget-related issues. When asked whose approach they prefer in dealing "with the tough choices involved in deciding on the federal budget for next year," 50% of respondents in last weekend's poll said President Clinton, compared to 35% who said the Republicans in Congress. Although Clinton's advantage is slightly lower than in previous polls, in the most general sense he has won on this type of budget question every time it has been asked since December 1995. In July 1995 the Republicans in Congress won by a 48%-to-42% margin on this question. The December 1995 poll was taken in the middle of a government shutdown caused by the inability of Congress and Clinton to agree on a budget. It is widely assumed that Clinton won that showdown and that it became a primary factor in his successful reelection over Bob Dole in 1996.

Both sides have agreed that they will not dip into the Social Security surplus, but Clinton seems to be urging increased taxes while Republicans have proposed an across-the-board tax cut. What does the public think?

In the most recent poll, Americans were asked if they favored or opposed each of these three different approaches to balancing the budget. It is clear that no one likes the idea of spending surplus Social Security funds, and only 16% of the public favor this alternative. Instead, the Republican plan—cutting government programs and agency spending—generates the most support from the public, with 55% supporting the idea, compared to 39% who oppose it. Only 43% of Americans say they favor the idea of increasing taxes and user fees, including an increase in the cigarette tax, while 55% oppose it. In short: Clinton wins over the Republicans in Congress when the public is asked whose approach they favor in a general sense. However, the Republicans' plan to cut government spending wins the most support of the three specific options tested, particularly when compared to the idea of tax and user fee increases.

Do Republicans and Democrats differ in favoring these options?

The biggest difference comes on the spending cut idea, which is favored by 66% of Republicans but only 47% of Democrats. The differences by party in support for the other two ideas are much less pronounced.

Everyone seems to agree that dipping into the Social Security surplus is not a good idea. Whom does the public trust more to protect Social Security funds—Clinton or the Republicans?

Clinton gets the nod here. Fifty percent of the public favors Clinton's approach to acting responsibly with government funds set aside for Social Security benefits, compared to 38% who have more trust in the Republicans in Congress.

By the way, Bill Clinton now has only about thirteen more months in office before a new president is inaugurated. How is his job approval rating holding up?

Clinton has a 59% job approval rating in Gallup's most recent poll, above the average for his administration and above the average for all other presidents since Harry S. Truman.

NOVEMBER 5
NUCLEAR TEST BAN TREATY

Interviewing Dates: 10/21–24/99
CNN/*USA Today*/Gallup Poll
Survey #GO 907190

Recently the U.S. Senate considered an international treaty, called the Comprehensive Test Ban Treaty, that would have banned testing of any nuclear devices by all countries in the world, including the United States. Had you heard about that treaty before, or not?

Heard about it 65%
Not heard about it 34
No opinion 1

Asked of those who have heard about it: How closely have you followed the arguments both for and against the treaty—would you say you have followed them very closely, somewhat closely, not too closely, or not at all?

Very closely 8%
Somewhat closely 30
Not too closely 22
Not at all 5
Not heard about it 35

Are you aware of whether or not the U.S. Senate recently voted to approve the treaty, or are you unsure what the Senate did? [Those who were aware were asked: What did the Senate do?]

Voted to defeat treaty 26%
Voted to ratify treaty 4
Other (volunteered) 1
No, not aware 60
No opinion 9

Regardless of what the Senate actually did, what do you think the Senate should have done—voted to ratify the treaty, or voted to defeat the treaty?*

Voted to ratify treaty 59%
Voted to defeat treaty 29
Other (volunteered) 1
No opinion 11

*Based on half sample

Regardless of what the Senate actually did, what do you think the Senate should have done—voted to ratify the treaty, withdrawn the treaty and considered it at a later time, or voted to defeat the treaty?*

Voted to ratify treaty 44%
Withdrawn it 21
Voted to defeat treaty 19
No opinion 16

*Based on half sample

Note: When the U.S. Senate voted last month against ratification of the Comprehensive Test Ban Treaty, which bans the testing of nuclear devices by all countries in the world, some Democrats vowed to make it an election issue in the year 2000, but a Gallup Poll taken the week after the Senate vote suggests that such an effort may be difficult. The poll shows that while most Americans support the general idea of the treaty, few are aware that it had just been rejected by the Senate. Barring a major communications effort by the treaty's proponents, by next year's election even fewer voters can be expected to remember the Senate action.

Conducted on October 21–24, the poll shows that about two-thirds of Americans have heard of the treaty, but only about half that number are closely following the issue, and only one-quarter know that the Senate had recently voted to defeat the treaty. When asked what the lawmakers should have done, 59% of respondents say that the Senate should have voted to ratify the treaty, with 39% saying that they feel strongly and the other 20% not strongly about the matter. Another 29% say that the Senate should have voted to defeat the treaty: 18% who feel strongly about the issue, and 11% who do not.

When given a third option—withdrawing the treaty to consider it at a later time—44% of respondents favor ratification of the treaty, 21% opt to withdraw it from consideration, and 19% say that the Senate should have defeated the treaty. The withdrawal consideration option was advocated by President Clinton once it became clear that there were not enough votes in the Senate for ratification, but Senate Republican leaders scheduled the vote anyway.

NOVEMBER 9
BERLIN WALL/EASTERN EUROPE

Interviewing Dates: 11/4–7/99
CNN/*USA Today*/Gallup Poll
Survey #GO 907193

Since the Berlin Wall separating East and West Germany fell ten years ago, do you think each of the following countries is better off or worse off:

Germany?

Better off	82%
Worse off	11
Same (volunteered)	2
No opinion	5

Russia?

Better off	50%
Worse off	40
Same (volunteered)	4
No opinion	6

The United States?

Better off	82%
Worse off	9
Same (volunteered)	6
No opinion	3

Now I'd like you to think about the changes that have taken place in Eastern Europe over the last ten years. First, do you think the economic well-being of people living in these countries has improved, or gotten worse?

	Nov. 4–7, 1999	Dec. 7–10, 1989*
Improved	48%	71%
Gotten worse	43	22
Remained the same (volunteered)	3	1
No opinion	6	6

Question wording: Do you think the economic well-being of people living in these [Eastern European] countries will improve, or will it get worse?

Next, do you think the people in Eastern Europe have more political freedom or less political freedom than ten years ago?

	Nov. 4–7, 1999	Dec. 7–10, 1989*
More freedom	78%	88%
Less freedom	16	7
Remained the same (volunteered)	2	1
No opinion	4	4

Question wording: Will people in Eastern Europe have more political freedom or less political freedom than they do now?

Next, do you think social problems like poverty, hunger, and alcoholism have increased or decreased in Eastern Europe as a result of the changes which have taken place over the last ten years?

	Nov. 4–7, 1999	Dec. 7–10, 1989*
Increased	65%	46%
Decreased	19	35
Remained the same (volunteered)	4	7
No opinion	12	12

Question wording: Do you think social problems like poverty, hunger, and alcoholism will increase or decrease in Eastern Europe as a result of the changes taking place there?

Note: The fall of the Berlin Wall ten years ago has had both positive and negative consequences, according to a new Gallup Poll. Americans agree that the dramatic events leading up to the reunification of Germany ended up being positive for Germany and for the United States but much less positive for Russia and the other nations of Eastern Europe.

The events of ten years ago are given midrange importance by Americans in the context of a scale that asked those responding to a new poll to rate a number of the century's most important events. About one-half (48%) say that the fall of the Berlin Wall in 1989 was one of the most important events of the century, about the same rating given the breakup of the Soviet Union that occurred shortly thereafter. This rating of the Berlin Wall is lower than the importance attached to other events of the century, including World War II, the Nazi Holocaust during World War II, dropping the atomic bomb, and women gaining the right to vote in the United States in 1920—all of which are seen as the most important events of the century by two-thirds or more of Americans.

Have the last ten years proved to be as promising as might have been imagined as the wall came down in 1989? For Germany and the United States, the American public's answer is yes. Over eight in ten say that both Germany and the United States have been better off since the Berlin Wall fell. The view is much more mixed concerning Russia, however: only 50% say that Russia is better off, while 40% say that things have actually gotten worse for Russia.

There are other signs in the poll suggesting that Americans recognize that not all has gone as well as might be imagined for Eastern Europe since the Berlin Wall fell. In December 1989, as the events in Berlin were unfolding, the public was asked if it thought that the economic well-being of Eastern European countries would improve or get worse as a result. At that time 71% predicted that the economy in Eastern Europe would get better. Now, looking back over the past ten years, only 48% say that the economic well-being of these nations has in reality gotten better, with almost as many (43%) saying that it has gotten worse.

Ten years ago, 46% of Americans said that social problems such as poverty, hunger, and alco-holism would increase after the wall fell, while 35% said that they would decrease. Now, looking back, 65% say that such problems have increased. However, there has been less change in terms of the dimension of political freedom. Eighty-eight percent of Americans ten years ago said that the people in Eastern Europe would have more freedom as a result of the fall of the wall. Now, ten years later, that number remains high, at 78%.

Germany as a country maintains a very positive image in the eyes of Americans, with 77% who have a favorable image of the country, compared to only 18% who have a negative image. This reply can be compared to Russia, which has a favorable image among only 38% of the public, while 58% of Americans give it an unfavorable image rating.

DECEMBER 6
THE FIVE MOST IMPORTANT EVENTS OF THE CENTURY—AN ANALYSIS*

What is the most important event of the twentieth century? Historians may ponder that question for years to come, but from the perspective of the people of the United States, it is World War II. In a recent Gallup Poll, Americans nominated the war in general, the Nazi Holocaust that occurred during the war, and the dropping of the atomic bomb on Japan that helped end it, as three of the top five events of the century. Rounding out the top five are two events that signaled major changes in human rights and equality: the granting of the right to vote to women in 1920, and the Civil Rights Act of 1964.

A Gallup Poll conducted earlier this fall first asked the American public to name the most important event of the century off the top of their head, without prompting. Gallup Poll analysts then took this list, deleted the "events" that in reality are more like sweeping advances (such as the computer), added additional events that have appeared on other lists, and created a new list of

*This analysis was written by Frank Newport, Editor in Chief; David W. Moore, Consulting Editor; and Lydia Saad, Managing Editor, The Gallup Poll.

eighteen events for the public to rate. These events were then read to a new random sample in November, and the respondents were asked to rate each of the events on the following scale:

1 = One of the most important events of the century
2 = Important but not the most important
3 = Somewhat important
4 = Not important

The eighteen events were then rank-ordered based on the percentage of Americans who placed each in the top category:

		One of the most important events
1.	World War II	71%
2.	Women gaining the right to vote in 1920	66
3.	Dropping the atomic bomb on Hiroshima in 1945	66
4.	Nazi Holocaust during World War II	65
5.	Passage of the 1964 Civil Rights Act	58
6.	World War I	53
7.	Landing a man on the moon in 1969	50
8.	Assassination of President Kennedy in 1963	50
9.	Fall of the Berlin Wall in 1989	48
10.	U.S. Depression in the 1930s	48
11.	Breakup of the Soviet Union in the early 1990s	46
12.	Vietnam War in the 1960s and early 1970s	37
13.	Lindbergh's transatlantic flight in 1927	27
14.	Launching of the Russian *Sputnik* satellites in the 1950s	25
15.	Korean War in the early 1950s	21
16.	Persian Gulf War in 1991	18
17.	Impeachment of President Clinton in 1998	15
18.	Watergate scandal involving President Nixon in the 1970s	14

The sections that follow look in greater detail at what polling showed about Americans' reactions to the top five events in the rankings as they were occurring and/or what the trend of American thought has been on the topic through the years of this century.

World War II—The Most "Just" War

According to the American public, not only was the Second World War one of the most important events of the twentieth century, but it was also the most "just" of all the major wars fought by the United States in its history. A Gallup Poll conducted shortly after the beginning of the Persian Gulf War in January 1991 showed that 89% rated World War II as a just war, compared with 76% who rated World War I that way, 75% the Revolutionary War, 74% the Persian Gulf War, and 70% the Civil War. Only about one-half (49%) rated the Korean War as just, with 32% saying it was not, and 19% unsure. Not surprisingly, only 25% rated the Vietnam War as just, while 65% said it was not, and another 10% were unsure.

Despite this retrospectively positive view of World War II, it may come as a surprise to learn that in the years leading up to the Japanese attack on Pearl Harbor, Americans were not inclined to become involved in fighting against either the Germans or the Japanese. In fact, so strong was American opposition to U.S. involvement that in October 1939, more than a month after the Germans had started World War II by attacking Poland, fully 68% said it had been a mistake for the United States to enter even the First World War, and only 16% said the United States should send our army and navy abroad to fight Germany in the war that was under way. This opposition to U.S. involvement persisted throughout the next two years. The last time before Pearl Harbor that Gallup asked a question about U.S. involvement in the war was in June 1941, when only 21% said the United States should go to war.

If Americans were reluctant for the country to become involved in actual fighting, they nevertheless wanted to take aggressive steps—short of war—to help England and France, and to thwart the buildup of power in Japan. In October 1941, about two months before the Japanese attacked the U.S. military in Hawaii, 64% of Americans said the United States should take steps "now" to prevent Japan from becoming more powerful, even if this action would mean risking a war with Japan, while just 25% were opposed. Even earlier, in October 1939, 62% said the United States should do everything possible, except going to war, to help England and France. But even this caveat was tempered by the willingness of the American public, in a June 1941 poll, to have the United States provide military escorts for ships carrying war materials to Britain, with 56% in favor and 35% opposed. Even more telling was the widespread support of Americans for allowing the U.S. Navy to shoot at German submarines and warships on sight, supported by a margin of 62% to 28%—these latter two clearly acts of war. One reason for the public's opposition may well have been its perception that U.S. involvement was not needed. When Americans were asked in August 1941 who would win the war between Germany and Britain, 69% said Britain, while just 6% said Germany.

The Atomic Bomb

In the days immediately following the bombing of Hiroshima and Nagasaki in August 1945, Americans overwhelmingly approved of the action, by a margin of 85% to 10%. And by a margin of 69% to 17%, Americans also said it was a good thing rather than a bad thing that the bomb had been developed at all. But in the years since, public opinion has become less supportive of both the development and use of the atomic bomb. The question about using the bomb on the Japanese cities was asked again in 1990, when barely half of the public (53%) said it approved of the dropping of the bomb, while 41% expressed disapproval. In the latest asking, on the eve of the fiftieth anniversary of the event in July 1995, the margin of approval increased from 1990 (with 59% approving of the use of the atomic weapon, and 35% disapproving), but it was still far below 1945 approval levels.

Even more dramatically, the 1995 Gallup Poll showed that 61% of Americans now thought it was a bad idea that the atomic bomb had been developed in the first place, with just 36% saying it was a good idea. These figures are similar to results of a 1990 Gallup Poll. The 1995 poll also showed that while 86% believed that dropping the atomic bomb saved American lives, the public was about evenly divided on whether it saved Japanese lives by shortening the war; 40% thought that it did, but 45% said that it cost more Japanese lives.

The Holocaust

Although the Holocaust is viewed by the American public as one of the most significant events of the twentieth century, there were no Gallup Poll questions about the Holocaust that were asked during or immediately after the Second World War. However, in 1993 the release of a poll by the Roper Organization led some people to believe that a substantial number of Americans simply did not believe that the Holocaust had ever occurred. The question asked of a national sample of respondents was as follows: "Does it seem possible, or does it seem impossible to you, that the Nazi extermination of the Jews never happened?" Fielded in November 1992, the poll was released in April 1993. It reported that 22.1% said "possible," 65.4% said "impossible," and 12.4% said "don't know." This suggested that more than one-fifth of all Americans had doubts about the occurrence of the Holocaust, and overall more than one-third either were unsure or had doubts.

Some observers expressed doubt about the results, suggesting that the double-negative structure of the question ("do you think it is impossible that the Holocaust never happened?") could have confused the respondents. In early 1994 a Gallup Poll sought to explore the extent to which respondents' doubt or lack of certainty was the result of question wording rather than an accurate reflection of what people believed. Half the sample in a January survey were asked the Roper question, and the other half of the sample were asked the following question: "As you know, the term 'Holocaust' usually refers to the killing of millions of Jews in Nazi death camps during World War II. In your opinion, did the Holocaust definitely happen, probably happen, probably not happen, or definitely not happen?" The findings from the Roper question in this survey showed that over one-third of respondents (37%) said it seemed possible that the Nazi extermination of the Jews never happened, very similar to the results of the original Roper survey. The findings from the second question, however, showed that only 2% said the Holocaust probably did not happen, and 1% said it definitely did not happen, while 83% said it definitely did happen and 13% said it probably occurred. Further follow-up questions, asking respondents why they felt the

Holocaust only "probably" happened or why it probably or definitely did not happen, showed that only about 1%–2% of all Americans were committed, consistent deniers of the Holocaust and that the doubts of others were reflective of their ignorance of history, not their denial of the event itself.

Women's Progress in This Century

In 1872, Susan B. Anthony was arrested and fined $100 for casting an illegal vote in the presidential election at a Rochester, New York, polling place. In a speech subsequent to her arrest, Anthony said: "It shall be my work this evening to prove to you that in thus voting, I not only committed no crime, but, instead, simply exercised my citizen's rights, guaranteed to me and all United States citizens by the National Constitution, beyond the power of any state to deny." Almost fifty years passed before Anthony and other members of the American suffrage movement succeeded in their cause. In 1920 the Nineteenth Amendment to the U.S. Constitution was finally ratified, stating: "The right of the citizens of the United States to vote shall not be denied or abridged by the United States or by any State on account of sex."

Although the issue of suffrage was decided before the establishment of The Gallup Poll in 1935, the collection of surveys since then documents a wide variety of attitudes relative to the role of women in society. The questions themselves serve as a helpful reminder of the wholesale changes that gender roles have undergone this century:

- **1936:** "Should a married woman earn money if she has a husband capable of supporting her?" (18% yes; 82% no)
- **1937:** "Are you in favor of permitting women to serve as jurors in your state?" (68% favor; 29% oppose)
- **1938:** "Would you favor the appointment of a woman lawyer to be a judge on the U.S. Supreme Court?" (37% favor; 59% oppose)
- **1939:** "A bill was introduced in the Massachusetts legislature prohibiting married women from working for the state or local government if their husbands earn more than $1,000 a year. Would you favor such a law in this state?" (66% yes; 31% no)

- **1942:** "If women replace men in industry, should they be paid the same wages as men?" (78% yes; 14% no)
- **1945:** "Do you think women should or should not receive the same rate of pay as men for the same work?" (77% yes; 17% no)
- **1948:** "Do you approve or disapprove of women of any age wearing slacks in public, that is, for example, while shopping?" (34% approve; 32% "indifferent"; 39% disapprove)
- **1949:** "Do you think a woman will be elected president of the United States at any time during the next fifty years?" (31% yes; 60% no)
- **1950:** "Would you favor or oppose drafting young women if there is another world war?" (30% yes; 66% no)
- **1951:** "Speaking in terms of their day-to-day activities, do you approve or disapprove of women in this community wearing shorts, in hot weather, on the street?" (21% approve; 75% disapprove)
- **1973:** "Do you approve or disapprove of the use of 'Ms.' as an alternative to 'Miss' or 'Mrs.'?" (30% approve; 45% disapprove)
- **1979:** "Do you strongly agree, somewhat agree, somewhat disagree, or strongly disagree that it would be a good thing if women were allowed to be ordained as priests?" (37% of Catholics say yes; 53% of Catholics, no)
- **1980:** "If a draft were to become necessary, should young women be required to participate as well as young men, or not?" (51% yes; 45% no)
- **1981:** "Do you favor or oppose passage of the Equal Rights Amendment (to the Constitution)?" (55% favor; 32% oppose)
- **1999:** "Do you consider yourself a feminist, or not?" (26% yes; 67% no)

Gallup trends on some of these questions show notable change over time. Perhaps the most dramatic example of the cultural shifts in gender-related attitudes is the question of voting for a woman president. When first asked in 1937, only one-third of the country would vote for a woman for president "if she qualified in every other respect." By 1955, majority support for this proposition had been reached, at 52%, but as recently as 1971 close to one-third of the country remained resistant to putting a woman in the Oval Office. In 1999 nearly unanimous support has been reached, with 92% saying they would support a woman candidate and only 7% saying they would not.

Attitudes about women in the workplace also seem to have undergone substantial change since Gallup began tracking them. When Americans were asked in 1953 whether they would prefer to work for a man or woman boss, two-thirds (66%) chose a man, while just one-quarter chose a woman, and only 5% said it would make no difference. The percentage choosing a male boss in the 1990s is now just 39%, while many more Americans (36%) now say that the gender of their boss would not matter.

In recent years, Gallup Poll questions dealing with women's rights have tended to focus on the perceived amount of progress in this area. Despite the major advances in legal rights for women in this century, a belief that women are at a cultural disadvantage to men persists. For example, only 26% told The Gallup Poll earlier this year that society today treats men and women equally. Sixty-nine percent said that society treats men better than women, while just 4% said that it treats women better than men. According to a 1993 Gallup survey focusing on gender issues, six in ten (including 69% of women and 50% of men) believed that men have the better life in this country; only 21% overall chose women, while 15% thought the genders have equal experiences. Similarly, only 39% indicated in the same survey that women and men have equal job opportunities, while 60% disagreed.

At the same time that Americans tend to be pessimistic about the progress made by women, there seems to be a clear recognition and appreciation for the positive impact made by the suffrage movement. As noted above, among the eighteen events of the century recently rated in terms of their importance, women gaining the right to vote in 1920 ranks number two, on a par with dropping the atomic bomb in World War II.

In a different survey assessing major events of the twentieth century that specifically affected women, the right to vote was ranked first out of a list of nine items rated, with 73% saying that the suffrage movement had the greatest impact on women. This event exceeds all other reforms listed, including those related to marriage, sexual reproduction, and work:

	Higher impact on women
Right to vote	73%
Birth control	63
Opportunity for higher education	56
Women's athletics	39
Women's movement	37
Changes in abortion law	37
Changes in divorce law	29
Access to jobs	29
Political representation	22

The Civil Rights Act of 1964 and Racial Attitudes

Some observers argue that the Civil Rights Act of 1964 was the most important civil rights legislation in U.S. history. The act was pushed through by President Lyndon B. Johnson, who declared almost immediately after assuming the presidency in November 1963 that the continuation of assassinated President John F. Kennedy's efforts on civil rights would be one of his highest priorities. Due in large part to Johnson's efforts, the Civil Rights Act was passed by the House of Representatives in February 1964; and after extraordinary debate in the Senate, it was passed by the upper chamber and signed into law in June 1964.

The heart of the bill was Title II, Section 201(a): "All persons shall be entitled to the full and equal enjoyment of the goods, services, facilities, privileges, advantages, and accommodations of any place of public accommodation, as defined in this section, without discrimination or segregation on the ground of race, color, religion, or national origin." How did the public react to this sweeping legislation that in parts of the country—particularly the South—upset social patterns that had been in place for centuries? Gallup Polls conducted at the time showed that reaction was generally positive. As far back as June 1961, in fact, Gallup asked the public to react to U.S. Supreme Court decisions that ruled against school segregation and segregation on trains, buses, and in public waiting rooms The majority at that time approved of the Court's decisions: all children, no matter what their race, must be allowed to go to the same schools (approve, 63%; disapprove, 32%); and racial segregation on trains, buses, and in public waiting rooms must end (approve, 66%; disapprove, 28%).

The Gallup Poll also tracked a question that summarized the thrust of the proposed new Civil Rights Act from 1963 through 1964. In a June 1963 poll, taken while Kennedy was still president, there was mixed reaction to the idea of racial equality in public places, with a slight plurality (49%) in favor, compared to 42% opposed. By August 1963 support had moved to 54%; and in January 1964, with LBJ in the White House and the Act moving through Congress, support shifted to 61%. After the civil rights legislation was passed, in two polls conducted in September and October 1964, roughly 60% of the public continued to approve of the measure, with roughly 30% disapproving.

As might be predicted, significantly different reactions to the new legislation by Americans of different races and regions of the country were noted by Gallup analysts at the time these surveys were conducted. For example, in the January 1964 poll, Gallup reported that 71% of whites outside of the South approved, compared to only 20% of whites living in the South who approved.

Despite the generally positive reaction to the new civil rights legislation, Gallup polling during the period of the civil rights movement captured mixed feelings among the public about the speed with which integration and civil rights legislation should be implemented. For instance, as far back as June 1961, it was obvious that the public wanted changes in racial laws and patterns to be implemented slowly, rather than all at once: "Do you think integration should be brought about gradually, or do you think every means should be used to bring it about in the near future?" (gradually, 61%; near future, 23%).

By October 1964, when polls were showing that about six in ten Americans supported the new civil rights legislation, almost the same percentage (57%) said that the pace of implementation of integration was too fast. And by February 1965, on voting rights and public access, the idea that the federal government was doing too much for the blacks in this country (34%) and was moving too fast (42%) had plurality support over the idea that

the federal government was not doing enough (24%) or was moving too slowly (25%).

Whether as a result of specific civil rights legislation or not, one of the most striking changes in American racial attitudes has been the alteration over time in the overt expression of racially negative attitudes. Gallup summarized these changes in a 1997 Gallup Poll Social Audit of the trends in racial attitudes: "Whites express tolerant racial views across a variety of measures, and a majority of whites indicate a preference for living, working, and sending their children to school in a mixed racial environment. A majority of whites say they would not object if blacks in great numbers moved into their neighborhood, or if their child went to a school which was majority black. Almost no whites would object to voting for a black for president, and six in ten now approve of interracial marriage. *The over time changes in a number of these attitudes have been profound.* There has thus been a significant decline in the past several decades in the number of whites who express overtly prejudicial sentiments."

In particular, the percentage of the American public willing to vote for a well-qualified black for president has shifted from just over one-third (in 1958) to over 90% (in 1999). The affirmative percentage in response to this question stayed below 40% until 1959, moved to about 50% in the early 1960s as the civil rights laws were being passed, and then jumped by the late 1960s to closer to 70%. By 1997 the percentage was at 93%; and in a 1999 poll, it was 95%.

Another major change in American attitudes over time has been the increase in the perception that blacks have the same chance as whites to get any type of job for which they are qualified. The major changes on this measure took place, significantly, in the years after the Civil Rights Act of 1964 was passed. Starting in 1963 with 43%, "blacks have same chance as whites" was in the mid- to upper-60% range in the 1970s and 1980s and rose to 75% in 1997.

Despite the types of progress in racial attitudes noted above, a persistent pattern of differential perceptions between blacks and whites of the state of race relations in the country continues. For example, in two polls conducted in 1997 and 1998, whites and blacks evinced two distinctly different views of how well blacks are treated in the local areas where they live. Three-quarters of whites felt that blacks were treated the same as whites in their local community, compared to only 43% of blacks.

As these findings suggest, in the final analysis, the passage of the Civil Rights Act of 1964 did not bring about a state in which all racial differences, or at least the perceptions of differences, were erased. Significantly, only about 48% in a recent Gallup Poll said that relations between whites and blacks in this country were at least somewhat good (44% said somewhat good, 4% very good), while 27% said that relations were bad (23% somewhat bad, 4% very bad), and 19% said somewhere in between.

Additionally, there is actually somewhat more, rather than less, pessimism now than there was in the early 1960s about the future of the relationship between the races. In a 1963 poll conducted by the National Opinion Research Company, 42% said that "relations between blacks and whites will always be a problem for the United States," while 55% said that a solution "will eventually be worked out." In 1998 the percentage feeling race relations will always be a problem was actually higher, at 56%, while only 41% said that a solution will eventually be worked out. This increased pessimism was at about the same level among both whites and blacks.

DECEMBER 9
RACIAL PROFILING

Interviewing Dates: 9/24–11/16/99*
CNN/*USA Today*/Gallup Poll
Special survey

*Based on 2,006 telephone interviews; margin of sampling error: ±4 percentage points. Parallel margins of sampling error are ±4 percentage points for the sample of 934 white respondents, and ±5 percentage points for the sample of 1,001 black respondents.

It has been reported that some police officers stop motorists of certain racial or ethnic groups because the officers believe that these groups are more likely than others to commit certain types of crimes. Do you believe that this practice, known as "racial profiling," is widespread, or not?

	Total	Whites	Blacks
Yes	59%	56%	77%
No	34	38	16
No opinion	7	6	7

Do you approve or disapprove of the use of "racial profiling" by the police?

	Total	Whites	Blacks
Approve	14%	15%	9%
Disapprove	81	80	87
No opinion	5	5	4

Have you ever felt that you were stopped by the police just because of your race or ethnic background?

	Total	Whites	Blacks
Yes	11%	6%	42%
No	89	94	57
No opinion	–	–	1

Asked of those who felt they were stopped by the police because of their race or ethnic background: How many times do you feel this has happened to you in your lifetime?

	Total	Whites	Blacks
One to two times	37%	53%	27%
Three to five times	30	17	39
Six to ten times	16	17	15
Eleven or more times	15	13	15
No opinion	2	–	4

Asked of blacks: Have you ever felt that you were stopped by the police just because of your race or ethnic background?

	Yes	No	No opinion
Men			
18–34 Years	72%	28%	–
35–49 Years	60	40	–
50 Years and Over	32	65	3

Women

18–34 Years	40	60	–
35–49 Years	34	65	1
50 Years and Over	14	82	4

Do you have a favorable or unfavorable opinion of each of the following:

Your local police?

	Total	Whites	Blacks
Favorable	81%	85%	58%
Unfavorable	17	13	36
No opinion	2	2	6

	Favorable	Un-favorable	No opinion
By Black Men			
18–34 Years	43%	54%	3%
35–49 Years	67	30	3
50 Years and Over	69	23	8
By Black Women			
18–34 Years	52	41	7
35–49 Years	60	36	4
50 Years and Over	64	27	9

The state police or state troopers in your area?

	Total	Whites	Blacks
Favorable	83%	87%	64%
Unfavorable	11	8	26
No opinion	6	5	10

	Favorable	Un-favorable	No opinion
By Black Men			
18–34 Years	55%	35%	10%
35–49 Years	66	28	6
50 Years and Over	81	9	10
By Black Women			
18–34 Years	57	36	7
35–49 Years	64	25	11
50 Years and Over	67	19	14

Do you feel you are treated fairly by each of the following, or not:

The local police in your area?

	Total	Whites	Blacks
Fairly	87%	91%	66%
Not fairly	10	7	27
Not applicable (volunteered)	3	2	5
No opinion	–	–	2

	Fairly	Not fairly	Not applicable; no opinion
By Black Men			
18–34 Years	43%	53%	4%
35–49 Years	71	23	6
50 Years and Over	68	22	10
By Black Women			
18–34 Years	67	26	7
35–49 Years	75	19	6
50 Years and Over	71	18	11

The state police or state troopers in your state?

	Total	Whites	Blacks
Fairly	86%	89%	69%
Not fairly	6	4	17
Not applicable (volunteered)	6	6	10
No opinion	2	1	4

	Fairly	Not fairly	Not applicable; no opinion
By Black Men			
18–34 Years	58%	29%	3%
35–49 Years	64	22	14
50 Years and Over	86	6	8
By Black Women			
18–34 Years	71	21	8
35–49 Years	75	16	9
50 Years and Over	67	8	25

The state police or state troopers in other states you travel through?

	Total	Whites	Blacks
Fairly	74%	78%	55%

	Fairly	Not fairly	Not applicable; no opinion
Not fairly 11		8	24
Not applicable			
(volunteered) 13		12	18
No opinion 2		2	3

	Fairly	Not fairly	Not applicable; no opinion
By Black Men			
18–34 Years 44%		41%	15%
35–49 Years 56		26	18
50 Years and Over 60		12	28
By Black Women			
18–34 Years 57		29	14
35–49 Years 54		27	19
50 Years and Over 62		6	32

Note: The majority of white, as well as black, Americans think that racial profiling is widespread in the United States today. In a new Gallup Poll Social Audit on Black/White Relations in the United States, 59% of a sample of national adults age 18 and older say that racial profiling is widespread. Racial profiling is defined in the question as the practice by which "police officers stop motorists of certain racial or ethnic groups because the officers believe that these groups are more likely than others to commit certain types of crimes." This definition, which is neutral in tone, leaves open the possibility that some people might see racial profiling in positive terms. This, however, is not the case: 81% of the public disapprove of the practice.

There are few regional differences in the perception of the incidence of racial profiling, although it is more likely to be considered widespread by those living in urban areas than by those living in suburban and rural America. The biggest differences are by race. Seventy-seven percent of blacks say that racial profiling is widespread, compared to 56% of whites. Eighty percent or more of both whites and blacks disapprove of the practice, however.

The incidence of having been stopped on the basis of skin color or ethnic background varies widely by age and gender within the black popula-

tion in this country. In particular, it is black men, and especially young black men age 18–34, who are most likely to report having been stopped because of their race. Almost three-quarters of young black men believe that they have been stopped by the police because of their race or ethnic background. This percentage can be compared to the much smaller number of young black women (40%) who perceive themselves to have been the victim of racial profiling, and with the small percentages of both black women and men ages 50 and older who say that they have been stopped because of their race. There are few differences in these self-reported numbers by education or income among blacks; well-educated, higher-income blacks are as likely to report being pulled over by the police as those with lower levels of education and lower incomes.

Americans were asked to give their opinion—either favorable or unfavorable—of the local police and the state police in their area. Although a good deal of the publicity about racial profiling has been focused on the state troopers who patrol America's major interstate highways, there appears to be slightly more animosity by black respondents toward their local police. There is very little difference in attitudes toward "your local police" and "state police or state troopers in your area" among whites—85% of whites have a favorable opinion of the former, and 87% of whites have a favorable opinion of the latter. Blacks, however, have a less favorable opinion of both: 58% have a favorable opinion of their local police, and 64% of state troopers. Looked at differently, about 36% of blacks have an unfavorable opinion of their local police, and 26% have an unfavorable opinion of their state police.

DECEMBER 10
TEENAGE CRIME

Interviewing Dates: 11/18–21/99
CNN/*USA Today*/Gallup Poll
Survey #GO 129182

Are you a parent?

Yes 77%
No 23

When a teenager commits a crime, which of the following do you think is most responsible, in addition to the teenager—the child's parents, the child's peers, the media, or the child's school?

Child's parents	60%
Child's peers	20
The media	9
Child's school	—
All equally (volunteered)	7
Other (volunteered)	2
No opinion	2

Next, we'd like to know your reaction to this statement: Parents are to blame when their child breaks the law. Do you strongly disagree, disagree, neither agree nor disagree, agree, or strongly agree?

Strongly disagree	12%
Disagree	30
Neither agree nor disagree	21
Agree	28
Strongly agree	8
No opinion	1

How do you feel about this statement: Parents should be punished when their child breaks the law. Do you strongly disagree, disagree, neither agree nor disagree, agree, or strongly agree?

Strongly disagree	21%
Disagree	43
Neither agree nor disagree	16
Agree	15
Strongly agree	3
No opinion	2

Asked of parents: Has any of your children ever had run-ins with the police?

Yes	18%
No	82

Many people have had experiences with delinquency when they were younger. When you were between the ages of 13 and 18, were you ever arrested?

Yes	9%
No	91

Note: Most Americans believe that parents are at least partially responsible when their teenage children commit crimes, but a majority is not ready to actually blame the parents, and only a small proportion advocates the most extreme measure designed to reduce teenage crime rates: punish the parents for the crimes their children commit. These issues have become particularly significant this year as the mass shootings and killings committed by teenagers at Columbine High School in Colorado and at other schools around the nation have focused attention on causes and possible solutions for these tragic occurrences.

According to a recent Gallup Poll, conducted on November 18–21, 60% say that when a teenager commits a crime, the people most responsible for that crime, in addition to the teenage perpetrator, are the parents. Another 20% say that the teenager's peers are most responsible and 9% cite the media, while 7% hold all three groups equally responsible. The key caveat to these results is that people hold parents and others responsible "in addition to" the teenager, as it is mostly the teenage miscreants whom people blame, not the parents. The poll shows that as most respondents (77%) are in fact parents themselves, they are not likely to assume blame for their children's crimes. When asked to agree or disagree with the statement that "parents are to blame when their child breaks the law," those who are not parents agreed by a margin of 43% to 34%, while parents disagreed by that same margin—an 18-point swing in sentiment based on whether one is or is not a parent.

DECEMBER 15
MOST ADMIRED PERSON

Interviewing Dates: 12/9–12/99
CNN/*USA Today*/Gallup Poll
Survey #GO 129321

What man whom you have heard or read about, living today in any part of the world, do you admire most? And who is your second choice?

The following are listed in order of frequency of mention, with first and second choices combined.

Bill Clinton
Billy Graham
Pope John Paul II
Ronald Reagan
Nelson Mandela
Bill Gates
Jimmy Carter
George Bush
Colin Powell
John McCain*

*Tied with twelve other men; see Note.

By way of comparison, the following are the results of the 1998 audit.

Bill Clinton
Pope John Paul II
Billy Graham
Michael Jordan
John Glenn
Colin Powell
Ronald Reagan
George Bush
Nelson Mandela ⎫
Bill Gates ⎭ tie

What woman whom you have heard or read about, living today in any part of the world, do you admire most? And who is your second choice?

Hillary Rodham Clinton
Oprah Winfrey
Margaret Thatcher
Elizabeth Dole
Madeleine Albright
Barbara Bush
Queen Elizabeth
Nancy Reagan ⎫
Barbara Walters ⎭ tie
Rosie O'Donnell

By way of comparison, the following are the results of the 1998 audit.

Hillary Rodham Clinton
Oprah Winfrey
Elizabeth Dole
Margaret Thatcher
Barbara Bush
Madeleine Albright
Maya Angelou
Queen Elizabeth
Janet Reno
Monica Lewinsky

Note: On the eve of the long-awaited year 2000, Gallup's annual measure of the world's most admired men and women reveals a marked decrease in public esteem for most well-known figures. While Bill Clinton retains the distinction of being the most admired man "living today in any part of the world," he is the first or second choice of only 10% of Americans, down from 18% in 1998. Hillary Rodham Clinton's rate of decline is even more precipitous: the choice of 28% in 1998, she retains the top spot among the most admired women in 1999 with only 14% support.

Despite President Clinton's tarnished personal image resulting from the Monica Lewinsky affair, he leads the field for the seventh consecutive year. This position is not unexpected; the sitting president has topped the list all but eight times since the inaugural poll in 1946. The First Lady's support last year, when she benefited greatly from her dignified demeanor during the Lewinsky scandal, was unusually high. In 1997 she topped the list of most admired women with 14%, exactly the same percentage as in 1999.

Other than the First Lady, who else comes to mind when Americans are asked about living women whom they admire? Oprah Winfrey retained second place on the list this year, named first or second by 6%—down from 8% in 1998. Other carryovers from 1998 include Margaret Thatcher, Elizabeth Dole, Madeleine Albright, Barbara Bush, and Queen Elizabeth. Janet Reno and Monica Lewinsky dropped off the list, while Nancy Reagan and Barbara Walters reappeared in a tie for eighth place, closely followed by Maya Angelou, Betty Ford, Rosa Parks, and three entertainers: Rosie O'Donnell, Celine Dion, and Madonna.

The Reverend Billy Graham's amazing tenure on the list of most admired men continues. In his thirty-sixth consecutive appearance, he is named by 7% this year as most admired, up from 5% a year ago and second only to President Clinton. Pope John Paul II is next on the 1999 list, which also includes three former presidents— Ronald Reagan, Jimmy Carter, and George Bush. Nelson Mandela, Bill Gates, and Colin Powell also make repeat appearances on the list. No less than thirteen men from a wide variety of occupations are tied for the tenth place, mentioned by 1% each: John McCain, Jesse Jackson, Texas Governor George W. Bush, Michael Jordan, Gordon Hinkley, the Dalai Lama, Bill Bradley, Christopher Reeves, Donald Trump, Tom Hanks, Rush Limbaugh, Ross Perot, and Hugh Hefner.

DECEMBER 16
SUPPORT FOR NASA

Interviewing Dates: 12/9–12/99
CNN/*USA Today*/Gallup Poll
Survey #GO 129321

How would you rate the job being done by NASA, the U.S. space agency—would you say it is doing an excellent, good, only fair, or poor job?

	Dec. 9–12, 1999	July 13–14, 1999
Excellent	13%	20%
Good	40	44
Only fair	31	20
Poor	12	5
No opinion	4	11

Now I'd like to ask you about government spending on NASA. In answering, please bear in mind that sooner or later all government spending has to be taken care of out of the taxes that you and other Americans pay. Do you think spending on the U.S. space program should be increased, kept at the present level, reduced, or ended altogether?

	Dec. 9–12, 1999*	July 13–14, 1999*
Increased	16%	18%
Kept at present level	49	45
Reduced	24	26
Ended altogether	10	8
No opinion	1	3

*Based on half sample

Do you think the federal government should or should not continue to fund efforts by NASA to send unmanned missions to explore the planet Mars?

Should continue	56%
Should not continue	40
No opinion	4

*Based on half sample

Note: As NASA engineers search for the cause of problems that doomed the space agency's latest attempts to study the surface of Mars, a new Gallup Poll finds that the American public's confidence in NASA has slipped. Slightly over one-half (53%) rate the job that NASA is doing as either excellent or good, while the percentage who rate it more negatively, as either fair or poor, has risen to 43%. By way of comparison, when last asked this question in July—coinciding with the thirtieth anniversary of the Apollo 11 lunar landing—64% rated NASA's performance in positive terms, and only 25% believed that it was doing less than a good job.

To put these ratings into perspective, it should be noted that NASA's highest positive rating in this decade came in 1998, when the country was focused on Senator John Glenn's historic return to space during a space shuttle mission. At that time, 76% gave NASA's job performance a positive rating, while just 21% rated it as fair or poor. The Glenn mission helped to give the space agency a much-needed boost in the eyes of the public. It should be noted that mission failures, for obvious reasons, have a tendency to erode the public's confidence. In 1993, NASA's positive rating slipped to 43% in the wake of another failed mission to Mars, the lowest rating in this decade.

While NASA's job performance rating fell between July and October, there is no significant change in support for funding of the space agency. In July, 18% supported an increase in the NASA budget, compared to 16% in the most recent poll. There is no change in the 34% who would prefer to cut the space budget, while 49% of those polled would keep NASA's budget as is—statistically similar to the 45% recorded in July. Interestingly, Republicans tend to support increases in the NASA budget slightly more than Democrats (19% to 11%).

The good news from this poll for NASA is that despite the decline in its job performance rating, there remains a solid base of support for continuing the exploration of Mars. A majority (56%) believe that the government should continue to fund Mars missions, while 40% would prefer to stop funding them altogether. This support is greater among those with higher levels of education: 75% of college graduates support funding unmanned missions to Mars, compared to 42% of those with a high-school education or less.

DECEMBER 17
ELIAN GONZALEZ

Interviewing Dates: 12/9–12/99
CNN/*USA Today*/Gallup Poll
Survey #GO 129321

As you may know, a 6-year-old Cuban boy recently found off the Florida coast is the only survivor of a group of people, including his mother, who were escaping Cuba for the United States by raft. He is now in Florida where his custody is being disputed. How closely have you followed the news about this story—very closely, somewhat closely, not too closely, or not at all?

Very closely.. 23%
Somewhat closely.. 45
Not too closely.. 18
Not at all.. 13
No opinion.. 1

Which of the following solutions do you think would be in the best interests of the boy—for

him to remain in the United States to live with relatives who have requested he stay here; or for him to live with his father in Cuba, as his father has requested?

Remain in United States.................................. 45%
Live with father in Cuba................................. 45
Other (volunteered) 3
No opinion.. 7

Note: The plight of 6-year-old Elián González has captured the attention of the American public. Almost two-thirds say that they are following the story of the Cuban boy somewhat or very closely, a relatively high number for a news item of this type.

What should be done? Should Elián be sent back to Cuba to be with his father, or should he stay in the United States with relatives? Respondents split right down the middle on the issue, with 45% saying that he should be returned, and 45% saying that he should remain in the United States. Unlike many issues that confront the public, there are relatively few differences in sentiment on the Cuban boy by partisanship: 49% of Republicans, 33% of independents, and 44% of Democrats say that he should go back to Cuba.

Public attention to the boy's situation ranks above average compared with other news events in this decade. Among the over fifty different news stories that Gallup has rated since 1991, the 1997 death of Princess Diana—closely followed by 85% of Americans—ranks highest. The 1994 popular vote in Japan for political reforms ranks lowest, with only 22% paying close attention. At 68% the close attention paid to the Cuban boy's story puts it above the average rating of 56%, on a par with attention to the NAFTA trade issue in 1993, the death of Mother Teresa in 1997, and, co-incidentally, the shooting down of two civilian airplanes by Cuba in 1996.

The entire incident may ultimately have diplomatic repercussions. The United States and Cuba currently do not have diplomatic relations, but recent Gallup polling suggests that the public is ready for this situation to change. While only 40% said that diplomatic relations should be resumed in a 1996 survey, earlier this year a Gallup Poll found that 69% said that relations should be resumed. Time will tell, of course, whether or not the current situation will affect the probability that Washington and Havana will start up a more normal diplomatic and trade relationship.

DECEMBER 22
Y2K COMPUTER PROBLEM

Interviewing Dates: 12/16–19/99
CNN/*USA Today*/Gallup Poll
Survey #GO 129384

How much have you seen or heard about the year 2000 computer bug problem, sometimes called the Millennium Bug or the Y2K Bug, before now—a great deal, some, not much, or nothing at all?

Great deal	67%
Some	21
Not much	8
Nothing at all	4
No opinion	*

*Less than 1%

Selected National Trend

	Great deal	Some	Not much	Nothing at all*
1999				
Nov. 18–21	70%	20%	6%	4%
Aug. 25–29	64	24	9	3
March 5–7	56	30	11	3
1998				
Dec. 9–13	39	40	13	8

*"No opinion"—at less than 1%—is omitted.

As you may know, most computer systems around the world have to be reprogrammed so that they can accurately recognize the date once we reach the year 2000. Do you think that computer mistakes due to the year 2000 issue will cause major problems, minor problems, or no problems at all?

Major problems	7%
Minor problems	70
No problems at all	21
No opinion	2

Selected National Trend

	Major problems	Minor problems	No problems at all	No opinion
1999				
Nov. 18–21	12%	71%	14%	3%
Aug. 25–29	11	71	15	3
March 5–7	21	65	12	2
1998				
Dec. 9–13	34	51	10	5

Do you think that computer mistakes due to the year 2000 issue will cause major problems, minor problems, or no problems at all for you personally?

Major problems	3%
Minor problems	44
No problems at all	52
No opinion	1

Selected National Trend

	Major problems	Minor problems	No problems at all	No opinion
1999				
Nov. 18–21	3%	50%	45%	2%
Aug. 25–29	7	52	40	1
March 5–7	9	56	32	3
1998				
Dec. 9–13	14	53	30	3

Overall, how concerned are you about the Y2K computer bug problem—very concerned, somewhat concerned, not too concerned, or not at all concerned?

Very concerned	4%
Somewhat concerned	25
Not too concerned	46
Not at all concerned	25
No opinion	*

*Less than 1%

Selected National Trend

	Very con- cerned	Some- what con- cerned	Not too con- cerned	Not at all con- cerned*
1999				
Nov. 18–21......	–	–	–	–
Aug. 25–29......	6	30	45	19
March 5–7	–	–	–	–
1998				
Dec. 9–13	16	40	31	13

*"No opinion"—at less than 1%—is omitted.

Form A. *Do you or does your household plan to take any steps to prepare or protect yourself from problems that might result from the Y2K computer bug? If "Yes," what specific actions or precautions are you planning to take as January 1, 2000, approaches?**

Stocking up on food 20%
Stocking up on water...................................... 20
Stocking up on household supplies
(candles, radio, firewood, etc.).................... 12
Having more cash on hand 9
Purchasing a generator, heater....................... 4
Stocking up on gasoline 4
Updating computer 3
Withdrawing cash from various accounts 3
Keeping better financial records; closer
monitoring of financial records 3
No air travel.. 1
Making sure everything is Y2K compliant 1
Saving more money... *
Other (miscellaneous)..................................... 8
No, do not plan to take any steps.................... 51
No opinion 3

*Total adds to more than 100% due to multiple replies.

Form B. *For each of the following, please say whether that is something you probably will or will not do in order to protect yourself against problems associated with the Y2K computer bug:**

	Yes, will do
Fill gas tank in your car, truck........................	75%

Avoid traveling on airplanes on or
around January 1, 2000 51
Obtain bank confirmation............................... 48
Stockpile food and water................................ 42
Stock up on gasoline....................................... 21
Withdraw and set aside a large
amount of cash.. 21
Buy a generator or wood stove....................... 12
Withdraw all your money from the bank 6

*Total adds to more than 100% due to multiple replies.

Thinking about the U.S. economy, which of the following statements best describes the possible effect you think the Y2K Bug will have on the economy—it will cause a total economic breakdown or catastrophe, it will cause serious problems in the economy such as slowing production or creating a recession, it will cause only minor problems in the economy, or it will have no negative impact on the economy?

Total breakdown.. 1%
Serious problems 8
Minor problems 60
No negative impact.. 30
Other (volunteered); no opinion 1

Selected National Trend

	Total break- down	Serious prob- lems	Minor prob- lems	No nega- tive impact*
1999				
Nov. 18–21......	–	–	–	–
Aug. 25–29......	2	13	63	20
March 5–7	–	–	–	–
1998				
Dec. 9–13	4	25	55	14

*"Other," "no opinion"—at 2% or less—are omitted.

Next, I'm going to read some specific problems. As I read each one, please say whether you think it likely or unlikely to occur as a result of Y2K:

	Likely to occur
Banking and accounting systems will fail......	34%

Air traffic control systems will fail 27
Food and retail distribution systems
    will fail 25
Emergency "911" systems will fail 22
Hospital equipment and services will fail 20
Nuclear power or defense systems
    could fail... 15
Passenger cars, trucks will fail 12

Note: The American public continues to show less and less concern about the potential impact of the Y2K computer problem as the new millennium approaches. A new Gallup Poll conducted for the National Science Foundation and *USA Today* finds a continuation in the trend of lessening concern over the last year, and there is now very little concern that Y2K will cause serious economic damage to the country. Attention to the computer programming problem began to accelerate last March, and by this past August about two-thirds of Americans indicated that they had heard a great deal about the year 2000 computer bug problem, a percentage that has stayed at about that level since then.

    As can be seen here, about half of those interviewed could not name anything they plan on doing. The top two steps have been, and continue to be, stocking up on food and water (20% each), followed by stocking up on other supplies (12%), and then getting more cash on hand (9%). The biggest change over time has been the slight increase in the percentage who say that they will be stockpiling water and other household supplies. The other half of the sample was asked to respond to a specific list of eight items and to indicate whether each item was something that they either had done already or planned on doing. The responses to these prompted questions reflect higher percentages than do the corresponding responses given to the unprompted question.

    The trends here are quite interesting. The percentage who say that they will avoid traveling on airplanes has stayed about the same over the past year, while interest in withdrawing large amounts of cash or in obtaining bank confirmation has dropped. Intentions to stockpile food and water, on the other hand, have actually gone up as the year has progressed, from 26% who said that they would last December, to 42% today. A small but still not insignificant number of respondents think that it is likely that banking systems will fail, that air traffic control systems will fail, that food and retail distribution systems will fail, that emergency "911" systems will fail, and that hospital services will fail. In all of these instances, the percentages who feel this way today are down from previous measurements. The least amount of concern expressed is for failures in nuclear power and passenger cars and trucks.

DECEMBER 28
TERRORISM ON NEW YEAR'S EVE

Interviewing Dates: 12/20–21/99
CNN/*USA Today*/Gallup Poll
Survey #GO 129385

How likely do you think it is that one or more terrorist attacks will occur in the United States on New Year's Eve or New Year's Day—very likely, somewhat likely, somewhat unlikely, or very unlikely?*

Very likely 22%
Somewhat likely 40
Somewhat unlikely 23
Very unlikely 12
No opinion 3

*Based on half sample

Strictly on the basis of concerns you may have about possible terrorism, would you say you are less likely or not less likely to attend large public gatherings on New Year's Eve or New Year's Day?*

Less likely 50%
Not less likely 43
No opinion 7

*Based on half sample

Note: With the recent publicity about the possibility of terrorist attacks in the United States on New Year's Eve, many Americans have reconsidered how they will celebrate the beginning of the new "millennium." According to a Gallup Poll conducted on

December 20–21, 50% say that because of concerns about possible terrorism, they are now less likely to attend a large public gathering on either New Year's Eve or sometime earlier in the day. Forty-three percent say that they will not be affected by such concerns, and 7% are unsure.

When asked to assess the likelihood of terrorist attacks actually occurring in the United States on New Year's Eve, 22% believe it is "very likely" that one or more such attacks will occur during that time period, while another 40% believe them to be "somewhat likely." In general, concerns about terrorism are shared about equally among most groups, with very little difference by age, gender, education, or partisan political orientation. However, people with higher incomes are less likely than those with lower incomes to say that they believe terrorist attacks will occur, and that they will avoid large public gatherings because of their fears of terrorism.

The poll shows that almost six in ten (58%) with household incomes of less than $50,000 per year are less likely to attend a large public gathering on New Year's Day, compared with just 36% whose household income exceeds $75,000 per year. Similarly, although almost two-thirds (66%) of lower income respondents think it is likely that terrorist attacks will occur on New Year's Eve, just 53% of higher income Americans make that prediction.

DECEMBER 31
MOST ADMIRED PERSON OF THE CENTURY—AN ANALYSIS*

Mother Teresa, the Roman Catholic nun who devoted her life to ministering to the poor and sick in India, is the Most Admired Person of the Century, according to new CNN/*USA Today*/Gallup Polls

*This analysis was written by Frank Newport, Editor in Chief, The Gallup Poll, based on a series of interviews conducted on December 20–21, 1999.

of the American people conducted this fall. Mother Teresa is followed in the Top 5 list by Martin Luther King, Jr., John F. Kennedy, Albert Einstein, and Helen Keller.

No Systematic Record of Whom Americans Admired for the Entire Century

There is no simple way to determine what single person has been most admired by average citizens of the country throughout the years from 1900 to the present. Modern-day polling was not instituted on a regular basis until the mid-1930s, so there is no systematic record of what the people thought for the first decades of the century. In fact, Gallup did not begin asking the public on a routine basis to name the man and the woman whom they most admired until 1948, meaning that contemporaneous data are available only for the second half of the century. Thus, any attempt to average what Americans thought throughout the entire century on a systematic, quantifiable basis is impossible.

The procedure that Gallup has followed, therefore, is based on retrospective admiration among the sample of adult Americans who are living as the century comes to a close. Earlier this fall, in October, a Gallup Poll asked a sample of Americans to name—without prompting—the man or woman who lived at any time in this century whom they most admired. All individuals who were mentioned by at least 1% of the public in response to that question, along with other historical figures who have appeared in Gallup's Most Admired lists since 1948, were combined into a list of eighteen potential candidates for the Most Admired Person of the Century award. This list was then read to a new random sample of Americans on December 20–21. Respondents in that poll were asked to classify each of the historical figures as: 1) one of the people you admire the most from this century; 2) a person you admire, but not the most; 3) a person you somewhat admire; 4) someone you do not admire at all. From these results, the eighteen personalities were rank-ordered based on the percentage placing them in the top category, "one of ten people you admire the most from this century."

Eighteen Most Admired People of the Century

The final list is as follows:

		One of the people I admire the most
1.	Mother Teresa	49%
2.	Martin Luther King, Jr.	34
3.	John F. Kennedy	32
4.	Albert Einstein	31
5.	Helen Keller	30
6.	Franklin D. Roosevelt	26
7.	Billy Graham	26
8.	Pope John Paul II	25
9.	Eleanor Roosevelt	22
10.	Winston Churchill	20
11.	Dwight Eisenhower	18
12.	Jacqueline Kennedy Onassis	18
13.	Mahatma Gandhi	18
14.	Nelson Mandela	17
15.	Ronald Reagan	17
16.	Henry Ford	15
17.	Bill Clinton	10
18.	Margaret Thatcher	9

As can be seen, the Top 5 list contains a fascinating blend of historical figures. The most admired person, Mother Teresa, devoted her life to helping others rather than acquiring personal power or wealth. It is interesting to note that in addition to receiving the most "most admired" votes when the list of eighteen names was read to respondents, Mother Teresa also was the top vote-getter when Gallup earlier asked Americans to name the person whom they most admired without prompting. Mother Teresa is No. 1 across all major demographic categories except those 18–29 years of age.

One additional figure in the Top 5 list also devoted his life to the betterment of others: civil rights leader Dr. Martin Luther King, Jr. He does very well among nonwhites in the sample, as would be expected, but King also does extraordinarily well among the youngest group in the sample, those 18–29 years of age, among whom he gets more votes than Mother Teresa. This fact is

very interesting in and of itself, since no one in this age group—the oldest of whom was born in 1970—was alive before King's assassination in 1968.

Five U.S. presidents made the list of eighteen finalists, and only one, John F. Kennedy, made it onto the Top 5 list. Kennedy was killed in 1963 and thus can only be remembered contemporaneously by those who are now in their 40s or older, but the mystique surrounding JFK apparently continues to this day. Some may attribute his high presence on the list to his martyrdom at the hand of an assassin, or perhaps to the publicity this year surrounding the tragic death of his son, John F. Kennedy, Jr., but it should be noted that JFK also generated high public opinion ratings while he was alive and serving in office. In fact, during his presidency, Kennedy received the highest average job approval ratings of any president since World War II. Kennedy also comes in near the top of any list generated when Gallup asks Americans to rate the best presidents in American history.

Albert Einstein, who died in 1955, did not appear routinely on Gallup's Most Admired lists while he was still alive. His presence as No. 4 on this list also was determined before the recent announcement of his designation as the Person of the Century by *Time* magazine. Einstein's appeal is roughly even across all demographic categories.

Helen Keller became the first deaf and blind individual to graduate from college when she was graduated with honors from Radcliffe College in 1904. She authored thirteen books and was a frequent contributor to magazines and newspapers, often writing on blindness, deafness, social issues, and women's rights. Keller is most admired by women and by older Americans 30 years of age and above, perhaps for her advocacy on behalf of the blind and disabled.

The sixth through tenth names on Gallup's Most Admired Person of the Century list include two religious figures—one Protestant, Billy Graham; and one Catholic, Pope John Paul II. The other three figures are at least partially associated with World War II: President Franklin D. Roosevelt, his wife Eleanor Roosevelt (who went on to establish a strong international career of her own in the years after her husband's death), and British Prime Minister Winston Churchill.

Life-Style

JANUARY 6

PROFESSIONAL BASKETBALL

Interviewing Date: 1/6/99
CNN/*USA Today*/Gallup Poll
Survey #GO 125721

Are you a fan of professional basketball, or not?

	Jan. 6, 1999	Oct. 9–12, 1998	March 11–13, 1994
Yes	29%	36%	32%
No	59	54	57
Somewhat of a fan (volunteered)	12	10	11

As you may know, there was a dispute between the professional basketball players' union and the NBA owners that caused the NBA to miss much of its current season. Which side in the dispute did you favor—the owners, or the players?

	Total	Fans only
Owners	32%	37%
Players	23	32
Neither (volunteered)	19	18
Both (volunteered)	2	3
No opinion	24	10

How much have you missed watching NBA basketball since the dispute started—a great deal, some, only a little, or not at all?

	Total	Fans only
Great deal	11%	23%
Some	12	23
Only a little	14	28
Not at all	60	25
No opinion	3	1

As you may know, the basketball players and owners have come to an agreement and the NBA will now hold a reduced schedule of games. Will you personally watch the remaining NBA games more often, less often, or about the same amount as you would have if the lockout had not occurred?

	Total	Fans only
More often	3%	4%
Less often	21	27
About the same	70	66
No opinion	6	3

Asked of basketball fans: Compared to last year's basketball season, are you just as interested today in NBA basketball as you were then, or are you less interested?

Just as interested 40%
Less interested 55
More interested (volunteered) 2
No opinion 3

JANUARY 30
SUPER BOWL

Interviewing Dates: 1/22–24/99
CNN/*USA Today*/Gallup Poll
Survey #GO 126280

Are you a fan of professional football, or not?

Yes 51%
No 39
Somewhat of a fan (volunteered) 10

Asked of football fans: Which team would you like to see win this year's Super Bowl game—the Denver Broncos, or the Atlanta Falcons?

Denver Broncos 41%
Atlanta Falcons 54
No preference (volunteered) 4
No opinion 1

Also asked of football fans: Regardless of whom you favor, which team do you think will win—the Denver Broncos, or the Atlanta Falcons?

Denver Broncos 74%
Atlanta Falcons 21
Too close to call (volunteered) 2
No opinion 3

Note: Is it the "Dirty Bird," or just the desire to see an underdog succeed in the Super Bowl? According to the latest Gallup Poll, football fans want to see the Atlanta Falcons upset football's defending champions, the Denver Broncos, when Super Bowl XXXIII kicks off on Sunday [January 31]. In the poll conducted on January 22–24, the Falcons took top honors when fans were asked which team they would like to see win the Super Bowl: 54% of those polled who described themselves as football fans favor the Falcons, while 41% back the Broncos.

However, reality sets in when the fans consider the strengths of both teams. When asked who they believe will win the Super Bowl, fans pick Denver to beat Atlanta by an overwhelming margin: 74% of those polled believe that the Broncos will win their second straight Super Bowl, while only 21% give the nod to the Falcons. While the fans expect Denver to repeat as Super Bowl champions, they could wind up with an upset. Last year, 61% of those polled projected that the Green Bay Packers would beat the Broncos, but John Elway led the Broncos to their first Super Bowl title with a 31-to-24 win over the Packers.

MARCH 1
SPENDING AN EVENING

Interviewing Dates: 11/20–22/98
CNN/*USA Today*/Gallup Poll
Survey #GO 124977

*What is your favorite way to spend an evening?**

Watching television 31%
Being with family, husband, wife 20
Reading 18
Dining out 15
Going to movies or theater 11
Resting, relaxing 10
Watching movies at home 7
Visiting friends or relatives 6
Entertaining friends or relatives 5
Listening to music 4

*Total adds to more than 100% due to multiple replies.

Note: The "watching movies at home" option is one that was, not surprisingly, much less likely to be mentioned in previous Gallup surveys before the widespread adoption of VCRs in American homes. The other major change that has occurred in the home in recent years has been the penetration of personal computers and the Internet. Still, only 3% of respondents volunteer that putting in time on their computers or on the Internet is their favorite way of spending an evening—not a high enough percentage to earn a place on the top ten list.

There are some differences by population segment in the popularity of these ways of spending an evening. Age, for example, makes an enormous difference when it comes to watching television, which is much less popular among young people than it is among older people. Sixty percent of those age 65 and older mention television as their favorite way, compared to only 21% of those age 18 to 29. Similarly, watching television is much more likely to be mentioned by those with lower levels of education than by those with college or postgraduate degrees. The better educated group is more involved in reading and dining out.

These results are from a survey conducted late last year that updated the replies to a very basic question asked by Gallup since 1938: "What is your favorite way to spend an evening?" In 1938, of course, there was no television, and reading and going out to the movies or theater topped the evening recreation list. By 1960, when Gallup next asked the question, television had sprinted to the top of the list, where it has remained.

MARCH 10
PROFESSIONAL FOOTBALL

Interviewing Dates: 3/5–7/99
CNN/*USA Today*/Gallup Poll
Survey #GO 127004

Are you a fan of professional football, or not?

Yes.. 47%
No 44
Somewhat of a fan (volunteered) 9

Asked of football fans: It has been proposed that the NFL reinstate the use of instant replay by the referees in NFL games. Do you favor or oppose this proposal?

Favor... 87%
Oppose.. 11
No opinion.. 2

Also asked of football fans: Which of the following do you favor—maintaining the current system by which NFL referees are part-timers who have other full-time jobs during the week; or changing the current system to have full-time NFL referees, as is the case in the National Basketball Association and major league baseball?

Maintain system of part-timers....................... 31%
Change system to full-timers........................... 64
No opinion.. 5

Note: In the latest Gallup Poll, 56% of those surveyed describe themselves as football fans. Of that percentage, 87% want the NFL to bring back instant replay, following a season of criticized calls and blown opportunities; only 11% oppose the idea. The NFL used instant replay from 1986 to 1991 but dropped the system after numerous complaints about game delays while officials in the press box reviewed videotapes of close plays. Under a system being considered by NFL officials, teams would have the opportunity to challenge two plays per game, with a team losing a time-out if a call is upheld. Twenty-four of the league's thirty-one owners would have to vote in favor of instant replay for the concept to be implemented.

There is also support for a major change in the NFL officiating ranks. Historically, NFL officials have been part-timers, working a regular job during the week and calling games on the weekends. However, the same type of criticisms that may well lead to the return of instant replay may also end that tradition. Several owners and coaches have called for a move to full-time officials, and 64% of the football fans surveyed want the NFL to follow the lead of the NBA and major league baseball in hiring full-time referees. Thirty-one percent support keeping the current system.

MARCH 19
BEST PICTURE OF THE YEAR

Interviewing Dates: 3/12–14/99
CNN/*USA Today*/Gallup Poll
Survey #GO 127085

Which one of the five movies nominated this year for best movie would you like to see win the Oscar award for Best Picture of the Year?

Life Is Beautiful	8%
Elizabeth	4
Saving Private Ryan	53
Shakespeare in Love	11
The Thin Red Line	7
None; other (volunteered)	4
No opinion	13

Note: The American public overwhelmingly would like to see Steven Spielberg's *Saving Private Ryan* win the Oscar this Sunday night [March 21] as the Best Picture of the Year in the annual Academy Awards ceremonies. When given a choice among the five movies nominated for Best Picture in a Gallup Poll conducted last weekend, *Saving Private Ryan* wins with 53% of the public's vote, followed in a distant second and third place by *Shakespeare in Love* with 11% and *Life Is Beautiful* with 8%. The other two nominated pictures, *The Thin Red Line* and *Elizabeth*, get only 7% and 4%, respectively.

One might be excused for thinking that there would be significant gender or generational differences in preference for the pictures nominated this year. *Saving Private Ryan* is a war picture from World War II, which would seem to have a special appeal to men and older Americans. Women, in particular, might be expected to disproportionately prefer either *Elizabeth* or *Shakespeare in Love*. However, none of these predictions bears out. The poll data show that the preference for *Saving Private Ryan* is almost as strong among women as among men, and on a relative basis is no stronger among those age 65 and older who lived through World War II than it is among younger people. Women have only slightly higher preferences for *Shakespeare* and *Elizabeth* than men do.

How closely do the preferences of the average American predict the votes of Academy mem-

bers? Last year, in 1998, the public was right on. Almost six in ten of those interviewed in a Gallup Poll in March 1998 selected *Titanic*, which went on to sweep not only the Best Picture Oscar but a large number of additional statues as well. Similarly, the public in a pre-Oscar poll overwhelmingly preferred Best Picture winner *Forrest Gump* as the 1994 winner.

In 1993, however, preferences for the eventual winner, *Schindler's List*, were more muted. The Spielberg picture received 34% of preferences, only slightly more than did *The Fugitive*, which received 26%. And the public missed the Best Picture winner altogether for the year of 1992. In that year, 34% wanted to see *A Few Good Men* win, and only 16% chose Clint Eastwood's *Unforgiven*, which went on to become Best Picture.

MARCH 24
EXHIBITION BASEBALL IN CUBA

Interviewing Dates: 3/19–21/99
CNN/*USA Today*/Gallup Poll
Survey #GO 127182

As you may know, the Baltimore Orioles will be playing an exhibition baseball game in Cuba this coming weekend. As far as you are concerned, do you approve or disapprove of the Orioles playing this game in Cuba this weekend?

	Total	Fans only
Approve	73%	79%
Disapprove	19	17
No opinion	8	4

Note: For the first time since 1959, American major leaguers will play in Cuba this coming weekend. The Baltimore Orioles have received special permission from the Clinton administration to schedule a home-and-home series with Cuba's national team. The two teams are scheduled to meet in Baltimore in early May.

While the exhibition games have been the subject of protests at the Orioles' spring training camp in Florida and major league umpires have threatened to not work the games, baseball fans overwhelmingly support the showdown. In a Gallup Poll conducted on March 19–21, 79% of those polled who describe themselves as baseball fans approve of the Orioles playing in Cuba, with 17% disapproving. Among the general population, 73% approve of the games, with 19% disapproving.

MARCH 29
GASOLINE PRICES

Interviewing Dates: 3/19–21/99
CNN/*USA Today*/Gallup Poll
Survey #GO 127182

One year from now, do you think the price per gallon of gasoline in this country will be much higher, higher, about the same, lower, or much lower?

Much higher	11%
Higher	54
About the same	31
Lower	3
Much lower	*
No opinion	1

*Less than 1%

If the price of gasoline went up to $1.50 per gallon, would you cut back your driving, or not?

Yes	41%
No	56
No opinion	3

Note: A Gallup Poll conducted on March 19–21 shows that many Americans will not be surprised if the low gas prices do not last much longer. Fifty-four percent of those polled project that gasoline prices will be higher a year from now, and another 11% predict that pump prices will be much higher. Only 31% think that prices will be about the same; and, reflecting perceptions that the market has likely bottomed out, just 3% think that prices will be lower a year from now.

However, even a sharp increase in gas prices will not necessarily end the love affair between Americans and their cars. When asked if a price hike to $1.50 per gallon would force them to cut back their driving, 56% of those polled reply "No," while 41% indicate that they would cut back. Not surprisingly, the increase in gas prices will hurt low-income households most: 51% of those making less than $20,000 per year say that $1.50 gas prices would curtail their driving, compared to only 29% of those making $75,000 or more.

APRIL 2
EASTER SUNDAY—AN ANALYSIS*

An estimated 100 million adults, or every other person age 18 and older, spent part of Easter Sunday at church services. This finding is based on Gallup data showing that typical weekly attendance swells from 40% to 50% on Easter Day.

Past analysis also reveals that the biggest surge in attendance occurs among young adults who are under 30 years of age and Catholics. Teen attendance, which Gallup Youth Surveys show to run about 10 points higher than adults in a typical week (averaging 50%), can also be expected to climb considerably this Sunday.

Only a Cultural Event?

When people do finally show up at church on Easter, the clergy often has its work cut out for it, because some in attendance may not fully appreciate why they are there. An earlier (1991) Gallup survey found that just eight in ten Protestant and Catholic adults understand the religious significance of Easter Sunday, while two in ten either misunderstood it or readily admitted that they could not even hazard a guess. In addition, as many as three in ten teenagers do not know the religious significance of Easter.

These findings point to a "knowledge gap" in Americans' religious condition—the gap between Americans' state of faith and their lack of the most basic knowledge about that faith. Surveys

*This analysis was written by George Gallup, Jr., Co-Chairman, The Gallup Organization.

show that many Americans do not know what they believe or why. Furthermore, despite the growing level of formal education in the United States, Biblical illiteracy remains.

There is also a gap between "believers" and "belongers." Millions of people of all faiths are believers, many devout, but they do not always participate in the congregational lives of their denominations. Americans tend to view their faith as a matter between them and God, to be aided, but not necessarily influenced, by religious institutions.

And finally, there is an ethics gap—the difference between the way we think of ourselves and the way we actually are. While religion is highly popular in this country, survey evidence suggests that it does not change people's lives to the degree one would expect from the level of professed faith.

Overlapping in Beliefs and Practices

Considerable overlapping is found in religious beliefs and practices. People tend to choose the items of belief that best suit them. Reginald Bibby, Canadian sociologist, calls this "religion à la carte." Substantial proportions of traditional Christians, for example, subscribe to non-Christian beliefs and practices such as reincarnation, channeling, astrology, and fortune telling.

Religion in America: Underlying Themes

Religion in America has been studied by Gallup for two-thirds of a century, because one cannot fully understand America if one does not have an appreciation of its spiritual and religious underpinnings. Gallup surveys have shown that the depth of religious commitment often has more to do with how Americans act and think than do other key background characteristics, such as level of education, age, and political affiliation.

The picture of religion in this country is a complex one, but certain underlying themes emerge:

- The widespread and continuing appeal or popularity of religion
- A higher percentage of persons attesting to orthodox Judeo-Christian beliefs and doctrines
- A glaring lack of knowledge about the Bible, basic doctrines, and the traditions of one's own church

- The inconsistencies and overlapping of beliefs—for example, evangelical Christians expressing belief in New Age practices
- The superficiality of faith, with many people not knowing what they believe or why
- At the same time, however, an eager searching for meaning in life, a hunger for God, and a belief in prayer and present-day miracles.

APRIL 5
PROFESSIONAL BASEBALL

Interviewing Dates: 3/19–21/99
CNN/*USA Today*/Gallup Poll
Survey #GO 127182

Are you a fan of professional baseball, or not?

Yes	34%
No	51
Somewhat of a fan (volunteered)	15

Selected National Trend

	Yes	No	Some-what of a fan
1998			
October 9–12	47%	39%	14%
September 14–15	45	37	18
June 22–23	34	56	10

Who would you say is the greatest baseball player of all time?

	Total	Fans only
Babe Ruth	31%	26%
Mickey Mantle	7	8
Hank Aaron	3	2
Joe DiMaggio	18	20
Willie Mays	3	5
Pete Rose	1	2
Lou Gehrig	2	2
Ted Williams	2	3
Ty Cobb	2	3
Other	17	21
No opinion	14	8

Do you think that any major league player will hit more than seventy home runs this season and break the new home run record?

	Total	Fans only
Yes	39%	39%
No	51	56
No opinion	10	5

Note: As the 1999 baseball season opens, a new Gallup Poll finds that most fans do not expect a repeat of last year's home run derby. After a season that saw both Mark McGwire and Sammy Sosa break the thirty-seven-year-old record for most home runs in a season, 51% of all of those surveyed and 56% of baseball fans do not believe that any big leaguer will break McGwire's new record of seventy homers this year. The home run race is being credited with sparking a resurgence of interest in baseball. However, the poll conducted on March 19–21 shows that most of last fall's high level of interest generated by McGwire and Sosa may have faded. Only 34% of those polled now describe themselves as baseball fans, while 15% are "somewhat of a fan."

By way of contrast, in October 1998, a Gallup Poll found a combined fan percentage of 61% (those who described themselves as fans or "somewhat of a fan"). That poll, along with a similar Gallup survey conducted the month before, generated the highest fan support for baseball since the 1994–95 major league players' strike. Since the strike, Gallup Polls other than those of last fall have found that about one-third of respondents consider themselves baseball fans, and the latest poll shows a return to that trend.

The latest poll also continues to suggest some trouble for the future of the sport, given that a slightly higher percentage of older people consider themselves to be fans than is the case for younger Americans (38% of those 65 and older, compared to 32% of those 18 to 29). Other sports, including in particular professional basketball, have fan profiles that skew younger.

As has been the case in Gallup Polls since 1949, Babe Ruth is considered the greatest baseball player of all time. In the latest poll, 31% give the Sultan of Swat the top honor—the same percentage as in the last Gallup Poll on the question

in 1990 but down from 1949, when 53% ranked Ruth number one.

MAY 6
NATIONAL DAY OF PRAYER—AN ANALYSIS*

The National Day of Prayer is Thursday, May 6, and Gallup Poll data suggest that many Americans do not just pray on special days like this, but on a regular basis. Overall, nine in ten Americans claim to engage in prayer, a proportion that has not changed over the last half-century of Gallup polling, and three out of four Americans say that they pray on a daily basis. An additional 15% of adults say that they pray at least weekly. Less frequent praying is reported by only 6%.

Why do people pray? The survey results indicate that people pray for a range of reasons—from asking for their family's well-being, to adoration of God, to winning the lottery. However, many reject the idea of using prayers to petition for material things. Nearly all Americans who pray believe that their prayers are heard and that their prayers have been answered. But 20% have been angered on at least one occasion because they believe their prayers have not been answered.

Pray to a Supreme Being

Americans who are most likely to report praying at least once daily are women, nonwhites, and residents of the South. Even among young adults under 30 years of age, 62% report daily prayers. Prayer is primarily a solitary event: more people (87%) say that they more often pray silently and alone than aloud and with others (11%).

Most adults say they pray to a supreme being, such as God, the Lord, Jehovah, or Jesus Christ. Only 1% each report that their prayers are

*This analysis was written by George Gallup, Jr., Co-Chairman, The Gallup Organization. Based on Gallup studies conducted for *LIFE Magazine*, 1994; the Mind/Body Institute of the Harvard Medical School, 1995; and in a special survey conducted in preparation for the book, *Varieties of Prayer,* by Margaret M. Poloma and George Gallup, Jr., published in 1991 by Trinity Press International.

in a New Age mode to a transcendent or cosmic force, to the "inner self," or to the "god within."

Prayers Are Conversational

A majority of Americans who pray—56%—say that their prayers are conversational in nature. Fewer people say their prayers usually are either meditative or reflective (15%), or more formal, such as reciting the Lord's Prayer (13%). Fourteen percent report they use a combination of all three approaches.

Reflecting the nature of their particular religious practices, Protestants are twice as likely as Roman Catholics to say they most often engage in conversational prayer (65% to 31%). Catholics, perhaps not surprisingly given the more formal nature of their religious ceremonies, are more likely than Protestants to report that their prayers are more formal expressions, such as the Lord's Prayer.

Saying Grace

Giving thanks to God before meals is fairly common in American homes, with 29% of those interviewed stating they always say grace, and 22% reporting it is a frequent occurrence. An additional 34% say it is an occasional practice; 14% report that saying grace before meals is never done.

Protestants are more likely than Catholics to report they always or frequently say grace, by a margin of 56% to 43%. Nonwhites are most likely to report that they say grace "always" or "frequently" (65%).

The Effectiveness of Prayer

In vast numbers and through a variety of prayer modes, Americans seek to relate to a power outside themselves. Respondents report that the effects are often profound, in terms of life satisfaction, finding purpose and meaning in life, involvement in social and political causes, and the ability to forgive others who have hurt them. Prayer not only comforts; it challenges the person praying to move toward a greater spiritual maturity.

A high proportion of the nine in ten people who say that they pray report experiencing a deep sense of peace and the strong presence of God through prayer. Survey respondents frequently report that they have received an answer to specific prayer requests. Still others say they have gained a deeper insight into some Biblical truth, and that they have been inspired or led by God to perform some specific action. Of those who pray, the vast majority report that they thank God for His blessings, talk to God in their own words, ask God to forgive their sins, and seek guidance for decisions.

MAY 25
DISASTER AID/FORECASTING THE WEATHER

Interviewing Dates: 5/7–9/99
CNN/*USA Today*/Gallup Poll
Survey #GO 127652

President Clinton has declared parts of several states as disaster areas because of the tornadoes, making residents of those areas eligible for federal disaster assistance. Do you think the amount of money the federal government spends on disaster aid is not enough, about right, or too much?

Not enough	33%
About right	52
Too much	5
No opinion	10

Do you think the official local weather bureau is doing a good, fair, or poor job of forecasting weather conditions for your area?

Good	70%
Fair	23
Poor	7
No opinion	*

*Less than 1%

Have you personally ever been in a tornado, or not?

Yes	27%
No	73

Have you personally ever been in a hurricane, or not?

Yes	32%
No	68

Note: A new Gallup Poll shows that 70% of Americans think their local National Weather Service forecasters do a good job of predicting the weather. That figure is up from 51% when Gallup interviewers asked the same question more than fifty years ago, in 1948.

Granted, much of the increase in accuracy (and public confidence) may be due to advanced weather forecasting technology not available in 1948. However, part of this increase in confidence may also be due to the ability of the public to get updated weather forecasts more quickly than was the case years ago. With twenty-four-hour forecasts available on cable television and immediate local updates constantly coming from local radio and television stations, Americans are better able to take advantage of weather forecasts than they were at the time of the 1948 poll, when forecasts were limited in scope and availability.

Tornadoes can strike without warning, tearing apart homes and families in their wake. Nearly three in ten respondents (27%) have been in a tornado, according to the May 7–9 Gallup Poll. The numbers are lowest in the East (10%); tornadoes tend to strike in the Midwest, where nearly four in ten have been the victims of a tornado. The numbers are also high in the South (31%) and the West (29%), and also among rural residents (37%) compared to urban (21%) and suburban residents (25%). Despite a stereotype that tornadoes seem to do more damage to lower-income housing, including trailer parks, the Gallup Poll shows that those earning $75,000 or more annually are more likely to have been in a tornado than are those earning less than $20,000, by a 28%-to-24% margin.

Virtually every U.S. state has recorded instances of tornadoes; the number of states that have been hit by hurricanes is more limited because of their basic nature—the need for proximity to a coastline. However, a slightly greater percentage have been in a hurricane in their lifetime (32%) than in a tornado. This may be due to increasing population in coastal states, or just the simple fact that hurricanes tend to be wideranging storms that can cover hundreds of square miles, while tornadoes tend to be small and fairly isolated. Perhaps, not surprisingly, 43% of Southerners claim to have experienced a hurricane, compared to 11% of Midwesterners. (Southerners may have the worst of both worlds; as noted, 31% of Southerners also say that they have been in a tornado.)

JUNE 2
TRAFFIC PROBLEMS

Interviewing Dates: 5/21–23/99
CNN/*USA Today*/Gallup Poll
Survey #GO 127701

Suppose you are traveling on a trip on an interstate highway in an unfamiliar area. If you found yourself in a traffic backup several miles long caused by construction, which of the following would you be most likely to do—take the nearest exit and try to find a way around the traffic, stay on the interstate but feel aggravated as you move slowly through the construction site, or stay on the interstate and not feel aggravated?

Take nearest exit... 40%
Stay on interstate, feel aggravated.................. 30
Stay on interstate, not feel aggravated........... 29
Other (volunteered); no opinion..................... 1

Asked of drivers: Which, if any, of the following types of traffic jams causes you the most trouble—those caused by highway construction, those caused by normal rush-hour traffic, or those caused by accidents?

Highway construction...................................... 38%
Rush-hour traffic 41
Accidents.. 17
None (volunteered)... 2
Doesn't apply (volunteered).......................... 1
No opinion.. 1

Also asked of drivers: When you get stuck driving in a traffic jam caused by highway construction, how often do you become angry because you feel it could have been avoided by better planning—every time, usually, rarely, or never?

Every time 10%
Usually... 24
Rarely 43
Never 21
Doesn't apply (volunteered)............................. 1
No opinion... 1

Note: The arrival of summer brings with it the arrival of barricades, cones, and hard-hatted flagmen on American roads. Nine in ten adults drive; and for more than one-third of them, highway construction is the type of traffic jam that causes them the most trouble.

Traffic jams are considered a key factor in so-called road rage, the violence that occasionally occurs when too many cars try to share too little road. However, a new Gallup Poll shows that only about one-third of respondents actually admit to getting angry behind the wheel during a construction-related traffic jam. Ten percent of those polled admit to getting angry every time they get caught in such a traffic jam because they believe that it could have been avoided by better planning, while another 24% of drivers admit that they usually get angry during construction-related jams; 64% rarely or never get mad because of construction. Young people apparently exhibit the most impatience with construction: 14% of those age 18 to 29 routinely get angry during construction-related traffic jams, while just 4% of those over 50 do.

The poll results suggest that more routine rush-hour traffic jams may be just as responsible for driver frustration as construction. Slightly over four in ten (41%) blame their traffic jams on normal rush-hour traffic. That percentage is lowest in the Midwest (30%) and highest in the West (50%), where traffic jams are a daily way of life in cities such as Los Angeles, San Francisco, and Seattle. By comparison, construction-related traffic jams rank highest in the Midwest (45%) and lowest in the West (23%). Rush-hour traffic jams are also cited most by those earning more than $75,000 annually (52%), compared to 36% of those earning less than $20,000—perhaps because those with the lowest incomes are least likely to commute to work in automobiles, or are retired and not in the work force.

JUNE 17
GAMBLING IN AMERICA, 1999: ADULTS AND TEENAGERS—A SOCIAL AUDIT*

Two-thirds of Americans approve of gambling, but serious reservations remain about the impact of legal betting on sports events, the effects of casinos on local communities, and the growth of youth gambling. Almost one-half of Americans favor keeping gambling at its current level, while the rest are divided over whether legalized gambling should be expanded, reduced, or banned altogether.

As the National Gambling Impact Study Commission prepares to release its report on the social and economic impacts of gambling in the United States, a new Gallup Poll Social Audit shows that nearly two-thirds (63%) of American adults approve of legalized gambling, while 32% oppose it. The poll also shows that teenagers are more evenly divided in their support for legalized gambling, with 52% of those age 13 to 17 in favor and 47% opposing it.

However, both teens and adults see problems with legalized gambling. Two-thirds of both groups believe that betting on sports events leads to cheating or "fixing" of games, and 57% of adults oppose legalized betting on sports events as a way to raise state revenues.

*The Social Audits group of The Gallup Poll continues the tradition begun six decades ago by Dr. George Gallup in support of his driving philosophy that in order for democracy to work, politicians, bureaucrats, policymakers, and community leaders must be able to hear the voice of the people. This poll was conducted by telephone in both English and Spanish among American adults 18 years and older along with teens ages 13 to 17 living in the continental United States between April 30 and May 23, 1999. For results based on samples of these sizes, one can say with 95% confidence that the error attributable to sampling and other random effects could be ±3 percentage points for adults and ±5 percentage points for teens.

Fifty-six percent of adults believe that casinos have a negative impact on family and community life in the cities in which they operate, even though the majority (67%) says that gambling helps the local economy. Twenty-two percent say that legalized gambling should be expanded, 47% say that it should stay at current levels, and 29% believe that it should be reduced or banned altogether.

Gambling Behavior

Nearly seven in ten adults and 26% of teens have taken part in some form of legal gambling, with lotteries being the favorite form of most Americans. Fifty-seven percent have purchased a lottery ticket within the last year, while 31% have gambled in a casino. However, only 26% of those who have gambled within the last twelve months claim to be "ahead" in their winnings, while 49% admit to losing money.

The Gallup results also counter a stereotype of gamblers as lower class and lower income. The results find that 75% of those earning at least $75,000 annually take part in some form of gambling, while 63% of those earning less than $25,000 do. The same trends hold for education, as 72% of college graduates report some form of gambling in the past year, compared to 61% of those who did not complete high school. Men tend to gamble more than women do; and among religious groups, Catholics are far more likely to gamble than Protestants and members of other religious groups.

Casinos and Communities

There is a clear distinction in Americans' minds about the economic benefits of casinos and the social impact on the communities in which they operate. Two-thirds (67%) of adults claim that casinos generally help a community's economy, but 56% believe that they damage everyday family and community life. Teens are more evenly divided on the economic impact (51% say they help, 45% say they hurt), but opposition is even stronger on the social impact—70% of teens believe that casinos hurt a community.

Problem Gambling

Eleven percent of adults say that they sometimes gamble more than they should, with that opinion more prevalent among men than women, and among those who report a family history of gambling problems. In addition, 9% of adults—up from 4% in a 1989 Gallup Poll—and 10% of teens report that gambling has caused problems in their family. Also, 41% of adults and 28% of teens know someone outside their family for whom gambling has become a problem.

Teen Gambling

The Gallup survey provides some justification for concerns about teen gambling: 20% of teens say that they gamble more than they should, compared to just 11% of adults. Teens also tend to be more positive about the success of their gambling: 61% claim to be "ahead" on their wagers over the last year, while only 26% of adults make the same claim. Finally, 29% of teen gamblers claim to have made their first wagers when they were 10 years old or younger, and a surprising number of teens bet on professional and college sports (27% bet on professional events, while 18% bet on college games), despite the fact that almost all legal gambling is restricted to those over 18 years of age.

Gambling as a Source of State Revenue

Lotteries have become an important source of funds for many states, and 75% of adults support this form of gambling as a way to raise state revenue. Bingo for cash prizes receives support from 74% of adults for this purpose, while 63% support casino gambling. Off-track betting on horse races, betting on professional sports events, and video poker all receive significantly less support.

Gambling and the Internet

There is far less support for gambling on the Internet than for other forms of legalized gambling. Three in four adults (75%) disapprove of online gambling, while 20% approve. In addition, 76% of adults and 70% of teens believe that it is easy for teens to gamble on the Internet, and a majority of both teens and adults believe that Internet access has increased gambling among teens. However, despite this perception, only 2% of teens report using the Internet to gamble.

JUNE 25
STAR WARS

Interviewing Dates: 5/21–23/; 6/4–5/; 6/11–13/99
CNN/*USA Today*/Gallup Poll
Survey #GO 127701; 127853; 127916

Have you, personally, seen the new Star Wars *movie called* The Phantom Menace?

	June 11–13, 1999	June 4–5, 1999	May 21–23, 1999
Yes	16%	15%	4%
No	84	85	96

Asked of those who saw The Phantom Menace: *How would you describe your reaction to the movie—did you think that it was one of the greatest movies you've ever seen, excellent, good, only fair, or poor?*

	June 11–13, 1999	June 4–5, 1999	May 21–23, 1999
One of the greatest	3%	5%	9%
Excellent	33	40	52
Good	40	32	32
Only fair	18	20	5
Poor	6	3	2

Asked of those who have children in Kindergarten through Grade 12: Has your child, or any of your children, seen The Phantom Menace?

	June 11–13, 1999	June 4–5, 1999	May 21–23, 1999
Yes	30%	29%	9%
No	70	68	91
Don't know	*	3	*

*Less than 1%

Note: Although films like *Austin Powers: The Spy Who Shagged Me* and Disney's *Tarzan* have now taken control of the nation's box offices, there is little question that this season's first and biggest blockbuster was *Star Wars Episode 1: The Phantom Menace*. And, now that the dust has finally settled from the early hype and initial negative reviews of the movie, Gallup polling indicates that 16% of Americans have seen the latest installment of the *Star Wars* film series, as of the weekend of June 11–13. An even larger number (30%) report that their children under age 18 have seen *The Phantom Menace*.

The movie clearly appealed to the young, with a steadily decreasing probability of having seen the movie as age increases. In fact, while 26% of those age 18 to 29 have seen it, only 1% of those 65 and older have done so. The movie has also been much more popular in the West than in the East, and it is more likely to have been seen by men than women.

JULY 6
FLAG BURNING

Interviewing Dates: 6/25–27/99
CNN/*USA Today*/Gallup Poll
Survey #GO 128120

Do you favor or oppose a constitutional amendment that would allow Congress and state governments to make it illegal to burn the American flag?

Favor	63%
Oppose	35
No opinion	2

	Favor	Oppose	No opinion
By Politics			
Republicans	73%	26%	1%
Democrats	60	38	2
Independents	60	38	2

Selected National Trend

	Favor	Oppose	No opinion
July 1995	65%	36%	2%
June 1990*	68	27	5
October 1989**	65	31	4
June 1989*	71	24	5

*Question wording: *Do you think we should pass a constitutional amendment to make flag burning illegal, or not?*
**Question wording: *Do you favor or oppose a constitutional amendment that would allow federal and state governments to make flag burning illegal?*

Note: With the bald eagle now off the endangered species list and no longer in need of federal preservation efforts, Americans are ready to give another symbol of national pride, the flag, special protection in the form of a constitutional amendment. A Gallup Poll taken on June 25–27 finds 63% in favor of a constitutional amendment that would allow Congress and state governments to make flag burning illegal. Just over one-third of the public (35%) are opposed to such an amendment

The flag-burning amendment has been a hot-button political issue since June 21, 1989, when the U.S. Supreme Court, by a 5–4 vote, ruled in *Texas vs. Johnson* that burning the American flag is free speech protected under the First Amendment, thus invalidating the laws of forty-eight states against flag desecration. Most recently, the U.S. House of Representatives approved a flag protection amendment last month that would allow Congress to prohibit the burning of Old Glory, or any act deemed to physically desecrate the flag. The bill now goes to the Senate where, if passed, it would be sent to all fifty states for ratification.

The current levels of support for an amendment prohibiting flag burning are slightly lower than those found when Gallup first polled on the subject in June 1989. At that time 71% were in favor of a constitutional amendment to make flag burning illegal, and only 24% were opposed. However, in subsequent Gallup surveys between October 1989 and July 1995, the public has expressed support levels for this measure ranging from 62% to 68%, similar to the 63% found today.

Opponents of a "flag-burning amendment" argue that prohibiting flag burning limits free expression and is antithetical to the American concept of liberty. According to the Gallup survey, however, a majority across nearly all gender, age, education, and even political lines seems to disagree with that sentiment, instead favoring flag protection.

JULY 8
GAMBLING IN AMERICA, 1999*

*Based on interviews conducted by telephone in both English and Spanish among American adults 18 years and older between April 30 and May 23, 1999

Please say whether you strongly agree, somewhat agree, somewhat disagree, or strongly disagree: The legal gambling industry is mostly based on taking advantage of poor people?

Strongly agree	20%
Somewhat agree	16
Somewhat disagree	25
Strongly disagree	37
No opinion	2

Please tell me whether or not you have done any of the following in the past twelve months:

	Yes, have done
Bought a state lottery ticket?	57%

By Income	Yes, have done
$75,000 and Over	56%
$50,000–$74,999	65
$25,000–$49,999	61
Under $25,000	53

	Yes, have done
Gambled at a casino?	31%

By Income	Yes, have done
$75,000 and Over	37%
$50,000–$74,999	37
$25,000–$49,999	34
Under $25,000	23

	Yes, have done
Participated in an office pool?	25%

By Income	Yes, have done
$75,000 and Over	36%
$50,000–$74,999	35
$25,000–$49,999	27
Under $25,000	13

Yes,
have
done

Played a video poker machine? 20%

Yes,
have
done

By Income
$75,000 and Over 22%
$50,000–$74,999 23
$25,000–$49,999 20
Under $25,000 17

Yes,
have
done

Bet on a professional sports event? 13%

Yes,
have
done

By Income
$75,000 and Over 16%
$50,000–$74,999 15
$25,000–$49,999 15
Under $25,000 9

Yes,
have
done

Played bingo for money? 11%

Yes,
have
done

By Income
$75,000 and Over 8%
$50,000–$74,999 10
$25,000–$49,999 12
Under $25,000 10

Yes,
have
done

Participated in riverboat gambling? 10%

Yes,
have
done

By Income
$75,000 and Over 13%
$50,000–$74,999 12

$25,000–$49,999 12
Under $25,000 6

Yes,
have
done

Bet on a horse race or dog race? 9%

Yes,
have
done

By Income
$75,000 and Over 14%
$50,000–$74,999 9
$25,000–$49,999 12
Under $25,000 5

Yes,
have
done

Bet on a college sports event? 9%

Yes,
have
done

By Income
$75,000 and Over 12%
$50,000–$74,999 11
$25,000–$49,999 11
Under $25,000 5

Yes,
have
done

Gambled for money on the Internet? ...... *

Yes,
have
done

By Income
$75,000 and Over 1%
$50,000–$74,999 .... *
$25,000–$49,999 .... *
Under $25,000 .... *

*Less than 1%

Note: One image of the legal gambling industry sometimes advanced by its critics is that it preys on ignorance or, at best, on the false hopes of those who live at the lower reaches of the economic spectrum. The results of the recently released Gallup Poll Social Audit Survey on Gambling in

America, however, show that most Americans disagree with this premise and that, in fact, the highest rates of gambling are found among those in higher income and education brackets.

Roughly six in ten adults disagree—most of them strongly—with the statement, "The legal gambling industry is mostly based on taking advantage of poor people." This figure includes 37% who strongly disagree with the anti-gambling charge, and another 25% who somewhat disagree. On the other side, 20% strongly agree and 16% somewhat agree that gambling victimizes the poor.

The public's self-reported participation in ten different types of gambling shows patterns that seem to justify these opinions. The types of gambling measured include betting on sports events, video poker, playing bingo for money, lotteries, and racetrack and casino gambling. Although the Gallup survey did not ask about frequency of gambling, lower-income respondents—defined as those in households with incomes below $25,000—are actually less likely to report having gambled in one or more of these ways in the past year than are those earning upward of $75,000 annually. Both groups report high rates of gambling, but the figure is 63% for those in the lowest income bracket, compared to 75% in high-income households. There is even less differentiation according to education. Respondents without college degrees are only slightly less likely to report having gambled in the past year than those with college degrees, by a 67%-to-72% margin.

JULY 14
RELIGION—AN ANALYSIS*

A special analysis of Gallup Poll data collected from 1992 to 1999, including interviews with more than 40,000 national adults, highlights the

*Based on an aggregated data set across Gallup Poll surveys conducted between 1992 and 1999, with a cumulative total of telephone interviews with 40,610 national adults. For results based on large sample sizes of 10,000 or higher, one can say with 95% confidence that the maximum error attributable to sampling and other random effects is ±1 percentage point.

general sociological finding that religious involvement and behavior increase in later stages of life. A fundamental question included in the analysis asks Americans to rate the importance of religion in their daily lives. Of the 18 to 29 year olds polled, 45% report that religion is very important in their daily lives. This percentage increases steadily with age, however, to 55% for those 30–49 years old, 70% for those 50 and older, and 77% among those 75 and older:

How important would you say religion is in your own life—very important, fairly important, or not very important?

	Very important	Fairly important	Not very important*
By Age			
18–29 Years	45%	39%	16%
30–49 Years	55	31	13
50–64 Years	66	23	10
65–74 Years	73	18	8
75 Years and Over	77	14	8

*"No opinion"—at 1% or less—is omitted.

There are similar patterns for other measures of religious participation and involvement. Membership in a church or synagogue, attendance, and intensity of belief, as evidenced by the acknowledgment that one is "born again," all increase with age. Weekly attendance at church or synagogue increases with age across the board, although these levels are much lower than church or synagogue membership. Only 23% of 18 to 29 year olds polled attend at least once a week, a number that rises to 46% who attend at least once a week among those 75 and older:

How often do you attend church or synagogue —at least once a week, almost every week, about once a month, seldom, or never?

	At least once a week	Almost every week	About once a month	Seldom*
By Age				
18–29 Years	23%	11%	19%	34%
30–49 Years	28	12	15	31
50–64 Years	38	10	14	26

65–74 Years 45	11	11	21
75 Years			
and Over...... 46	11	12	19

*"Never," "no opinion"—at 14% or less—are omitted.

Sixty-one percent of 18 to 29 year olds surveyed say that they are members of a church or synagogue, a figure that increases in all subsequent age brackets, with 66% of 30 to 49 year olds reporting membership, 76% of those 50 and older, 79% of those 65 and older, and a high of 81% for those 75 and older. The age trend is not as pronounced among those who describe themselves as "born again" or evangelical Christians. Over one-third of respondents in each age bracket polled declare themselves to be "born again," including 43% of those 50 and older, 38% of those in the 30–49 age bracket, and 37% of those age 18–29. In response to a different question, 70% of 18 to 29 year olds say that religion is losing its influence in American life, compared to only 46% of those 75 and older who share this view.

JULY 16
PROFESSIONAL BASEBALL

Interviewing Dates: 7/13–14/99
CNN/*USA Today*/Gallup Poll
Survey #GO 128278

As you may know, former major league player Pete Rose is ineligible for baseball's Hall of Fame due to charges that he had gambled on baseball games. Do you think he should or should not be eligible for admission to the Hall of Fame?

	Total	Fans only
Should..	59%	62%
Should not...................................	38	36
No opinion	3	2

As you may know, Shoeless Joe Jackson is ineligible for baseball's Hall of Fame due to charges that he took money from gamblers in exchange for fixing the 1919 World Series.

Do you think he should or should not be eligible for admission to the Hall of Fame?

	Total	Fans only
Should..	38%	44%
Should not...................................	55	52
No opinion	7	4

How about the use of domed stadiums in some cities—has this been a change for the better, a change for the worse, or has it not made a difference?

	Total	Fans only
Change for better	52%	55%
Change for worse..........................	16	21
No difference	24	21
No opinion	8	3

Would you prefer to watch a baseball game in an open-air stadium, a domed stadium, or a stadium with a retractable roof?

	Total	Fans only
Open-air......................................	47%	53%
Domed	9	8
Retractable roof	30	31
Don't care; don't attend...............	12	7
No opinion	2	1

Note: Even though Baseball Commissioner Bud Selig says that Pete Rose can forget about reinstatement to the game, baseball fans think that the all-time hits leader should be in the Baseball Hall of Fame. In a Gallup Poll conducted on July 13–14, 59% say that Rose should be eligible for the Hall, despite allegations that he gambled on baseball games while managing the Cincinnati Reds. Support is even stronger among those who identify themselves as baseball fans; 62% say that he should be eligible for induction.

However, legendary ballplayer Shoeless Joe Jackson does not receive majority support from the public, despite efforts by Ted Williams and other baseball legends to end Jackson's eighty-year-long ban for his role in the 1919 World Series "Black Sox" scandal. Only 38% of respondents—and 44% of fans—say that Jackson merits induction into the Hall of Fame, despite allegations that he took money from gamblers to fix games in the 1919 World Series.

JULY 21
READING BOOKS

Interviewing Dates: 7/13–14/99
CNN/*USA Today*/Gallup Poll
Survey #GO 128278

During the past year, about how many books, either hardcover or paperback, did you read either all or part of the way through?

	July 13–14, 1999	Dec. 13–16, 1990
None	12%	16%
One to five	24	32
Six to ten	18	15
Eleven to fifty	34	27
Fifty-one plus	10	7
No opinion	2	3
Mean:	20	–

Do you have a favorite author?

	July 13–14, 1999	Dec. 13–16, 1990
Yes	42%	39%
No	56	–
No opinion	2	–

Asked of those who have a favorite author: Who is your favorite author?

	July 13–14, 1999	Dec. 13–16, 1990
Stephen King	14%	18%
Danielle Steele	8	9
Louis L'Amour	2	4
Sidney Sheldon	1	4
James Michener	*	3
V. C. Andrews	*	3
Charles Dickens	*	2
Mark Twain	*	2
Ernest Hemingway	*	2
John Steinbeck	*	2
William Shakespeare	*	2
Tom Clancy	6	2
John Grisham	6	–
Mary Higgins Clark	1	–
Dean Koontz	1	–
Other	59	44
No opinion	2	3

*Less than 1%

Next, if you can, please tell me the name of the author for each of the following books:

The Great Gatsby?

F. Scott Fitzgerald (correct)	15%
Incorrect; don't know	85

The Old Man and the Sea?

Ernest Hemingway (correct)	29%
Incorrect; don't know	71

The Firm?

John Grisham (correct)	26%
Incorrect; don't know	74

The Cat in the Hat?

Dr. Seuss (correct)	72%
Incorrect; don't know	28

A Tale of Two Cities?

Charles Dickens (correct)	18%
Incorrect; don't know	82

Have you ever read a book by Ernest Hemingway?

	July 13–14, 1999	Dec. 13–16, 1990
Yes	51%	64%
No	44	36
No opinion	5	–

As far as you are concerned, was Ernest Hemingway one of the greatest authors of all time, or not?

Yes... 49%
No 33
No opinion..................................... 18

Note: Today [July 21] marks the 100th anniversary of Ernest Hemingway's birth. A July 13–14 Gallup Poll shows that 51% of Americans claim to have read a book by Hemingway, and that 49% cite Hemingway as one of the greatest authors of all time. However, less than 1% say that Hemingway is their favorite author.

While one-half of respondents have read a Hemingway book, his novels are not universally recognized. Only 29% could correctly identify Hemingway as the author of *The Old Man and the Sea*, and only 18% recognized *A Farewell to Arms* as one of his novels. These results compare to 72% who know that Dr. Seuss wrote *The Cat in the Hat*, 48% who state that Mark Twain/Samuel Clemens wrote *Huckleberry Finn*, and 42% who recognize Stephen King as the author of *The Shining*. Hemingway's contemporary, F. Scott Fitzgerald, was recognized as the author of *The Great Gatsby* by only 15% of respondents, and only 12% knew that Herman Melville wrote *Moby-Dick*.

Respondents with higher levels of education are most likely to be Hemingway fans. Fifty-six percent of those with some form of graduate-level education consider Hemingway one of the greatest authors of all time, compared to 46% of those with a high-school education or less. This more positive opinion of Hemingway may stem from greater exposure to his work. Eighty percent of respondents with a postgraduate education have read one of Hemingway's books, compared to only 35% of those with a high-school education or less.

Older people are also more likely to have read a book by Hemingway than are younger ones. Fifty-four percent of those 65 years and older have read a Hemingway book, compared to just 44% of those age 18–29. Hemingway, who originally hailed from Illinois, is called one of the greatest authors of all time by 55% of Midwest respondents, compared to 45% in the East, 48% in the West, and 49% in the South.

JULY 27
JOHN F. KENNEDY, JR.

Interviewing Dates: 7/22–25/99
CNN/*USA Today*/Gallup Poll
Survey #GO 128335

How closely have you followed the news about the plane crash and death of John F. Kennedy, Jr., and the Bessette sisters—very closely, somewhat closely, not too closely, or not at all?

Very closely.................................... 39%
Somewhat closely........................... 42
Not too closely............................... 16
Not at all 3
No opinion..................................... *

*Less than 1%

How would you describe the reaction you had to John F. Kennedy, Jr.'s, death when you first heard about it—were you as upset as if someone you knew personally had died; or were you sad, but not as upset as if it were someone you personally knew?

Upset.. 19%
Sad, but not upset 74
Not sad (volunteered) 6
No opinion..................................... 1

What is your opinion of the amount of news coverage given in the past week to the death of John F. Kennedy, Jr.—has there been too much coverage, or has the amount of coverage been appropriate?

Too much.. 58%
Appropriate.................................... 40
Too little (volunteered).................. 1
No opinion..................................... 1

From what you have seen, heard, or read, do you have a favorable or unfavorable opinion of the way in which the news media are covering the John F. Kennedy, Jr., situation?

Favorable....................................... 57%
Unfavorable................................... 39
No opinion..................................... 4

Overall, do you feel that the news media have acted responsibly or irresponsibly in this situation?

Responsibly 75%
Irresponsibly 22
No opinion 3

Note: As America's news media return to routine coverage after spending much of the past ten days devoted to the plane crash that killed John F. Kennedy, Jr., his wife Carolyn, and her sister Lauren Bessette, how did the public react to the story? In a Gallup Poll conducted on the weekend after the funerals (July 22–25), 19% said that they were as upset about Kennedy's death as if a member of their own family had died. Another 74% were saddened, but not as upset as if it had been someone they personally knew. Women were much more likely than men to react to Kennedy's death as if he were someone they knew personally, as were older Americans, particularly those 65 and above. By way of comparison, a Gallup Poll conducted on September 4, 1997, immediately after the death of Princess Diana in a Paris traffic accident, found that 27% of Americans said that her death upset them as much as the death of someone they knew personally, a percentage that dropped to 15% nearly a year after the crash.

With all of the media coverage, it was hard for almost anyone to miss the story completely. Thirty-nine percent told Gallup interviewers that they followed the story very closely, with another 42% claiming that they followed the news coverage somewhat closely. Gallup routinely asks this question about major news events, and the percentage that followed the Kennedy story very closely is among the highest in this decade. The death of Princess Diana was followed very closely by 55% of Americans in a September 1997 Gallup Poll, and 53% followed the start of the 1991 Desert Storm ground war in Iraq very closely. The JFK Jr. tragedy is third on this list, receiving more short-term attention than the Clinton-Lewinsky scandal (33% in an August 1998 Gallup Poll), the Kosovo crisis (30%), and the 1997 death of Mother Teresa (31%).

A majority (58%) viewed the amount of media coverage of the Kennedy story as excessive, while 40% thought that the amount of time devoted to the story was appropriate. Again, in comparing the Kennedy story to the death of Princess Diana, more Americans believed that the media spent too much time on the Kennedy tragedy. In the 1997 poll following Diana's death, 49% thought that there was too much coverage, while 48% thought that the level of coverage was appropriate.

However, the public gives the media high marks for the way they covered the Kennedy tragedy, perhaps because many media outlets tried to be respectful of the family's privacy. Nearly six in ten (57%) have a favorable opinion of the media's coverage of the Kennedy crash, while 39% have an unfavorable opinion. In addition, 75% believe that the news media acted responsibly in their coverage, compared to 22% who consider the coverage irresponsible.

AUGUST 4
VACATIONS

Interviewing Dates: 7/16–18/99
CNN/*USA Today*/Gallup Poll
Survey #GO 128287

Do you plan to take, or have you already taken, a vacation this summer?

Yes 53%
No 46
No opinion 1

Asked of those who are planning/have taken a vacation: Are you taking one single vacation this summer, or are you taking several different vacations at different times during the summer?

One single vacation 49%
Several vacations 50
No opinion 1

Also asked of those who are planning/have taken a vacation: How much money do you think you and your family have spent or will spend on your vacation this summer?

$300 or less	10%
$301–$500	14
$501–$1,000	26
$1,001–$1,500	6
$1,501–$2,000	15
$2,001–2,500	4
$2,501–$3,000	7
$3,001 or more	16
No opinion	2

Mean: $1,820

If you were trying to design a perfect vacation on a trip away from home, would each of the following be something you would try to do, or not:

Read a book?

Try to do	58%
Not do	42

Get a suntan?

Try to do	43%
Not do	57

Engage in vigorous exercise?

Try to do	39%
Not do	61

Shop?

Try to do	72%
Not do	28

See a museum, play, or other cultural activity?

Try to do	82%
Not do	18

Seek out good food and restaurants?

Try to do	92%
Not do	8

Try to meet new people?

Try to do	73%
Not do	27

Spend time with friends or family you normally don't see?

Try to do	80%
Not do	20

Participate in a sport or hobby you regularly engage in?

Try to do	63%
Not do	37

Participate in a sport or activity you don't normally have the chance to do?

Try to do	59%
Not do	41

Note: Despite the historic tradition of summertime vacations, almost half of Americans interviewed in a recent Gallup Poll will not be taking a vacation this summer. Only 53% have already taken at least one vacation so far or plan to do so before the end of the summer. The rest will apparently stay put or keep working. Of those who will be taking a vacation, a lucky 50% will manage to sneak in more than one. August is the most popular month, with 44% of those planning a getaway this summer scheduling it for this month.

Thirty-seven percent of those planning a vacation this summer will take between one and seven days off. Another 35% will take up to two weeks, and 26% have the good fortune to be able to take more than two weeks off. The average family will spend $1,820 on vacation this summer—up from $1,368 in a 1991 Gallup Poll—and 64% will travel outside their home state. Only 12% will travel outside the United States, however. When Americans were asked which of the fifty states they would most like to visit on vacation, Hawaii (17%) and California (12%) were the most popular choices, followed by Alaska and Florida at 10%. All four states fell in popularity from Gallup's 1991 poll, when 21% selected either Hawaii or California, 13% chose Alaska, and 12% selected Florida.

What do Americans want to do when they go on vacation? One of the biggest choices is between going to one area and staying put, or traveling around from place to place. Respondents seem to prefer the latter, more active option. Two in three say that their ideal vacation would be to keep moving, while 31% prefer to spend it in just one place. Similarly, two-thirds would prefer to be involved in activities and sightseeing in their ideal vacation, while just one-third would prefer to rest and relax.

AUGUST 12
MOVIE CONTENT

Interviewing Dates: 7/16–18/99
CNN/*USA Today*/Gallup Poll
Survey #GO 128287

We'd like to know how you would feel about certain types of content in movies. If you happened to go to a movie and it included any of the following, how offensive, if at all, would you find that—extremely offensive, very offensive, only somewhat offensive, not too offensive, or not offensive at all:

Frequent profanity, meaning swear language?

Extremely offensive 24%
Very offensive 25
Somewhat offensive 27
Not too offensive 11
Not offensive at all 13
No opinion .... *

*Less than 1%

Graphic violence?

Extremely offensive 27%
Very offensive 27
Somewhat offensive 25
Not too offensive 9
Not offensive at all 12
No opinion .... *

*Less than 1%

Nudity?

Extremely offensive 19%
Very offensive 19

Somewhat offensive 26
Not too offensive 14
Not offensive at all 22
No opinion .... *

*Less than 1%

Sexual activity?

Extremely offensive 24%
Very offensive 21
Somewhat offensive 25
Not too offensive 13
Not offensive at all 16
No opinion 1

Negative racial stereotypes?

Extremely offensive 31%
Very offensive 31
Somewhat offensive 22
Not too offensive 8
Not offensive at all 7
No opinion 1

Negative gender stereotypes?

Extremely offensive 20%
Very offensive 27
Somewhat offensive 29
Not too offensive 9
Not offensive at all 11
No opinion 4

Note: Potentially offensive content in movies has sparked debate about the standards used to determine movie ratings and the obligation of theater owners to limit youth's access to R-rated films. A Gallup Poll conducted on July 16–18 measured public reaction to potentially offensive movie content. The findings reveal that Americans are most offended by racial stereotypes or graphic violence and somewhat less offended by frequent profanity or gender stereotypes; they are least offended by nudity or sexual content.

The public frowns most heavily on negative racial stereotypes in movie content, as 62% find such material extremely or very offensive. Another

22% find it somewhat offensive, while only 15% think that negative racial stereotypes in movies are not too offensive or not offensive at all. There is little difference between whites and nonwhites in their reactions. Sixty-seven percent of nonwhites find negative racial stereotypes offensive in movies, compared to 61% of whites.

Graphic violence in movies is very or extremely offensive to 54% of the public, while only 21% tend not to be offended. Frequent profanity (swear language) on screen is extremely or very offensive to 49%, while only 24% say that such "blue language" is not too offensive or not offensive at all. Negative gender stereotypes in movies also receive bad reviews. Forty-seven percent find negative gender stereotypes very or extremely offensive, while just 20% find them not too offensive or not offensive at all.

Gender plays a role in the opinions of the public about gender stereotypes, profanity, and graphic violence in movie content. Men find all of these issues less offensive than do women. Fifty-three percent of women find gender stereotypes extremely or very offensive, while 42% of men have the same reaction. This 11-point gap persists with regard to profanity in movies, as 54% of women find it extremely or very offensive, compared to 43% of men. Sixty-five percent of women find violent content in movies extremely or very offensive, while only 40% of men react the same way—the largest difference observed by gender.

It should be noted that respondents' income and education are also related to offensive movie content. For example, 71% of those with postgraduate education (master's degree or higher) find negative racial stereotypes in movies extremely or very offensive. This percentage drops to 56% among those with a high-school education or less. Additionally, where negative gender stereotypes in movies are concerned, 42% of those with incomes over $75,000 find such content extremely or very offensive, while 52% of those making under $20,000 feel the same way.

AUGUST 15
WEIGHT AND BODY IMAGE

Interviewing Dates: 7/22–25/99
CNN/*USA Today*/Gallup Poll
Survey #GO 128335

How would you describe your own personal weight situation right now—very overweight, somewhat overweight, about right, somewhat underweight, or very underweight?

	July 22–25, 1999	Oct. 11–14, 1990
Very overweight	4%	7%
Somewhat overweight	35	41
About right	53	46
Somewhat underweight	6	5
Very underweight	1	1
No opinion	1	*

*Less than 1%

Would you like to lose weight, put on weight, or stay at your present weight?

	Total	Women	Men
Lose weight	52%	58%	44%
Put on weight	9	5	13
Stay at present weight	39	37	43
No opinion	*	*	*

*Less than 1%

Selected National Trend

	Lose weight	Put on weight	Stay at present weight	No opinion
1996	55%	4%	41%	*
1990	52	7	40	1
1955	37	13	48	2
1953	35	14	48	3

*Less than 1%

How often do you worry about your weight— would you say that you worry all of the time, some of the time, not too often, or never?

	Total	Women	Men
All of the time	15%	20%	10%
Some of the time	27	32	21
Not too often	34	29	41
Never	24	19	28
No opinion	*	*	*

*Less than 1%

At this time, are you seriously trying to lose weight?

	Total	Women	Men
Yes	20%	24%	16%
No	80	76	84

Selected National Trend

	Yes	No
1996	26%	74%
1990	18	82
1955	17	83
1953	25	75
1951	19	81

Note: A recent Gallup Poll update of weight and body image trends records some interesting changes over the past decade, suggesting that Americans are losing the battle of the bulge but seem resigned to it. The average self-reported weight of the nation's adults is up nearly 10 pounds since 1990, but fewer respondents now consider themselves to be overweight. Despite the extra weight, most people remain satisfied with the way their bodies look. Perhaps as a result, the percentage who want to lose weight has remained the same, and there has been no significant change in the percentage who actually report serious efforts to lose weight.

According to respondents' reports about their own weight in a July 22–25 Gallup telephone survey, the typical American woman today weighs 150 pounds and the typical American man weighs 190 pounds. Both of these figures have increased since 1990 when, on average, women claimed to weigh 142 pounds and men claimed to weigh 180 pounds. At the same time, their conceptions of their own ideal weight have also increased. Today, the average ideal body weight cited by women is 136 pounds and the average ideal weight cited by men is 180 pounds. Both of these figures have increased since 1990 as well, when the average ideal weights for women and men were 129 pounds and 171 pounds, respectively.

The public may be heavier than in the past, but just as conceptions of ideal weight have increased since 1990, the percentage describing themselves as overweight has dropped, from 48%

in 1990 to 39% today. Both the percentage who reportedly weigh more than their target ideal (62%) and the percentage who want to lose weight (52%), however, have remained unchanged since 1990.

SEPTEMBER 2
LABOR UNIONS

Interviewing Dates: 8/24–26/99
CNN/*USA Today*/Gallup Poll
Survey #GO 907169

Do you approve or disapprove of labor unions?

	Aug. 24–26, 1999	March 5–7, 1999
Approve	65%	66%
Disapprove	28	29
No opinion	7	5

In the labor disputes of the last two or three years, have your sympathies, in general, been on the side of the unions or on the side of the companies?

Unions	45%
Companies	37
Neither (volunteered)	5
Both (volunteered)	6
No opinion	7

Note: While just 13% of Americans are personally members of labor unions, a new Gallup Poll on labor issues shows that 65% approve of labor unions, not that different from the 72% who approved of labor unions when Gallup first asked the question over sixty years ago in 1936. A majority have, in fact, answered in the affirmative whenever the labor union approval question has been asked in the years since. At the same time, however, this generalized approval of unions does not automatically translate into favoring the labor side in strikes and other work actions. When asked where their sympathies lie in labor disputes over the last two or three years, 45% pick the unions, compared to 37% who choose the companies involved in those disputes. These results are comparable to Gallup data from 1952, when slightly more than four in ten favored the unions over the companies.

OCTOBER 14
CIGARETTE SMOKING

Interviewing Dates: 9/23–26/99
CNN/*USA Today*/Gallup Poll
Survey #GO 128808

Have you, yourself, smoked any cigarettes in the past week?

	Yes
National	23%

Selected National Trend

	Yes
1998	28%
1997	26
1994	27
1990	27
1986	31
1981	35
1977	38
1972	43
1969	40
1957	42
1954	45
1949	44
1944	41

Asked of smokers: About how many cigarettes do you smoke each day?

Less than one pack	55%
One pack	35
More than one pack	9
No answer	1

Selected National Trend

	Less than one pack	One pack	More than one pack	No answer
1997	48%	32%	19%	1%
1996	43	38	16	3

1990	51	32	14	3
1988	40	38	20	2
1987	48	32	18	2
1981	38	37	24	1
1977	41	31	27	1

Also asked of smokers: At what age did you begin smoking?

Under 16	36%
16 to 18	35
Over 18	29
No answer	*

*Less than 1%

Selected National Trend

	Under 16	16 to 18	Over 18	No answer
1994	32%	37%	29%	2%
1991	34	36	29	1

Also asked of smokers: All things considered, would you like to give up smoking, or not?

Yes	76%
No	23
No opinion	1

Selected National Trend

	Yes	No	No opinion
1997	74%	24%	2%
1996	73	26	1
1990	74	24	2
1988	68	27	5
1987	77	20	3
1986	75	22	3
1981	66	30	4
1977	66	29	5

Also asked of smokers: Have you ever made a really serious effort to stop smoking, or not?

Yes	65%
No	35

	Yes	No
1997	62%	38%
1996	74	26
1991	64	36
1990	67	33
1989	60	40
1988	70	30

Also asked of smokers: Do you feel you would be able to quit smoking if you made the decision to do so, or not?

Yes	77%
No	20
No opinion	3

Selected National Trend

	Yes	No	No opinion
1990	78%	16%	6%
1980	66	27	7

Also asked of smokers: Do you consider yourself addicted to cigarettes, or not?

Yes	72%
No	28

Selected National Trend

	Yes	No
1997	73%	27%
1996	69	31
1990	61	39

Also asked of smokers: If you had to do it over again, would you start smoking, or not?

	Sept. 23–26, 1999	July 6–8, 1990
Yes	13%	13%
No	85	83
No opinion	2	4

Do you think cigarette smoking is harmful, or not?

Yes	95%
No	4
No opinion	1

Selected National Trend

	Yes	No	No opinion
1990*	96%	3%	1%
1981	91	7	2
1977	90	7	3
1954	70	23	7
1949	60	33	7

Question wording: Do you think cigarette smoking is harmful to your health?

Have you heard or read anything recently to the effect that cigarette smoking may be a cause of cancer of the lung?

Yes	85%
No	15

Selected National Trend

	Yes	No
1954		
June 12–17	90%	10%
January 9–14	83	17

What is your own opinion—do you think cigarette smoking is one of the causes of lung cancer, or not?

Yes	92%
No	6
No opinion	2

Selected National Trend

	Yes	No	No opinion
1990	94%	4%	2%
1981	83	10	7
1977	81	11	8
1972	70	13	17
1971	71	16	13
1969	70	11	19
1960	50	28	22

1958 44	30	26
1957		
Nov. 28–		
Dec. 4................. 47	32	21
June 27–		
July 2 50	24	26
1954		
June 12–17.............. 39	29	32
Jan. 9–14................. 41	31	28

What is your own opinion—do you think cigarette smoking is one of the causes of heart disease?

Yes... 80%
No 13
No opinion... 7

Selected National Trend

	Yes	No	No opinion
1990	85%	9%	6%
1981	74	14	12
1977	68	17	15
1969	60	15	25
1960	34	38	28
1958	33	37	30
1957			
Nov. 28–			
Dec. 4.................	36	42	22
June 27–			
July 2	38	34	28

How about cancer of the throat?

Yes.. 90%
No 6
No opinion.. 4

Selected National Trend

	Yes	No	No opinion
1981	81%	10%	9%
1977	79	10	11

How about birth defects?

Yes.. 67%
No 21
No opinion.. 12

Selected National Trend

	Yes	No	No opinion
1990	68%	16%	16%
1981	54	23	23
1977	41	30	29

In general, how harmful do you feel second-hand smoke is to adults—very harmful, somewhat harmful, not too harmful, or not at all harmful?

Very harmful 43%
Somewhat harmful 39
Not too harmful 11
Not at all harmful 5
It depends (volunteered)................................. 1
No opinion.. 1

Selected National Trend

	Very harmful	Some-what harmful	Not too harmful	Not at all harmful*
1997	55%	29%	9%	5%
1996	48	36	9	5
1994	36	42	12	6

*"It depends," "no opinion"—at 4% or less—are omitted.

What is your opinion regarding smoking in public places—should they set aside certain areas, should they totally ban smoking, or should there be no restrictions on smoking in each of the following:

Hotels and motels?

Set aside areas 70%
Totally ban.. 24
No restrictions 6
No opinion.. *

*Less than 1%

Selected National Trend

	Set aside areas	Totally ban	No restric-tions	No opinion
1994	68%	20%	10%	2%
1991	70	17	12	1

1990	73	18	8	1
1987	67	10	20	3

Workplaces?

Set aside areas 61%
Totally ban... 34
No restrictions 4
No opinion... 1

Selected National Trend

	Set aside areas	Totally ban	No restrictions	No opinion
1994	63%	32%	4%	1%
1991	67	24	8	1
1990	69	25	5	1
1987	70	17	11	2

Restaurants?

Set aside areas 56%
Totally ban... 40
No restrictions 4
No opinion... *

*Less than 1%

Selected National Trend

	Set aside areas	Totally ban	No restrictions	No opinion
1994	57%	38%	4%	1%
1991	66	28	5	1
1990	66	30	4	–
1987	74	17	8	1

Which of the following statements best describes your view of who's to blame for the health problems faced by smokers in this country—the tobacco companies are completely to blame, the tobacco companies are mostly to blame, smokers are mostly to blame, or smokers are completely to blame?

	Sept. 23–26, 1999	May 6–7, 1997
Tobacco companies completely....	9%	5%
Tobacco companies mostly	21	20
Smokers mostly	31	38
Smokers completely	24	26
Smokers and tobacco companies equally (volunteered).............................	13	10
No opinion...................................	2	1

As you may know, this week the U.S. Justice Department filed a lawsuit against the tobacco industry seeking to recover billions of dollars in federal health costs for smoking-related illnesses. The tobacco companies being sued have stated that the charges have no merit and should be dismissed. Which side do you agree with more in this lawsuit—the Justice Department, or the tobacco companies?

Justice Department 51%
Tobacco companies 42
Both equally (volunteered)............................ 2
Neither (volunteered) 2
No opinion.. 3

Has smoking ever been a cause of serious health problems in your family?

Yes... 45%
No 54
No opinion.. 1

Note: While Philip Morris, the nation's largest cigarette maker, now acknowledges that smoking is harmful to the health of those who smoke, Gallup Polls show that for the past three decades, the vast majority of Americans have recognized the harmful effects of smoking. The most recent Gallup survey on smoking, conducted on September 23–26, shows that today virtually everyone (95%) thinks that cigarette smoking is harmful, about the same number as recorded in a 1990 Gallup Poll but substantially higher than that recorded one-half century ago, when the question was first asked. In 1949, 60% said that cigarette smoking was harmful to their health, although followup questions asked in both 1949 and 1954 suggest that their definition of harm at that time was less serious than what people believe today. The new poll shows that when asked specifically if cigarette smoking is one of the causes of lung cancer, nine in ten today say "yes," compared with just four in ten who felt that way when the question was first asked in 1954. By the 1960s, one-half of the public said that smoking was a cause of lung cancer. Thirty years ago, in a 1969 Gallup Poll, 70% said that smoking caused cancer; by the 1980s, the proportion had climbed to 80%. Respondents are less convinced that cigarette smoking is the cause of some other diseases, although in each case the percentage well exceeds a majority. Nine in ten believe that smoking causes throat cancer, eight in ten believe smoking to be a cause of heart disease, and about seven in ten say that smoking causes birth defects.

Americans are more likely to blame smokers than tobacco companies for the health problems associated with smoking, but tobacco companies are not viewed as blameless. Overall, 55% say that smokers are completely or mostly to blame, compared with 30% who think that tobacco companies are mostly or completely to blame. An additional 13% volunteer that the two groups are equally at fault. Compared with similar figures obtained in a 1994 Gallup Poll, the new figures suggest that the public may be shifting the blame somewhat toward the tobacco companies. Five years ago, the Gallup Poll showed that only 25% put the major blame on tobacco companies, 5 percentage points lower than today, while 64% blamed smokers, 9 points higher than in the current poll. Despite these figures, respondents adopt a more critical stance against the tobacco companies when asked about the recent U.S. Justice Department lawsuit filed against the tobacco industry that seeks to recover billions of dollars in federal health costs for smoking-related illnesses. Just over one-half (51%) support the lawsuit, while 42% take the tobacco companies' view that the charges have no merit and should be dismissed.

While eight in ten say that second-hand smoke is harmful, most nevertheless endorse smoking in public places when areas are specifically set aside for that activity. Only about one-quarter of the public (24%) would ban smoking completely in hotels and motels, but one-third would do so in workplaces, and four in ten would do so in restaurants. These views are little changed from five years ago but represent at least a twofold increase in opposition to smoking in public places over that recorded in a Gallup Poll in 1987, when the questions were first asked. At that time, only 10% wanted a total ban on cigarette smoking in hotels and motels, and 17% wanted a total ban both at the workplace and in restaurants.

According to the new poll, 23% of Americans currently smoke cigarettes, down slightly from the 26% reported in 1997. For thirty years after 1944, when Gallup first asked the public about smoking habits, the rate of smoking apparently remained fairly steady, with about four in ten indicating that they were smokers. Over the next decade and one-half, the number of self-reported smokers declined gradually, so that by the end of the 1980s only about three in ten smoked cigarettes. Among smokers, more than half (55%) generally smoke less than a pack per day, while 35% say a pack per day, and 9% say more than that. The average reported number of cigarettes smoked per day is fourteen. Most smokers start young, with 36% starting before age 16, and another 35% between the ages of 16 and 18. On the other hand, more than three-quarters of all smokers would like to give up smoking, and two-thirds have made a serious effort to do so. Although 72% of smokers say that they are addicted to cigarettes, 77% of smokers believe that they could quit if they made a decisions to do so. The difficulty of quitting, however, is highlighted by the fact that only 13% of smokers say that if they had to do it all over again, they would take up the smoking habit.

OCTOBER 29
HALLOWEEN—AN ANALYSIS*

Is the custom of giving out treats at the door on Halloween widespread in this country?

Yes. Sixty-nine percent of all Americans said in a Gallup Poll conducted last weekend that they would be "giving out Halloween treats from the

*This analysis was written by Frank Newport, Editor in Chief, The Gallup Poll, based on interviews conducted on October 21–24, 1999.

door of their home on Halloween" this year, exactly the same number as in the ABC/*Washington Post* poll from 1985. Interestingly, the custom is much more prevalent among white households: 72% of white adults interviewed in the poll said they will give out treats, compared to only 52% of those in nonwhite households. Additionally, Americans living in the South are somewhat less likely to be giving out treats than are those living elsewhere across the country.

There is usually talk of the dangers of trick-or-treating. Any sign that fewer kids will be out now than in the past?

No. A very large number of kids will apparently be out and about this Halloween. Two-thirds of parents of children under the age of 15 said that their child would be going out trick-or-treating door to door on Halloween. This is actually a somewhat larger number than in the past. When an ABC/*Washington Post* poll asked the same question back in 1985, a slightly smaller number of Americans (60%) said their children would be trick-or-treating.

What are kids' favorite costumes this year?

Costumes this year are going to be widely varied, but here are the top five choices when Gallup asked parents of children under 15 what their child would be wearing on Halloween:

1. Batman
2. *Star Wars* character
3. Witch
4. Pokémon
5. Disney characters

What else will kids be wearing?

All types of things. Here's the rest of the list of costumes that 1% or more of the parents said that their children would be wearing: princess, ghost, M&M, angel, clown, athlete, pumpkin, cowboy/cowgirl, fireman, ninja, Spiderman, cheerleader, Tigger, devil, Cinderella, Blue's Clues, Barbie, vampire, Grim Reaper, monster, and ladybug.

Are there differences in choice of costume by subgroup around the country?

There are not dramatic differences by region, although *Star Wars* characters seem to be a little more prevalent in the West, and witches and ghosts in the East. It is interesting to note that higher-income families are slightly more likely to say their kids will be Disney characters, while lower-income families are more likely to have kids dressed up as Batman.

There are some individuals who are opposed to Halloween on religious grounds, saying that it is in reality a celebration of the devil. How widespread is this?

About 12% of Americans say that they have objections to celebrating Halloween on religious grounds. These objections are most common among conservatives and Republicans.

Finally, do Americans really believe in witches and ghosts?

Some do. In the most recent poll, 33% of Americans said they believe in ghosts, and 22% said they believe in witches. These numbers represent increases from twenty years ago, but we are unsure what that change really means, although one clue may be found in the fact that belief in ghosts is much higher among younger Americans than among older Americans. Over half (54%) of those 18–29 say they believe in ghosts, compared to only 8% of senior citizens 65 and older.

NOVEMBER 3
ALCOHOLIC BEVERAGES

Interviewing Dates: 9/23–26/99
CNN/*USA Today*/Gallup Poll
Survey #GO 128808

Do you have occasion to use alcoholic beverages such as liquor, wine, or beer, or are you a total abstainer?

Yes.. 64%
No, total abstainer.. 36

Asked of those who drink: When did you last take a drink of any kind of alcoholic beverage?

Within past 24 hours.. 35%
Over one day to one week ago 25
Over one week ago 39
Don't know.. 1

Asked of those who had an alcoholic beverage within the last week: Approximately how many drinks of any kind of alcoholic beverage did you drink in the past seven days?

None 40%
One to seven 47
Eight to nineteen... 8
Twenty plus 4
Don't know.. 1

Asked of those who drink: Do you most often drink liquor, wine, or beer?

Liquor 19%
Wine 34
Beer 42
All about equally (volunteered)....................... 4
Other.. *
No opinion.. 1

*Less than 1%

Also asked of those who drink: Do you sometimes drink more alcoholic beverages than you think you should?

Yes.. 24%
No 76

Also asked of those who drink: Have you ever made a really serious effort to stop drinking, or not?

Yes.. 15%
No 80
Don't want to quit (volunteered).................... 4
No opinion.. 1

Has drinking ever been a cause of trouble in your family?

Yes.. 36%
No 64

All things considered, which of the following products do you think creates the most problems for society—cigarettes, or alcohol?

Cigarettes... 12%
Alcohol 77
Both equally (volunteered)............................. 9
No opinion.. 2

Note: Over one-third of Americans report that drinking has been a cause of trouble in their family, the highest percentage in response to this question in the more than fifty years it has been asked. About two-thirds of respondents are drinkers; and, of these, about one-fourth sometimes drink more than they should. Fifteen percent of drinkers report having made a serious effort to stop.

The percentage of the population who drink alcoholic beverages has fluctuated greatly over the past sixty years, ranging between 55% and 71%. The lowest percentage who reported that they drink came in the 1950s, while the highest was registered in Gallup Polls conducted in the mid-1970s. In Gallup's most recent survey on this issue, conducted on September 23–26, 64% of the adult population say that they have taken an opportunity to drink, remarkably similar to the 58% who reported drinking in 1939, when Gallup first asked Americans about their drinking habits. Persons most likely to drink include men, those with higher incomes, those under age 65, those who do not attend church regularly, those living in regions of the country other than the South, and self-identified liberals.

Most respondents who drink report alcohol consumption habits that could be viewed as light to moderate. About four in ten drinkers say that the last drink they had was more than a week before the time at which they were interviewed. Among those who did drink in the past week, the number of drinks they report consuming (six) averages less than one per day. At the same time, a significant minority of drinkers report behaviors that might suggest a problem: 24% sometimes drink more alcohol than they think they should, and 15% have at some time made a serious effort to stop drinking (and apparently failed).

Beer is the most popular alcoholic beverage, favored by 42% of drinkers, followed by wine and hard liquor, favored by 34% and 19%, respectively. There are big differences in favorite alcoholic beverages by demographic variables:

- Men strongly prefer beer (60% of men say that beer is their favorite drink), while women's favorite is wine
- Beer drinking drops significantly with age. Beer is the favorite choice of 52% of 18–29-year-old drinkers but drops to only 21% among those 65 and older
- Wine as the favorite beverage increases with age; it is the favorite choice for 57% of those 65 and over
- Wine is the favorite beverage of those making more than $75,000 per year, while beer is the favorite of lower-income drinkers

An increasing number of respondents are telling Gallup that drinking has been a problem in their family, particularly in recent years. In 1947, when Gallup first asked the question, only 15% said that drinking had been a problem in their family. That number climbed into the 20% range during the 1970s and remained at one-quarter of the public into the 1990s. As recently as 1994 the rate of self-reported problems was just 27%. However, this figure rose to 30% in 1997 and reached 36%—the all-time high—in this most recent survey.

There could be several explanations for this increase in self-reported family drinking problems, including a real-world increase in alcoholism, a greater willingness to admit such problems, and a possibly broadened understanding of what "drinking problems" means. It is not possible to say which single or combined explanation is true in relation to this survey, but data trends since 1996 offer a couple of clues that point in the direction of perception, rather than reality. First, there has been no significant change in the percentage of drinkers reporting that they sometimes drink more than they should. And second, the rate of self-reported family drinking problems has increased most dramatically among 18 to 29 year olds, from 17% in 1996 to 42% today. Among older people, whose views of what constitutes "alcoholism" may be more set, the increase in reported drinking problems is just 9 percentage points.

DECEMBER 24
RELIGION

Interviewing Dates: 12/9–12/99
CNN/*USA Today*/Gallup Poll
Survey #GO 129321

Which of the following statements comes closest to describing your beliefs—you are religious, you are spiritual but not religious, or you are neither?

Religious 54%
Spiritual but not religious 30
Neither 9
Both religious and spiritual (volunteered) 6
No opinion 1

Which of the following statements comes closest to your belief about God—you believe in God, you don't believe in God but you do believe in a universal spirit or higher power, or you don't believe in either?

Believe in God 86%
Believe in higher power 8
Don't believe in either 5
Other (volunteered) 1
No opinion .... *

*Less than 1%

Which of the following statements comes closer to the way you decide how to conduct your life—you pay more attention to God and religious teachings, or you pay more attention to your own views and the views of others?

More to God and religious teachings 48%
More to your own views and
    views of others 45
Other (volunteered) 5
No opinion 2

*Asked of those with a religious preference:
Do you think there is any religion other than your own that offers a true path to God?*

Yes 75%
No 20
No opinion 5

Asked of those who replied in the affirmative: Do you think your religion is the best path to God, or are others equally good?

Own religion is best path................................. 16%
Others are equally good.................................. 82
No opinion... 2

Next, as I read a list of statements about religion, please say whether you agree or disagree with each one:

Religions have unnecessary rules and responsibilities?

Agree 52%
Disagree... 46
No opinion... 2

There are a lot of things taught in my religion that I don't really believe?

Agree 39%
Disagree... 59
No opinion... 2

If you are a good person, you will go to Heaven whether or not you believe in God?

Agree 44%
Disagree... 50
No opinion... 6

There will be a day when God judges whether you go to Heaven or Hell?

Agree 79%
Disagree... 19
No opinion... 2

Note: A new Gallup Poll shows that Americans remain intensely religious in many conventional ways but at the same time embrace nontraditional approaches to religion. Gallup has been tracking religious attitudes and behavior for decades. As has been the case for many years, its basic measures continue to show remarkably high levels of religiosity. Some of the key trends, as updated in the latest survey conducted on December 9–12, are as follows:

- Six in ten say that religion is very important in their life, and another three in ten say that it is fairly important; only 11% say that religion is not at all important. The "very important" percentage was as low as 52% at one point in the late 1970s and was at 70% in 1965, but it has generally been in the high-50% to low-60% range in recent years.
- About two-thirds of respondents claim to be a member of a church or synagogue, a number which too has not changed much over the years. Additionally, when asked to state their religious preference, only 9% say "none"; the rest are connected enough, however loosely, with a religion or denomination to be able to name it in response to this question.
- Only 8% say that they never attend church or synagogue. Another 28% attend religious services "seldom," which means that about two-thirds of the population claim to attend services at least once a month or more often, while 36% attend once a week. Similarly, when asked if they attended church or synagogue in the last seven days (before the interview), 45% say "yes." This measure of church attendance has been one of the most remarkably stable measures in Gallup Poll history, staying at roughly the same level—in the high-30% to low-40% range—for thirty years.
- Almost nine in ten (86%) believe in God, even when given the choice of saying that they "don't believe in God but do believe in a universal spirit or higher power" (chosen by only 8%). In fact, only 5% of the population choose neither of these options and thus claim a more straightforward atheistic position.
- When given a choice between saying that "religion can answer all or most of today's problems," or that "religion is largely old-fashioned and out of date," 68% pick the former, while only 19% choose the "old-fashioned" response. This breakout has stayed roughly the same for over twenty-five years.
- Seventy-nine percent agree with the statement, "There will be a day when God judges whether you go to Heaven or Hell."

At the same time, the responses to several new questions suggest that some people approach religion in less than conventional ways. For example, one question asked Americans if they would define themselves as religious, or as "spiritual but not religious." Only 54% choose the straight "religious" label, while 30% would define themselves as "spiritual but not religious." Even 20% of those who say that religion is very important in their daily lives define themselves as spiritual but not religious.

The results of the survey also suggest that despite their outward affiliation with a religion and frequent church attendance, less than one-half of respondents lead their daily lives strictly by the code or teachings of their religious faith. While 48% say that they pay more attention "to God and religious teachings" in deciding how to conduct their lives, almost as many (45%) say that they pay more attention to their "own views and the views of others." Although those who say that religion is very important in their lives are most likely to pay more attention to God and religious teaching, one-quarter rely more on their own views or on others'. Groups that are most likely to pay more attention to their own views than God's include men, younger people (including 65% of those 18–29), and those living on either coast. Along the same lines, about one-half (52%) say that religions have unnecessary rules and responsibilities. (Catholics are more likely than Protestants to have this belief, by a 59%-to-46% margin.)

There is clear evidence from the survey results that many respondents, although personally devout, do not view their religion as the only true path to God. Seventy-five percent say that there is a religion "other than their own that offers a true path to God," and of that number a substantial majority believe that this other path is equally as good as their own. Additionally, although the vast majority say that there will come a day when God judges people and decides whether they will go to Heaven or Hell, the poll finds that 44% believe that a good person will go to Heaven whether or not he or she believes in God.

DECEMBER 30
CONCERNS FOR NEW YEAR'S EVE

Interviewing Date: 12/28/99
CNN/*USA Today*/Gallup Poll
Survey #GO 129386

As you may know, most computer systems around the world have to be reprogrammed so that they can accurately recognize the date once we reach the year 2000. How likely do you think it is that there will be major problems in the United States this New Year's as a direct or indirect result of the Y2K computer problem—very likely, somewhat likely, somewhat unlikely, or very unlikely?

Very likely	7%
Somewhat likely	30
Somewhat unlikely	32
Very unlikely	30
No opinion	1

How do you feel about the warnings that have been in the news about possible Y2K computer problems—do you consider these warnings unnecessary overreactions or necessary precautions?

Unnecessary overreactions	38%
Necessary precautions	59
No opinion	3

How likely are you to change your behavior or take special precautions this New Year's because of concerns you may have relating to the Y2K computer problem—very likely, somewhat likely, somewhat unlikely, or very unlikely?

Very likely	11%
Somewhat likely	25
Somewhat unlikely	20
Very unlikely	43
No opinion	1

Now thinking about other countries around the world, how likely do you think it is that there will be major problems in other countries this New Year's as a direct or indirect result of the Y2K computer problem—very likely, somewhat likely, somewhat unlikely, or very unlikely?

Very likely	22%
Somewhat likely	48

Somewhat unlikely 16
Very unlikely 9
No opinion 5

How likely do you think it is that one or more terrorist attacks will occur in the United States on New Year's Eve or New Year's Day—very likely, somewhat likely, somewhat unlikely, or very unlikely?

	Dec. 28, 1999	Dec. 20–21, 1999
Very likely	21%	22%
Somewhat likely	40	40
Somewhat unlikely	24	23
Very unlikely	13	12
No opinion	2	3

How do you feel about the warnings that have been in the news about possible New Year's Eve terrorist problems—do you consider these warnings unnecessary overreactions or necessary precautions?

Unnecessary overreactions 17%
Necessary precautions 80
No opinion 3

How likely are you to change your behavior or take special precautions this New Year's because of concerns you may have about terrorism—very likely, somewhat likely, somewhat unlikely, or very unlikely?

Very likely 13%
Somewhat likely 20
Somewhat unlikely 17
Very unlikely 49
No opinion 1

Finally, do you think U.S. cities should or should not cancel large public gatherings which they currently have scheduled for New Year's Eve?

Should cancel 24%
Should not cancel 71
No opinion 5

Note: As New Year's Eve approaches, a new Gallup Poll conducted on Tuesday evening [December 28] finds that more Americans are convinced that a Y2K terrorist attack will occur in the United States than think that Y2K-related computer failures will wreak societal havoc. Almost two-thirds (61%) believe that one or more terrorist attacks are likely to happen on New Year's, while just 37% think that major disruption from computer errors awaits us. However, a much smaller percentage think that either of these prospects is very likely to occur. Perhaps as a result, only one-third or so indicate that they will adjust their behavior or take other precautionary steps—a sign that public alarm is at low levels.

On the same day that the special Gallup pre-New Year's survey was taken, Seattle municipal leaders announced that they were canceling a downtown New Year's celebration because of fears of terrorism. However, the news had no immediate impact on respondents' concerns. In a Gallup Poll taken last week [December 20–21], prior to the Seattle decision, 22% said that it was "very likely" that one or more terrorist attacks would occur on New Year's Eve, while another 40% said "somewhat likely." Roughly one-quarter viewed the possibility as "somewhat unlikely," and 12% considered it "very unlikely." When the question was asked again this week, the figures were almost identical, with 21% predicting that such terrorism is very likely, and 40% as somewhat likely.

DECEMBER 31
THE NEW MILLENNIUM

Interviewing Date: 12/28/99
CNN/*USA Today*/Gallup Poll
Survey #GO 129386

As far as you know, which date will officially mark the beginning of the new millennium—January 1, 2000, or January 1, 2001?

January 1, 2000 .... 49%
January 1, 2001 45
No opinion 6

Regardless of when you think the new millennium will begin, which date do you think deserves the bigger celebration—January 1, 2000, or January 1, 2001?

January 1, 2000.. 68%
January 1, 2001.. 19
Both equally (volunteered)............................ 4
Neither (volunteered) 4
No opinion.. 5

Do you, personally, expect to have a good time or a bad time this New Year's Eve?

Good time... 90%
Bad time 3
No opinion.. 7

Next, please say whether each of the following describes or does not describe the way you are likely to feel on New Year's Eve this year:

Excited?

Yes, likely... 67%
No, not likely... 32
No opinion.. 1

Apprehensive or fearful?

Yes, likely... 22%
No, not likely... 77
No opinion.. 1

Annoyed by the New Year's hype in advertising and the media?

Yes, likely... 40%
No, not likely... 59
No opinion.. 1

Bored?

Yes, likely... 11%
No, not likely... 88
No opinion.. 1

Reflective?

Yes, likely... 61%
No, not likely... 34
No opinion.. 5

Joyous?

Yes, likely... 79%
No, not likely... 19
No opinion.. 2

Looking ahead to next year, are you more hopeful or more fearful about what the year 2000 holds in store:

For you personally?

More hopeful 85%
More fearful.. 6
Equally mixed (volunteered)......................... 5
No opinion.. 4

For the world in general?

More hopeful 68%
More fearful.. 22
Equally mixed (volunteered)......................... 5
No opinion.. 5

Note: While the date of the official beginning of the new millennium is somewhat controversial—with the calendar suggesting January 1, 2001, as the actual beginning, while virtually the whole world seems ready to celebrate on January 1, 2000—most Americans are ready to celebrate the occasion now on this January 1, not one year from now. Because the calendar starts with the year "1" rather than the year "0," the end of the year 2000 would seem to be the completion of the second millennium rather than the beginning of the third. But a new Gallup Poll, conducted on December 28, shows that respondents are about evenly divided over the matter: 49% say that the new millennium officially begins with the year 2000, while 45% say that it begins a year later. Still, when asked which year deserves the bigger

celebration, the public agrees, by a margin of 68%
to 19%, that this coming New Year's Eve, rather
than the one a year from now, is the time to celebrate the end of the old millennium and the beginning of the new one. Despite this consensus, just
28% expect to do something different on this New
Year's Eve. Thus, for most people, while they
may be toasting or acknowledging the new millennium, their celebration of the New Year will be
about the same this time as it has been in previous
years.

INDEX

Bush, George W. (Texas governor) (*continued*)
    know enough about, 63
    knows how to get things done in Washington,
        as important for a president, 105
    likely to support, 71, 118
        trend, 71, 118
    likely to support, if Buchanan were not
        running, 99
    likely to support, if McCain beats him in early
        primaries, 117
    likely to vote for, 84, 119
        trend, 119
    likely to vote for Bradley or, 119
        trend, 119
    likely to vote for Gore or, 72, 119
        trend, 72, 119
    Medicare dealt with by, 81
    more likely to vote for him because he allows
        concealed weapons, 66
    more likely to vote for him because he believes
        that juveniles should be prosecuted as
        adults, 67
    more likely to vote for him because he is
        opposed to abortion, 66
    more likely to vote for him because he requires
        students to meet minimum requirements,
        66
    more likely to vote for him because he
        supported property tax cut, 66–67
    more likely to vote for him because he would
        increase penalties for hate crimes, 66
    moving country in right direction, 96
    opinion of, 45
        trend, 45
    problems of raising children dealt with by, 81
    and Republican party [note], 87–88
    Republicans in Congress or, to have more
        influence over Republican party, 91
    shares your values, 82
    Social Security dealt with by, 81
    as strong and decisive leader, 65
    as strong and decisive leader, as important for
        a president, 105
    taxes dealt with by, 81
    tough enough for the job, 82
    vote for Gore, Buchanan, or, 88–89, 99
    vote for Gore, Trump, or, 89
Business and industry
    confidence in big business, 210
    confident that large businesses have upgraded
        computer systems, 158
    confident that small businesses have upgraded
        computer systems, 158
    worried about environment, 171

Business executives
    honesty rating, 148

C

Cabinet
    homosexuals should be appointed as members
        of, 169
Campaign finance reform
    important to your vote for Congress, 132
    presidential candidate's position on, as priority
        in voting for him, 69
    as top priority issue in Congress, 98
Campaign financing and fund-raising
    Gore engaged in unethical, 58
    less likely to vote for Gore because he engaged
        in unethical, 59
    needs complete overhaul, 98
Carpenters
    honesty rating, 148
Cars
    likely that cars and trucks will fail as result of
        Y2K problem, 247
    likely to buy or lease new or used, 144
Car salesmen
    honesty rating, 148
Carter, Jimmy
    as most admired man, 242
    as outstanding president, 77
Catholics
    vote for Catholic presidential nominee, 53
        trend, 54
The Cat in the Hat (Dr. Seuss)
    name the author of, 267
Children
    amount of violence that they are exposed to in
        lyrics to popular music, 202
    amount of violence that they are exposed to in
        movies, 202
    amount of violence that they are exposed to in
        television programming, 202
    amount of violence that they are exposed to in
        video or computer games, 202
    enough information about violence content in
        lyrics to popular music, 203
    enough information about violence content in
        movies, 202
    enough information about violence content in
        television programming, 203
    enough information about violence content in
        video or computer games, 203
    hold parents legally responsible if children
        commit crimes with parents' guns, 201
    not raised right, as most important problem, 194
        trend, 195

Clergy
  homosexuals should be hired as, 169
  honesty rating, 148
Clinton, Bill
  approval rating, 12, 43
    Gallup analysis, 74–75
    trend, 12, 43
  approval rating, as person, 95
  approve of House decision to impeach him, 16
  approve of Senate Democrats' handling of
    impeachment proceedings, 7
    trend, 7
  approve of Senate Republicans' handling of
    impeachment proceedings, 6
    trend, 6–7
  approve of Senate's decision to acquit him, 13,
    16
    trend, 16
  approve of Senate's decision to continue his
    impeachment trial, 5–6
  approve of Senate's handling of impeachment
    trial, 9
  budget deficit handled by, 44
  budget surplus to be used for Social Security or
    for other government programs, 69–70,
    132–33
  can get things done, 47
  charges more serious against Clinton in
    Lewinsky controversy than against Nixon
    in Watergate, 76
  charge that he committed perjury before Starr's
    grand jury as serious enough for removal,
    3–4
  charge that he committed perjury before Starr's
    grand jury as true, 2–3, 9
  charge that he influenced testimony of Lewinsky,
    his secretary, and others in Paula Jones law
    suit as serious enough for removal, 4
  charge that he influenced testimony of
    Lewinsky, his secretary, and others in Paula
    Jones lawsuit as true, 3, 9
  confidence in him as military leader, 27
  confidence in him or Republicans in Congress
    to set policy toward Yugoslavia, 27
  confidence in him to handle Kosovo situation,
    31–32
    trend, 32
  confident that Congress and president will pass
    budget in time to avoid government
    shutdown, 141
  confident that Congress and president will pass
    budget that you approve of, 142
  confident that Congress and president will stay
    within spending limits, 142

Congress fairly conducted its charges against, 16
crime handled by, 44
delighted with Senate's decision to not remove
  him, 13
deserves credit for Kosovo peace agreement, 36
dissatisfaction with, as most important
  problem, 195
  trend, 195
economy handled by, 44
  trend, 44
education handled by, 44
environment handled by, 44
favor his sending ground troops into Kosovo, 25
  trend, 25–26
foreign affairs handled by, 43
  trend, 43–44
Gallup analysis of battle over federal budget
  between Republicans and, 228–30
gender gap, *Gallup analysis*, 11
Gore's stands on issues would be too close to
  his, 58
Gore went too far in defending him during
  Lewinsky controversy, 58
has gotten fair trial in Senate, 9
health-care policy handled by, 44
his actions concerning Kosovo as significant
  foreign policy achievement, 34
as honest and trustworthy, 47
how harmful was impeachment process to
  country, 17
if Democratic-sponsored bill to cut taxes is
  passed, should he sign it, 218
if Democratic-sponsored bill to expand
  Medicare to include prescription drugs is
  passed, should he sign it, 218
if Republican-sponsored bill to cut taxes is
  passed, should he sign it, 218
if Senate votes not to remove him, he will have
  received sufficient punishment in Lewinsky
  matter, 10
impeachment of, as most important problem,
  195
  trend, 195
impeachment trial (unit), 1–17
  Gallup analysis of, 11–12
Iraq situation handled by, 44
Kosovo situation, administration has clear
  policy on, 25
Kosovo situation handled by, 36
less likely to vote for Gore because Gore's
  stands on issues would be too close to his, 59
less likely to vote for Gore because Gore went
  too far in defending him during Lewinsky
  controversy, 59

Lewinsky controversy, as most important
    problem, 195
  trend, 195
like to see next president continue with his
    policies, 95
Medicare, confidence in Republicans or, on
    handling, 204
  trend, 204–5
Medicare handled by, 44
as most admired man, 242
as most admired person of the century, 248–49
moving country in right direction, 91, 96
  trend, 91, 96
news media acted responsibly in impeachment
    process, 15
news media biased in favor of him, 15
opinion of, 12, 44
  Gallup analysis, 74–75
  trend, 12–13, 44–45
as outstanding president, 77
poverty and homelessness handled by, 44
prefer approach of Republicans in Congress or,
    to cut taxes and maintain federal programs,
    132
prefer approach of Republicans in Congress or,
    to federal budget, 92
  trend, 92
Puerto Rican nationalists, agree with his offer
    of clemency to, 224
Puerto Rican nationalists, followed news about
    his offer of clemency to, 223–24
Puerto Rican nationalists, offered clemency to,
    to win support for Hillary among
    Hispanics, 224
race relations handled by, 44
rather see Senate censure him or drop
    Lewinsky matter, 13
Republicans in Congress or, have acted more
    responsibly on federal budget, 92
  trend, 92
Senate censure acceptable which condemns his
    behavior in Lewinsky matter, 10
Senate censure acceptable which states that he
    committed crimes in Lewinsky matter, 10
Senate's decision to acquit him vindicates him,
    13
shares your values, 47
should be charged with crime after he leaves
    office, 16
sincere when he said he was "profoundly
    sorry" for Lewinsky matter, 13–14
Social Security handled by, 44
taxes handled by, 44
tired of anyone associated with, 95

want Senate to censure Clinton if not removed
    from office, 8
want Senate to remove him from office, 1–2
  trend, 2
would commit adultery again if he could get
    away with it, 14
Clinton, Hillary Rodham
  appropriate for her to move to New York
    where she can run full time for Senate,
    111–12
  appropriate for her to run for Senate while First
    Lady, 111
  approval rating, 44
    trend, 44
  Clinton offered clemency to Puerto Rican
    nationalists to win support for her among
    Hispanics, 224
  concerned that duties of First Lady are not
    being met if she runs for Senate, 62
  like to see her run for Senate in New York, 62
  as most admired woman, 242
  opinion of, 45
    Gallup analysis, 74–75
    trend, 45
  qualified to be U.S. senator, 111
Cobb, Ty
  as greatest baseball player, 256
Columbine High School. *See* Littleton, Colorado,
    school shootings; Students (age 13 to 17),
    asked of
Computer industry
  confidence in, 210
Computer industry executives
  honesty rating, 148
Computers
  amount of violence that children are exposed
    to in computer games, 202
  enough information for children about violence
    content in computer games, 203
  use personal computer at home, work, or
    school, 145
  See also Internet; Microsoft Corporation; Y2K
    computer problem
Computer salesmen
  honesty rating, 148
Congress
  approval rating, 47
    trend, 47
  approve of House decision to impeach Clinton,
    16
  campaign finance reform as top priority issue
    in, 98
  conducted its charges against Clinton fairly, 16
  confidence in, 209

likely to support [list], 72
    trend, 72
Democrats in Congress
    approval rating, 91
        trend, 91
    approve of their handling of impeachment
        proceedings, 7
        trend, 7
    benefiting the rich or middle class with tax
        cuts, 133–34
    if Democratic-sponsored bill to cut taxes is
        passed, should Clinton sign it, 218
    if Democratic-sponsored bill to expand
        Medicare to include prescription drugs is
        passed, should Clinton sign it, 218
Dentists
    honesty rating, 148
Dickens, Charles
    name the author of *A Tale of Two Cities*, 267
    as your favorite author, 267
DiMaggio, Joe
    as greatest baseball player, 256
Dining out
    as favorite way of spending evening, 252
    would seek out good food and restaurants on
        perfect vacation, 270
Disaster aid
    amount federal government spends on, 258
Doctors
    allow them to assist patient to commit suicide
        when person has incurable disease, 161
        trend, 161
    homosexuals should be hired as, 169
    honesty rating, 148
    vote for making marijuana legally available for
        them to prescribe, 170
Dole, Elizabeth
    Gallup analysis of G. W. Bush and, 78–80
    Gallup analysis of her candidacy, 94
    likely to support, 71
        trend, 71
    likely to support, if Buchanan were not
        running, 99
    likely to vote for, 84
    as most admired woman, 242
    opinion of, 45
        trend, 45
Domestic problems
    confidence in government's handling of, 49
        trend, 49–50
Drivers and driving
    cut back your driving if price of gasoline went
        up to $1.50 per gallon, 255
    See also Traffic problems

Drought
    experiencing, in your area, 217
Druggists
    honesty rating, 148
Drugs and drug abuse
    drugs as serious problem at school, 221
    important for a president to have never used
        illegal drugs, 106
    as most important problem, 195
        trend, 195
    vote for legalization of marijuana, 170
    vote for making marijuana legally available for
        doctors to prescribe, 170
Duke University
    recognized as best university, 219–20

E

Eastern Europe
    people have more political freedom in, 231
    people's economic well-being has improved in,
        231
    social problems have increased in, 231
Easter Sunday
    Gallup analysis of public's understanding of
        significance of, 255–56
East Timor
    favor sending in troops to, 225
    followed news about conflict in, 224
    peaceful solution to conflict in, as U.S. foreign
        policy goal, 225
Economic conditions
    getting better or worse, 48
    rated today, 48, 129–30
        trend, 48, 130
Economic policy
    G. W. Bush knows enough about, to be a good
        president, 116
    Gore knows enough about, to be a good
        president, 116
    increase U.S. economic aid to Israel, 215
Economy
    dealt with by G. W. Bush, 80
    Gore or G. W. Bush can keep economy strong,
        65–66
    handled by Bush, 63
        trend, 63
    handled by Clinton, 44
        trend, 44
    handled (dealt with) by Gore, 57, 80
    immigrants help, by providing low-cost labor,
        160

F

Families
  being with family as favorite way of spending
    evening, 252
  breakdown of family blamed for Littleton
    shootings, 192
  decline in family as most important problem,
    194
    trend, 195
  spend time with friends or family on perfect
    vacation, 270
  See also Children; Parents
Financial situation, personal
  better off next year than now, 48
    trend, 48
  better off now than year ago, 48
    trend, 48
  gotten better or worse in past three years,
    140
The Firm (Grisham)
  name the author of, 267
Flag, American
  constitutional amendment to make it illegal to
    burn, 262
    trend, 262
Food safety
  believe that foods produced using biotech-
    nology pose health hazard, 226
  confidence in federal government to ensure
    safety of food supply, 226
  confident that food at grocery stores is safe to
    eat, 226
  confident that food served at restaurants is safe
    to eat, 226
  heard or read about genetic modification of
    food, 226
  support use of biotechnology in agriculture and
    food production, 226
  willing to pay more for food with labels
    indicating biotechnology use, 226
Football
  fan of, 252, 253
  maintain NFL referees as part-timers, 253
  proposal that NFL reinstate use of instant
    replay by referees, 253
  See also Super Bowl
Forbes, Steve
  likely to support, 71, 118
    trend, 71, 118
  likely to support, if Buchanan were not
    running, 99
  likely to support, if McCain defeats G. W.
    Bush in early primaries, 117
  likely to vote for, 84

opinion of, 46
  trend, 46
Ford, Henry
  as most admired person of the century, 248–49
Foreign affairs
  best for future of country if we take active part
    in world affairs, 39
    trend, 39
  G. W. Bush knows enough about, to be a good
    president, 116
  Clinton's actions concerning Kosovo as
    significant foreign policy achievement, 34
  dealt with by G. W. Bush, 81
  Gore knows enough about, to be a good
    president, 116
  handled by Clinton, 43
    trend, 43–44
  handled (dealt with) by Gore, 57–58, 80
  as most important problem, 195
    trend, 195
Foreign aid
  as most important problem, 195
    trend, 195
Foreign policy
  important for a president to have experience in,
    106
  peaceful solution to conflict in East Timor as
    U.S. foreign policy goal, 225
  peaceful solution to Kosovo situation as U.S.
    foreign policy goal, 214
  peaceful solution to Northern Ireland situation
    as U.S. foreign policy goal, 214
  peaceful solution to Palestinian/Israeli situation
    as U.S. foreign policy goal, 214
Foreign trade. *See* China; Cuba; Trade deficit;
  Trade relations
Friends
  entertaining, as favorite way of spending
    evening, 252
  visiting, as favorite way of spending evening,
    252
Funeral directors
  honesty rating, 148

G

Gambling
  bet on college sports event, 264
  bet on horse or dog race, 264
  bet on professional sports event, 264
  bought state lottery ticket, 263
  Gallup social audit of gambling by adults and
    teenagers, 260–61
  gambled at casino, 263

knows how to get things done in Washington, as important for a president, 105
lacks vision, 58, 59
less likely to vote for him because he doesn't inspire you, 59
less likely to vote for him because he engaged in unethical campaign fund-raising, 59
less likely to vote for him because he is a tax-and-spend liberal, 59
less likely to vote for him because he lacks vision, 59
less likely to vote for him because he went too far in defending Clinton during Lewinsky controversy, 59
less likely to vote for him because his stands on issues would be too close to Clinton's, 59
less likely to vote for him because of his extreme positions on environment, 59
as liberal or moderate, 113
as likeable, 102
likely to support, 72
   trend, 72
likely to support Bradley or, 118
   trend, 118
likely to vote for, 57, 84
likely to vote for because he cares about needs of people like you, 60
likely to vote for because he has necessary experience to be president, 60
likely to vote for because he is good husband and father, 60
likely to vote for because he is honest and trustworthy, 60
likely to vote for because he would continue policies of Clinton administration, 60
likely to vote for G. W. Bush or, 72, 119
   trend, 72, 119
likely to vote for McCain or, 119–20
like to see debate between Bradley and, between now and February primary, 102–3
Medicare dealt with by, 80
moving country in right direction, 96
not a typical politician, 102
opinion of, 45, 101
   trend, 45
positions on environment are too extreme, 58
as presidential, 102
problems of raising children dealt with by, 80
shares your values, 81
as sincere, 102
Social Security dealt with by, 80
stands on issues would be too close to Clinton's, 58, 59

as strong and decisive leader, 65, 102
as strong and decisive leader, as important for a president, 105
support him strongly, 101
as tax-and-spend liberal, 58, 59
taxes handled (dealt with) by, 58, 80
as thoughtful, 102
tough enough for the job, 82
understands the nation's problems, 101–2
vote for Bradley or, in New Hampshire Democratic primary, 101
vote for G. W. Bush, Buchanan, or, 88–89, 99
vote for G. W. Bush, Trump, or, 89
watched Bradley and, in New Hampshire town meeting, 101
went too far in defending Clinton during Lewinsky controversy, 58, 59
would continue policies of Clinton administration, 60
would do better job than Bradley of improving health care, 102
Government, federal
amount spent on disaster aid, 258
confidence in, to ensure safety of food supply, 226
confidence in Executive branch, 50
   trend, 50
confidence in its handling of domestic problems, 49
   trend, 49–50
confidence in its handling of international problems, 49
   trend, 49
confidence in Judicial branch, 50
   trend, 50
confidence in Legislative branch, 50
   trend, 50
confident that it has upgraded computer systems to correct Y2K problem, 158
continue to fund NASA efforts to send unmanned missions to Mars, 243
dissatisfaction with, as most important problem, 195
   trend, 195
do more to regulate violence in movies, 179
do more to regulate violence in popular music, 179
do more to regulate violence in video games, 179
do more to regulate violence on Internet, 179
do more to regulate violence on television, 179
Republican party has gone too far in criticisms of, 87

law in your state should cover homosexuals, 154

law in your state should cover racial minorities, 154

law in your state should cover religious and ethnic minorities, 154

law in your state should cover women, 154

more likely to vote for G. W. Bush because he would increase penalties for, 66

worried about being victim of, 154

Health care

dealt with by G. W. Bush, 81

dealt with by Gore, 80

Gore or Bradley would do better job of improving system, 102

handled by Clinton, 44

important to your vote for Congress, 131

likely that hospital equipment and services will fail as result of Y2K problem, 158, 247

as most important problem, 195
trend, 195

presidential candidate's position on costs as priority in voting for him, 69

satisfied with family and medical leave benefits your employer offers, 137

side more with Justice Department or tobacco companies in lawsuit to recover federal health costs, 277

See also HMOs (health maintenance organizations)

Health insurance

satisfied with benefits your employer offers, 137

Heart disease

think that cigarette smoking is cause of, 276
trend, 276

Hemingway, Ernest

ever read book by, 267

name the author of *The Old Man and the Sea*, 267

as one of greatest authors, 267–68

as your favorite author, 267

Heston, Charlton

opinion of, NRA president, 178

Hispanics

Clinton offered clemency to Puerto Rican nationalists to win support for Hillary among, 224

members of violent groups at school as dangerous to, 189

members of violent groups at school talk about hatred of, 189

HMO managers

honesty rating, 148

HMOs (health maintenance organizations)

concerned that Democrats' reform plan would go too far, 211

concerned that Republicans' reform plan would not go far enough, 211

confidence in, 210

important to your vote for Congress, 131

need to be completely overhauled, 211

Republican or Democratic party's approach to regulation of how HMOs treat patients, 211

Holocaust

Gallup analysis of five most important events of century including, 232–38

Homelessness

handled by Clinton, 44

as most important problem, 195

trend, 195

Homosexuality

as acceptable life-style, 169

Homosexuals

hate crime law should cover, 154

members of violent groups at school as dangerous to gay students, 189

members of violent groups at school talk about hatred of gays, 189

relations between consenting adults should be kept legal, 168–69

should be appointed to president's cabinet, 169

should be hired as clergy, 169

should be hired as doctors, 169

should be hired as elementary-school teachers, 169

should be hired as high-school teachers, 169

should be hired as salespersons, 169

should have equal rights in job opportunities, 169

should serve as members of armed forces, 169

vote for homosexual presidential nominee, 54

trend, 54

Honesty and ethics rating

of forty-five occupations [list], 148

House of Representatives

confidence in, 50
trend, 50

Human rights

link human rights issues in China to U.S.-China trade policy, 197–98

rate job government of China does in respecting, 197

Human rights atrocities

military action in Yugoslavia will prevent other governments from committing, 38

U.S. should use military more often to stop, 40

Hunger

has increased in Eastern Europe, 231

Hurricane
ever personally been in, 258
Hyde, Henry
opinion of, 46

I
Illegal aliens
as most important problem, 195
trend, 195
Immigrants
become productive citizens, 159–60
trend, 160
help economy by providing low-cost labor, 160
how many live in your area, 160
take jobs that Americans want, 160
Immigration
as most important problem, 195
trend, 195
should be kept at present level, 159
trend, 159
Income, personal
expect next pay raise will be larger than last, 135
expect to receive pay raise, 135
expect your income to go up more than prices, 134
trend, 135
satisfied with amount of money you earn, 137
Independents
Gallup analysis of the independent voter, 55–57
Inflation
as most important problem, 194
trend, 195
Insurance salesmen
honesty rating, 148
International issues
confidence in government's handling of, 49
trend, 49
as most important problem, 195
trend, 195
See also Foreign affairs; Foreign policy
Internet
blamed for Littleton shootings, 179, 192
confidence in news on, 210
controlling, could prevent another incident like Littleton shootings, 192
ever bought anything on, 126
ever get onto, through computer or Web TV, 126
ever invested in any Internet companies, 126
ever used, for financial information, 126
ever used, to conduct trading in financial markets, 126
gambled for money on, 264

government should do more to regulate violence on, 179
honesty rating of journalists who publish only on, 148
how well have your investments in Internet companies done, 126
invested currently in Internet companies, 126
invested first in Internet company in what year, 126
invested in Internet companies long-term or short-term, 126
investing in Internet companies more risky than in other stocks, 127
likely to invest in Internet companies in future, 126–27
likely to use for Christmas shopping, 150
percentage of your portfolio invested in Internet stocks, 127
percentage return from Internet companies higher than in other stocks, 127
reasons why you invested in Internet companies, 127
stop violence in schools by restrictions on, 173
who recommended that you invest in Internet companies, 127
Iraq situation
handled by Clinton, 44
as most important problem, 195
trend, 195
Israel
Arab nations and, will be able to live in peace, 215
favor independent Palestinian state on West Bank and Gaza Strip, 185
importance of outcome of Israeli elections to U.S., 184
increase U.S. economic aid to, 215
increase U.S. military aid to, 215
opinion of, 185
peaceful solution to Palestinian/Israeli situation as U.S. foreign policy goal, 214
prefer to see Prime Minister Netanyahu reelected or replaced, 184
U.S. should pressure Palestinian Arabs and, to implement terms of Wye River peace accords, 214
your sympathy more with Israelis or Palestinian Arabs, 214–15

J
Jackson, Jesse
likely to support, 72
trend, 72

opinion of, 29–30
    trend, 30
Jackson, Shoeless Joe
    should be eligible for baseball's Hall of Fame,
        266
Jewelers
    honesty rating, 148
Jews
    vote for Jewish presidential nominee, 53
        trend, 53
Jobs
    employed full-time, part-time, retired, or
        unemployed, 136
    employee of private company, government
        employee, or self-employed, 137
    homosexuals should have equal rights in job
        opportunities, 169
    immigrants take, 160
    more trade between U.S. and China would
        increase jobs for American workers, 151
    as most important problem, 194
        trend, 195
    presidential candidate's position on job avail-
        ability as priority in voting for him, 69
    satisfaction with your job, 136
    satisfied with amount of stress, 137
    satisfied with amount of work required, 136
    satisfied with amount you earn, 137
    satisfied with boss, 136
    satisfied with chances for promotion, 137
    satisfied with family and medical leave
        benefits, 137
    satisfied with flexibility of hours, 136
    satisfied with health insurance, 137
    satisfied with job security, 136
    satisfied with opportunity to grow, 136
    satisfied with recognition you receive, 137
    satisfied with relations with co-workers, 136
    satisfied with retirement plan, 137
    satisfied with safety of workplace, 136
    satisfied with vacation time, 136
    see yourself as high achiever, workaholic, or
        underachiever, 137
    See also Workplace
John Paul II
    as most admired man, 242
    as most admired person of the century,
        248–49
Jones, Paula
    charge that Clinton influenced Lewinsky's
        testimony in lawsuit as serious enough for
        removal, 4
    charge that Clinton influenced Lewinsky's
        testimony in lawsuit as true, 3, 9

Jordan, Michael
    as most admired man, 242
Jordan, Vernon
    approve of Senate calling him as witness in
        impeachment trial, 6
Journalists
    honesty rating, 148
Judges
    honesty rating, 148
July 4th
    what event is celebrated on, 206
Justice Department
    side more with Microsoft or, 128, 145
    side more with tobacco companies or,
        277

K

Kasich, John
    likely to support, 71
        trend, 71
    opinion of, 46
Keller, Helen
    as most admired person of the century, 248–49
Kennedy, John F.
    as most admired person of the century, 248–49
Kennedy, John F., Jr.
    death of, and Clinton opinion rating in *Gallup
        analysis*, 74–75
    followed news about plane crash and death of,
        268
    news media acted responsibly in covering his
        death, 269
    opinion of news media in covering his death,
        268
    too much news coverage given to his death,
        268
    your reaction to his death, 268
Kerrey, Bob
    likely to support, 72
        trend, 72
Kerry, John
    likely to support, 72
        trend, 72
    opinion of, 46
Kevorkian, Dr. Jack
    approval rating, 162
    followed news about, 162
Keyes, Alan
    likely to support, if Buchanan were not
        running, 99
    likely to support, if McCain defeats G. W. Bush
        in early primaries, 117

King, Martin Luther, Jr.
  as most admired person of the century, 248–49
King, Stephen
  as your favorite author, 267
Koontz, Dean
  as your favorite author, 267
Kosovo situation
  air strikes' outcome represents victory for
    U.S., 37–38
  approve of ending all military action, 32
  approve of suspending air strikes to negotiate,
    32
  Clinton administration has clear policy on, 25
  Clinton deserves credit for peace agreement,
    36
  Clinton's actions concerning, as significant
    foreign policy achievement, 34
  confidence in Clinton or Republicans in
    Congress to set policy toward Yugoslavia,
    28
  confidence in Clinton to handle, 31
    trend, 31–32
  confident that U.S. will accomplish its goals
    with few casualties, 22
    trend, 22
  confident that U.S. will accomplish its goals
    without sending in ground troops, 22–23
  continue action against Yugoslavia until
    Milosevic complies with terms acceptable
    to NATO, 29
  crisis (unit), 19–41
  favor call-up of U.S. reservists to NATO air
    war on Yugoslavia, 26
  favor committing U.S. troops to peacekeeping
    force, 19
  favor helping U.S. rebuild area that refugees
    will return to, 34
  favor helping U.S. rebuild Serbian areas
    bombed by U.S. in Yugoslavia, 34
  favor presence of U.S. ground troops in peace-
    keeping force, 37
  favor (approve of) sending U.S. ground troops,
    25, 27, 32, 35
    trend, 25–26, 27
  favor (approve of) sending U.S. ground troops
    if peace agreement is worked out, 27
  favor terms of peace agreement, 37
    trend, 37
  favor U.S. being part of NATO attacks against
    Serbs in Yugoslavia, 31
  handled by Clinton, 36
  handled by Congress, 27
  likely that Milosevic will comply with peace
    agreement, 34

  likely that new Cold War will break out as
    result of disagreements between NATO
    countries and Russia on NATO action in
    Yugoslavia, 183
  military action in Yugoslavia will prevent
    other governments from committing human
    rights atrocities, 38
  as most important problem, 195
    trend, 195
  NATO military action in Yugoslavia has been
    success, 26
    trend, 26
  NATO military action in Yugoslavia has made
    situation better, 23
  NATO military action in Yugoslavia will be
    success, 26
    trend, 26
  NATO military action in Yugoslavia will have
    made situation better, 23
  open your home to ethnic Albanian refugees,
    30
  peace agreement probably will work, 35
  peaceful solution to, as U.S. foreign policy
    goal, 214
  peace possible in Yugoslavia only if Milosevic
    is removed, 38
  presidential candidate's position on, as priority
    in voting for him, 68
  Serbian government or NATO more
    responsible for ethnic Albanian refugees
    leaving Kosovo, 23–24
  support decision to bring ethnic Albanian
    refugees to U.S., 30
  U.S. air strikes in Yugoslavia justified by
    Serbian attacks on civilians, 24
  U.S. air strikes in Yugoslavia justified by
    threat to U.S. strategic interests, 24
  U.S. and NATO doing everything to minimize
    civilian casualties, 32
  U.S. and NATO military action against
    Yugoslavia has been too aggressive,
    28–29
  U.S. and NATO or Serbs in Yugoslavia have
    won more in peace settlement, 33
  U.S. and NATO should continue military
    action in Yugoslavia until Milosevic is
    removed, 33
  U.S. has moral obligation to help keep peace, 20
    trend, 20
  U.S. made mistake sending forces to
    Yugoslavia, 33
  U.S. needs to be in Kosovo to protect its own
    interests, 20
    trend, 20

U.S. through NATO air attacks will
accomplish its objectives, 21–22
worth going to war over, 34–35

L

Labor union leaders
honesty rating, 148
Labor unions
approval rating, 273
confidence in organized labor, 209
your sympathies on side of unions or of
companies, 273
L'Amour, Louis
as your favorite author, 267
Lawyers
honesty rating, 148
Leisure time
favorite way [list] of spending evening, 252
Lewinsky, Monica
approve of Senate calling her as witness in
impeachment trial, 6
charges more serious against Clinton in
Lewinsky controversy than against Nixon
in Watergate, 76
charge that Clinton committed perjury about
his relationship with her as serious enough
for removal, 3–4
charge that Clinton committed perjury about
his relationship with her as true, 2–3, 9
charge that Clinton influenced her testimony in
Paula Jones lawsuit as serious enough for
removal, 4
charge that Clinton influenced her testimony in
Paula Jones lawsuit as true, 3, 9
controversy over, as most important problem,
195
trend, 195
Gore went too far in defending Clinton during
Lewinsky controversy, 58
if Senate votes not to remove Clinton, he will
have received sufficient punishment, 10
less likely to vote for Gore because he went
too far in defending Clinton during
Lewinsky controversy, 59
as most admired woman, 242
opinion of, 46
trend, 46
Senate censure acceptable which condemns
Clinton's behavior, 10
Senate censure acceptable which states that
Clinton committed crimes, 10
Life Is Beautiful (movie)
like to see it win Oscar, 254

Littleton, Colorado, school shootings
any of your children expressed worry about
feeling unsafe since, 176, 220
blame gun availability for, 179
blame Internet for, 179
blame media coverage of similar incidents for,
180
blame parents for, 179
blame schools for, 179
blame social pressures on youths for, 179–80
blame television programs, movies, and music,
179
criminal charges should be filed against
parents, 176
Gallup analysis of teen violence and, 174–75
government and society can take action to
prevent, 173
as indication of something seriously wrong in
country, 172
likely to happen in your community, 172
news media have acted responsibly about, 176
talked with child about, 176
what could be done [list] to prevent another
incident, 192
why did this happen [list], 192
See also Students (age 13 to 17), asked of
Lott, Trent
opinion of, 46
trend, 46
Lotteries
bought state lottery ticket, 263
Lung cancer
heard or read that cigarette smoking is cause
of, 275
trend, 275
think that cigarette smoking is cause of, 275
trend, 275–76

M

Mandela, Nelson
as most admired man, 242
as most admired person of the century, 248–49
Mantle, Mickey
as greatest baseball player, 256
Marijuana
vote for legalization of, 170
vote for making it legally available for doctors
to prescribe, 170
Mays, Willie
as greatest baseball player, 256
McCain, John
likely to support, 71, 118
trend, 71, 118

McCain, John (*continued*)
    likely to support, if Buchanan were not running, 99
    likely to support, if he defeats G. W. Bush in early primaries, 117
    likely to vote for, 84
    likely to vote for Bradley or, 120
    likely to vote for Gore or, 119–20
    as most admired man, 242
    opinion of, 45
      trend, 45
Media
    confidence in, in reporting news fairly, 51
      trend, 51
    likely to feel annoyed by New Year's hype in, 285
    as most important problem, 195
      trend, 195
    parents, peers, media, or school are responsible when teenager commits crime, 241
    See also by type; News media
Medical system
    confidence in, 209
Medicare
    confidence in Clinton or Republicans on handling, 204
      trend, 204–5
    dealt with by G. W. Bush, 81
    dealt with by Gore, 80
    handled by Clinton, 44
    if Democratic-sponsored bill to include prescription drugs is passed, should Clinton sign it, 218
    important to your vote for Congress, 132
    as most important problem, 195
      trend, 195
    needs to be completely overhauled, 205
    prefer larger tax cut and smaller increases in spending on, 133
    presidential candidate's position on, as priority in voting for him, 68
    use budget surplus to increase spending on, 69–70, 132–33
Men
    find gender stereotypes offensive in movies, 271
    Gallup analysis of most admired person of the century, 248–49
    most admired man [list], 242
Michener, James
    as your favorite author, 267
Microsoft Corporation
    as monopoly, 129
    opinion of, 128, 145
      trend, 128

opinion of Bill Gates, 46, 128
    trend, 46–47, 128
    positive effect on computer industry, 128–29
    require it to break up into several smaller companies, 145
    side more with Justice Department or, 128, 145
Middle-class people
    Democrats in Congress benefiting the rich or, with tax cuts, 134
    middle-income people paying their fair share in federal taxes, 123–24
    Republicans in Congress benefiting the rich or, with tax cuts, 133–34
Middle East situation
    Israel and Arab nations will be able to live in peace, 215
    peaceful solution to Palestinian/Israeli situation as U.S. foreign policy goal, 214
    your sympathies more with Israelis or Palestinian Arabs, 214
Military
    amount government should spend for, 153
      trend, 153
    approve of American troops in peacekeeping forces under NATO command, 40
    approve of American troops in peacekeeping forces under UN command, 40
    confidence in, 208–9
    favor sending in troops to East Timor, 225
    homosexuals should serve as members of armed forces, 169
    important for a president to have served in, 106
    increase U.S. military aid to Israel, 215
    U.S. only uses air strikes for vital strategic purposes, 40
    U.S. should use more often, to stop human rights atrocities, 40
    which branch of armed services should be built up, 153
    See also Kosovo situation
Millennium
    January 1, 2000, or January 1, 2001, as date beginning new, 284
    January 1, 2000, or January 1, 2001, deserves bigger celebration, 285
    hopeful or fearful about the year 2000 for world in general, 285
    hopeful or fearful about the year 2000 for you personally, 285
Milosevic, Slobodan
    continue action against Yugoslavia until he complies with terms acceptable to NATO, 29

likely that he will comply with peace
agreement, 34
as most important problem, 195
trend, 195
objective of NATO action in Yugoslavia
should be his removal from power, 30
opinion of, 30
peace possible in Yugoslavia only if he is
removed, 38
U.S. and NATO should continue military
action in Yugoslavia until he is removed,
33
Minorities
hate crime law should cover racial, 154
members of violent groups at school as
dangerous to, 189
members of violent groups at school talk about
hatred of, 189
MIT (Massachusetts Institute of Technology)
recognized as best university, 219
Morals and morality
important for a president to have good moral
character, 105
lack of morals blamed for Littleton shootings,
192
moral decline as most important problem, 194
trend, 195
raising morals could prevent another incident
like Littleton shootings, 192
Republican party has been too pessimistic
about moral standards, 87
Mormons
vote for Mormon presidential nominee, 54
Mother Teresa
as most admired person of the century, 249
Movies
amount of violence that children are exposed
to in, 202
blamed for Littleton shootings, 179, 192
blame teenage crimes on violence in, 179
enough information for children about violence
content in, 202
find gender stereotypes offensive in, 271
find graphic violence offensive in, 271
find nudity offensive in, 271
find profanity offensive in, 271
find racial stereotypes offensive in, 271
find sexual activity offensive in, 271
going to, as favorite way of spending evening,
252
government should do more to regulate
violence in, 179
like to see [list] win Oscar for Best Picture,
254

stop violence in schools by regulation of
violence in, 173
watching at home, as favorite way of spending
evening, 252
Music
listening to, as favorite way of spending
evening, 252
Music, popular
amount of violence that children are exposed
to in lyrics to, 202
blamed for Littleton shootings, 179, 192
enough information for children about violence
content in lyrics to, 203
government should do more to regulate
violence in, 179

N

NASA (National Aeronautics and Space
Administration)
continue to fund efforts to send unmanned
missions to Mars, 243
Gallup analysis of space exploration and,
212–14
rated, 243
spending on space program should be
increased, 243
National Day of Prayer
Gallup analysis of habits of prayer, 257–58
NATO (North Atlantic Treaty Organization)
approve of American troops in peacekeeping
forces under NATO command, 40
See also Kosovo situation
Netanyahu, Benjamin
opinion of, 45
prefer to see him reelected or replaced, 184
News media
acted responsibly in Clinton impeachment, 15
acted responsibly in covering death of John F.
Kennedy, Jr., 269
acted responsibly in Littleton shootings, 176
biased in favor of Clinton, 15
blame media coverage of similar incidents for
causing Littleton shootings, 180
confidence in, in reporting news fairly, 51
trend, 51
open Senate impeachment debate to, 8
opinion of, in covering death of John F.
Kennedy, Jr., 268
read or heard about Internet companies in, 127
too much coverage given to death of John F.
Kennedy, Jr., 268

News media (*continued*)
too much coverage given to Littleton
shootings, 176
Newspaper reporters
honesty rating, 148
Newspapers
confidence in, 209
confidence in, in reporting news fairly, 51
trend, 51
New Year's Eve
expect to have good or bad time, 285
likely to feel annoyed by hype, 285
likely to feel apprehensive, 285
likely to feel bored, 285
likely to feel excited, 285
likely to feel joyous, 285
likely to feel reflective, 285
See also Millennium; Terrorism; Y2K
computer problem
Nixon, Richard
charges more serious against Clinton in
Lewinsky controversy than against Nixon
in Watergate, 76
familiar with Watergate affair during Nixon
administration, 75
trend, 75
his actions regarding Watergate serious enough
to warrant his resignation, 75
trend, 75–76
as outstanding president, 77
Watergate serious because it revealed
corruption in Nixon administration, 75
trend, 75
Northern Ireland situation
peaceful solution to, as U.S. foreign policy
goal, 214
Notre Dame University
recognized as best university, 219–20
NRA (National Rifle Association)
opinion of, 177–78
opinion of president Charlton Heston, 178
Nuclear power
how safe are plants that produce electric
power, 166
likely that systems could fail as result of Y2K
problem, 158, 247
name plant in Pennsylvania [Three Mile
Island] with breakdown, 166
Three Mile Island plant breakdown is likely to
happen again, 166
worry about threat of accidents, 166
Nuclear Test Ban Treaty
aware of whether Senate voted to approve, 230
followed arguments closely, 230

heard about, 230
Senate should have voted to ratify, 230
Senate should have voted to ratify or
withdrawn treaty, 230
Nudity
find it offensive in movies, 271
Nurses
honesty rating, 148
Nursing home operators
honesty rating, 148

O

O'Donnell, Rosie
as most admired woman, 242
Officeholders, local
honesty rating, 148
Officeholders, state
honesty rating, 148
The Old Man and the Sea (Hemingway)
name the author of, 267
Onassis, Jacqueline Kennedy
as most admired person of the century, 248–49

P

Palestinian Arabs
favor independent Palestinian state on West
Bank and Gaza Strip, 185
Israel and, will be able to live in peace, 214
peaceful solution to Middle East situation as
U.S. foreign policy goal, 214
U.S. should pressure Israel and, to implement
terms of Wye River peace accords, 214
your sympathies more with, in Middle East
situation, 214–15
Parents
any of your children had run-ins with police,
241
are you a parent, 240
parental involvement could prevent another
incident like Littleton shootings, 192
parental rights taken away, as most important
problem, 195
trend, 195
parents are to blame when their child breaks
the law, 241
parents should be punished when their child
breaks the law, 241
parents, peers, media, or school are responsible
when teenager commits crime, 241
poor parenting blamed for Littleton shootings,
192

Reform party
   prefer Buchanan or Trump to win party
      nomination, 89
   would participate in its presidential primary,
      89
   See also Beatty, Warren; Buchanan, Pat;
      Trump, Donald; Ventura, Jesse; Weicker,
      Lowell
Rehnquist, William
   opinion of, 47
Religion
   any religion other than yours that offers true
      path to God, 281
   attend church or synagogue how often,
      265–66
   believe in God or higher power, 281
   blamed for Littleton shootings, 192
   confidence in church or organized, 208
   Gallup analysis of habits of prayer on National
      Day of Prayer, 257–58
   Gallup analysis of public's understanding of
      significance of Easter Sunday, 255–56
   Gallup analysis of religious involvement,
      265–66
   God judges whether you go to Heaven or Hell,
      282
   good person will go to Heaven, 282
   hate crime law should cover religious and
      ethnic minorities, 154
   important for a president to attend religious
      services regularly, 106
   important in your own life, 265
   pay more attention to God or your own views,
      281
   putting prayer back in school could prevent
      another incident like Littleton shootings,
      192
   religions have unnecessary rules, 282
   as religious or spiritual in your beliefs, 281
   things taught in my religion that I don't
      believe, 282
   your religion as best path to God, 282
   See also Prayer in public schools
Reno, Janet
   as most admired woman, 242
Republican party
   approach of Democratic or, to regulation of
      how HMOs treat patients, 211
   G. W. Bush or Republicans in Congress to
      have more influence over, 91
   can do better job on gun control, 196
   concerned that Republicans' HMO reform plan
      would not go far enough, 211
   gone too far in criticisms of government, 81

not compassionate enough about needs of the
   poor, 87
opinion of, 45, 114
   trend, 45, 114-15
too pessimistic about moral standards, 87
vote for its candidate in elections for Congress,
   114
   trend, 114
Republican presidential nominees
   Gallup analysis of G. W. Bush and "also-
      rans," 78–80
   Gallup analysis of candidates after Iowa straw
      poll, 77–78
   Gallup analysis of Republican front-runner,
      109–11
   likely to support [list], 71
      trend, 71
   likely to support [list], if Buchanan were not
      running, 99
Republicans in Congress
   approval rating, 91
      trend, 91
   approve of their handling of impeachment
      proceedings, 6
      trend, 6–7
   benefiting the rich or middle class with tax
      cuts, 133–34
   budget surplus to be used for Social Security or
      for other government programs, 69–70,
      132–33
   G. W. Bush or, to have more influence over
      Republican party, 91
   Clinton or, have acted more responsibly on
      federal budget, 92
      trend, 92
   confidence in Clinton or, on handling
      Medicare, 204
      trend, 204–5
   confidence in Clinton or, to set policy toward
      Yugoslavia, 28
   dissatisfaction with, as most important
      problem, 195
      trend, 195
   Gallup analysis of battle over federal budget
      between Clinton and, 228–30
   if Republican-sponsored bill to cut taxes is
      passed, should Clinton sign it, 218
   moving country in right direction, 91
      trend, 91
   prefer approach of Clinton or, to cut taxes and
      maintain federal programs, 132
   prefer approach of Clinton or, to federal
      budget, 92
      trend, 92

censure acceptable which condemns Clinton's
behavior in Lewinsky matter, 10
censure acceptable which states that Clinton
committed crimes in Lewinsky matter, 10
Clinton has gotten fair trial in, 9
confidence in, 50
trend, 50
delighted with its decision to not remove
Clinton, 13
if it votes not to remove Clinton, he will have
received sufficient punishment in Lewinsky
matter, 10
its decision to acquit Clinton vindicates him,
13
open impeachment debate to news media, 8
rather see it censure Clinton or drop Lewinsky
matter, 13
should have voted to ratify Nuclear Test Ban
Treaty, 230
should have voted to ratify or withdrawn
Nuclear Test Ban Treaty, 230
vote to censure Clinton if not removed from
office, 8
vote to remove Clinton from office, 1–2
trend, 2
Senators
honesty rating, 148
Serbs and Serbia. *See* Kosovo situation
Sexual activity
find it offensive in movies, 271
Shakespeare, William
as your favorite author, 267
Shakespeare in Love (movie)
like to see it win Oscar, 254
Sheldon, Sidney
as your favorite author, 267
Shepherd, Cybill
view her as serious presidential candidate,
90
Simpson, Nicole Brown. *See* Simpson, O. J.
Simpson, O. J.
charges that he murdered Nicole Brown
Simpson and Ron Goldman are true, 199
feel sympathetic toward, 199
should continue to be given legal custody of
his children, 199
Smith, Bob
likely to support, 71
trend, 71
opinion of, 46
Socialism
becoming socialistic as most important
problem, 195
trend, 195

Social Security
allow savings to be used for mortgages and
education as well as retirement, 125
dealt with by G. W. Bush, 81
dealt with by Gore, 80
handled by Clinton, 44
have savings managed by government or
workers, 125
important to your vote for Congress, 131–32
as most important problem, 195
trend, 195
overhaul system, 125
prefer to manage own savings, 125
presidential candidate's position on, as priority
in voting for him, 68
put third of tax now paid into savings for
retirement, 125
use budget surplus for, 69–70, 132–33
Space exploration
Gallup analysis of NASA and, 212–14
Stanford University
recognized as best university, 219
Starr, Ken
charge that Clinton committed perjury before
grand jury as serious enough for removal,
3–4
charge that Clinton committed perjury before
grand jury as true, 2–3, 9
Gallup analysis of his negative image, 93–94
opinion of, 46
trend, 46
Star Wars: The Phantom Menace (movie)
has your child seen *The Phantom Menace*,
262
have you seen *The Phantom Menace*, 262
your reaction to *The Phantom Menace*, 262
Steel, Danielle
as your favorite author, 267
Steinbeck, John
as your favorite author, 267
Stockbrokers
honesty rating, 148
Stock market
have money invested now in, 142–43
trend, 143
investing in, if you had thousand dollars to
spend, 143
trend, 143
stock prices will go higher in next six months,
143
See also Internet
Students (age 13 to 17), asked of
able to tell who violent groups are by what
they wear, 189

Tobacco companies (*continued*)
  See also Cigarette smoking and smokers
Tornado
  ever personally been in, 258
Trade deficit
  as most important problem, 194
    trend, 195
Trade relations
  as most important problem, 194
    trend, 195
Traffic problems
  if in traffic backup on interstate highway, take
    nearest exit, 259
  when stuck in traffic jam, how often do you
    become angry, 259–60
  which types of traffic jams cause you the most
    trouble, 259
Tripp, Linda
  opinion of, 46
Trucks
  likely to buy or lease new or used, 144
Trump, Donald
  Gallup analysis of his candidacy, 85–86
  likely to vote for, if he runs as Reform party
    candidate, 99
  opinion of, 47
    trend, 47
  prefer Buchanan or, to win Reform party
    nomination, 89
  view him as serious presidential candidate, 89
  vote for Gore, G. W. Bush, or, 89
Twain, Mark
  as your favorite author, 267

U

UCLA (University of California at Los Angeles)
  recognized as best university, 219–20
Unemployment
  as most important problem, 194
    trend, 195
United Nations
  approve of American troops in peacekeeping
    forces under UN command, 39–40
United States
  better off since fall of Berlin Wall, 231
  satisfaction with way things are going in, 47
    trend, 47–48
Universities
  recognize [list] as best, 219–20

V

Vacations
  plan to take vacation this summer, 269

satisfied with amount of vacation time you
  receive, 136
spend how much money on your vacation this
  summer, 269–70
taking one single vacation this summer, 269
would engage in vigorous exercise on perfect
  vacation, 270
would get suntan on perfect vacation, 270
would participate in sport you don't normally
  do on perfect vacation, 270
would participate in sport you regularly engage
  in on perfect vacation, 270
would read a book on perfect vacation, 270
would seek out restaurants on perfect vacation,
  270
would see museum or play on perfect vacation,
  270
would shop on perfect vacation, 270
would spend time with friends or family on
  perfect vacation, 270
would try to meet new people on perfect
  vacation, 270
Ventura, Jesse
  and *Gallup analysis* of third-party movement,
    73–74
  likely to vote for, 84
  opinion of, 47
    trend, 47
  view him as serious presidential candidate, 89
Veterinarians
  honesty rating, 148
Video games
  amount of violence that children are exposed
    to in, 202
  controlling, could prevent another incident like
    Littleton shootings, 192
  enough information for children about violence
    content in, 203
  government should do more to regulate
    violence in, 179
Violence
  blamed for Littleton shootings, 192
  as most important problem, 194
    trend, 195
  See also Children; Government, federal;
    Movies; School violence; Workplace

W

Walters, Barbara
  as most admired woman, 242
War
  as most important problem, 195
    trend, 195

Watergate affair
  charges more serious against Clinton in
      Lewinsky controversy than against Nixon
      in Watergate, 76
  familiar with, 75
      trend, 75
  Nixon's actions serious enough to warrant his
      resignation, 75
      trend, 75–76
  serious matter or just politics, 75
      trend, 75
Weather conditions
  amount the federal government spends on
      disaster aid, 258
  any air conditioning where you live, 217
  ever been in hurricane, 258
  ever been in tornado, 258
  ever known summer as hot as this one, 217
  experiencing drought in your area, 217
  hot this summer compared to previous
      summers, 217
  job that local weather bureau is doing of
      forecasting, 258
Weicker, Lowell
  opinion of, 47
Weight
  describe yourself as overweight, 272
  trying to lose weight, 273
      trend, 273
  worry about your weight how often, 272
  would like to lose weight, 272
      trend, 272
Welfare
  as most important problem, 195
      trend, 195
Wellstone, Paul
  likely to support, 72
      trend, 72
Williams, Ted
  as greatest baseball player, 256
Winfrey, Oprah
  as most admired woman, 242
  view her as serious presidential candidate, 89
Women
  find gender stereotypes offensive in movies, 271
  Gallup analysis of five most important events
      of century including women's suffrage and
      progress, 232–38
  Gallup analysis of most admired person of the
      century, 248–49
  hate crime law should cover, 154
  most admired woman [list], 242
  vote for woman presidential nominee, 54
      trend, 54

Workplace
  ban cigarette smoking in, 277
      trend, 277
  know anyone capable of violence at your, 216
  worried about violence by co-worker in your,
      216
  See also Jobs
World Trade Organization
  favor agreement between China and U.S. to
      allow China to join, 150
World War II
  Gallup analysis of five most important events
      of century including, 232–38
Wye River peace accords
  U.S. should pressure Israel and Palestinian
      Arabs to implement terms of, 214

Y

Y2K computer problem
  avoid traveling on airplanes on January 1, 157,
      246
  buy generator or wood stove, 157, 246
  computer mistakes due to year 2000 issue will
      cause major problems, 156, 245
      trend, 245
  computer mistakes due to year 2000 issue will
      cause major problems for you personally,
      156, 245
      trend, 245
  concerned about, 245
      trend, 246
  confident that foreign governments of
      developed countries have upgraded
      computer systems, 159
  confident that foreign governments of Third
      World countries have upgraded computer
      systems, 159
  confident that large businesses have upgraded
      computer systems, 158
  confident that small businesses have upgraded
      computer systems, 158
  confident that U.S. government has upgraded
      computer systems, 158
  confident that your local government has
      upgraded computer systems, 158
  confident that your state government has
      upgraded computer systems, 158
  confirm bank balances, 157, 246
  consider warnings about possible problems as
      overreactions, 283
  fill gas tank in your car, 246
  how long will computer problems last, 156

ISBN 0-8420-2699-1

9 780842 026994

90000 >